writers and revolution

New Viewpoints
A Division of Franklin Watts, Inc.
New York, 1974

renee winegarten

writers and **REVOLUTION** *the fatal lure of action*

Library of Congress Cataloging in Publication Data

Winegarten, Renee.
    Writers and revolution; the fatal lure of action.

    Includes bibliographical references.
1. Authors—Political and social views.
    2. Literature and revolutions.   I. Title.
PN51.W57 1975   809'.933   74-3464
ISBN 0-531-06368-2
ISBN 0-531-06500-6 (pbk.)

Cover design by Brian Ganton

Text design by Diana Hrisinko

To the memory of my father

It is no great matter, supposing that Italy could be
liberated, who or what is sacrificed. It is a
grand object—the very poetry *of politics.*

BYRON

.... revolution
Alone can save the earth from hell's pollution.

BYRON

Romantic poetry . . . is the expression of the secret
attraction to a chaos which lies concealed in the
very bosom of the ordered universe, and is
perpetually striving after new and marvelous births . . .

A.W. SCHLEGEL

.... the roar of thy Democracies,
Thy reigns of Terror, thy great Anarchies,
Mirror my wildest passions like the sea . . .

OSCAR WILDE

contents

part 2. *the religion of revolution*

part 3. *confrontations and reactions*

part 4. *the phase of aesthetic nihilism*

foreword

I affix here what assumes largely the aspect of a testament of friendship rather than a purely formal list of acknowledgments. Without the inspiration of Neal Kozodoy, to whom I owe so much, this book would not exist. It was during one of our periodic discussions in New York, in the autumn of 1969, that the idea arose. In its first form, as an essay on "Literary Revolutionism," it appeared in *Commentary,* thanks to the editor, Norman Podhoretz, whose unfailing kindness and encouragement I have been privileged to experience. I am indebted to Joseph Epstein for (among other things) directing me toward Alexander Herzen. From Desmond Stewart there came, apart from the thread that guided me to Swinburne, invaluable help and stimulus arising from long correspondence and pleasurable hours of conversation. With characteristic verve and generosity Moshe Pearlman imparted much helpful practical advice. My dear friend of many years, Professor Yakov Tal-

mon, has unstintingly given me the benefit of his experience as a historian of r
olution, and it affords me great pleasure to have the opportunity to acknowled
publicly all that I owe to his learning and humanity. My heartfelt thanks are (
to my husband, who has patiently sustained me throughout all my literary vici
tudes. Suffice it to add, however, that I alone am responsible for the opini
expressed in the pages that follow.

London, 1974.

writers and revolution

prologue:

*writers and salvation
through revolution*

Revolution: that awesome cry of expectation has fascinated and haunted creative writers—poets, novelists, dramatists, essayists—for more than two hundred years. When the Bastille fell in 1789 there was scarcely a poet whose heart did not beat faster as he glimpsed a vision of humanity reborn. One, so it is said, dared to wear the red Phrygian cap in the London streets, while in Württemberg another was rumored to have danced with his friends around a tree of liberty. From being a mark of the generous aspirations of an intellectual and spiritual elite in the days of Blake and Hölderlin, revolution has become a catchword, a criterion of artistic excellence, even a cliché in advertisements or a means of adventitious excitement. How has this decline come about?

Evidently, dissatisfaction with society and its abuses was, and remains, the chief ostensible reason for advocating revolution. An age of privilege, child labor, press gangs, slavery, and disproportionate punishment could not but arouse indignation in those capable of thought and feeling, and awaken their desire for change. But what was the primary urge which at first made a complete overthrow seem more attractive than anything else? Some deeper need than the desire for social change and improvement underlies the passion for revolution. It is the yearning for salvation both for the individual and for society, through a total transformation of man and his world.

This yearning may be traced in the work of imaginative writers who subscribed to revolution. But their attitude rarely remained constant. If some were faithful to their early enthusiasm in spite of everything, some modified their views under the pressure of experience, and some reneged. Some reveal how the desire for an ideal can lead by insensible degrees to its opposite. Others manifest contradictions that cannot be satisfactorily reconciled. Yet others are tempted by irresistible impulses. There are few whose tensions, paradoxes, and temptations do not throw light on present-day attitudes.

The intention here is not to write an exhaustive history of the interaction of literature and revolution. It is to examine, through key figures and moments, the attraction of revolution for men of letters at various times since 1789, the reasons for it, and the vagaries to which it gives rise. Why men of letters? In what way do they differ from other thinkers?

The fact is that creative writers can often provide a key that is not to be found, or may be found only with great difficulty, in the more rebarbative writings of political philosophers or men of affairs. The dreams and visions of poets, their intuitions and premonitions are expressed in powerful and haunting language, and can make an indelible effect on the imagination. The cry of Schiller's Karl Moor in *The Robbers,* "It is liberty that giveth birth to Titans . . . Put me at the head of a troop of men like myself, and I will make Germany a republic beside which Rome and Sparta would seem like a convent of nuns," may well have inspired bored young Germans to attitudes of revolt. It may also have stirred the youthful Coleridge to exclaim, "My God! Southey! Who is this Schiller? This convulser of the Heart?" [1] But on a lifelong revolutionary of intense poetic susceptibility like Alexander Herzen, Schiller's plays had a profound formative influence. Still, we shall be concerned here not so much with the influence of poets as with their insights and their inner conflicts and contradictions.

After 1789, moreover, men of letters were seen as having a new and vital importance in the Western world. Their role had changed during the course of the eighteenth century, wrote Madame de Staël in her book *On Literature Considered in Its Relations with Social Institutions* (1800). Literature, she noted rather sweepingly, had ceased to be an art, and had become instead a means to an end, "a weapon in the service of the spirit of man." [2] Some years later, the writer-politician Alexis de Tocqueville, reflecting on this theme, wondered why men of letters were so influential in the eighteenth century though others were performing the actual work of government. His view was that the spectacle of so many absurd privileges and bizarre institutions made them wish to rebuild society entirely anew by the light of individual reason. No experience tempered their ardor for change: "they had no idea of the dangers which always accompany the most necessary revolutions. . . . And so they became much bolder in their novelties, more enamoured of general ideas and of systems, more contemptuous of ancient wisdom. . . ." [3] The same ignorance also gave them "the ear and the heart" of the crowd.

This view was not so very different from Edmund Burke's complaint in 1790: "Your literary men, and . . . the whole clan of the enlightened among us . . . have no respect for the wisdom of others; but they pay it off by a very full measure of confidence in their own." And Burke added that "duration is no object to those who think little or nothing has been done before their time, and who place all their hopes in discovery . . . they are at inexpiable war with all establishments." [4] In short, while eighteenth-century men of letters were accused of self-conceit, imprudence, audacity, a passion for novelty, and a boundless impatience, they also had ascribed to them a vast and dangerous influence. Although this assessment of their influence would doubtless be modified by present-day historians and critics, the important fact from our standpoint is that this opinion was widely held toward the end of the eighteenth century and during the century that followed.

Consequently, many writers took to wearing the Pindaric mantle of seer, or regarded themselves as visionary bards, prophets, and leaders whose duty it was to guide those who were not gifted with antennae like their own. And with the decline of established religion, such figures became, as it were, members of a secular clergy. Especially in countries where repression was hard, writers were to provide not only inspiration but comfort and consolation. In this respect, they often saw themselves (and were seen by their readers) as Promethean—either because, like the rebel Titan Prometheus, they suffered agony of soul and even exile, torment, and persecution in order to bring benefits to mankind; or because, like him, they defied authority and challenged the very injustice of the universe established and governed by Olympian Zeus.

At the end of the eighteenth and beginning of the nineteenth century, the imaginative artist's growing sense of his high standing was consecrated notably in the speculative theories of German writers on the fine arts, in particular Schiller and the brothers Schlegel. The creative activity of the genius was conceived as analogous to that of God himself. Like the God of Genesis, the genius was seen as being able to create his world out of nothing; or, like Plato's Demiurge, he could create it according to an eternal pattern. In either case, the emphasis was on the element of the divine or quasi-divine in the genius and his creative activity. Writers of genius were placed upon a pedestal of remarkable elevation, and some of their glory reflected upon imaginative writers in general, enhancing their value and importance.

In the light of the analogy between artistic and divine creativity, it was believed that the artist should strive for many-sidedness, for totality on the divine model. Schiller, in his *Letters on the Aesthetic Education of Man* (1795), wrote: ". . . we must surely call divine any tendency which has as its unending task the realization of that most characteristic attribute of Godhead, viz., absolute manifestation of potential (the actualization of all that is possible), . . ." [5] There should be no limit to the development and expression of potentialities. Indeed, according to A. W. Schlegel, the artist revealed his genius in the extent of his receptivity, diversity, and many-sidedness. The ambition to be all-embracing in the divine image could readily turn into its opposite, an admiration for single-mindedness.

Yet a further analogy between the genius and God was freedom from constraint. Friedrich Schlegel, writing in the *Athenaeum* (1798), observed that "the freedom of the poet shall suffer no law to be imposed upon it." [6] No longer was the artist bound by theories of imitation, by rules, by conventions of decorum and taste. All that mattered was that he should produce and communicate whatever lay within. For some, the desire for freedom for themselves as artists moved them to seek freedom for all, or, as Schiller expressed it, "A noble nature is not content to be itself free, it must also set free everything around it . . ." ; [7] for others, freedom from constraint inspired a nostalgia for discipline and order. Consequently advocates of boundless diversity and liberty in the field of literature could be found lost in admiration for the ruthless authoritarian ruler. Madame de Staël would remark upon the way the Germans of her day combined great freedom and daring of thought with an inclination to obedience in politics. This tendency would not be confined to some German idealists; it would be found among intellectuals everywhere who would somehow manage to reconcile the claims of unfettered freedom with the acceptance of various forms of autocracy.

The exaltation of creativity, the drive to many-sidedness, and freedom from constraint on the divine model were signs that the writer was conceiving his role and function as those of a substitute divinity. As respect for institutional religion declined, the cult of self-expression finally displaced the ideal of service to the glory of God. The principle of endless striving for a goal that could never be attained, which at first had seemed a censurable aspect of the modern spirit, now began to look more remarkable than the ideal of completion and fulfillment. The strain of activity and upheaval now appeared more dramatic and stimulating than a divinely fixed order of the universe where each individual knew his place and could, perhaps, derive from that knowledge some quietude of mind. Above all, such delight in movement and restlessness struck observers as being new and modern.

Equally new in Europe, at least according to Saint-Just, was the ideal of happiness. However, with the individual's right to happiness came the right to a full life as distinct from mere existence, a challenging distinction that Rousseau had emphasized when he declared, "Life consists less in length of days than in the keen sense of living," or "Live while you are alive," or "We are born . . . twice over; born into existence, and born into life." [8] The demand for a full life led to a perpetual quest for enrichment of experience, and to an insatiable yearning for they knew not what.

Besides, it was supposed that at some time in the distant past man and his world had been in harmony. But modern man was obviously far from this happy condition. As Schiller, after Rousseau, expressed it: "Everlastingly chained to a single little fragment of the Whole, man himself develops into nothing but a fragment; everlastingly in his ear the monotonous sound of the wheel that he turns, he never develops the harmony of his being, and instead of putting the stamp of humanity upon his own nature, he becomes nothing more than the imprint of his occupation or of his specialized knowledge." [9] How to recover the mythical lost harmony and wholeness of the Greeks, in whom every aspect of life seemed to have been in accord? (Or at least so it appeared to those prepared to overlook the existence of a slave society.) How to achieve the full humanity, "the harmony of his being," that belonged to every individual as of right? Clearly it followed that much in the world as it was actually experienced would have to be radically transformed. And as Schiller himself maintained, for man "a complete revolution in his whole way of feeling is required, without which he would not even find himself on the way to the ideal." [10] Schiller's aesthetic view of full humanity is thought to have helped to shape the outlook of Marx on alienation, and traces of it can certainly be found among writers today.

What Schiller had to say about the crisis of modern civilized man in general applied even more forcibly to the crisis of the modern writer, with his extreme degree of self-absorption and self-awareness. In Schiller's distinction, the modern "sentimental" poet, unlike the "naive" poet at one with himself and his world, was fully conscious of the rift between himself and his environment as well as of the rift within his own soul. For the tormented "sentimental" poet, unity within and without was no longer a reality, but an ideal for which he must strive. The connection between Schiller's insight into the "sentimental" artist and the writer's revolutionary outlook has been aptly pointed out: "He is Amfortas and seeks peace, salvation, the healing of his own or his society's secret and patent wounds. He cannot be at rest. . . . Hence the effect of the sentimental artist is not joy and peace, but tension, conflict with nature or society, insatiable craving, the notorious neuroses of the modern age, with its troubled spirits, its martyrs, fanatics and rebels, and its angry, bullying subversive preachers, . . . offering not peace but a sword." [11]

One of the subjects that particularly bothered the writer conscious of his inner discord and division was the search for his true self. Where was it to be found? Full self-expression demanded the quest for authenticity, for the truly genuine, natural, instinctive, spontaneous, as opposed to the artificial, spurious, conventional, hypocritical, and calculating. Anger and disgust with ruse, cant, and falsity, with the world as it exists and with society as it is constituted, could provide a powerful stimulus. For some, the test of authenticity was to lie in full involvement and action, regardless of where these might lead—even, if need be, to violence, bloodshed, and crime. The call of action for its own sake began to haunt men of letters, aware of their own inaptitude for action or the unpropitiousness of the moment. It was partly their obsession with action that made Hamlet, so melancholy and vacillating, a theme of endless fascination for them. But the real trial of an author's attitude toward action often lay in his response to the Jacobin Terror—and less to the incorruptible Robespierre than to the handsome, youthful, charismatic figure of Saint-Just, "the archangel of the Terror," who made so lasting an impression on writers from Stendhal to Malraux and Camus.

Such a response could be equivocal, or it could develop and change. Most writers were utterly repelled by the Terror, and under its impact some came to the conclusion that men were not yet ready for political liberty. So Schiller could insist that the long-term ennoblement of man through art should precede political improvements. On the other hand, Madame de Staël (who found the Terror an inexplicable horror) felt that in some historical circumstances those strong passions which lead to crimes are "necessary" to wind the clock of society. It is through such passions that ideas are discovered which otherwise would not have been heard of: "Violent upheavals are necessary to bring the human spirit to entirely new purposes; they are earthquakes, subterranean fires, which reveal to man's gaze buried riches; time alone would not have sufficed to excavate the path to these." [12] For her, powerful and generous impulses serve as an excuse; they cause one to overlook criminal excesses "provided the mark of greatness is imprinted on the brow of the offender." [13]

Some years later, however, at the height of her opposition to Bonaparte, her standpoint was quite different. "When at the bloodiest period of the Revolution, they wanted to sanction every crime, they called the government the Committee of Public Safety; thereby proclaiming the well-known maxim, that the welfare of the people is the supreme law. The supreme law is justice." And she went on to quote her beloved Rousseau as saying that a nation should not "purchase the most desirable Revolution with the blood of a single innocent person." [14] To use evil means for an end that one believed to be good was, she insisted, vicious, since men could know nothing either of the future or of themselves.

But to return to the consequences of the urge for self-expression. Self-expression demands the new. The man of letters, no longer dependent on models, must now discover what is uniquely individual, new, and original for him. With the French Revolution of 1789, the new in all things became the order of the day. In the Assembly, Jean-Paul Rabaut de Saint-Etienne (who would die by the guillotine in 1793) declared: "All establishments in France crown the misery of the people: to make the people happy it must be regenerated; its ideas, its laws, its customs must be changed, . . . men must be changed, . . . everything must be destroyed since everything is to be created anew." [15] Here is expressed the obligation to destroy in order to start again from scratch. It was Saint-Just himself who went even further: "In a time of innovation, all that is not new is pernicious," he observed. [16] For him, the old was automatically bad, and the new a value in itself. Henceforward, the new could be regarded less as the outcome of natural growth or development than as the consequence of a break with the past or as an aim to be striven for consciously and deliberately. The end of this process is by no means in sight.

Such extreme statements about the new voiced by French revolutionaries make it clear that the desired change applied to everything, not just the political order. A total transformation was envisaged, in some instances embracing social and sexual morality as well as the world of art and literature. Thus, for example, the father of modern philosophic anarchism, William Godwin, opposed domestic tyranny as much as the tyranny of privilege— not only in his *Enquiry Concerning the Principles of Political Justice* (1793) but in his gripping novel of pursuit, *Caleb Williams* (1794), both written when he was feeling shattered by the blood bath of the Terror in France. Exceptional women like Mary Wollstonecraft (the first Mrs. Godwin) or Madame de Staël sought to free their sex from the disabilities they themselves had to suffer. Such spirits felt that there must be a revolution which would change ideas concerning the disadvantageous position of women in the eyes of the law and the unequal relations between the sexes.

Similarly, the view was widely held that a revolution in letters must accompany the political and social revolution. The changed situation required a different kind of literature. "Nothing in art must be stationary, and art becomes petrified when it ceases to change," [17] wrote Madame de Staël, who felt that twenty years of revolution had imparted new needs to the imagination, needs totally different from those which could be satisfied by an earlier form of literature. There were others—a Goethe, for instance—who, while recognizing the need for change in literature, were nonetheless opposed to violent political overthrow.

These three aspects—the political, the moral, and the aesthetic—are three forms of the total revolutionary outlook. They will recur, though it will be found that they do not always recur together and in harmony. In spite of this commitment to change in all spheres, the myth or tradition of revolution itself, its language and rhetoric, are embedded in romanticism. The appeals to the people, the legendary popular heroism of the barricades would continue to exert a powerful force of attraction down to our own day. Their aura cannot be separated from romanticism and in this sense they remain fundamentally conservative.

It seems strangely significant that the word "revolution" was not used in June 1789, when the oath was taken at the Tennis Court, this being the essential revolutionary act which led to all the rest. The Assembly spoke of "national regeneration," and only fifteen months later did "revolution" appear in a proclamation.[18] The idea of regeneration was certainly present in Rabaut de Saint-Etienne's mind when he listed the aspects of life awaiting radical transformation. Others like him envisaged humanity cleansed, purified, renewed. Indeed, it was just this "air of tending to the regeneration of the human race" that, according to de Tocqueville, gave the revolution of 1789 its unique similarity to the revolution caused by Christianity in the ancient world.[19]

While in the eyes of some the revolution meant the destruction of Christianity, for others this awe-inspiring event appeared as the fulfillment of Christian teaching. It was of the latter party that the poet André Chénier spoke disapprovingly in April 1791, castigating the Illuminati and the Rosicrucians who preached liberty and equality like the Eleusinian or Ephesian mysteries, which became fashionable around 1790. Such spirits had their parallels in England and Germany. Chénier (who—in his revolutionary sympathies, opposition to extremism, and death by the guillotine the day before the end of the Terror—epitomizes the fate of the martyred literary revolutionary) is thought to have had in mind a sermon on the harmony between the Christian religion and revolutionary liberty.

The preacher, using the slogans of the day, maintained that God had prescribed "democratic" government for the Jews, and that Jesus, who had come to announce "the rights of man," was the "friend of the people." In this way, thought André Chénier, political disputes succeeded scholastic and theological quarrels, but they were being "treated in the same manner, with the same sophistry (for the character of the human species does not change in the slightest), . . ."[20] Certainly, later revolutionaries and some of their literary sympathizers were to see themselves as not so very different from the small elite groups of early Christians, preserving the true faith and working for the day.

"Regeneration," as employed by the early French revolutionaries, provides a clue to the central metaphor of revolution. It expressed a constant yearning, doubtless as old as man, who has been perennially dissatisfied with himself and his circumstances. "For behold, I create new heavens and a new earth: and the former things shall not be remembered, nor come into mind." (Isaiah 65:17) "And I saw a new heaven and a new earth: for the first heaven and the first earth were passed away. . . . And he that sat upon the throne said, Behold, I make all things new. . . ." (Revelation 21:1,5) ". . . Except a man be born again, he cannot see the kingdom of God." (John 3:3) "Therefore if any man be in Christ, he is a new creature: old things are passed away; behold, all things are become new." (2 Corinthians 5:17) The longing for rebirth, renewal, regeneration—in religion naturally referring to spiritual rebirth—becomes transferred (as Chénier had perceived in a related connection) to the political, social, and aesthetic spheres.

In both the Old and the New Testament the promise of rebirth and salvation is preceded by dreadful punishments and catastrophes. From this arises the potent notion of the "necessary" catastrophe. Salvation cannot be attained by the precious remnant of the righteous or the saints without passage through the refining fire, and without the previous elimination of all those wicked people whose sins are not only delaying the day of deliverance but have placed the unrepentant evildoers themselves beyond redemption.

So the destruction of the dehumanized enemy of salvation (whether in the shape of idolaters and sinners; of Satan/Antichrist and his monstrous train in the Book of Revelation; of the Tyrant; and, nearer our own day, of the Bourgeois, the Capitalist, the Imperialist, existing-bourgeois-society-as-a-whole) has to precede the establishment of peace and harmony, when wolf and lamb will feed together and when (as in the fantasies of the Golden Age of classical antiquity) there will be no more conflict and no more war. The necessary purificatory terror resembles the necessary catastrophe of the Bible. On the death of one or many to achieve the desired end, both Charlotte Corday and her victim Marat were agreed. And as we have seen, even the liberal-minded Madame de Staël, foreshadowing Auden's aberrant "necessary murder," could momentarily find excuses for the "necessary" political crime and the "necessary" violent upheaval.

Catastrophe itself, provided it is on the grand cosmic scale, has a very potent attraction for a certain kind of imagination. "And I will shew wonders in the heavens and in the earth, blood, and fire, and pillars of smoke. The sun shall be turned into darkness and the moon into blood, before the great and the terrible day of the Lord comes." (Joel 2:30, 31) In this ancient example, one among many, blood and fire are the key images which return again and again down the ages: blood with its associations of violence, human sacrifice, and fertility; fire which equivocally both destroys and purifies, as do flood and storm, equally common images of catastrophe.

Very often in the use of these images one detects a certain note of complacency in the contemplation of impending doom, a wallowing (almost) in the idea of destruction, the cataclysmic night of upheaval and disaster that precedes purification and the freshness of the new dawn. There comes a moment when destruction is virtually welcomed in order to hasten the hour of release. This note becomes more and more marked as time goes on and as the romantic imagination revels in the sheer dramatic excitement of images of disaster, hurricanes, earthquakes. Rousseau foreshadowed this trend when he observed somewhat wryly that "it is revolutions and catastrophes that make history interesting"; [21] and they did so presumably by adding an element of heightened drama to the otherwise even tenor of events.

There is another sense in which destruction and death are necessary. Without them there can be no regeneration or resurrection. "Thou fool, that which thou sowest is not quickened, except it die." (1 Corinthians 15:36) In this sense, creation and destruction are inseparable, as they are inseparable attributes of the godhead. Those who desired universal renewal might well be tempted to sweep all away in order to achieve it, and think the cost worthwhile. Some might view this destruction with exaltation, others with regret. Moreover, the actual process of resurrection as described by St. Paul is rapid in the extreme: "In a moment, in the twinkling of an eye, at the last trump: for the trumpet shall sound, the dead shall be raised incorruptible, and we shall be changed." (1 Corinthians 15:52) The transmutation from the old to the new spiritual state "in the twinkling of an eye" is clearly paralleled in a secular mode in the desire for complete and swift transformation from the old to the new order. Any slow movement of gradual change would thus fail to satisfy the deep longing to be rid of the old, the known, the botched, and the rotten.

The coming of the Savior-Redeemer breaks the tragic human cycle of sin and death. But where previously redemption was achieved through the Suffering Servant or the Lamb, now it is to be achieved through the people, and later through the proletariat, or the colonized, or the self-sacrificing revolutionary who takes upon himself the world's suffering. The powers that were formerly attributed to a divine messenger or divine being were now assumed by a self-deceiving human agent. This tendency, seen in a number of heretical medieval millenarian movements where popular leaders and their followers imagined themselves to be the elite saving remnant of the millennium and believed themselves to be messiahs or even incarnate gods, appears as a recurrent temptation of the human spirit. It would not be a simple matter to eradicate traces of centuries of religiously directed thought and feeling, inspired by some of the deepest human urges and aspirations.

The years before, during, and after the French Revolution were characterized by intense spiritual upheaval. If rationalism governed one current in this period, the struggle to combat rationalism and materialist philosophy governed another. Mysticism, often in heretical forms, served as a weapon in this battle. Indeed, mysticism and politics could sometimes be blended together in a strange brew. Meanwhile apocalyptic millenarianism, based on the Revelation of St. John and related biblical and apocryphal texts, flourished. Many felt they were living in the Last Days. The fondness for interpreting "the signs of the times" and judging on the basis of such texts led to the French Revolution's being considered by a Klopstock as the reign of Antichrist and by a Lavater as the advent of the millennium.[22]

One of the most enduring and aesthetically satisfying of apocalyptic systems, invented by a medieval Calabrian monk, Joachim di Fiore, was persistently to find its obscure way into literature. Not surprisingly, since his prophetic doctrine of an ascent through three ages—the age of the Father, the age of the Son, and the age of the Holy Spirit, has been characterized as the most influential one before Marxism. According to Joachim, the third age, or kingdom, had not yet arrived, but it was to be the culmination of human history, when direct revelation would replace the New Testament. Direct revelation would be made through the "everlasting gospel" which, on the authority of the Book of Revelation, was to be preached to all peoples in the Last Days. This system clearly envisages a time when the New Testament and even Jesus himself will be transcended. In the third age, men would live together in innocence, freedom, joy, peace, and love. There would be no private property and no institutional authority. Joachim's system of the three ages may be traced in poets and writers who perhaps were not always aware of the source of their ideas.

Among the attributes of the Joachite third age were guiltlessness and freedom from suffering. It resembled in this the moment of redemption in Isaiah when "the Lord God will wipe away tears from off all faces" or in the Revelation of St. John when "God shall wipe away all tears from their eyes; and there shall be no more death, neither sorrow, nor crying, neither shall there be any more pain. . . ." For those medieval millenarians—like the initiates of the Free Spirit and their heirs, the seventeenth-century Ranters, who believed that they were already living in the Joachite third age of innocence and love—there could be no sin if they did as they pleased and indulged in anarchic eroticism. Moreover—and this is a lasting dream—the fantasies of some were such that they thought there could be neither sickness nor death in the third age. And it is curious how devotees of reason could be carried away by millennial fantasies: Condorcet (who was to poison himself to escape the guillotine in 1794) suggested that the progress of enlightenment toward a new golden age would eventually bring immortality, while Godwin too believed that ill-health, disease, and possibly even death would eventually be transcended at some stage in the future course of humanity.

Besides the longing for freedom from guilt, pain, and death, a potent force in apocalyptic and heretical movements from the Middle Ages onward, was the contrast between the teachings of Jesus on poverty and the austere simplicity of the primitive Church on the one hand, and on the other the wealth and worldliness of some manifestations of ecclesiastical authority. There seemed to be no connection between the abuses of the Church of the day and the words that Jesus speaks to the wealthy ruler, ". . . sell all that thou hast, and distribute unto the poor, and thou shalt have treasure in heaven. . . . How hardly shall they that have riches enter into the kingdom of God!" (Luke 18:22, 24) Moreover, in the Gospel could be found an account of the primitive Church where the early Christians "had all things in common"; those who were rich sold what they owned "and distribution was made unto every man according as he had need." (Acts 4:32,35)

The notion that the social teachings of Jesus were being betrayed was to prove of great emotive power. An eighteenth-century Swabian pietist like Oetinger (who influenced Hölderlin as well as Hegel) deduced from the New Testament his program of reform, which included the suppression of absolutism and private property and the restoration of liberty and equality under Christ. This trend toward what was believed to be a truly Christian anarchism would be repeated in our own day. However, the distinction drawn between the essential purity of the teachings and way of life of Jesus, his apostles and disciples, and the wealth and conduct of the established churches or of conventional believers, was not confined solely to the social aspect. Nietzsche was to stress the irony of what he called the Church's perversion of the Gospel into its opposite, and was to give this view a renewed life among creative writers in the twentieth century. It is a view that has often occurred to poets.

Another tendency working against established religion in its received or socially accepted institutional forms was theosophy, which claims to understand and reveal the hidden workings of the divinity. Here were blended together occultism, the esoteric doctrines of Neoplatonism, Christianized cabala, alchemy, magic, and Christian mysticism, often in forms condemned as heretical. All these made for a kind of nonorthodox spirituality. Some writers were in search of a universal religion that might accord with their idea of man as a being intrinsically capable of spiritual insight regardless of his creed or lack of it. In Germany, mysticism was greeted as the universal theology known to Adam, and as the spiritual basis of all religions. So philosophers and poets were able to proclaim a universal revelation that had been given to all humanity at the beginning of time. Indeed, this view was not so very different from that of the second-century Christian apologist Tertullian, who expressed the opinion that, besides the supernatural revelation, there was another, older, natural revelation originally implanted in the soul of Adam, never wholly lost, and accessible to all.

The rediscovery in Germany of the condemned medieval mystic Eckhart and the seventeenth-century mystic cobbler-theosopher Boehme (whose works were already well known in the Low Countries and in England), together with the "revelation" of the Swedish visionary Swedenborg, which was understood as a continuation and elaboration of biblical revelation, fortified the conviction that the Absolute is not outside but within the soul. For the daring mystic of this tinge, the attributes of God are thus transferred to a deified self. And this conception connects both with the artist's speculation concerning the analogy between divine and artistic creativity and with the radical millenarian's idea of himself as an incarnation of the divine. However, for many writers the words of Rousseau's Savoyard Vicar, "Let me follow the Inner Light, . . ." were to be the guiding thread. If the light is within you, if God is within you, you do not need to bother with laws, rites, and ceremonies; and the inner perception of an "eternal Christianity" can be contrasted with the outward forms of a temporary and temporal Church.

Because writers who fell under the spell of these sentiments ceased to believe that salvation was to be found in obedience to ecclesiastical authority, this did not mean that they had ceased to yearn for salvation for their own souls and for humanity at large. They probably yearned for it all the more in their uncertainty, and tended to look for it in any manifestation that promised purgation, redemption, and renewal. Revolution seemed to hold out such a promise. The advent of peace and love, harmony and universal brotherhood, prophesied in the Bible, continued to be the desired ideal, now to be sought for by the "Inner Light" and with the guidance of direct revelation to the individual or the "everlasting gospel." These were the instruments of that singular visionary William Blake, whose insights into the new world born of political and industrial revolution prefigure many current aspects of literary revolutionism. For his era saw the dawn of our own. It is therefore to him and to the English romantic poets—the grand archetypes—that we turn first in order to observe the effects of the French Revolution at one remove from the central upheaval, as they work upon the imagination, the mind, and heart of the writers who were changed by the wash of the great wave.

part

the lyrical illusion

Are not Religion and Politics the Same Thing?

WILLIAM BLAKE

chapter 1

the apocalyptic vision of
William Blake

*It is in the poetry of William Blake that the literary connection between regen*eration, salvation, and revolution can be perceived with striking clarity. The headlong and tormented fall from harmony and wholeness, the violent severity and terror of the Last Judgment, the sudden blazing glory of resurrection and restoration—these haunt Blake's imagination and occupy a dominant place in the poems that express his early revolutionary hopes, as well as in his later work. Yet even when his revolutionary sympathies were at their height, political revolution was never an end in itself for Blake; it simply formed part of his cosmic vision of human regeneration, involving every aspect of man's psyche in the corporeal and the spiritual universe, here and hereafter. As has been well said, what Blake sought was "the achievement of true liberty, which would be, not a political order, but a visionary order with necessary political and social consequences." [1]

By an odd coincidence, in 1757, the year of Blake's birth, yet another Joachite third age of the spirit—inaugurating a new heaven, a new church, and a new dispensation with the Last Judgment—was proclaimed by Swedenborg. In the new Swedenborgian age, worship of God as man (the Divine Humanity) was to replace that of the invisible God. The coincidence between his date of birth and the beginning of the new age was not lost on Blake, who remarked on the event thirty-three years later, at a time when his admiration for the Swedish theologist-philosopher was qualified by reservations. The quirky, opinionated, and genial poet and painter, who said he loved laughing and fun, was commenting on the Swedenborgian revelation with a characteristic blend of sly satire and deep seriousness in one of his most subversive works, *The Marriage of Heaven and Hell,* whose paradoxical reversal of values anticipates Nietzsche. Certainly, for Blake the apocalyptic moment of judgment and regeneration, associated with his birth through the Swedenborg Society (to which he belonged for a while), was not a final crisis but an event to be constantly renewed.

"Are not Religion and Politics the Same Thing?" Blake was to inquire rhetorically some years later in his long, abstruse prophetic poem *Jerusalem.* [2] He was born into an age when the vocabularies of religion and politics were often interchangeable, when a leading radical nonconformist minister like Dr. Richard Price (who is chiefly remembered for having aroused Edmund Burke's ire) could welcome the French Revolution in 1789 with the words of Simeon's prayer, "Lord, now lettest thou thy servant depart in peace, for mine eyes have seen thy salvation," thus echoing the very sentiments expressed by the Reverend Hugh Peters at the downfall of Charles I. The parallel between these two revolutionary divines rejoicing at the dismay of kings was noted by Burke, who saw in Dr. Price "a man much connected with literary caballers, . . . with political theologians, and theological politicians, both at home and abroad." [3] Blake may have met Dr. Price at the weekly dinners given by

Joseph Johnson, the radical printer and bookseller who published the first and only extant book of Blake's poem *The French Revolution.*

Johnson numbered among his guests such radical luminaries as Dr. Joseph Priestley, the chemist, Presbyterian preacher, and author of *A History of the Corruptions of Christianity;* Tom Paine, cosmopolitan fighter for human rights in America and France, who, according to Blake, attacked the "perversions" of Christ's words and acts; and William Godwin, for whom religion that aroused phantoms of guilt was accursed, and who said that "God himself has not a right to be a tyrant." [4] Blake shared the mingled interest in radicalism and religion among this circle, natural enough at a time when religion often served as an instrument of state and a means of keeping the lower orders in ignorance and submission. He shared, too, their indignation at social injustice and their unlimited hopes for a better and more humane world—hopes whose expansiveness then had the excuse of innocence as yet largely untainted by contact with practical obstacles or repeated disillusion.

When the most astonishing revolution that has ever occurred, as Burke called it, broke out in 1789, only a hundred years had passed since the "bloodless" English revolution of 1688 and another forty since the Puritan revolution of 1648. It is scarcely surprising, then, that English Jacobins and anti-Jacobins should look back with respect or aversion to the Puritan precedent, when liberty and apocalyptism went together. Moreover, all his life Blake felt a unique personal tie with John Milton, the republican, the visionary recorder of the councils of heaven and hell, of paradise lost and regained, as distinct from the puritanical figure "clothed in black, severe and silent." [5] And although evidence of direct influence is lacking, Blake's writings reveal, too, a close affinity with the apocalyptic libertarians on the extreme radical wing of the Commonwealth, especially the Ranters, the Muggletonians, and others, some of whom persisted in small conventicles among the London tradespeople as late as the eighteen-twenties. [6] The son of a moderately prosperous hosier, Blake grew up among London artisans and shopkeepers, and he remained all his days a craftsman, an engraver, a man who worked with his hands.

The adherents of such extreme radical dissenting sects were antinomian: they believed the moral laws were not binding on Christians. Like their millenarian forerunners, the medieval Brethren of the Free Spirit and the Anabaptists of sixteenth-century Münster, they imagined they were living in the Last Days, in the Joachite third age of the spirit, when God is within man, and therefore established churches, laws, and moral codes are superfluous. As the Ranter Abiezer Coppe (who advocated "have ALL THINGS common") wrote in *A Fiery Flying Roll* in 1650, "But behold, behold, he is now risen . . . who by his mighty Angell is proclaiming . . . . That Sin and Transgression is finished and ended; and everlasting righteousnesse brought in; and the Everlasting Gospell preaching; which Everlasting Gospell is brought in with most terrible earth-quakes, and heaven-quakes, and with signs and wonders following." [7] The Everlasting Gospel, foretold in the Book of Revelation, grants a new direct revelation and dispensation, and is invisible alike to conventional churchmen and to deists like Paine, thought Blake. As Blake saw it, all peoples had originally shared one language and one religion: "this was the religion of Jesus, the Everlasting Gospel." [8] To this religion they should return.

Blake, then, was quite as attuned to this native antinomian tradition, where millenarianism and radicalism are united, as he was versed in the Neoplatonic "perennial philosophy," in alchemy and cabala, and the theosophy of Boehme and Swedenborg. He thought of himself as a prophetic bard who sees past, present, and future—"Hear the voice of the Bard!"—and who calls his hearers to a new birth and a new dawn. He understood the prophet to be one who does not utter prophecies in the void but who perceives and points out the consequences of human actions, both private and public: "Thus: If you go on So, the result is So. He never says, such a thing shall happen let you do what you will. A prophet is a Seer, not an Arbitrary Dictator." [9] In this way, the prophetic poet glimpses the hidden connections between political actions and their spiritual and moral causes and effects: "A tyrant is the worst disease, and the cause of all others." [10] He knows that the moral pestilence bred by tyranny and imperialism inevitably redounds at last upon all those who support them and profit by them, as well as upon the innocent.

For everything is interrelated. If one aspect is out of joint, the rest must follow. And this applies as much to nations as to individuals. Blake expressed this sense of interrelatedness most memorably in his poem "Auguries of Innocence,"

> A Robin Red breast in a Cage
> Puts all Heaven in a Rage . . .
> A dog starv'd at his Master's Gate
> Predicts the ruin of the State . . . [11]

or later, more evangelically, in *Jerusalem,*

> For not one Sparrow can suffer and the whole Universe not suffer also
> In all its Regions. . . .[12]

As Blake himself insisted, he moved not in the world of historians like Gibbon and Voltaire who discussed logical cause and effect (which did not interest him) but in accordance with an older tradition, in the world where what he called "spiritual agency" reigned.[13]

It is within this biblical framework that Blake sees revolution and revolutionary liberty. All his sympathies lay with the American colonists in revolt and with the French people; the revolutions in America and France appeared to him as twin aspects of the same phenomenon, the annunciation of a universal movement of redemption that would spread to Spain, Italy, and England, to Mexico and Peru. The tyrannous old order, which promoted oppression, injustice, cruelty, and war, would vanish in the new dawn of humanity. For Blake, revolution was only partially an historical event; it was a terrifying yet wonderful apocalyptic prelude to the salvation and regeneration of mankind.

The revolutionary dawn of the messianic age of peace and freedom breaks in images of resurrection:

> The morning comes, the night decays, the watchmen leave their stations;
> The grave is burst, the spices shed, the linen wrapped up;
> The bones of death, the cov'ring clay, the sinews shrunk and dry'd
> Reviving shake, inspiring move, breathing, awakening,

Spring like redeemed captives when their bonds and bars are burst.
Let the slave grinding at the mill run out into the field,
Let him look up into the heavens and laugh in the bright air;
Let the inchained soul, shut up in darkness and in sighing,
Whose face has never seen a smile in thirty weary years,
Rise and look out; his chains are loose, his dungeon doors are open;
And let his wife and children return from the oppressor's scourge.
They look behind at every step and believe it is a dream,
Singing: "The Sun has left his blackness and has found a fresher morning,
And the fair moon rejoices in the clear and cloudless night;
For Empire is no more, and now the Lion and Wolf shall cease.[14]

Revolution in Blake frequently merges with resurrection in a violent but triumphant agony that defies paraphrase as the grave becomes fertile and shrieks with delight in the carnal act of conception and the process of birth; the rattling dry bones join together, and all flesh rises naked from the dead dust.

But with revolutionary resurrection there must be a Last Judgment, and for this the source of his imagery is the apocalyptic vision of divine vengeance, the furious and bloody treading of the winepress in Isaiah, the human harvest and vintage in the Revelation of St. John, when blood rises to the level of the horse bridles. The poet whose hatred of cruelty and bloodshed is one of his most notable and touching qualities nonetheless lingers in imagination over torrents of gore, over "golden chariots raging with red wheels dropping with blood." [15]

Why does Blake return time and again to the terrors and horrors of apocalyptic judgment and vengeance? He himself provided an explanation, insisting that a Last Judgment is "necessary" for hindering the oppressor: "A Last Judgment is Necessary because Fools flourish. . . . A Last Judgment is not for the purpose of making Bad Men better, but for the Purpose of hindering them from oppressing the Good with Poverty and Pain. . . ." And he went on, "Christ comes, as he came at first, to deliver those who were bound under the Knave, not to deliver the Knave. He comes to deliver Man, the Accused, and not Satan, the Accuser." [16] So in his poem *Vala, or the Four Zoas,* the oppressed "pursue like the wind"; and when the unjust judge appeals for mercy, the prisoner who had seen his father tortured scorns such hypocrisy and "dash'd him with his foot." [17]

Throughout his work, Blake insists on the separation of sheep and goats. One of his early comments on the bland aphorisms of the Swiss poet and theologian Lavater was that "Severity of judgment is a great virtue." [18] Where Lavater nobly argued that one must never lose sight of the human being in one's enemy, since the most inhuman person still remains a man, Blake remarked: "None can see the man in the enemy; . . . I cannot love my enemy, for my enemy is not man, but beast or devil, if I have any." [19] This note of Blake's is extremely revealing. He relieved his aggressive feelings in savage private epigrams scourging those false friends whom he felt, perhaps with justice, had betrayed, wronged, or harmed him. The tigers of wrath might be wiser than the horses of instruction, but it was doubtless his growing realization of the equivocal nature of his own angry impulses which lay at the heart of his impassioned devotion to the doctrine of forgiveness of sins. Yet this devotion did not interfere with his equally firm belief in the necessity of the implacable Last Judgment, and in his early works revolution itself serves partly as the destructive Last Judgment that must precede the inauguration of true liberty, in both its narrow political and wider spiritual sense.

Revolutionary severity is rooted in the conviction that paradise has been lost and can be regained only by a fiery purgation. One must be powerfully certain that something wonderful has gone, to be ready to embrace destruction for the sake of restoring it. Blake looks back to the innocence of a vanished Eden—"O times remote!" when none were thought sinful and impure—to the idyllic Golden Age of the youth of the world. He plainly avows that "The Nature of my Work is Visionary or Imaginative; it is an Endeavour to Restore what the Ancients call'd the Golden Age." [20] The paradise of infancy—fearless, happy, joyfully nestling for delight in laps of pleasure—was lost, and in its place stood a prison, the hell ruled by canting, aged ignorance with its repressive laws. How to regain the joyous lost paradise of childhood and youth, the lost wholeness of man, the lost vision of which all are capable if only they would realize it, and cleanse the doors of perception? Then doubtless—as in climes of eternity—rocks, clouds, and mountains would speak again, and the lamb reply to the infant voice.

What Blake saw around him was a "ruin'd world" which he believed had been brought about by excessive reliance on abstract reasoning and analysis at the expense of the vaulting and reconciling powers of imagination and vision. This mistaken trust in analytical reasoning transformed life into sordid mechanics and was the fateful origin of the miseries spread by the factories and furnaces of the industrial revolution. Instead of the ecstatic, free, angelic harmony of Ezekiel's wheels within wheels, he found repressive mechanization and the separation of faculties that should be blending in unison:

> I turn my eyes to the Schools and Universities of Europe
> And there behold the Loom of Locke, whose Woof rages dire,
> Wash'd by the Water-wheels of Newton: black the cloth
> In heavy wreathes folds over every Nation: cruel Works
> Of many Wheels I view, wheel without wheel, with cogs tyrannic
> Moving by compulsion each other, not as those in Eden, which,
> Wheel within Wheel, in freedom revolve in harmony and peace.[21]

It was the visionary concord of the Hebrew prophet that Blake sought to recover: he yearned to reintegrate the divided elements both within man and in man's present discordant way of life.

Originally, in climes of eternity, man was androgynous or ambisexual. Then separation took place and the resulting sexual disharmony was the source of all social disharmony, of the cruelty, violence, and war into which man's repressed and unsatisfied sexual energies were diverted. Blake wrote in defense of sexual freedom, against concealment and false shame, against repression and unacted desires. He would have liked to break the chains of loveless marriage. There seems little doubt that, in common with later utopian revolutionary spirits, he associated his revolutionary hopes with sexual liberty and with the recovery of "the lineaments of gratified desire." In his private mythology, the virgin Oothoon, raped by the tyrant Bromion and as a result abandoned by Theotormon, her conventional lover, mournfully utters a paean to free love:

> I cry: Love! Love! Love! happy happy Love! free as the mountain wind!
> Can that be Love that drinks another as a sponge drinks water,
> That clouds with jealousy his nights, with weepings all the day, . . . ?
> Such is self-love that envies all, a creeping skeleton
> With lamplike eyes watching around the frozen marriage-bed.
> But silken nets and traps of adamant will Oothoon spread,
> And catch for thee girls of mild silver, or of furious gold.
> I'll lie beside thee on a bank and view their wanton play
> In lovely copulation, bliss on bliss, with Theotormon: . . .[22]

The syntax of the last two lines, as so often in Blake, may leave the precise action somewhat dubious and obscure, but the gist and intention seem clear enough.

Allusions in Blake's poetry to unanswered male sexual demands, to jealousy, female possessiveness, and the will to dominate, have suggested to some an autobiographical note. The poem "William Bond," where the self-sacrificing wife's humble and agonized acceptance of a concubine leads to a change of heart in the unfaithful spouse and to reconciliation between husband and wife, has been interpreted in a personal sense. The Germanophile Henry Crabb Robinson alleged in his diary in 1826, the year before the poet's death, and in German for discretion, that Blake told him he advocated community of women, having deduced it from the Bible. Furthermore, in fantasies of the Golden Age it was quite customary for women to be held in common, on the pretext of obviating jealousy and lust. There is, too, the story, hotly denied, that Blake's patron Thomas Butts discovered the young poet and his wife sitting naked in their Lambeth garden. "Come in!" cried Blake, "it's only Adam and Eve, you know!" [23] This tale has given rise to the view that Blake may have been practicing the ritual nakedness of the Adam cult popular among the Brethren of the Free Spirit and their later followers, including the Ranters, and justified by their belief in the restoration of innocence under the higher dispensation of the Last Days.

If Blake's revolutionary hopes were fixed on a change in sexual attitudes and conduct, they also went much deeper and embraced the whole sphere of repressive conventional morality, of which the sexual aspect was but a part. Sexual hypocrisy was merely one facet of general hypocrisy. "Alas, in cities where's the man whose face is not a mask unto his heart?" inquired Blake before he was twenty, and of whom his devoted admirer the painter Samuel Palmer was to say that he was "a man without a mask." [24]

For Blake, the origin of canting self-righteousness and pharisaic holiness was the cruel deity who ruled over this world, and whom he called variously the Elohim, Urizen, Satan, and Nobodaddy, the last inspiring a particular excremental disrespect somehow associated with the German religious epic poet Klopstock. This malevolent divinity (after Gnostic tradition) was quite distinct from the true God: he was the tyrant of tyrants, the inventor of iron laws that "no flesh nor spirit could keep," laws that forbid and restrict, inspire fear and punish, whereas in truth "everything that lives is Holy" and a ceaseless spring of joy and delight. The instruments of this hateful deity were established religion and the established church, or the Synagogue of Satan: "The Modern Church Crucifies Christ with the Head Downwards," he declared, thereby expressing his feeling that religious orthodoxy was a perversion of spiritual truth. [25]

True Christianity, as he conceived it, is a revolutionary force. It has no connection with the conventionally pious, with those who talk of virtue with hardened hearts, who think well of themselves because they dispense a grudging charity "with cold usurious hand," but whose ill-gotten wealth is founded on exploitation, on Negro slavery and the labor of little children. And in Blake's eyes, Jesus is a revolutionary spirit, oddly resembling himself in having a snub nose and sharing his world-view. In a typically challenging reversal, one of his friendly devils explains how Jesus revolted against the Ten Commandments: ". . . did he not mock at the sabbath and so mock the sabbath's God? murder those who were murdered because of him? turn away the law from the woman taken in adultery? steal the labour of others to support him? . . . I tell you, no virtue can exist without breaking these ten commandments. Jesus was all virtue, and acted from impulse, not from rules! " [26] So wrote Blake between 1790 and 1793 in *The Marriage of Heaven and Hell,* but these ideas remained with him all his life, and were expressed in similar words many years later, about 1818, in *The Everlasting Gospel.*

In this poem, only fragments of which remain, whose order is irrecoverable, Blake could roundly declare to orthodox believers:

> The Vision of Christ that thou dost see
> Is my Vision's Greatest Enemy. . . . [27]

By this he meant that the humble, gentle Jesus born of the Virgin was a false invention whom he called "Creeping Jesus" or even Antichrist; whereas he felt that the true Jesus must needs have been born of a harlot to fulfill his mission, that this spiritual Savior spoke with disturbing and challenging authority, "used the Elders and Priests like dogs," cursed the rulers before the people, and

> His Seventy Disciples sent
> Against Religion and Government: . . .[28]

Here is Blake's plainest formulation of revolutionary anarchism, based (like certain later manifestations of political anarchism, notably in Spain) upon a revolutionary interpretation of Christianity.

In Blake it is the revolutionary spirit—whether Orc or Jesus—that stamps to dust the stony law of sexual, moral, and spiritual repression and hypocrisy. The revolutionary urge is seen as a form of energy, and in the voice of Blake's subversive devil (which may be understood as one of the poet's inner voices), "Energy is the only life. . . . Energy is Eternal Delight." [29] Yet Blake's vision of energy is ambiguous. His revolutionary spirit, named Orc (after Orcus or hell), is "the new-born terror," "red Orc," "terrible Orc," a demon, "a serpent of fiery flame," a figure who is bound in chains like Prometheus, the bearer of equivocal gifts that do both good and harm. The poet, who once said he preferred active evil to passive good, would not flinch from the "thick-flaming, thought-creating fires of Orc," fires which consume but which can also reveal life in all its holiness. Orc, the fierce ambivalent liberator, blends in Blake's private mythology with Luvah, or love, and so sometimes even with Jesus himself, whom he calls "the God *of Fire* and Lord *of Love.*" [30]

When Samuel Palmer tried to describe Blake many years after the poet's death, he recalled that "He was energy itself. . . . His eye was the finest I ever saw: . . . it flashed with genius, or melted in tenderness. It could also be terrible." [31] With these words Palmer conveys a glimpse of Blake's enduring energetic powers and of his inner division between the tender and the awe-inspiring. Blake himself spoke of the "terrific" and the "gentle" parts of his poetry in the preface to the first section of *Jerusalem.* It was Blake who wondered whether destructiveness is as much a part of the divine design as compassion, in "The Tiger," a poem whose ambivalence leaves the reader torn between exaltation at the beauty of animal energy and terror at its savagery.

Blake answered the question about the tiger—"Did he who made the Lamb make thee?"—in the affirmative when he wrote that beasts of prey and the destructive sword are portions of eternity, too great for the eye of man. Here also, perhaps, is the core of Blake's feeling about revolution, a feeling divided between inexorable destruction and bottomless pity, between elation and dread. Nothing indicates more clearly the ambivalence of the fascination exerted by revolution upon Blake and on many who came after him. He is, above all, the supreme poet of the double face of humanity in *Songs of Innocence* and *Songs of Experience.* In one version of "The Divine Image," Mercy has a human heart, Pity a human face, while in the other Cruelty has a human heart, Jealousy a human face, and Terror the human form divine. Doubtless he was moved to write these potent lyrics from observation, not only of others but of himself.

His poetry strives to resolve contraries in his nature rather than marking the achievement of resolution and reconciliation. Blake's dialectic of contraries—"Without Contraries is no progression . . ." [32]—may therefore be seen as the consequence of his own inner divisions no less than as a heritage of his reading of the Neoplatonists or Boehme. Similarly his stress on the concept of wholeness and harmony, on the restora-

tion of vision, can be regarded as the result of a private sense of deprivation of vision which he mentioned in a strange letter addressed to
William Hayley on October 23, 1804, as having lasted for twenty years,
years during which he nonetheless produced many of his finest poems.

Rarely averse to astonishing his prosaic interlocutors by allusions to
his frequent colloquies with spirits of the eminent dead or by his idiosyncratic opinions on sex and religion, Blake united great boldness of
thought with considerable public caution. The dark atmosphere of reaction and repression in England was perhaps sufficient to justify his nervous fears, and he had before him the example of those leaders of the
Reform movement who were sentenced to transportation in 1793 and
1794. If Godwin courageously spoke out on behalf of Holcroft, Horne
Tooke, and the other leading members of the Corresponding Society who
had been accused of treason, and by his action saved their lives, he simply
points out the contrast between the active thinker and the poetic visionary.

Blake preferred not to risk publishing his more daring thoughts; and
this inclination was reinforced after he had been accused of sedition in
1803 and brought to trial in January 1804. A soldier whom he had
ejected from his garden in Felpham asserted that the poet had not only
shouted "Damn the King" but had declared the soldiers and the poor
were all slaves, and had expressed defeatist sentiments concerning a possible Napoleonic invasion—and all this in time of war. Blake denied the
charge and was acquitted, to general acclamation in court, but the an-
timonarchical opinions and social criticism of which he stood accused
could be found in his works. His fear of spies became almost paranoid
after this experience, which left him badly shaken.

Gradually Blake no longer directly expressed revolutionary sympathies, and the fiery liberating demon Orc ceased to loom so large in his
poetry. True, as a poet he did not think in terms of policies and reforms
but in terms of deep social concern, of the new dawn, and regeneration
and salvation. When he envisages a new society, it is one where there
would be neither poverty nor injustice, where all would be joyful, selfless,
and spiritually whole, and where the arts would flourish. While endless

mental battle must be waged to achieve this new Jerusalem, a certain disillusion with purely political revolutionary aims becomes evident. In "The Grey Monk," for instance, which dates from 1801–1804, Blake sees in libertarian vengeance merely the substitution of one tyrant for another:

> The hand of Vengeance found the Bed
> To which the Purple Tyrant fled;
> The iron hand-crush'd the Tyrant's head
> And became a Tyrant in his stead.[33]

And by 1810 he was declaring publicly, "I am really sorry to see my Countrymen trouble themselves about Politics. If Men were Wise, the Most arbitrary Princes could not hurt them. If they are not wise, the Freest Government is compell'd to be a Tyranny," [34] a comment which (like the opinion of Schiller or Godwin) implies that the acquisition of wisdom should take precedence over political solutions.

At about the same time, he wrote in similar vein: "Many Persons, such as Paine and Voltaire, . . . say: 'we will not converse concerning Good and Evil; we will live in Paradise and Liberty.' You may do so in the Spirit, but not in the Mortal Body as you pretend, till after the Last Judgment. . . ." [35] Here Blake dissociates himself in public from Paine whom he had defended so warmly (though in private) in 1798. The celebrated lines in *Jerusalem,*

> He who would do good to another must do it in Minute Particulars:
> General Good is the plea of the scoundrel, hypocrite and flatterer, . . .[36]

likewise imply disillusion not just with philanthropy but with Jacobin declarations of intent.

Despite these saddened reflections, Blake's later works share the same hatred of cruelty and war as his early writings, the same indignation at hypocrisy, the same pity for the innocent victims of injustice, the same misery at the deleterious effects of the industrial revolution, the same yearning to break through "the mind forg'd manacles." What has happened is that Blake has moved away from the idea of regeneration and salvation through revolution toward a spiritual rebirth brought about by a change of heart, the annihilation of selfhood, the restoration of wholeness of vision, and the acceptance of the doctrine of forgiveness of sins. His concern with regeneration and salvation has not changed, only the means whereby they are to be attained. The total transformation of man that Blake requires is a form of inner transfiguration, ultimately spiritual in nature, and in its way no less revolutionary than his earlier standpoint. Since there is a constant falling off from the ideal, there must always be a Last Judgment which he thus unexpectedly conceives not as a final event but as a recurring process (for he holds that every time an individual rejects error, a Last Judgment passes upon that individual). Where a later revolutionary was to speak of permanent revolution, Blake's vision rests on a permanent apocalypse.

At first, then, it would seem that Blake restores the longing for regeneration and salvation to the field of discourse in which it truly belongs, namely religion. But this is to overlook the singular nature of Blake's religion. Often using familiar religious vocabulary and concepts, but interpreting the Bible in a "spiritual sense" (as Crabb Robinson noted), Blake ends with something quite unsystematic and subtly distinct from what is usually understood by these concepts. So devoted was Blake to art that he believed Jesus, his apostles and disciples were all artists, and he could not envisage religion dissociated from visionary art. For him, Jesus is the imagination, the visionary power in man as well as the all, or the divine image. When Crabb Robinson asked Blake what he thought about the divinity of Jesus, the poet's disconcerting reply was reported as follows: "He said—*He is the only God*—But then he added—'And so am I and so are you.' " [37] This would suggest a more daring step on the path to self-deification than the Christian text would warrant.

Blake was at war with all authorities and establishments, including those of church, state, and art. He was on the side of youth against age. He sought for social regeneration through sexual harmony. Above all, he longed to recover what he believed had once existed but had now been lost, an idyllic childlike innocence and wholeness of vision. Indeed, his function as prophetic bard was to restore the Golden Age. To this end, he strove to destroy Babylon and build the new Jerusalem of true spiritual liberty.

To many of his contemporaries—even those who, like Wordsworth, admired his poems—Blake appeared crazed. He was born, as he sadly knew, with a "different face" from theirs, and not until recent times has his profound foreshadowing originality become manifest, awakening a somewhat distorted echo in the proselytizing sensuality of Gide and D. H. Lawrence, both of whom recognized in him a kindred spirit. In his awareness of the etiolation caused by industrial advancement, his hatred of materialism and distrust of analytic reasoning, his rejection of false benevolence (a form of antiliberalism), his loathing for repression in all its forms, sexual and moral, physical and spiritual, his longing for the total transformation and regeneration of mankind, Blake anticipates the redemptive urge of the anarchic revolutionary literature of the present day. "The road of excess leads to the palace of wisdom" is one proverb of hell that might serve as a modern motto. Not for one moment does Blake doubt that the path to regeneration and salvation, whether attained by revolution or by some private overthrow of selfhood, leads through the terrors of the apocalypse.

chapter **2**

the God that failed:
Wordsworth and Coleridge

odyssey of a revolutionary enthusiast: Wordsworth

Of all the major English Romantic poets, William Wordsworth was the only one
who was actually *there,* in France, during some of the most exhilarating
and bloody moments of the French Revolution. How this happened was
in the beginning the result of mere chance, and few with his remote upbringing among the northern hills and lakes might seem, at first sight,
likely material for a revolutionary sympathizer. Yet it is frequently
among such compassionate idealists, with a lofty conception of man's capabilities for self-transformation and for transforming the world, that literary revolutionists are to be found.

Unworldly, visionary, apolitical, uninformed, a young man of strong and deep feelings who knew he wanted to be a poet and was reluctant to commit himself to the professions of either Church or law, he managed (much to the distress of his guardians) to spend the years 1790 to 1794 ostensibly doing nothing. But during that period he underwent the shattering experiences that were to help transform him from a solitary and imitative young man into a revolutionary poet, experiences that marked him for life, both for good and ill. Moreover, as the exponent of "the egotistical sublime," he was the first poet to describe in minute detail all the varied stages of his emotional and intellectual progress into and out of revolution.

It was on July 13, 1790, the day before the first anniversary of the fall of the Bastille, that Wordsworth crossed the Channel and set foot in France on a walking tour with a Welsh friend, a fellow undergraduate at Cambridge. As they continued on their way, they met the delegates returning from the festivities of Federation Day in Paris. All was dancing and gaiety in the first flush of freedom. Wordsworth and his companion were honored and made welcome. The original version of *Descriptive Sketches,* the poem which gives an account of the tour and of the poet's reactions to the joyous celebration of liberty, was not written until two years later, at the height of Wordsworth's revolutionary enthusiasm. In this poem, published by Joseph Johnson in 1793, Wordsworth sees the flames of revolution as "innocuous": from them springs a new earth with its own virtues, a virgin reign of love and truth. When he reverted to the same moment in the sixth book of *The Prelude,* he spoke of Europe filled with rejoicing, of France standing on the top of golden hours, and, significantly, of human nature seeming reborn—and he derived lessons of genuine brotherhood from what he saw and felt.

Only in later revisions of *Descriptive Sketches* did Wordworth tone down his excitement. (No longer is there truly a new and lovely birth from the revolutionary flames; it merely seems "as if" a new heaven and earth were called into being.) But for a long while to come he would not abandon the hopes and the ideals of that glorious and happy time, and then only after painful inner struggles. The poem reveals what Wordsworth in his early twenties expected from revolution: the victory of freedom over imperialism and privilege, over persecution, oppression, and famine, ambition and conquest, discord and war; and the utter ruin of monarchs who opposed the new dispensation.

Unlike Blake, Wordsworth did not envisage this new dispensation as having effect in some equivocal terrain, part here and now, part idyllic Eden or restored Golden Age, part within the transformed human psyche, and totally within a world of united flesh and spirit. Wordsworth meant, quite unambiguously, the world around him. It was during this same walking tour, though in a passage written some years later in the sixth book of *The Prelude,* that Wordsworth conceived the apocalypse not in a Christian context (however idiosyncratic), as Blake does, but through the universe of wild nature. The lines occur in that mysterious and unforgettable episode on the Simplon Pass, where the poet and his companion by mistake ascend the mountain instead of descending it, and find they have crossed the Alps without realizing they have done so.

At this moment the poet perceives, in an imaginative flash which reveals the invisible world, that human destiny

> Is with infinitude, and only there;
> With hope it is, hope that can never die,
> Effort, and expectation, and desire,
> And something evermore about to be.[1]

After this mighty parenthesis, the friends hurry on through a gloomy path among woods decaying, though never to be decayed, past hurtling torrents and lofty crags, and it seems to the poet as if

> Tumult and peace, the darkness and the light
> Were all like workings of one mind, the features
> Of the same face, blossoms upon one tree,
> Characters of the great Apocalypse,
> The types and symbols of Eternity,
> Of first, and last, and midst, and without end.[2]

For Wordsworth, then, it is the natural world that reveals terror and glory and eternity to the receptive imagination; and Blake, while admiring his poetry, thought him often an atheist for worshipping the natural world which he (Blake) regarded as a Satanic illusion.[3]

Coleridge, too, in the early years of their friendship, found Wordsworth a republican and "at least a *semi*-atheist," that is, not anti-Christian but rather a person unconcerned by Christianity.[4] Nor could Blake tolerate the passage in *The Recluse* where Wordsworth passes Jehovah and the angelic host "unalarmed": it gave him terrible pains in the bowels. But if Wordsworth could feel unmoved by divine terror it was because— as he declares in his poem—chaos, hell, and nothingness did not inspire so much awe in him as did the mind of man, "the main region of my song." For to the discerning intellect, Wordsworth believed, paradise, Eden, and Elysium are not a myth but a "simple produce of the common day."[5]

That Wordsworth in his French period believed in a concrete, rational, and secular world-transformation is made clear in the celebrated lines of *The Prelude* (quoted here throughout in the less polished and less familiar but early version of 1805), where he writes that the new thinkers and revolutionary spirits had "plastic" material to hand which they felt they could mold to their heart's desire. Moreover, they

> Were call'd upon to exercise their skill,
> Not in Utopia, subterranean Fields,
> Or some secreted Island, Heaven knows where,
> But in the very world which is the world
> Of all of us, the place on which, in the end,
> We find our happiness, or not at all.[6]

From this it would seem perfectly plain that for "mild schemers" like these whose feelings Wordsworth shared, happiness is to be found in this world alone. Such a view need not clash with the idea that human fate is romantically involved with "something evermore about to be."

The young man who came home after his first journey abroad, stirred by the delights the wider world had to offer, and touched by what he had witnessed, was still uninvolved. His second stay in France was to be of longer duration and more far-reaching consequences. While in Paris from November 30 to December 5, 1791, he saw the sights, gained admission to the National Assembly and the Jacobin Club, visited the ruins of the Bastille, and, as an "enthusiast," pocketed a stone for a souvenir; but (he maintained) he affected more emotion than he felt, and was still looking for something he could not find. Lacking political education, he remained as before, unconcerned, like a spectator at a play.

On December 6 he traveled on to Orléans, where he intended to stay to study French. Deeply moved, he could observe the self-sacrificing patriotism of the volunteers leaving family and home to defend their country. Their conduct proved

> that 'twas a cause
> Good, and which no one could stand up against,
> Who was not lost, abandon'd, selfish, proud,
> Mean, miserable, wilfully deprav'd,
> Hater perverse of equity and truth! [7]

So righteous was the cause, its opponents must needs be evil. At the same time he met two people who changed his life. He fell in love with Annette Vallon, who was to bear him a daughter. And he won the friendship of a republican officer, Michel Beaupuy, who, together with the volunteers, appeared to him the supreme embodiment of the nobility and justice of the revolutionary ideal.

Everything about the future General Beaupuy was attractive to Wordsworth. Not only was he a man of action who (unlike his royalist fellow officers) realized that the clock could never be turned back; he was also endowed with a deep sense of humanity and respect for human dignity. On one of their long walks together, they encountered a listless "hunger-bitten girl" with a cow tied to her arm, and Beaupuy turned to him, saying,

> " 'Tis against *that*
> Which we are fighting," . . .[8]

Nothing was more likely to win Wordsworth's regard.

From an early age, the poet had learned to love and reverence human nature as embodied in the lowly shepherds and wanderers of his native hills. For him human nature was "a spirit"; and no dark side, no vice, guilt, debasement, or misery could destroy his trust in "what we *may* become." [9] Kindred souls, then, Wordsworth and Beaupuy walked along the Loire and talked endlessly about the goals and the best forms of government, about the relative claims of tradition and change. The friends believed that abject poverty such as they had seen personified by the wretched cow-girl would vanish "in a little time," established institutions of privilege and pomp would be blotted out, abuses like imprisonment without trial would be abolished, the people would be allowed to participate in framing the country's laws—and that these improvements would mean better times for all mankind. [10]

It is to the enriching period of his association with Beaupuy that these oft-quoted lines refer:

> O pleasant exercise of hope and joy!
> For great were the auxiliars which then stood
> Upon our side, we who were strong in love;
> Bliss was it in that dawn to be alive,
> But to be young was very Heaven; . . .[11]

This euphoria could not endure. During the massacres of September 1792, Wordsworth was in either Orléans or Blois, and he arrived in Paris on October 29, the day Louvet attacked (but failed to dislodge) Robespierre in the Convention. He passed by the empty Tuileries and the Temple, where Louis XVI and his family were imprisoned, and he remained firmly convinced of the king's guilt. But the crimes and massacres were over, never to return, as he told himself in an effort at justification; they were

> Ephemeral monsters, to be seen but once;
> Things that could only shew themselves and die.[12]

All the same, in his lonely room at the top of a tall mansion, he felt in what world he was placed. Paris appeared to him

> Defenceless as a wood where tigers roam.[13]

He could scarcely avoid hearing the demagogic denunciations of Marat, and learned to hate the Jacobins and the mob.

In deep sadness he witnessed the ineffectualness and indecision of the Girondists, with whose aims he sympathized. Like so many others, he felt that only a benevolent dictator, "one paramount mind," could save the day.[14] Meanwhile, apparently on the brink of total commitment, or so he hints, Wordsworth found his funds cut off and was forced to return to England. Otherwise, he says, he would have made common cause with the Girondists who perished, and might even have suffered the same fate, a mere poet in embryo.

Some idea of Wordworth's revolutionary views at this time can be gleaned from his letter to the Bishop of Llandaff, composed early in 1793 but published posthumously. They are stronger than he admits in his poem. The months following the execution of Louis XVI on January 21, 1793, marked the peak of Wordsworth's period of austere Roman republicanism. He reproached the bishop for attaching too much importance to the personal sufferings of the late monarch at a time when the very fate of the human race was being decided. Besides, he informed the bishop, the safety of the people was the supreme law.

The proponents of liberty (Wordsworth believed then) could sometimes be obliged to adopt the methods of despotism in order to overthrow it, and, while deploring such stern necessity, must establish liberty by violence. War between the oppressed and the oppressors must of necessity disturb and confuse ideas of morality. He maintained that political virtues are established at the expense of moral ones; that pity is dangerous when traitors are to be punished. (Saint-Just would say no less when he told his hearers that, since they were striving not for themselves but for the people, they had not the right to show clemency to traitors.) However, Wordsworth allowed that pity was too often suppressed. But, he inquired rhetorically, was all this unpleasantness sufficient reason to blame an upheaval out of which a fairer order will spring? He concluded that the struggle for liberty was necessarily accompanied by the elimination of many talented human beings. With such arguments did the poet counter reaction and complacency at home.

Wordsworth had arrived in England to find the opponents of the slave trade still smarting under their defeat, but he himself was not excessively perturbed by it, because he retained his faith in the good and pure cause whose ultimate success would destroy all such abuses. He had found, in short, the ideological panacea for all ills. If France prospered, he reasoned, the rotten branch of slavery would fall, "together with its parent tree." [15] Several catastrophes followed which shook him to the core and embittered his feelings, but did little to disturb his faith.

The first and greatest of these shocks was the crusading war against France, which left him torn between loyalty to his country and to his ideal. To see Englishmen fighting against the France of Beaupuy and the volunteers was more than he could bear, and he compared himself to the once-happy green leaf (later the harebell), now tossing in the whirlwind. He even rejoiced at English defeat, and bitterly denounced the government for undermining the patriotic loyalty of "the best youth of England," to whom (as he put it in religious terms)

> apostasy from ancient faith
> Seem'd but conversion to a higher creed, . . . [16]

Besides, he opposed the war because it served the Jacobins as an excuse for their crimes.

The second test of his faith was the Jacobin Terror:

> Head after head, and never heads enough
> For those who bade them fall: . . .[17]

It was a lamentable time for mankind, and especially tragic for those whose hopes survived the shock, and who preserved their "trust in man." [18] Among these was Wordsworth himself. He struggled not too convincingly to find some consolation in the honorable conduct of the victims which might never have existed without such tribulations. He refused to recant, to join with those who regarded the Terror as the inevitable outcome of popular government and the doctrine of equality. On the contrary, he attributed the disaster not to human fallibility nor to mistaken ideology, but to a terrible reservoir of guilt and ignorance which had been accumulating down the ages and which had finally overflowed.

The poet may have returned to France sometime during the Terror at the end of September or early October 1793, for in conversation with Carlyle, many years later, he remarked that he had witnessed the execution of the journalist and deputy Antoine Gorsas, which took place on October 7, 1793. Gorsas (with an equally influential journalist named Carra) is mentioned in *The Prelude,* but not in the account of the Terror; his name occurs in connection with Wordsworth's first visit to Paris and Orléans. If Wordsworth was an eyewitness of the slaughter, it would help to account for his disturbed nights, his "ghastly visions" of despair long after the atrocities were over, his nightmares of pleading before unjust tribunals. And the dread vision of the sacrificial altar of the druids, which he later saw on Salisbury Plain, fed with "living men," could be attributed as much to personal experience as to literary sources.[19]

The downfall and execution of Robespierre on July 28, 1794, inspired Wordsworth to an exultant hymn of vengeance. Those who had preached that nothing but rivers of blood could cleanse the Augean stables, those who had set the revolutionary ideal on an evil course and had dimmed its luster, had been swept away in their turn. The monster who had betrayed the revolution had met with his just deserts. Now the revolution could return to its pristine origins, now the golden times could begin like the fresh morning, and earth "March firmly towards righteousness and peace," for the mighty "renovation" would be able to continue.[20] His own confidence was unimpaired:

> in the People was my trust
> And in the virtues which mine eyes had seen, . . .[21]

He knew the triumphs of the young republic would be in the end "Great, universal, irresistible." [22] Unhappily for him, further shocks were to follow, however: the French had moved from defensive war to a war of conquest. While suffering from disappointed idealism and striving to hide his dismay, the poet clung all the more tenaciously to his beliefs.

About this time, in the years 1794–1795, Wordsworth came under the influence of William Godwin, enjoying the idea of shaking off the "accidents of nature, time, and place," rejecting restraints, and adopting as sole guide the inspiration of the individual independent intellect. He longed to see man emerge from his "worm-like state" and nobly aspire to become "Lord of himself." But by dint of questioning everything he ended by yielding up moral questions "in despair." [23] In his 1795 drama, *The Borderers,* the Godwinian Iago, Oswald, prevails upon the luckless Marmaduke to murder, with the best intentions, a perfectly innocent old man—and stands condemned. The play marks the limits of Godwin's influence (though the two writers continued to meet socially from 1795 until Godwin's death in 1836, long after their political opinions diverged). It was the French invasion of Switzerland in 1798 that completed Wordsworth's disillusion. The coronation of Bonaparte as emperor in 1804 he would call the "last opprobrium" as the French people imitated "the dog returning to his vomit." [24]

Thus Wordsworth scrupulously traced, in a model trajectory, the course of his emotions and opinions from the early thrill of revolutionary exultation to the final sense of human folly and tragic failure, by way of every degree of noble loyalty, pained exculpation, proud obstinacy, and blind self-deception. He had even momentarily considered dangerous commitment to a foreign political party, and had rejoiced at his own country's defeat. No wonder this disappointed internationalist would end as a devout exponent of nationalism.

We know what his hopes and expectations were, how he yearned for a mighty renovation of mankind; we know the windings of the path and the obstacles he encountered and surmounted, only to find others blocking his way. We know, too, his reluctance to recant, for, after all, one does not easily surrender what one believes to be the key to human redemption. He who had approached the shield of human nature "from the golden side," who had trusted so ardently in "what we *may* become" that he had expected the man of the future to be "parted as by a gulph" from the man of former times, now grieved to think "What man has made of man." [25] The sight made him turn inward, to try to preserve and enlarge freedom within himself: "For this alone is genuine Liberty." [26]

Coleridge and the fascination of revolution

Coleridge, more than two years younger than Wordsworth, followed a different road, but by the time they became friends he had reached a similar point of gloom and withdrawal. Recalling the moral and intellectual upheaval caused by the French Revolution, the fascination it exerted which he refused to discount, he wrote: "My feelings . . . and imagination did not remain unkindled in this general conflagration; and I confess I should be more inclined to be ashamed than proud of myself, if they had! I was a sharer in the general vortex, though my little World described the path of its revolution in an orbit of its own." [27] As a schoolboy at Christ's Hospital he had written an ode celebrating the "Destruction of the Bastille," hoping that France's example would be universally followed. And in his undergraduate days at Cambridge he acquired the reputation of a republican, leveler, and Jacobin. This label stuck, and he later spent a good deal of his time trying to prove its inaccuracy. Unlike Wordsworth at the same age, Coleridge was politically aware, memorizing the pamphlets of the day as they issued hot from the press. There is no doubt where his emotional and idealistic sympathies lay at that period.

Already, at Cambridge, his gift for mismanaging his life manifested itself. Mounting debts encouraged him in the folly of enlisting in the King's Light Dragoons under the improbable pseudonym of Silas Tomkyn Comberbacke, and he had to be bought out by his brothers. While on vacation in Oxford in the summer of 1794, he met Southey, and the encounter had at least one lasting consequence: the two poets rushed to collaborate on a tragedy called *The Fall of Robespierre,* hatched together a utopian scheme for founding a colony in America, and, less transiently, became brothers-in-law. In the autumn of 1794, Coleridge sent a copy of their play (of which he composed only the first act) to Miss Brunton with a poem on the French Revolution, where his imaginative commitment, now tinged with some qualifications, is evident:

> When slumbr'ing Freedom rous'd by high Disdain
> With giant Fury burst her triple chain!
> Fierce on her Front the blasting Dog star glow'd;
> Her banners, like a midnight meteor, flow'd;
> Amid the yelling of the storm-rent Skies
> She came, and scattered Battles from her eyes!
> Then Exultation woke the patriot fire
> And swept with wilder hand th'empassion'd Lyre.
> Red from the Tyrant's wounds I shook the Lance,
> And strode in joy the reeking plains of France!
>
> In ghastly horror lie th'Oppressors low—
> And my Heart akes though Mercy struck the Blow! [28]

These lines reveal the note of exultation that frequently characterizes imaginative participation in bloody revolutionary action.

He later felt the need to defend this kind of imaginative excess, though in connection with another poem. It was, he maintained, the product of the poet's "seething imagination, and therefore impregnated with that pleasurable exultation which is experienced in all energetic exertion of intellectual power, . . ." [29] Yet at the same time as he joyfully strides the reeking plains of France in his imagination, Coleridge cannot help expressing his sorrow at the bloody deed. Characteristically, he is torn: from one point of view, it is mercy for the victims of oppression that strikes down oppressors, but the terrible end of the latter, as victims in their turn, inspires him with horror and pity.

A little later, in his poem "Religious Musings," allegedly composed on Christmas Eve 1794, Coleridge still saw the revolution in apocalyptic imagery such as might have been employed by Blake, of whom Coleridge would say self-deprecatingly, ". . . verily I am in the very mire of common-place compared with Mr. Blake, apo- or rather ana-calyptic Poet, and Painter!" [30] After an invocation to the sorrowing Galilean, Coleridge passed to the oppression suffered by the "wretched Many," telling them that "More blood must stream, or ere your wrongs be full," though the day of retribution is at hand. This day arrives when the Lamb opens the fifth seal and the French Revolution begins, marking the destruction of the union of religion with power, a combination that particularly offended Coleridge. The revolution ushers in the millennium, conceived in terms of Pantisocracy, where "the vast family of Love" enjoys the equally distributed produce of common toil, and Coleridge's saints of the hour—Newton, Hartley, and Priestley—enter into paradise as the earth is "renovated." [31]

Coleridge's approach to Pantisocracy lay through humanitarian indignation at social injustice. Pity inspired his pantisocratic enthusiasm. As he wrote with biting irony: "It is *wrong,* Southey! for a little girl with a half-famished sickly baby in her arms to put her head in at the window of an inn—'Pray give me a bit of bread and meat!' from a party dining on lamb, green peas, and salad. Why? Because it is *impertinent* and *obtrusive!*" Or so Coleridge's companion felt, a cultivated man who professed humanitarianism: "yet such are the unfeeling remarks, which the lingering remains of aristocracy occasionally prompt." [32]

Pantisocracy would change all that. The young ass, with its wretched mother tied by a shortened chain within sight of lush meadows, and whose hard and thoughtless master is as wretched as they, personifies the misery of the poor:

Poor little Foal of an oppresséd race!
I love the languid patience of thy face:
And oft with gentle hand I give thee bread,
And clap thy ragged coat, and pat thy head. . . .

Poor Ass! thy master should have learnt to show
Pity—best taught by fellowship of Woe!
For much I fear me that *He* lives like thee,
Half famish'd in a land of Luxury! . . .
Innocent foal! thou poor despis'd forlorn!
I hail thee *Brother*—spite of the fool's scorn!
And fain would take thee with me, in the Dell
Where high soul'd Pantisocracy shall dwell!
Where Mirth shall tickle Plenty's ribless side, . . .[33]

The Dell of Pantisocracy lies not far from the Land of Cockayne in this poem. Here the true gentleness of Coleridge's nature contrasts with the violent flights of his exultant imagination and revolutionary rhetoric in a juxtaposition of opposites that never ceased to astonish the poet himself, endlessly brooding on the mystery of his favorite proverb, "Extremes meet."

As intended by Coleridge, Pantisocracy was an experiment in human perfectibility, rooted in Godwinian justice, in "all that is good in Godwin."[34] An elite of twelve young men and twelve young ladies would found an agricultural commune on the banks of the Susquehanna. The desire to emigrate and found a utopian colony implied the rejection of the established order with all its ills, as well as the impulse to seek escape from a personal impasse through flight. It also implied the necessity for changing human nature before the world can be changed. The idea was that the noble example of the ideal commune would radiate its regenerating rays upon the world at large. That the advancement of humanity was to come from personal action and individual effort remained one of Coleridge's constant beliefs. Selfishness and greed were to be removed by the abolition of private property, or by "such similarity of Property, as would amount to a *moral Sameness,* and answer all the purposes of *Aboli-*

tion." [35] The simple innocence of the age of the biblical patriarchs was somehow to be beautifully combined with the refinements of European culture.

The scheme foundered when, to Coleridge's dismay, Southey suggested not only that they take along children who, Coleridge feared, were already inculcated with superstition and the prejudices of society, but that they should be accompanied by servants, too. "Is every family to possess one of these unequal equals, these Helot Egalités?" cried Coleridge indignantly. [36] By the summer of 1795 he was writing to Southey of the realization of Pantisocracy as something distant, "perhaps a miraculous Millennium." [37] All that he gained from his considerable proselytizing efforts on its behalf was his disastrous marriage to Sarah Fricker (to which he was persuaded by an overstrained sense of honor and duty), together with an "insight into the nature of individual man" and of social relations, which he had previously lacked and which would now color his entire thinking. [38] This insight was to be reinforced by the increasing sense of his own shortcomings, his growing dependence on drugs, and his inability to reconcile conception and aspiration with will.

Despite his early distaste for established religion and his bewildering changes of opinion, Coleridge remained essentially a Christian spirit. Where Blake saw politics and religion as the same thing, Coleridge longed to restore their unity:

> I therefore go, and join head, heart, and hand,
> Active and firm, to fight the bloodless fight
> Of Science, Freedom, and the Truth in Christ. [39]

He felt a deep need for Christian truth that could never really be satisfied by any nonreligious system. The doubts that worried him, he felt, could be turned just as well toward the pursuit of faith as toward the confirmation of skepticism. And indeed for him Pantisocracy was in essence a form of religious ideal: "What I dared not expect from constitutions of government and whole nations, I hoped from Religion and a small company of chosen individuals. . . ," he said afterward. [40] By which he doubtless meant that he anticipated the inner spiritual and moral improvement of the members of the commune in a state of relative isolation from the temptations of a corrupt world.

In the first of several political lectures, given in Bristol in 1795, in which he discussed the French Revolution and the Terror, Coleridge saw religion as offering the only universally efficient means of raising the overworked poor. For the French Revolution, while it was the beacon of freedom, also illuminated the dangers along the road. Among these pitfalls was "the dangerous and gigantic error of making certain evil the means of contingent good." [41] Robespierre ardently considered the end, and either overlooked or did not scruple about the means. But Coleridge did not regard the end for which Robespierre was working as "wicked." He acutely perceived that to Robespierre "the distant prospect, to which he was travelling, appeared to him grand and beautiful; but that he fixed his eye on it with such intense eagerness as to neglect the foulness of the road." [42] In the end, power (which Coleridge always viewed with suspicion) shaped and depraved the Incorruptible's character.

Coleridge then went on to discuss the consequences of "enthusiasm," its tendency to promote cruelty and fanaticism. Speaking no doubt from personal experience, and perhaps recalling his own joyous progress in imagination through the reeking plains of France, he declared: "Enthusiasm, even in the gentlest temper, will frequently generate sensations of an unkindly order. If we clearly perceive any one thing to be of vast and infinite importance to ourselves and all mankind, our first feelings impel us to turn away with angry contempt from those who doubt and oppose it. The ardour of undisciplined benevolence seduces us into malignity: and whenever our hearts are warm, and our objects great and excellent, intolerance is the sin that does most easily beset us." [43] And intolerance, cruelty, indifference to truth were what he came to loathe. He noted elsewhere, on more than one occasion, the parallel between the fanaticism of the Anabaptists of Münster and that of the French Jacobins, "which differed only . . . by the substitution of theological for philosophical jargon." [44]

He divided "enthusiasts," or "professed friends of liberty," into four categories. First come the half-baked, whose benevolence is matched by their indecisiveness. Then there are those whose hatred of the oppressor and lust for revenge "would make the altar of freedom stream with blood, while the grass grew in the desolated halls of justice." [45] Coleridge appreciated that "terrible charms" lay in the idea of retribution. He recognized, too, that it was small wonder if men lacked humanity when they lacked all the circumstances of life which humanize. While he deprecated the vengefulness of the wronged and injured, he could understand their motives and urge reforms. What he could not bear was that men of "dissimilar opportunities," who lacked the excuse of poverty and misery, should express hair-raising sentiments of vengefulness. He disliked equally those who were ready to uproot "mouldering establishments" but who did nothing actively to improve the lot of the wretched. [46] Only disinterested Godwinian patriots (like himself), who put illumination before revolution, met with his undivided approval. And he ended his lecture urging that all things be done in the spirit of love, echoing the constant invocations to love in his poems.

The fact is that Coleridge never overlooked the fascination of revolution, having experienced that appeal personally. "It is bad policy to represent a political system as having no charm but for robbers and assassins, and no natural origin but in the brains of fools or mad men, when experience has proved, that the great danger of the system consists in the particular fascination it is calculated to exert on noble and imaginative spirits; on all those who, in the amiable intoxication of youthful benevolence, are apt to mistake their own best virtues and choicest powers for the average qualities and attributes of the human character." [47] Coleridge was only too well aware of the errors into which the poet could be led by "the fascinations of his own ideal world." [48]

At the same time he admonished the selfish reactionary who rejects reform. He reminded his readers that "every speculative error which boasts a multitude of advocates, has its *golden* as well as its dark side; that there is always some Truth connected with it, the exclusive attention to which has misled the Understanding, some moral beauty which has given it charms for the heart." [49] Thus Coleridge wished less to deny the merit and attractiveness to be found in the revolutionary ideal than to point to its double face and to the dangers besetting a view of man that took insufficient account of the light and shade of his nature.

For Coleridge, as for Wordsworth, the French invasion of Switzerland in 1798 had marked the end of his illusions. In "France: An Ode" (February 1798) he reviewed the progress of his emotions during the revolutionary years: his joy at the beginning of the revolution, his shame at the crusading war against the champions of freedom, his view of the Terror as a passing storm occasioned by former despotism and superstition, his fears and his hopes that, by her example, France would still be able to "compel the nations to be free." But now the act of French aggression against a free country forced him to recant:

> The Sensual and the Dark rebel in vain,
> Slaves by their own compulsion! In mad game
> They burst their manacles and wear the name
> Of Freedom, graven on a heavier chain!
> O Liberty! with profitless endeavour
> Have I pursued thee, many a weary hour;
> But thou nor swell'st the victor's strain, nor ever
> Did'st breathe thy soul in forms of human power.[50]

The pure ideal of human freedom, glimpsed through the phenomena of nature, is almost anarchic and cannot be attained through "forms of human power," which the poet distrusts, but only by the individual insofar as he is able to commune with free nature, "Possessing all things with intensest love."

By March 1798, Coleridge was writing to his brother George that rulers are much the same in all ages, "as bad as they dare to be"; that the French Revolution was like the great wind, the earthquake, and the fire in none of which God was to be found, and that he was waiting for "the still small voice." He asserted his most steadfast belief in original sin, adding that only the spirit of the Gospel could prove the cure for inherent human depravity. ". . . I have snapped my squeaking baby-trumpet of Sedition and the fragments lie scattered in the lumber-room of Penitence. I wish to be a good man and a Christian—but I am no Whig, no Reformist, no Republican. . . ." He told his brother he had withdrawn to reflect on fundamental causes, and could write: "I love fields and woods and mountains with almost a visionary fondness." [51] In short, by then he was inspired by Wordsworth, whom he had met briefly in Bristol in 1795. Two years later they became neighbors in Somerset and enjoyed together the marvelous year 1797–1798 that saw the birth of a new poetic taste.

poetic revolution

If Wordsworth and Coleridge were disappointed in their hopes of changing the world, they did succeed in bringing about a poetic revolution when they published the *Lyrical Ballads* anonymously in 1798. Rightly or wrongly, it was the first ultimately successful literary revolution to be linked in the critical mind with political revolution. Where later critics would seek and find precursors in Burns, Cowper, Crabbe, and others, the enlightened contemporaries of Wordsworth and Coleridge had not the slightest doubt that an important change had taken place, whether they approved of it or not. Disapproval was strong enough so that Wordsworth was long refused the recognition that was his due—a refusal which (it was said) isolated him and reinforced both his virtues and his faults of character.

Contemporary criticism centered to an extraordinary extent upon Wordsworth's choice of members of the lower orders for his heroes, and the elevation of these lowly born stoic characters seems to have offended the readers' preconceived standard of dignity and decorum even more than the controversy about poetic diction. According to De Quincey, who was very proud of the fact that he had recognized Wordsworth's merits many years before the public came to accept his poetry, Wordsworth's "revolutionary principles of composition" had earned him only scorn and insolence. [52] And De Quincey went on to speak of the hatred aroused by all new and important systems of truth which work against the grain of ancient prejudices.

It was Hazlitt who, in a celebrated passage, made the most emphatic and elaborately pointed connection between the poetry of Wordsworth and Coleridge and the French Revolution, perhaps because he wanted to contrast their former revolutionary sympathies with what he liked to call their later "apostasy." As a young man, Hazlitt had visited the poets at Nether Stowey and Alfoxden in 1798 and had been stirred by the new style and the new spirit in poetry. Years later, after personal and political differences had arisen, he declared that what he named the Lake school of poetry "had its origin in the French Revolution, or rather in those sentiments and opinions which produced that revolution. . . . The change in the belles-lettres was as complete, and to many persons as startling, as the change in politics, with which it went hand in hand. . . . According to the prevailing notions, all was to be natural and new. Nothing that was established was to be tolerated. . . . It was a time of promise, a renewal of the world and of letters; and the Deucalions, who were to perform this feat of regeneration, were the present poet-laureate and the two authors of the Lyrical Ballads. . . . They founded the new school on a principle of sheer humanity, . . ." [53]

This was one of Hazlitt's favorite themes. Elsewhere, in an essay on Wordsworth's poetry, Hazlitt elaborated this view: "It is one of the innovations of the time. It partakes of, and is carried along with, the revolutionary movement of our age: the political changes of the day were the model on which he formed and conducted his poetical experiments. His Muse . . . is a levelling one." [54] While there is something too deliberate in Hazlitt's account of a school, and in his picture of the poet's intentions—for Wordsworth's faith in human dignity precedes the French Revolution—there is a basic element of justice in his estimate that the new poetry derived from the climate of opinion that produced the revolution of 1789.

According to Hazlitt, it was Coleridge who told him on their jaunt along the Bristol Channel in 1798 that "the Lyrical Ballads were an experiment about to be tried by him and Wordsworth, to see how far the public taste would endure poetry written in a more natural and simple style than had hitherto been attempted. . . ." [55] This turn of phrase invites comparison with the gist of the involved opening of Wordsworth's preface to the second edition of the *Lyrical Ballads,* where he states that the collection was "published, as an experiment," to try to find how far poetic pleasure might ensue from fitting meter to "a selection of the real language of men in a state of vivid sensation."

As Wordsworth maintained, to provide a systematic defense of the theory on which the poems were based would require "retracing the revolutions, not of literature alone, but likewise of society itself." It was a theme he did not choose to pursue. Yet evidently disapproval of the established order, of privilege and social injustice, inspired the search for a form of poetry more closely in keeping with his ideals and his hopes. The preface shows him in the role not only of poet but of social prophet, one of the first to recognize the "multitude of causes, unknown to former times" that were now acting to blunt discrimination. Among these causes he named the movement of men into cities, "where the uniformity of their occupations produces a craving for extraordinary incident." He saw his poetry as an attempt to counteract "this degrading thirst after outrageous stimulation." [56]

Hazlitt was surely justified, though, in seeing one of Wordsworth's outstanding contributions to the new poetry as a deep and all-embracing humanity. For Wordsworth the poet must be "a man speaking to men." It was Wordsworth who perceived the qualities of suffering social outcasts whom the world barely considered human. As he expressed it movingly in *The Prelude,* the uncouth vagrants or madmen he encountered on the lonely roads led him to see

> into the depth of human souls,
> Souls that appear to have no depth at all
> To vulgar eyes. [57]

Only when he conceived such figures as being somehow more human than others did he seem to go too far.

Already in 1798, Coleridge had found cause to lament to Hazlitt about some aspects of Wordsworth's poetry. Although Coleridge said that

Wordsworth's preface to the second edition of the *Lyrical Ballads* arose out of such frequent conversations that (with rare exceptions) it would be difficult to ascribe to either of them any particular thought, he also remarked that he was far from agreeing with Wordsworth on all points. By 1802 he suspected a "radical difference" in their theoretical opinions on poetry.[58] But in reality their differences in poetics concealed deeper differences of temperament which grew more marked with the years, exploding in an episode hurtful to Coleridge's pride; and the formal and uneasy reconciliation that eventually took place never restored their earlier intimacy.

the concept of man's potentialities

It was on the nature of man that Wordsworth and Coleridge fundamentally differed. This divergence ostensibly expressed itself through religion: ". . . we found our data dissimilar," wrote Coleridge, and having uncovered this difference of opinion as regards religion, the poets thereafter chose to remain silent and never reverted to the subject.[59] Where Coleridge's personal experience convinced him of original sin, of inherent human depravity that could be redeemed only through religion, Wordsworth had always approached humanity "from the golden side," with a trust in man's own potentialities for improvement, in "what we *may* become." What Coleridge wanted from Wordsworth was a great philosophical poem which (so Coleridge hoped) was to deal with "a Fall in some sense" and a scheme of redemption (in short, the pattern of his own poem, *The Rime of the Ancient Mariner*).[60] The fall of man could not be eluded because it was attested by experience and conscience, that is, by the experience and conscience of Coleridge. He was expecting, then, the philosophical poem he himself could potentially have written, but which Wordsworth, given his view of man, could not.

Now in *The Excursion* (published in 1814), which so signally failed to satisfy Coleridge's expectations, Wordsworth again attempted to cope with the effects of the French Revolution, this time through the experience of the Solitary and the consolatory advice of the Wanderer-Sage, who are both aspects of himself. The Solitary recalls the great upsurge of revolutionary hopes, followed by the excesses which led to dejection and despondency and want of confidence in the virtue of mankind. The Wanderer-Sage, on the contrary, states the ground for continuing hope, stressing the need for patience where the course of great revolutions is concerned, and he observes:

> For that other loss,
> The loss of confidence in social man,
> By the unexpected transports of our age
> Carried so high, that every thought, which looked
> Beyond the temporal destiny of the Kind,
> To many seemed superfluous—

just as there was no cause for such exalted confidence in man, so there was now none for despair.[61] Reason must disown both extremes; and

> if, with sharp recoil, from one
> You have been driven far as its opposite,
> Between them seek the point whereon to build
> Sound expectations . . .[62]

The Wanderer therefore proposes a more soundly based hope, rooted neither in excessive trust nor in excessive mistrust of human nature.

Considering those who triumph now in Europe, the Wanderer maintains that their victory was due to superior energies, and to firmer faith in their "unhallowed principles." In his view, the bad

> Have fairly earned a victory o'er the weak,
> The vacillating, inconsistent good.[63]

For himself, he waits patiently and hopefully to see the moment when the defenders of the right will prove as zealous in striving for the just and righteous cause as their opponents have been in pursuing their evil ends. When that happens, mankind will at last be redeemed:

That spirit only can redeem Mankind;
And when that sacred spirit shall appear,
Then shall *our* triumph be complete as theirs.[64]

True, should this event fail to take place, he will bear disappointment with stoic fortitude, yet plainly the Wanderer still expects the redemption of man to occur through the efforts and the zeal of the virtuous fighters for the right. He still conceives the "complete" triumph of humanity and liberty to be attainable through human devotion.

This concept of the potentialities of mankind could not but arouse doubts in Hazlitt who, while an unswervingly ardent supporter of the libertarian ideal, preserved (like Coleridge) a religious awareness of the human condition inherited from the tradition of dissent, and disliked any assessment of man which overlooked the complexities of his nature. Wordsworth's hopes for the "complete" triumph of humanity and liberty struck Hazlitt as inconceivable: "For this purpose, we think several things necessary which are impossible. It is a consummation which cannot happen till the nature of things is changed, . . . till the love of power and of change shall no longer goad man on to restless action, till passion and will, hope and fear, love and hatred, and the objects proper to excite them, that is, alternate good and evil, shall no longer sway the bosoms and the businesses of men." [65] Hazlitt could remember longingly the bright youthful dream, the glad revolutionary dawn, the springtime of the world; he could believe that traces of the dream still lingered behind; he could despise the reactionaries who destroyed these high hopes; but he was convinced that "evil is inseparable from the nature of things." [66] This did not mean giving up the struggle; but only by taking man's evil propensities into account would it be possible to arrive at some amelioration of political, social, and economic abuses.

Perhaps it was partly because Hazlitt felt Wordsworth's excessively high estimation of human potentialities finally inclined the poet, by the swing of the pendulum, to dark reaction that the essayist was so severe on his elder's "apostasy." A juster assessment of man and his fallible nature might have avoided this development. So the visionary and libertarian

Wordsworth dwindled by slow degrees, imperceptible to himself, into the civil servant, the sycophantic agent of a peer, the dismal reactionary who pained his liberal-minded contemporaries. While he never lost his compassion for the poor and wretched, and unfailingly condemned the consequences of heartless industrialization, his nervous fear of change and of the mob grew sharper. With advancing years, the shadow of revolution seemed to haunt him the more. The ideals of his young manhood became to him the "pestilence" of revolution, "monstrous theories of alien growth." [67] Finally, the tragic loss of several much-loved members of his family led him to the Church, and he began changing his early poems to conform with his later beliefs.

Meanwhile Coleridge, once the idealistic pantisocrat, the enemy of private property, became the defender of the property principle, the antidemocratic contemner of "fool-and-knave-ocracy," the independent conservative political philosopher. Where formerly he had expressed distaste for received religion, he now saw the established Church as the main bulwark for toleration. [68]

As a disciple of Burke, Coleridge voiced the objections to revolution drawn from religion and tradition. He condemned particularly in the French revolutionaries their presumptuous and irreligious philosophy, the way they overrated the knowledge and power given by the advance of art and science, their conceit in believing that governments and states ought to be constructed like machines whose every movement could be foreseen, and their "remorseless arrogance" in seeking to realize their plans whatever the cost in human rights and human lives. In his view, they preferred abstract reason to "the lights of specific experience, and the modifications of existing circumstances." [69] It was their audacity in refusing to recognize man's limitations that offended his deeply religious nature. If Coleridge's development appears less depressing than that of Wordsworth, it is because the poet of "Kubla Khan" remained primarily a seeker after truth, favoring intuition rather than concept, and suspicious of systems, who, in the extremely moving note written as he lay dying on July 10, 1834, associated the improvement of mankind with the glory of God.

Thus, in the attitudes of these poetic luminaries who outlived the visionary gleam, there can be found not only the traditional progress of the impassioned idealist through various shades of painful adjustment to gradualism, conservatism, or reaction, but also the debate on the assessment of human nature which governs belief in what revolution can or cannot achieve. The trust in a total transformation of human nature by the elimination of antisocial failings or vices, in the redemption of mankind through mankind alone, in the complete and final triumph of liberty and humanity, confronts the awareness of human complexities and inadequacies or the religiously grounded view of human nature and its need for spiritual redemption. Evidently this does not mean that all hope of human improvement has to be jettisoned; it means (for Coleridge or Hazlitt) that expectations of man's ability to change his nature should not be pitched too high. And it was just this disinclination to preserve a balance between dream and feasibility that Hazlitt disliked in Shelley, the apostle of Satanic-Promethean revolt against the flaw in the universe.

chapter 3

the anarchist response: Shelley

When Hazlitt turned his penetrating and embittered gaze on the extremist rebels and revolutionaries of his day, on those who maintained that whatever is, is wrong, he did not fail to include Shelley among them. Discounting Shelley's complex fluctuation between opposing and contradictory drives and urges, Hazlitt saw the poet of *Prometheus Unbound* principally in his rebellious stance—as spokesman of those who were striving to erase the past, to overturn all established creeds and systems, and who cared little for the accumulated wisdom of the ages or the common consent of mankind. So extreme an attitude, the essayist felt, brought discredit on the cause it purported to serve. As poets live mainly in an ideal world of their own, "it would perhaps be as well if they were confined to it" was Hazlitt's sour comment.[1]

What Hazlitt, with his fondness for the dramatic, apparently failed to remark was that Shelley rebelled not merely against the system, the existing order of society, but against the very order of the universe. The one was but the mirror of the other. Kings, priests, and statesmen were earthly tyrants, but God was the supreme tyrant, the "prototype of human misrule." [2]

From his precocious early youth and the period of his obsession with romantic Gothic horror, spirits, alchemy, and the occult, Shelley was haunted by the mysterious figure of the mage Ahasuerus, the Wandering Jew, hurling defiance at the Christian God whose banners he saw stained with the blood of Christians as well as infidels down the ages. Shelley's Ahasuerus is akin to his Prometheus: they are rebels against the omnipotent tyrant in the name of suffering humanity. Ahasuerus prefers the freedom of hell to the servitude of heaven, echoing the Satan of *Paradise Lost,* who cried,

> Better to reign in Hell, than serve in Heav'n.

Such was the boast of Milton's apostate angel, though "rackt with deep despare," who dared to oppose the "Tyranny of Heav'n." Milton's Satan conceived the relationship between God and himself as that between master and slave, scorned and rejected it; so does Shelley's Ahasuerus, while his Prometheus sees man and God bound together as slave and master. (This view would be shared by the arch-romantic, antireligious anarchist Bakunin and by his enemy, the Prometheus-haunted Marx, who proclaimed with the Titan of Aeschylus that it was better to be chained to the rock than bound in the service of Zeus.)

For Shelley, Milton's Satan was morally far superior to his God because Satan stood steadfast and defiant, despite indescribable suffering, in the face of a vengeful, cold-blooded, and all-powerful tyrant. The figure of Satan, in Shelley's view, was excelled only by Prometheus, who shared Satan's wrongs but not, significantly, his faults, being the ideal champion of mankind, "the type of the highest perfection of moral and intellectual nature, impelled by the purest and the truest motives to the best and noblest ends." [3] Shelley's Prometheus was the loftiest poetic expression of that romantic metaphysical revolt on behalf of oppressed man, and that imaginative ideal revolutionary action of which the poet himself was the supreme incarnation and exponent.

Shelley presents an outstanding instance of the young rebel born to affluence, of revolt against the father reinforcing revolt against the father figures of monarch and deity. The only son of Sir Timothy Shelley, a wealthy member of the new landed gentry, Shelley could easily have followed in his father's footsteps, adopted the political career anticipated for him, and entered Parliament. Instead he developed into a confirmed angry rebel, seething with indignation at every injustice, solicitous to relieve the miseries of the poor. As he speaks through one of his poetic personae,

> *Me*—who am as a nerve o'er which do creep
> The else unfelt oppressions of this earth, . . . [4]

He became known as the author of radical and antireligious propaganda, the agitator for Irish liberties and outspoken friend of world liberation and revolution, the devoted enemy of political, religious, and domestic tyranny personified in his poetic drama by a vicious parent like Count Cenci (whose murder at the hands of his injured daughter Beatrice also attracted the attention of the father-hating Stendhal).

Sir Timothy's opposition to his son's antireligious views and misalliance with Harriet Westbrook, a girl of lower social standing, served to confirm the poet in his role of outcast (a role he would maintain when he later fled abroad with Godwin's daughter Mary). At the height of the clash with Sir Timothy, Shelley roundly (and probably excessively) declared that he had never loved his father. This was in a letter to William Godwin, his master and future father-in-law. But where the poet and his father were concerned, the gap between the generations seemed unbridgeable. Sir Timothy, though well-intentioned enough, was a worldly conformist to whom his son's refusal to conform appeared as a blot on the escutcheon and as treachery to his own class.

While still a schoolboy, Shelley had experienced a spiritual crisis: his prayers to God being unanswered, he suddenly felt another presence which filled him with ecstasy. To this presence he dedicated himself and his life, rejecting the "poisonous names with which our youth is fed." [5] He called this spiritual force variously freedom, justice, love; it was the religion of humanity which replaced the vacuum left by the rejected faith.

There was a strong element of mutual rejection in his attitude, for it was said that Shelley could not bear to be thwarted in any sphere. When at seventeen his engagement to his cousin Harriet Grove was broken off because of his anti-Christian opinions, this blow inspired an extraordinary petulant outburst: "Oh! I burn with impatience for the moment of Xtianity's dissolution, it has injured me; . . . Indeed I think it is to the benefit of society to destroy the opinions which *can* annihilate the dearest of its ties." [6] Here Shelley characteristically argues from the personal to the general. And shortly before the publication of *The Necessity of Atheism,* a tract which caused him and his friend and co-author Thomas Hogg to be sent down from Oxford in March 1811, he wrote on the same theme: ". . . here I swear that never will I forgive Christianity! . . . Oh how I wish I *were* the Antichrist, that it were *mine* to crush the Demon, to hurl him to his native Hell never to rise again—." [7] His emphatic passion bridges the years from Voltaire to Nietzsche.

So besides compassion it was loathing for tyranny—domestic, institutional, social, governmental, religious, and cosmic—that caused Shelley to raise his "solitary voice" in angry protest against all injustice, custom, precedent, received opinion, and authority. An order of society and of the universe that blights young love must be hated, overturned, and crushed. He felt he must break through the crust of outworn opinions to a world where love could flourish, where youth could overcome the faults of age, indeed where the spirit of youth would be eternal.

After Godwin, Shelley thought free love would not lead to promiscuity, although it seemed to him, as to Godwin, impracticable in the present state of society where the position of the woman would be made unbearable: hence his two marriages. Among an emancipated elite of noble kindred souls, however, a man should not, in theory, mind sharing his wife with his best friend. Shelley, in an episode with homosexual undertones, professed to have no objection to sharing his first wife, the ill-starred Harriet Westbrook, with Hogg; it was she who demurred, he maintained disingenuously. A less stormy experiment in free love was attempted with Mary Godwin as the third member of the trio. His ideal revolutionary hero and heroine, Laon and Cythna, brother and sister in one version, would daringly unite in incestuous bliss, incest being then as now the supreme taboo to be challenged. Women must be liberated in order to prevent male repression and recourse to prostitutes, for

> Can man be free if woman be a slave? [8]

And although, at a time when universal female suffrage was a controversial issue, Shelley thought votes for women premature, he made it plain that he would be "the last to withhold his vote from any system which might tend to an equal and full development of the capacities of all living beings." [9]

To Shelley, the enemy of this goal of full humanity was a creature all of a piece, evil personified. Life appeared to him as a conflict between powers of good and ill. In one sense, the enemy is incapable of improvement. The tyrant willfully remains a tyrant and, by his monstrous actions, actually obliges the liberator to shed his blood: "So dear is power that the tyrants themselves, neither then, nor now, nor ever, left or leave a path to freedom but through their own blood." [10] Nevertheless, in another sense, evil and its representatives are as nothing: they are shapes molded by false opinions, to be swept away by the sword of the merciful destroyer, or to vanish by process of nature like wrecks of a dissolving dream.

Evil and the acceptance of evil are, then, in this view, merely the consequence of wrongly directed will:

> This need not be; ye might arise, and will
> That gold should lose its power, and thrones their glory;

> That love, which none may bind, be free to fill
> The world, like light; and evil faith, grown hoary
>   With crime, be quenched and die. —Yon promontory
> Even now eclipses the descending moon!—
>   Dungeons and palaces are transitory—
> High temples fade like vapour. —Man alone
> Remains, whose will has power when all beside is gone.[11]

"Ye might arise, and will . . .": here is the essence of the belief that man himself, by his own willpower, can establish a realm of love on earth. According to Mary Shelley's illuminating note to *Prometheus Unbound,* "Shelley believed that mankind had only to will that there should be no evil, and there would be none. . . . That man could be so perfectionized as to be able to expel evil from his own nature, and from the greater part of the creation, was the cardinal point of his system." [12] Naturally, in this transformation of the human personality and of the world, it was the transition from evil to good, from hatred to love that remained vague.

Having reached the conclusion that the riddle of the origin of evil was insoluble by man in his present state, Shelley resolved to concentrate in his poetry upon ideas that ennoble humanity, on conjectures concerning "the condition of that futurity towards which we are all impelled by an inextinguishable thirst for immortality." [13] The advance of science, in which Shelley was passionately interested, would clearly play a large part in eliminating present flaws and in establishing future bliss. Still, as he knew only too well, "to anticipate however darkly a period of regeneration and happiness is a more hazardous exercise of the faculty which bards possess or feign." [14] It was nonetheless a theme to which he reverted many times in his early verse, in *Queen Mab* as well as in some of his finest passages in *Prometheus Unbound* and *Hellas.*

Usually there is a sudden break, without transition, from the hell of things as they are under the present system to the restoring and inspiriting vision of the heaven of things as they should and will be:

Let the axe

Strike at the root, the poison-tree will fall;
And where its venomed exhalations spread
Ruin, and death, and woe, where millions lay
Quenching the serpent's famine, and their bones
Bleaching unburied in the putrid blast,
A garden shall arise, in loveliness
Surpassing fabled Eden. [15]

Where once was sterility and lifelessness, all suddenly grows fresh and green—"Green stalks burst forth." [16] The basic pattern does not change: you get rid of tyrants and despots, "those ringleaders of the privileged gangs of murderers and swindlers, called Sovereigns" [17] (or whoever may be the diabolic enemy of the moment), and hell turns to paradise. This swift, magical transformation from the old to the new order may be seen as the fulfillment of an imaginative instinct, impulse, or yearning for rebirth, regeneration, resurrection, "an inextinguishable thirst for immortality," which subsists at the same time as Shelley discusses more soberly in prose the need for enlightenment and reforms to be accomplished over many generations.

What Shelley resisted with all the fervor of his generous nature was the flaw in the universe whereby there is no unmixed good or evil, each gain involves a loss, and right often wars with right. He prophesied the swift and sure arrival of the age when the unbounded frame of the cosmos

Will be without a flaw
Marring its perfect symmetry. [18]

In a letter of protest to the Chief Justice, Lord Ellenborough, at the harsh sentence passed on Daniel Eaton for "blasphemy" in publishing Part Three of Paine's *The Age of Reason,* the freethinker's bible, Shelley foretold the time when Christianity would be obsolete and men would find the concept of original sin as absurd as the metamorphoses of Jupiter. It was not original sin, that common excuse of the reactionary, which caused the taints in man's nature, but unnatural political institutions. Not human nature but the system is to blame for all ills, corrupting the child, inculcating antisocial opinions and superstitions and the acceptance of exploitation and war.

In *Prometheus Unbound,* the Spirit of the Earth perceives the wonderful change wrought when all things put away their evil nature. Here is the everlasting yearning for the death of evil, for renewal and the restoration of innocence expressed later by Victor Hugo in the apotheosis of *Ce que dit la bouche d'ombre,* when hells become paradises, and Jesus and Satan are no longer distinguishable:

> Le mal expirera: les larmes
> Tariront. . . .

For Shelley, evil will perish and tears cease to flow, not at the last trump but when man freely returns to simplicity and innocence.

None has given more potent expression to this immortal dream than he in his vision of anarchist bliss conveyed by the Spirit of the Hour in *Prometheus Unbound:*

> And behold thrones were kingless, and men walked
> One with the other even as spirits do,
> None fawned, none trampled; . . .
> The loathsome mask has fallen, the man remains
> Sceptreless, free, uncircumscribed, but man
> Equal, unclassed, tribeless and nationless,
> Exempt from awe, worship, degree, the king
> Over himself; just, gentle, wise; but man
> Passionless?—no, yet free from guilt or pain
> Which were, for his will made or suffered them,
> Nor yet exempt, tho' ruling them like slaves,
> From chance, and death, and mutability, . . .[19]

In this future paradise, there is neither hypocrite nor sycophant, neither oppressed nor oppressor, neither religion nor rule: man is now kind and loving, lord of himself, free at last from guilt and pain and suffering, and at least unmoved by accident, death, and change (for if he were free of these he would be god). Among the vital elements of this vision are the release from the burden of guilt and suffering, and the advent of the time when there shall be no more tears and death itself shall have lost its sting.

When Shelley discussed Christian redemption in his "Essay on Christianity," he had used very similar language: "There shall be no misery, no pain, no fear. The empire of evil spirits extends not beyond the boundaries of the grave. . . . This is Heaven, when pain and evil cease, and when the Benignant Principle, untrammelled and uncontrolled, visits in the fulness of its power the universal frame of things." [20] It is scarcely necessary to underline the parallel: Shelley's future golden age strikingly resembles, in its absence of evil, guilt, and suffering, the Christian paradise of the blessed and the redeemed. His beautiful new order rises from the blood and chaos of the world as from a resurrection.

Indeed, Shelley paradoxically shares the respect shown by bitterly antireligious rebel anarchists for primitive Christianity. For this family of spirits, Jesus often appears as the revolutionary reformer betrayed by orthodox and conventional believers. Shelley comes to see Jesus in this light as a kind of Jean-Jacques Rousseau of the ancient world, preaching egalitarianism, and he naturally quotes in support of his contention the text ". . . sell all that thou hast, and distribute unto the poor," and the passage in Acts describing how all things were held in common by the early Christians. These doctrines, Shelley felt, were reversed by the later followers of Jesus. The labor of the impoverished many for the luxury of the few (and especially the new aristocracy based on money instead of chivalry) aroused Shelley's disgust. The work of regeneration and the redemption of the human race could never occur unless something were done to put an end to inequality. The ultimate if extremely remote goal should be "equality in possessions which Jesus Christ so passionately taught." [21] Meanwhile he proposed a bold program to reduce the economic burdens of the poor.

Like his master, Godwin, Shelley did not regard himself as an anarchist. With Godwin he employed "anarchy" in its negative sense, though both preferred it to despotism because they believed that where despotism was lasting, anarchy was transitory. Shelley also liked to apply the word ironically to God, king, and law: thus tyrants were "anarchs." Godwin, however, was quite clear that "since government even in its best state is an evil, the object principally to be aimed at is that we should have as little of it as the general peace of human society will permit." [22] The author of *An Enquiry Concerning Political Justice* firmly condemned institutions, associations, and organized societies. Here Shelley was at variance with him, since he hoped that nuclei, or groups, of illumined souls might bring about the peaceful regeneration of mankind. Where he agreed with Godwin was in believing that the virtuous man abhors both rule and submission, and neither commands nor obeys.

Precisely what Shelley meant by "revolution" is not always absolutely clear and varies according to his mood—now extreme, now moderate, now imaginative, now reasonable. Sometimes he was thinking of revolution in terms of class war as the scarcely avoidable consequence of the blindness of the tyrannical oppressor who would be overthrown by popular vengeance: "This is the age of the war of the oppressed against the oppressors. . . ." [23] On an earlier occasion he had expressed hopes that a violent overthrow might be averted, since the practical as well as the tender aspects of his nature shrank from popular insurrections and revolutions, though if these came he said he would be on the side of the people. In such instances, revolution might be regarded as manmade, forged by the dialectic of oppressor and oppressed, rather than presented as it is through his poetic imagery in the shape of a natural and ineluctable force, like a hurricane or earthquake.

Again, at times Shelley would speak of revolution as if it meant solely beneficent change (though at others he viewed it as a Janus-headed phenomenon that would bear both good and evil gifts). In this sense of change-for-the-good, revolution was not far off from reform: "Call it reform or revolution, as you will, a change must take place; one of the consequences of which will be, the wresting of political power from those who are at present the depositaries of it." [24] Yet if it were a question of reform, Shelley was prepared not to think in terms of a rapid transformation, but was ready to work toward an amelioration that would only take place long after he was dust. The lesson he learned from the French Revolution was the urgent need to institute reforms before it was too late.

While Blake, Wordsworth, and Coleridge lived through the years when the French Revolution was actually taking place, Shelley, who was born in 1792, knew only the long period of harsh reaction in England, the Napoleonic wars, the restoration of the European monarchies, and the sporadic struggles for national independence. For Shelley, the French Revolution was a mighty presence whose long shadow dominated everything. He was haunted by it, studying the course it took and the reasons for the failure of its high hopes. It seemed to him that he was living in the sultry and oppressive atmosphere of the approaching storm, which, as his poetry reveals, he half longed for and half dreaded. The revolutionary storm would leave a wreck in its wake; at the same time it would clear the air and make all things fresh and new. This oscillation between repulsion and attraction helps to explain why, in an essay in which he stresses the necessity for reform, Shelley also conducts a sanguine survey of the progress of world revolution. This survey embraces not only the countries of Europe ("everything . . . wears in Germany the aspect of rapidly maturing revolution") but South America, India, Asia ("The Great Monarchies of Asia cannot, let us confidently hope, remain unshaken by the earthquake . . ."), Persia, and the Near East.[25]

To Shelley, the French Revolution was "the master-theme of the epoch."[26] Certainly it provides the ground base of many of his poems where the theme of revolution is either explicit or implicit. The fact is that for Shelley there were two revolutions. One was the actual historical French Revolution which in the name of liberty had passed through the searing crucible of the Terror to culminate inconceivably and ironically in the absolute rule of Napoleon, the "anarch" of liberty's own "bewildered powers."[27] So tragic a development had spread panic and despair among the thinking men of Europe. This era of despair Shelley envisaged as drawing to a close around 1817, when he composed the preface to *Laon and Cythna, or the Revolution of the Golden City,* revised under the more familiar title of *The Revolt of Islam.*

In this preface he suggested that the dismay aroused by the excesses of the French Revolution was unwarranted. There was no need to lose hope because a people that had been enslaved for so long had behaved ferociously once it was partially freed from its fetters. This was already a familiar argument. Besides, hopes had been excessive: ". . . such a degree of unmingled good was expected as it was impossible to realize." [28] (Here his sense of practical possibilities diverges from his magical poetic dreams and prophetic yearnings.) And Shelley curiously employed an argument similar to that used by the devout to explain and justify the presence of evil in the universe: namely, that if the revolution had succeeded in all aspects, everything would have been morally too easy. The lesson taught by the French Revolution was that the crushed and debased slave cannot turn liberal and tolerant overnight. For this transformation to come about, "the systematic efforts of generations of men of intellect and virtue" are required.[29] So Shelley argued in order to preserve unsullied his hopes for the redemption of the human race.

The other revolution in Shelley's purview was the ideal revolution, as depicted, for instance, in *The Revolt of Islam,* what he called "the *beau ideal,* as it were, of the French Revolution. . . ." [30] This revolution is inspired and led from above by two noble, loving, emancipated, illumined spirits, by the dedicated revolutionary hero and heroine, who are missionaries and finally martyrs of the religion of humanity. If they fail, they need not lose faith and die in despair, since others will surely follow in their footsteps. The revolution does fail through excessive magnanimity to the tyrant, who not unnaturally takes advantage of the hero's generosity to stage a counterrevolution. But though the noble enterprise fails, it offers a model of the spirit of love in which the true revolution should be conducted.

Clearly, in *The Revolt of Islam,* Shelley portrayed his own secret longing to bring tidings of redemption to the human race. His gospel is poetry, which, through its imaginative and creative power, will help to free man who, though he has enslaved the elements by science, remains himself a slave. Shelley conceived poetry as the "unfailing herald, companion and follower of the awakening of a great people to work a beneficial change in opinion or institution." [31] Moreover, the role of poets and great writers in the modern age was for him not very different from that of poetry: they were teachers, prophets, visionaries, "the companions and forerunners of some unimagined change in our social condition or the opinions which cement it"; they were "the hierophants of an unapprehended inspiration; the mirrors of the gigantic shadows which futurity casts upon the present; . . . the unacknowledged legislators of the world." [32] In his conception of his role as poet he was, as it were, at once the St. John the Baptist, the Messiah, and the St. Paul of some mysterious religion of humanity, the religion of the future.

The greatest incarnation of the revolutionary religion of humanity in Shelley's poetry is the Titan Prometheus. He represents the ideal grandiose rebel-redeemer, Satanic in his steadfast defiance, Christlike as the gentle and forgiving savior of suffering man:

> To suffer woes which Hope thinks infinite;
> To forgive wrongs darker than death or night;
>   To defy Power, which seems omnipotent;
> To love, and bear; to hope till Hope creates
> From its own wreck the thing it contemplates . . . [33]

The religion of humanity of which the poet-Prometheus is the visionary redeemer appears as the one to which Shelley had dedicated himself as a boy, the one which filled the vacuum left by the silence of God. And it is unquestionably a substitute faith, since

> ". . . We are assured
> Much may be conquered, much may be endured,
> Of what degrades and crushes us. We know
> That we have power over ourselves to do
> And suffer—what, we know not till we try;
> But something nobler than to live and die—
> So taught those kings of old philosophy
> Who reigned, before Religion made men blind;
> And those who suffer with their suffering kind
> Yet feel their faith, religion. . . ." [34]

as Julian-Shelley, charged with utopianism, tells Maddalo-Byron, whom he believed capable of being "the redeemer" of his country.

It is not difficult to see in a number of Shelley's poems his dream-fulfillment of an active revolutionary role. There he can figure, masked, as the farsighted and self-sacrificing hero who awakens and leads the suffering multitude to redemption, and who, like Laon, stands bravely steadfast amid the "cleansing fire" and the destructive earthquake caused by the awakened masses. Action is one pole to which he tends; the other marks withdrawal from human society, his longing to embark with a female kindred soul—Emilia Viviani or his wife Mary and their child—for a far Eden, some lonely island paradise where vestiges of the simple life of the Golden Age remain and whence famine, disease, war, and earthquake are banished. No sooner is he there in imagination than he contemplates devoting himself to oblivion or future generations and dreams of forming a nucleus of like-minded spirits, "a society of our own class, . . . in intellect or in feelings." [35] These two extremes indicate the precarious balance of commitment and withdrawal in Shelley (repeated in many another romantic revolutionist). He likes the idea of the role of revolutionary prophet and leader; on the other hand, the falsity and corruption of society repel him and he feels unhappy at having to touch pitch. The beautiful poetic hopes and ideals hide the desolation and desperation of a sensitive and passionate nature appalled at the hellish state of society as he knows it.

Once, as a young man, Shelley had attempted without much success to play an active part in politics. This was in Ireland, where he had sought to rouse both peasantry and gentry. When, completely shattered by the depth of human misery in Dublin, he described the Irish populace as "one mass of animated filth," scarcely higher in the scale of intellectual being than the oyster, Godwin (daring in speculation but otherwise far from rash) warned him against exhorting men in such a condition to redress their own grievances: "Shelley, you are preparing a scene of blood!" And Shelley wrote back to say that had he lived through the French Revolution like Godwin, he would probably have been more cautious. [36]

While suggesting at times the inevitability of bloodletting, Shelley never ceased, in his poems, to urge the claims of nonviolence and passive resistance. The ideal revolutionary disarms his opponent with a lofty Godwinian stance:

> "What hast thou to do
> With me, poor wretch?"— [37]

thus causing the dagger to fall from the assailant's hand; while in *The Mask of Anarchy,* inspired by the massacre of Peterloo, Shelley counsels the people to withstand the soldiery with folded arms, for such moral courage will force the foe to melt away shamefacedly. Yet in the same poem he seems to be urging the people to resort to arms—

> Rise like Lions after slumber. . . .
> Ye are many—they are few. [38]

The fascination that tyrannicide and insurrection exerted upon his literary imagination from his early youth vies with his hatred of fighting and bloodshed for any cause, even that of self-sacrifice for the religion of love and humanity.

This movement of imaginative attraction and rational repulsion can be glimpsed in his poetic imagery. In an early poem, "The Crisis," he wrote of his hopes for the arrival of the consummating hour, "Dreadfully, sweetly, swiftly . . . ," where the twofold reaction of sweet pleasure and dread horror is manifest. [39] And in a poem on a painting of the Medusa, he spoke of "the tempestuous loveliness of terror," of horror, beauty, and death inextricably intertwined, in language that betrays the dark irrational aspects of romanticism, the association of beauty and terror defined by Mario Praz as "the romantic agony": "The very objects which should induce a shudder—the livid face of the severed head, the squirming mass of vipers, the rigidity of death, . . . all these give rise to a new sense of beauty, a beauty imperilled and contaminated, a new thrill." [40] This element in romanticism, the fascination of the abhorrent, the perverse spell of blood, pain, and death, together with the exaltation of vast upheaval and catastrophe, will come to form a notable aspect of the thrill of revolution. It is an aspect which can perfectly well co-exist, as it does in Shelley, with a deep concern for humanity.

Basic to Shelley's imagery is the notion of light arising out of darkness, peace out of desolation, a theme already present in "The Crisis" and elaborated in the posthumously published poem "Liberty." Freedom is born out of a mighty catastrophe, out of the ruin of the terrible storm, out of the fiery mountains, the tempestuous oceans, the earthquake that reduces whole cities to ashes. It is swifter and more blinding than the lightning or the volcanic eruption, and when its dazzling day dawns, tyrants and slaves vanish like darkness before the morning light. Thus for Shelley the process of change to freedom through destruction and renovation is a natural one, resembling the peace and renewal after the destructive tempest, or the freshness of morning after the gloom of night. The grandiose, terrifyingly beautiful, and annihilating disaster must come before renewal can take place.

Another favored way of expressing this phenomenon is through the life cycle of the seasons. In the opening lines of Canto V of *Queen Mab*, Shelley described the death and birth of generations (a process of change and renewal that is itself as indestructible, unchanging, everlasting as the eternal universe in which he believed as a pantheist), through the image of rotting leaves. These fertilize the land—as blood may fertilize the tree of liberty—until the time when a new forest of youth and beauty springs up, to perish in its turn and make way by its destruction for another. In this manner the reign of virtue and love can arise naturally out of the soil of ugliness and selfishness and corruption. Here the trace of the pagan notion of fertilization through destruction and sacrifice seems evident.

The concept of natural change through horror and destruction to rebirth reaches its finest expression in the great "Ode to the West Wind." This resonant poem may doubtless be understood in various ways, one of them concerned with the theme of revolution as resurrection. The autumnal wind that drives the dead leaves like ghosts fleeing from an enchanter, or like pestilence-stricken multitudes, appears as a revolutionary force, "destroyer and preserver"—preserver because it bears the winged seeds that will lie buried like corpses until spring resurrects them. By associating the wind with a fierce maenad, reminiscent of a wildly dancing figure seen in an art gallery, with her uplifted hair merging into the "locks of the approaching storm," Shelley reinforces the hint of revolution conveyed by his vision of a tempest of rain, fire, and hail. And in the final verses invoking the wind—

> Be thou me, impetuous one!
>
> Drive my dead thoughts over the universe
> Like withered leaves to quicken a new birth!
> And, by the incantation of this verse,
>
> Scatter, as from an unextinguished hearth
> Ashes and sparks, my words among mankind!
> Be through my lips to unawakened earth
>
> The trumpet of a prophecy! O, Wind,
> If Winter comes, can Spring be far behind? [41]—

the poet gives vent to his own spiritual yearning for renewal and regeneration, his own longing that his prophetic poetry may quicken the world into a new birth.

Only at the end of *Hellas* does he intimate dissatisfaction with the cyclical process of death and resurrection, destruction and renewal:

> The world's great age begins anew,
>   The golden years return,
> The earth doth like a snake renew
>   Her winter weeds outworn:
> Heaven smiles, and faiths and empires gleam,
> Like wrecks of a dissolving dream.
>
> . . . Oh, cease! must hate and death return?
>   Cease! must men kill and die?

> Cease! drain not to its dregs the urn
>   Of bitter prophecy.
> The world is weary of the past,
> Oh, might it die or rest at last! [42]

Here Shelley appears to wish for the end of the recurring cycles of seasonal death and rebirth. The last lines suggest the world death-wish of the rebel whose revolt might easily turn to nihilism, as indeed would prove the case with later literary revolutionists of similar anarchic tinge.

Through Shelley's imagery, which embodies his subconscious drives and urges in language of incantatory lyric power, we can glimpse certain recurring and enduring elements in the mind and heart of revolution-haunted man. Dominated by the enormous, single, unassimilable fact of the French Revolution, as an early Christian must have been dominated by the fact of the Crucifixion, Shelley believed, with the perfect faith of a disciple of Godwin and Condorcet, that it is possible for men eventually to create by their own efforts a timeless ideal world where love will reign supreme, where men and women will live in innocence and simplicity, without hypocrisy, hatred, and guilt, without conflict and war, without pain, sickness, and suffering. This beautiful ideal, which he felt he must keep before the eyes of his readers as a model and inspiration, formed the reverse of the world of ugliness, falsity, corruption, and suffering whose agony he found hard to tolerate. He was also convinced that this ideal world of regenerated and totally transformed man, which resembles in so many aspects the vision of immortal life after resurrection for which he thirsted, can arise either as a result of human will or, like the Christian resurrection, as a swift natural process requiring and accepting the necessity of the death of the individual and of others, and the destruction of things as they are.

Intellectually and emotionally the most daring radical rebel poet of his day, Shelley sought to overturn not only the system of society as he knew it but the ethos upon which it was based, in the name of an ethos that differed remarkably little from the one to be established in the Christian millennium. Was he not a blasphemer of the sort which needs and preserves God as the sole worthy antagonist? Shelley's untimely death in the waters off Leghorn prevents one from knowing what course he might have taken, and whether he might have ended an activist like Byron (who said Shelley was to have accompanied him to Greece), a conservative like Wordsworth, or, as Browning thought, a Christian. Sensible rationalist, audacious dreamer, he stands as the prophetic poet whose imagery strangely illuminates the dark currents that flow into the mainstream of the idea of revolutionary rebirth. His poetry betrays the fascination of the beauty of crisis and terror, the Medusa of revolution who has the power to turn her compassionate but hypnotized beholders to stone.

chapter 4

the lure of action:
Keats

Although less obviously involved with the problems of society, with politics and revolution than Shelley, Keats has been qualified as "more the child of the Revolutionary Idea than we commonly suppose." [1] Obliquely and by contrast, Keats presents a critique of revolutionary ideals and revolutionary action. He was on the same side as Shelley, the side of radical reform, following with keen sympathy the fate of prosecuted deists and martyred patriots, and was deeply disturbed by poverty and by exploitation in mines and factories as symbolized by the actions of the ruthless brothers of the hapless Isabella. He, too, was concerned about the nature and manner of revolutionary change, and he never ceased to feel an intense yearning to do some good to suffering humanity. "I would jump down Aetna for any great Public good," he told one of his friends, [2] and this was a theme to which he often reverted.

What he never managed to resolve to his own satisfaction during his brief and tragic life was which form such a commitment should take, whether it should lie through poetry or through humanitarian action. At one time, when harassed by financial problems and frustrated in his poetical ambitions and his love for Fanny Brawne, he even contemplated (like Byron) joining one of the South American wars of liberation, if not serving as a surgeon on an Indiaman. Having set out upon the career of medicine, which he studied and practiced as an apprentice surgeon-dresser with some success, he abandoned it for poetry. But he remained torn between certainty of his poetic vocation and posthumous fame, on the one hand, and, on the other, doubts about whether he was on the right path, even sometimes about whether he was a poet at all. He felt divided between belief in the value of poetry for humanity and preference for an ideal of direct action, regarded as superior to poetry; between the pull of the imagination and the pull of "real things" that would sweep him off course "like a muddy stream."

This dilemma carried him away from the field where his true gifts lay, where the cultivation of the senses would lead him triumphantly into embalmed darkness and the murmurous haunt of flies on summer eves. As early as "Sleep and Poetry," published in 1817, he anticipated leaving the realm of Flora and Pan, the realm of sensuality:

> And can I ever bid these joys farewell?
> Yes, I must pass them for a nobler life,
> Where I may find the agonies, the strife
> Of human hearts: . . .[3]

The nobler life—writing to Richard Woodhouse about his aims, Keats said: "I am ambitious of doing the world some good: if I should be spared, that may be the work of maturer years—in the interval I will assay to reach to as high a summit in poetry as the nerve bestowed upon me will suffer. . . . All I hope is, that I may not lose all interest in human affairs— . . ."[4] He was then envisaging commitment to public good as a project for his maturity, and therefore as a higher ambition than poetry, though he would meanwhile strive for the highest poetic achievement with complete devotion and integrity. Yet he feared lest poetry might detach him from the goaded world of sighs and suffering.

These veerings between senses and thought, poetry and doing good, sometimes led Keats into inextricable confusion. But it is through the very nature of this confusion that one may glimpse the hesitations and temptations besetting a certain kind of poetic temper. Nowhere more readily than through Keats's dilemma can one sense the poet's irrepressible feeling that he ought really to be doing something other than writing poetry, something nobler, more heroic, and more useful for humanity; that he ought to be participating in the real world of life, where changes and improvements are effected, rather than confining himself to the world of the imagination alone. This feeling would often provide the impetus to political and revolutionary activism in others, although (despite the fact that he was haunted by it and despite his various projects including one for journalism in the liberal and reformist cause) it did not do so in the case of Keats himself.

Perhaps because of his self-doubt, Keats tended to define his own position at any given moment by contrast with his contemporaries. His poems and letters draw a graph of the growth of the poet and the human being, a graph that admittedly is not always easy to interpret because it expresses rapidly changing moods. Of modest origins, Keats lacked the superb gentlemanly assurance of Shelley, whom he met at Leigh Hunt's cottage in Hampstead in December 1816; there he heard the author of *Queen Mab* shrilly proclaiming his provocative antireligious and revolutionary views.

Keats's own political and religious opinions were less obsessive and extreme: unlike Shelley, he was no metaphysical rebel. These opinions were largely derived from regular reading of Leigh Hunt's radical weekly, *The Examiner,* and he may even have been compromised by his reputation as Leigh Hunt's disciple in what was then called the Cockney school of poetry and politics. "He was of the sceptical and republican school," wrote George Felton Mathew, one of Keats's many friends, "an advocate for the innovations which were making progress in his time; a fault-finder with everything established." [5] All the same, Keats maintained a certain independent reserve toward Shelley: it was attributable in part not merely to self-consciousness about his slight physique but also to a sense of class difference. Both of these marked his attitude toward Byron, whom he first admired, then repudiated, and to whom he was alluding when he commented wryly, "You see what it is to be under six foot and not a lord." [6]

Certainly in the beginning Keats had no objection to the treatment of social and political themes in poetry. Following in the steps of Wordsworth and his own patron, Leigh Hunt (whom he called "Libertas"), he seems to have felt that it was his poetic duty to introduce patriotic libertarian subjects, to defy "vulgar superstition," condemn "abject Caesars," and to try to "startle princes from their easy slumbers." [7] Those whom he regarded as the great spirits of the day—Wordsworth, Leigh Hunt, and the painter Haydon—would be joined by others, including doubtless Keats himself, who would give the world another heart. But Keats's attempts at political themes, possibly because they run counter to his true poetic gifts as distinct from his liberal and reformist opinions, are usually weak, the most notorious example being the awkward condemnation of the lords of the earth that opens the third book of *Endymion.*

Gradually Keats began to feel dissatisfied with poets who pressed opinions of any sort upon the reader, and the first to fall under criticism was his admired master, Wordsworth, whose metamorphosis into a submissive and conformist civil servant shocked Keats when he witnessed it for himself: ". . . are we to be bullied into a certain Philosophy engendered in the whims of an Egotist? . . . We hate poetry that has a palpable design upon us, and, if we do not agree, seems to put its hand into its breeches pocket. Poetry should be great and unobtrusive . . ." [8] Leigh Hunt was included in this judgment. Keats was not denying the worth of these poets (though the association now seems a curious one in terms of anything except a reputation for loving liberty), but he was challenging what he felt to be the obtrusive expression of personal views in poetry, and especially self-regarding reflection, "the whole of anybody's life and opinions" as found in the fourth canto of Byron's *Childe Harold.* [9]

Shelley, too, later met with disapproval on a similar score. Provoked by a rather patronizing though well-intentioned letter from Shelley inviting him to stay in Pisa, Keats (who was already in the grip of a fatal consumption) queried whether modern poetry must have a purpose: "You, I am sure, will forgive me for sincerely remarking that you might curb your magnanimity, and be more of an artist, and load every rift of your subject with ore." [10] Two distinct conceptions of poetry are at issue here: Shelley, who declared in the Preface to *Prometheus Unbound* that he abhorred didactic poetry, nonetheless liked to keep before the reader a vision of ideal perfection as a stimulus to betterment and action; while Keats toward the end of his short life rejected poetry-with-a-purpose in favor of his own conception of loading every rift with ore, the poetic ideal embodied in the great odes of his miraculous year.

It was vis-à-vis others, not only poets but public men and benefactors of humanity, that Keats tried to define his own poetic nature. In the course of doing so he illuminates some basic recurring aspects of the literary character faced with the challenge of "real things," action and commitment. One of these aspects is the poet's feeling that he lacks identity, a feeling which often stimulates him to look for some activity other than poetry which will grant him the sense of identity he so greatly desires. Keats gave memorable expression to this feeling. Comparing men gifted with creative imagination with men of power, he observed that whereas the former have no sense of individuality, the latter are endowed with a proper self: "Men of Genius are great as certain ethereal Chemicals operating on the Mass of neutral intellect—but they have not any individuality, any determined Character—I would call the top and head of those who have a proper self, Men of Power." [11] This insight goes some way to explain the attraction of power for the poet or the imaginative writer, since the pursuit of power means the attainment of "a proper self."

The poet's lack of a sense of identity may well be balanced by the gift of heightened insight, of empathy, or even of metamorphosis into another being, as when Keats shares in the existence of the sparrow outside his window and picks about the gravel. Yet the man who feels himself both uniquely gifted and deprived is bound to be attracted as well as repelled by his opposite, the man of power. Perhaps, too, he is even at times secretly envious of the latter's "proper self" and conduct in the sphere of "real things" (as distinct from the imagination), which in some moods he would like to emulate.

Keats tried to turn his own sense of a lack of identity and of firm commitment to a philosophy or party into a virtue, telling his beloved brothers George and Tom about a quality that was the reverse of partisanship: "I mean *Negative Capability,* that is, when a man is capable of being in uncertainties, mysteries, doubts, without any irritable reaching after fact and reason . . . ," and he added, "with a great poet the sense of Beauty overcomes every other consideration, or rather obliterates all consideration." [12] Keats misjudged Coleridge in this context, thinking him incapable of remaining in a state of enriching doubt, and he went on to allude to "poor Shelley," whose poem on the ideal revolution, *Laon and Cythna* (which he had not yet read), had just appeared and was thought likely to arouse as much opposition as *Queen Mab.* It looks as if Shelley enters into the association of ideas in Keats's mind here as a negative instance of the view that considerations of poetic beauty should prevail over all others. Keats was later to say of one who could not feel he had a personal identity unless he had made up his mind about everything, and who was obsessed with Godwinian political justice, that a man's first political duty should be the happiness of his friends and that the mind should be "a thoroughfare for all thoughts, not a select party." [13]

The question of identity arose again when Keats attempted to establish the quality of his own poetic nature, not as opposed to the character of the man of power but in comparison with a poetic temperament different from his own, that of his lofty predecessor, Wordsworth: "As to the poetical character itself (I mean that sort, of which, if I am anything, I am a member; that sort distinguished from the Wordsworthian, or egotistical Sublime; which is a thing per se, and stands alone), it is not itself—it has no self—It is every thing and nothing—It has no character —it enjoys light and shade; . . . It has as much delight in conceiving an Iago as an Imogen. What shocks the virtuous philosopher delights the chameleon poet. It does no harm from its relish of the dark side of things, any more than from its taste for the bright one, because they both end in speculation." [14] Here Keats elaborates upon the theme of the poet's lack of identity while introducing a new element: the pleasure of the poetic imagination in the dark side of life and, as he proposes, the harmlessness of this pleasure since it has no effect in reality.

For the poetic imagination is not necessarily either moral or concerned with doing good (his repeatedly avowed ambition), and this was plainly one of the things that sometimes bothered him about poetry. He had doubtless reflected upon the remarkable observations of his friend Hazlitt on *Coriolanus.* Hazlitt had said in his lecture on Shakespeare's play that the language of poetry naturally falls in with the language of power, and in his reply to the critic William Gifford, who had challenged this opinion, he clarified his views. It was Hazlitt's reply to Gifford that Keats quoted at length, and with evident zest and enthusiasm, in a journal-letter to his brother George and his sister-in-law in America: "I affirm, Sir," wrote Hazlitt to Gifford, "that Poetry, that the imagination, generally speaking, delights in power, in strong excitement, as well as in truth, in good, in right, whereas pure reason and the moral sense approve only of the true and good. I proceed to show that this general love or tendency to immediate excitement or theatrical effect, no matter how produced, gives a Bias to the imagination often inconsistent with the greater good, that in Poetry it triumphs over principle, and bribes the passions to make a sacrifice of common humanity." [15]

Hazlitt's analysis of the "subtle sophistry of the human mind" in this regard, an analysis highly lauded by Keats, stresses the excitement felt by the literary imagination in particular at the idea of vast upheaval, destruction, and bloodshed, already noted in connection with Blake, Coleridge, and Shelley. Hazlitt would write, more generally, some years after Keats's death, on the pleasure of hating, that "a whole town runs to be present at a fire, and the spectator by no means exults to see it extinguished." [16] If men like Hazlitt and Keats were particularly fascinated by this kind of perverse inclination, it may be assumed that they had been struck by it in their contemporaries and sensed it in themselves with a degree of awareness that later writers who experienced the same tendency would not always share.

Keats approached the problem of morality and the attitude of the poetic imagination toward power and destruction from another angle later on in the same journal-letter to his brother and sister-in-law: he observed that very few men, with the exception of Socrates and Jesus, "ever arrived at a complete disinterestedness of Mind: very few have been influenced by a pure desire of the benefit of others,—in the greater part of the Benefactors of Humanity some meretricious motive has sullied their greatness—some melodramatic scenery has fascinated them." [17] (The sullied secular benefactors of humanity may well include the French revolutionaries.) This reflection was prompted by his disquiet at being unable to feel as deep a grief for the approaching death of the father of his friend William Haslam as he felt for the painful death of his own younger brother, Tom. Moreover, Keats could not help believing that the triumph of pure disinterestedness would actually disturb the balance of nature, which he understood to mean the inclusion of cruelty, pain, death, and destruction.

He had already broached this subject the previous year when Tom was dying of tuberculosis, in the "Epistle to John Hamilton Reynolds":

>   . . . I was at home
> And should have been most happy,—but I saw
> Too far into the sea, where every maw
> The greater on the less feeds evermore.—
> But I saw too distinct into the core
> Of an eternal fierce destruction, . . .
> Still do I that most fierce destruction see,—
> The Shark at savage prey,—the Hawk at pounce,—
> The gentle Robin, like a Pard or Ounce,
> Ravening a worm,—Away, ye horrid moods!
> Moods of one's mind! You know I hate them well. [18]

Now, writing to George and his wife on the unlikelihood of complete disinterestedness, Keats brooded on the theme of destruction once again—"For in wild nature the Hawk would lose his Breakfast of Robins and the Robin his of Worms." [19] He compared man to the hawk, but instead of conceiving such violent images of predator and victim to be the consequence of a morbid and depressive mood, as he had before in his poem to Reynolds, he now found a certain pleasurable wonderment in observing the alertness of the stoat and the anxiety of the deer.

The thought struck him that there might even be superior beings as entertained in a nonmoral way by men-hawks and men-victims as he was by stoat and deer: "Though a quarrel in the Streets is a thing to be hated, the energies displayed in it are fine; . . . By a superior Being our reasonings may take the same tone—though erroneous they may be fine. This is the very thing in which consists Poetry, and if so it is not so fine a thing as philosophy—for the same reason that an eagle is not so fine a thing as a truth." [20] Like so many of his contemporaries, Keats recognized the attraction of all manifestations of energy and power divorced from moral ends. By analogy, he saw that the pleasure of poetry could be of a similar kind, that it might be nonmoral though otherwise full of grace. But admitting so much, he could not but feel that poetry might prove inferior to truth—that is, to the unadulterated "true and good" approved by the moral sense, as Hazlitt put it in his reply to Gifford, as well as to the pursuit of humanitarian action.

Just as pleasure in light and dark, in mutually opposed forces in life, made Keats question the value of poetry itself, so the willed acceptance of death and destruction as ineluctable elements in nature obliged him to resist the facile optimism of the theorists of human perfectibility. For Keats, reflecting on such extremes of humanity as the primitive American Indian and the civilized Frenchman under Louis XIV, "Man is originally a poor forked creature subject to the same mischances as the beasts of the forest, destined to hardship and disquietude of some kind or other." [21] As he saw it, each ascent of the rungs of civilization merely brings fresh disadvantages, and death remains the end of all. Perfect earthly happiness would only make death harder to bear. Consequently, unlike Godwin and Shelley, Keats could not conceive of undiluted earthly happiness or perfection, any more than he could envisage total disinterestedness: "But in truth I do not at all believe in this sort of perfectibility—the nature of the world will not admit of it—. . . ." [22] While seeking a system of salvation that would not affront reason and humanity, a system "grander . . . than the Christian religion," Keats arrived at the same kind of criticism leveled by the devout at those convinced of the possibility of revolutionizing human nature and human circumstances.

All the same, Keats had shown concern for growth and advance through change when he remarked that Wordsworth's anxiety for humanity appeared greater than Milton's. He recognized three great changes in English history. The first, for the better, was the gradual abolition of the tyranny of the nobles. The second, for the worse, occurred when kings forgot their obligations to the people. The English revolutionary example in the seventeenth century and the activity of liberal writers in England and France "sowed the seed of opposition to this tyranny, and it was swelling in the ground till it burst out in the French Revolution. That has had an unlucky termination." [23] The unfortunate course of the French Revolution stopped the growth of free opinion in England, served as a pretext to undermine freedom, and encouraged reactionary fears of innovation and improvement. But now, after the massacre of Peterloo, roused by their own misery, the English people were struggling to destroy reaction.

Since he had come to feel that suffering is a spur to moral and spiritual growth, Keats could write: "Perhaps, on this account, the present distresses of this nation are a fortunate thing though so horrid in their experience. You will see I mean that the French Revolution put a temporary stop to this third change—the change for the better—Now it is in progress again, and I think it an effectual one. This is no contest between Whig and Tory, but between right and wrong." [24] Curiously, on this subject Keats showed none of the doubts or the concern with light and shade which he felt essential to his fulfillment as a poet. Indeed, this very contrast underlies the frustration of his efforts in his most ambitious heroic poem, "Hyperion."

When he tried to express his views on poetry and life in "Hyperion," which has been seen as "under allegoric forms, the epic of the Revolutionary Idea," [25] Keats twice ended in an impasse. The first version of the poem depicts the rebellion of "son against his sire," the necessity of creative mutation and growth, the progress from sterility to creativity through painful change, and thus contains within itself not merely the revolt of Olympians against Titans, Saturn deposed by Jove, and Hyperion displaced by Apollo, but the old regime ousted by a new order, the old system of poetry replaced by the new, or the old Keats by the new Keats tempered in the fire of suffering. Thus it presents change as inevitable and natural in history, politics, literature, and the individual spirit, indeed in every sphere.

The poem opens with the terrible lifelessness and sterility of the doomed old forms, as dethroned Saturn longs for beautiful things made new, yet cannot fashion them:

> But cannot I create?
> Cannot I form? Cannot I fashion forth
> Another world, another universe,
> To overbear and crumble this to nought? [26]

Unlike Saturn in his hopelessness, Hyperion, the dazzling Titan of the sun, aims at resistance, intending a counterrevolution against the rebel gods in order to restore Saturn to his throne, but in vain. Oceanus, on the contrary, evolves a philosophy of change and urges its acceptance:

> We fall by course of Nature's law, not force
> Of thunder, or of Jove. [27]

Supreme power, says Oceanus, blinds the ruler or the possessor of it to the difficult truth that all dominion is transitory:

> So on our heels a fresh perfection treads,
> A power more strong in beauty, born of us
> And fated to excel us . . . [28]

There follows the proclamation of the dubious

> eternal law
> That first in beauty should be first in might:
> Yea, by that law, another race may drive
> Our conquerors to mourn as we do now. [29]

So, through Oceanus, Keats envisages an endless series of inevitable revolutions.

The new poetic force, Apollo, attains godhead through knowledge that embraces

> Names, deeds, grey legends, dire events, rebellions,
> Majesties, sovran voices, agonies,
> Creations and destroyings . . .[30]

But in acquiring the heroic certainty of the knowledge that suffering and destruction are necessary for creation and growth, the poet-Apollo ceases to be the kind of poet whose gift depends on the ability to preserve nuance and uncertainty. Apollo dies into new life through initiation into the harsh reality of suffering and destruction, and at the moment when "Apollo shriek'd," Keats was obliged to break off, doubtless because he found he was denying a part of himself and was being carried into a realm where he could no longer see clearly.

The pressure of what he was trying to say forced Keats to make another attempt later in 1819 in the fragment called "The Fall of Hyperion: A Dream." In this poem he sought to establish a distinction between the poet and the active humanitarian, and again came to a dead end. There are, he begins, three kinds of dreamer: fanatics, who weave a "paradise for a sect" (and who may be counted as both religious and revolutionary dreamers), savages who have no poetry, and poets:

> Whether the dream now purpos'd to rehearse
> Be poet's or fanatic's will be known
> When this warm scribe, my hand, is in the grave.[31]

This distinction between poet and fanatic at once strikes a discordant note, since one would not associate Keats with those who weave a "paradise for a sect," and it hints at his difficulties.

Now it is the poet himself, not Apollo, who shrieks as he dies into new life, mounting in a vision the steps of an ancient sanctuary. He is mystified to find himself there alive, and asks the temple's guardian spirit, the awe-inspiring goddess Moneta, to enlighten him:

> "High prophetess," said I, "purge off,
> Benign, if so it please thee, my mind's film."
> "None can usurp this height," return'd that shade,
> "But those to whom the miseries of the world
> Are misery, and will not let them rest." [32]

And Moneta adds that if any others, save these humanitarians, approached the temple, they would die.

The poet, still puzzled to know why he has survived in that case, inquires whether there are not thousands who love their fellowmen, who "feel the giant agony of the world," and who, moreover, labor for the good of humanity. Why, then, is he here alone? Moneta replies that such active humanitarians are neither visionaries nor dreamers, and do not think of approaching the temple. She proceeds to cut the poet down to size:

> And thou art here, for thou art less than they.
> What benefit canst thou do, or all thy tribe
> To the great world? Thou art a dreaming thing,
> A fever of thyself: think of the earth . . . [33]

The poet is therefore less than the active humanitarian; he can do nothing for the world; he is a mere dreamer who "venoms all his days." Still, useless dreamers such as he, though unworthy, are sometimes admitted to the temple, it appears.

Keats has expressed here the poet's terrible sense of inadequacy vis-à-vis the committed and active humanitarian in a time of upheaval. The injunction to think of the earth is surely unnecessary: he does think of it, and is propelled out of his proper sphere by the secret pressure of commitment and action.

However, in a number of lines that Keats seems to have intended to erase, the poet tries to challenge Moneta and to justify and defend the poet's role and usefulness:

> . . . sure not all
> Those melodies sung into the world's ear

> Are useless: sure a poet is a sage;
> A humanist, physician to all men.[34]

Then the awful doubt crosses his mind, whether he himself can be counted among the true poets. Moneta calls him a dreamer, repeating what she had said before, but now distinguishes between poets and dreamers as complete opposites: true poets console humanity, while false ones (dreamers) trouble it. There follows a condemnation of bad lyric poets and self-worshippers, and with this Keats probably realized that he had lost the thread of his argument. Not long after, he again abandoned the poem.

The quandary that Keats personified may seem at first to be on the fringe of the problems raised by literary revolutionism, but in reality it is central to them. In the age of revolution the poet longs to benefit the great world, but what contribution can he make? Only too often he feels inferior to the man of action and power who, unlike himself, seems to have a proper sense of identity. Only too often he feels that composing works of imagination is less worthy than doing active good in the world of real suffering and oppression. Perhaps it was only Keats's distaste for the limitations of partisanship, and his belief that the flaw in the universe provides the stimulus to spiritual growth (to say nothing of tragic lack of time), which prevented him from treading the path that would be taken by many others who either shared his respect for action, like Byron, or who inherited his doubts and his dilemma.

chapter **5**

_revolution as personal
salvation: Byron_

When Lord Byron died at Missolonghi in April 1824, *half murdered by the in-*
competence and stupidity of his doctors and suffering not only from fever
but from unrequited love for a Greek youth, he consecrated revolutionary
commitment and, by the example of his dramatic sacrifice and martyrdom, he endowed the revolutionary cause with a romantic aura it has
never lost. The Greek expedition was the last in a long line of libertarian
causes that had beckoned him, from the reformist movement at home to
revolutionary intrigues against the Austrians in North Italy, where a spy
referred to him as "this revolutionary fellow." [1] What brought him not
merely to place his name and wealth at the disposal of foreign activists
but to risk his life in perilous political enterprises? Among the most powerful motives was dissatisfaction with himself and with the world, the

feeling that he was trapped, that he had made a mess of his life, that he had not fulfilled his capabilities and potentialities, and that only some bold, grand gesture of defiant service could redeem him.

Despite much that now seems pure pose in himself, or rings hollow in his serious verse (as distinct from his diverting satires and his letters, where we feel we can hear his speaking voice), Byron remained absolutely true to his contradictory impulses. Indeed, in his extremes of melancholy and gaiety he was probably what would now be called a manic-depressive. He candidly transcribes his obscure strivings as well as his conscious attitudes. With one part of his being he was as devoted to "that which is" as Stendhal, whom he encountered briefly in the latter's beloved Milan in 1816. "My first object is truth even at my own expense," wrote Byron, and John Cam Hobhouse, a lifelong friend, commented in the margin, "Very true." [2] Throughout Europe a good many of his contemporaries and successors recognized themselves in the frustrated sensibility he revealed, aspects of which have become so well absorbed in the modern makeup that their Byronic source is all but forgotten.

Byron was obsessed by thoughts of destruction and self-destruction. The incongruity between man's limitless aspirations and his limited condition inspired him with nostalgia for the abyss. It was not only Manfred who favored heights and yearned after the flight of the bird of prey, but Julien Sorel and countless others (fictional and actual) who would risk all to push back the social limits or the earthbound frontiers of human existence. As you look down over the precipice, Byron noted, you feel an awful wish to plunge within it. He called this the "lurking bias" to the *unknown,* "a secret prepossession" to plunge—but where? (He himself uses the word "plunge" twice.) [3] Besides this temptation to self-destruction (he was haunted by instances of suicide among his wild ancestors), Byron had extraordinary prophetic visions of a world totally destroyed:

> I had a dream which was not all a dream, . . .
> . . . .   The world was void,
> The populous and the powerful was a lump,
> Seasonless, herbless, treeless, manless, lifeless . . . [4]

He was attracted by the theory of worlds repeatedly destroyed—baked, fried, burned, or drowned, as he once cheerfully put it. Such visions and inclinations reveal his secret and frustrated aggression. He liked to sleep with sword or pistols by his bedside. His sudden inexplicable rages were notorious.

To the misfortune of his lameness (mark of destiny's disfavor to a deeply superstitious mind that attributed everything to the goddess Fortune and carefully studied the auguries) was added his premature sexual initiation at the age of nine by a Calvinist maid, an experience which he felt had made him "anticipate life." Byron himself was to add various other burdens to these, including several bitter precocious disappointments in love; homosexual inclinations, sublimated in the case of the choirboy Edleston-Thyrza, then indulged during the latter part of his first journey to the Eastern Mediterranean; clandestine relations, so it is believed, with his half-sister Augusta; and the flaunted Don Juan-ism, dissipation, and debauchery from which he was rescued by Countess Guiccioli. Small wonder that his sable-curled, sneering heroes carry a guilt complex of alarming proportions—a weight of mysterious unmentionable sins and nameless crimes, and an "uneradicable taint of sin" so dreadful that it cannot be cleansed by repentance and redemption.[5] Religion itself is powerless against such guilt, and the respected man of the cloth falls back helpless as the doomed Satanic hero defiantly pursues his desperate path to perdition.

The Byronic hero accumulates sins out of defiance. For while airing a superficial Voltairean skepticism and deism, Byron was haunted by damnation, by the somber Calvinist view of predestined damnation without the sinner's fault. He called himself "Methodist, Calvinist, Augustinian" to Shelley,[6] and it is this Calvinist tinge which distinguishes his form of revolt from that of the pagan-inspired poet of *Prometheus Unbound.* Shelley, whose friendship with Byron began during their Genevan exile in 1816, would have liked to eradicate from Byron's mind "the delusions of Christianity, which in spite of his reason, seem perpetually to recur. . . ."[7] Though Byron did not share Shelley's anti-Christian stand, he thought Shelley possessed "one of the first Christian virtues, charity and benevolence." [8] Byron seems to have regarded himself as more deeply Christian than many conventional believers because he felt more warmly charitable in outlook: he resisted the idea of eternal damnation for infidel, heretic, and sinner in an age when not only was narrow fundamentalism rife but even a Blake insisted upon apocalyptic vengeance.

If Christianity is truly the religion of forgiveness, why is there not salvation and redemption for all, including Satan? So inquires one of Byron's political protagonists, the Doge Faliero. In such a view, Lucifer himself appears in *Cain* as the Promethean champion of suffering mankind against divine cruelty and injustice: for unlike the solitary deity, Lucifer knows that damned spirits like himself and unhappy men at least sympathize with each other, and by their mutual sympathy make their sufferings more endurable. Man may well be wretched and foredoomed, but he can resist: that is the meaning of Satanic Promethean revolt for Byron, and it is here, in the resistance of the damned of the earth against divine and human hardheartedness, that sentimental Byronic Satanist rebellion meets and merges into revolution.

Standing as "a stranger in this breathing world," [9] the Byronic hero becomes one of the principal models for all those rebellious outsiders who were to follow down to our own day. Yet at the same time that Byron's outlaw heroes remain estranged from the hostile world, the peopled desert, by the cruel marks of a jealous destiny as much as by their own willful acts, they have latent capacities for good. The trouble is that they have been "warped" by the world itself. Byron derives from Rousseau the notion that human failings are chiefly due to the insufferable state of society. The world, or established society, is characterized by hypocrisy, which Byron—with his ideal of pre-Adamite innocence, purity, and sincerity—qualifies as the crying sin, perhaps remembering the Calvinist maid who had poisoned the springs of his existence. "The truth is, that in these days the grand *'primum mobile'* of England is *cant;* cant political, cant poetical, cant religious, cant moral; but always *cant,* multipled through all the varieties of life," he complained. [10]

It seems as if there can be no escape either from the agonized self or from the oppressive, damaging, hypocritical world-as-it-exists: all traditional outlets are blocked. One refuge alone remains. Self-disgust and disgust at shoddy, corrupt society inspire a yearning for action in some good cause that will prove purifying, cathartic, redemptive, a cause that will somehow wipe the slate clean and give the individual and humanity a chance to start afresh. The revolutionary cause is all the more attractive to Byron because it offers a glimpse of the purgation that he felt Calvinism would deny him.

While he had no great opinion of Keats, whose poetry he once called "a sort of mental masturbation," it so happens that, true to Keats's assessment of one variety of poetic temper, Byron admitted to having "no character at all. . . . I am so changeable, being every thing by turns and nothing long"; [11] and he never ceased to urge the prestige of action against the claims of literature. The fact was that with the publication of *Childe Harold's Pilgrimage* in 1812, he became famous overnight. Fêted, lionized, for a brief period he reigned. Governed as he was by inordinate pride and by the longing for fame and glory (he wrote to his mother from school at Harrow that he was determined to carve himself the passage to grandeur), he may well have felt that his poetic triumph seemed too easily acquired. Therefore, with his love of difficulty, he professed not to value poetic laurels as much as the laurels of action which he had not won.

This attitude was more than mere lordly disdain for the profession of letters. Not long after he had achieved fame as a poet, he claimed that he did not rank poetry or poets high in the scale of intellect, that he preferred the talents of action "to all the speculations of those mere dreamers. . . ." [12] In his journal he observed that he no longer considered authorship so important as he had done when younger. The great fuss about scribbling and scribes, made by themselves and others, was in his opinion a sign of effeminacy and degeneracy: "Who would write, who had anything better to do? 'Action—action—action'—said Demosthenes: 'Actions—actions', I say, and not writing,—least of all, rhyme." [13] Only great writers who were courageous, active citizens were excluded from this scathing judgment on his art and its practitioners.

When the scandal surrounding the breakup of his disastrous marriage to Annabella Milbanke caused him to be cut dead in the salons where formerly he had been lionized, a literary reputation consecrated by so despicable and canting a crew seemed of little worth. "If I live ten years longer," he wrote wildly to the Irish poet Thomas Moore from voluntary exile in Venice, "you will see, however, that it is not over with me—I don't mean in literature, for that is nothing; and it may seem odd enough to say, I do not think it my vocation. But you will see that I shall do something or other—. . . ." [14] That "something" which would puzzle and astonish the world would imply doing more for mankind than write verses.

What Byron would have liked from the first was the role of public benefactor and leader of the reformist cause. His maiden speech in the House of Lords in February 1812, just before *Childe Harold's Pilgrimage* appeared, had taken up the cause of the Luddites in the neighborhood of his own estate, the Nottingham framebreakers. Here was an instance of the sacrifice of human beings to the new industrial machinery which, by allowing one man to do the work of seven, put six men out of work. "I have seen the state of these miserable men, and it is a disgrace to a civilised country," he told the moderate Whig leader, Lord Holland. The wretches deserved pity rather than punishment. Then, feeling he had perhaps gone too far, he added a postscript: "I am a little apprehensive that your Lordship will think me too lenient towards these men, and half a *framebreaker myself.*" [15]

Such social timidity distinguishes Byron the patrician rebel from an unswerving rebel-on-principle like Shelley. For in contrast with Shelley, Byron did not seek to undermine existing religious, social, and moral conventions even while he flouted them, any more than he wanted to undermine literary tradition—believing, as an admirer of Pope, that he himself and nearly all the post-Wordsworthian poets were following "a wrong revolutionary poetical system, or systems." [16] Certainly Byron's social and political standpoint was not the result of audacious reflection, as was Shelley's; rather it figures partly as a form of *noblesse oblige.*

His attitude would remain highly equivocal. He confided to his journal on November 23, 1813, that if he had any ambition it was to be Caesar or nothing. Then he enlarged upon the kind of Caesar he had in mind: "To be the first man—not the Dictator—not the Sylla, but the Washington or the Aristides—the leader in talent and truth—is next to the Divinity!" This note makes one suppose that he fancied the role of father and redeemer of his country, a role which Shelley would conceive as lying within his friend's powers. Yet after adding Franklin and Penn to Washington as desirable exemplars, Byron moved on to the tyrannicides Brutus and Cassius, ending surprisingly with the sanguinary Saint-Just. "I shall never be any thing, or rather always be nothing," he brooded. "The most I can hope is, that some will say, 'He might, perhaps, if he would.' " [17] He felt that only his own indolence was preventing him from fulfilling himself as man of action and leader, like some of his own poetic heroes.

While in his poems the outlaws of every creed and race discuss visionary schemes and are distinguished for their fraternity and solidarity among themselves and their enmity to outsiders, the Chief "mingles not but to command." [18] He alone has the art of rule that dazzles and chills the vulgar. On the other hand, a superior spirit like Manfred might once, in his youth, have had noble aspirations to be the "enlightener of nations," but Coriolanus-like he could not bring himself to sue for men's support—

I disdain'd to mingle with
A herd, though to be leader— . . . [19]

Byron, in short, moved between the glamor of rule and command and a scarcely concealed distaste for those to be commanded.

Even while he approved of the constitutional reform of abuses, he had a poor view of democracy, defining it as an aristocracy of blackguards. The demagogues admired by the *canaille* disgusted him and put him off the reformist cause at home ("If we must have a tyrant, let him at least be a gentleman who has been bred to the business . . .").[20] He was not impressed by the bungling Italian conspirators, and even less by the disputatious and mercenary Greeks, who inspired the comment that "we must not look always too closely at the men who are to benefit by our exertions in a good cause, or God knows we shall seldom do much good in this world." [21] The cause mattered more to him than those who would ultimately profit from its success.

If in Byron's political outlook there was love of the *beau rôle* and the heroic ideal, there was also a contrariness, a spirit of opposition. When young, he said he loved liberty because his mother was so despotic, and later he certainly loved it because it was the forbidden fruit in that age of reaction and restoration. He was anti-establishment, whatever its color, as he frankly owned: "As for me, by the blessing of indifference, I have simplified my politics into an utter detestation of all existing governments; and, as it is the shortest and most agreeable and summary feeling imaginable, the first moment of an universal republic would convert me into an advocate for single and uncontradicted despotism. The fact is, riches are power, and poverty is slavery all over the earth, and one sort of establishment is no better nor worse for a *people* than another." [22] His loyalty to his chosen party arose more from a sense of honor than from political principle. As he put it succinctly ten years later in *Don Juan,* "I was born for opposition," and repeated his contention that the triumph of democracy would drive him to the side of the royalists. [23]

By revolution, Byron intended either the overthrow of existing monarchical regimes and their replacement by a republican form of government or the achievement of national independence from foreign oppression. His low opinion of men as wolves meant that he did not envisage that change would bring Utopia. There might be new times, but there would still be the same old tears and crimes. Nonetheless, he realized that after the French Revolution nothing could be quite the same again: the veil of ancient forms and traditions had been torn, never to be repaired. Much that was good had been overthrown with the bad. But he believed that the elite who lead revolutions, while abhorring bloodshed, should not make the mistake of confusing the Terror (a passing phenomenon and the inevitable consequence of long oppression) with the revolutionary cause, which was good and glorious in itself. Revolutions are not to be made with rosewater, as he was fond of repeating after Marmontel. Still, while some blood may and must be shed for the cause, it need not be *"clotted."* [24] How moderation is to be achieved he does not say.

Some idea of Byron's private hesitations and reservations about revolutionary action may be surmised from his resonant drama *Marino Faliero*, finished in 1820 when Italy was on the eve of an uprising that would prove abortive and when he himself was becoming involved with the Carbonari in the Romagna. Although his play deals with the fourteenth-century conspiracy of the Doge Faliero, impelled by trivial-seeming personal grievance, against the government of which he is the titular head, the theme is the moral conflict between the claims of humanity and the use of violence in revolutionary situations.

The reluctant doge sees the despotic Venetian state as a specter "which must be exorcised with blood," [25] but he vacillates when he remembers all the personal ties that bind him to the patricians on the Council, ties which he feels the plebeian patriots with whom he is allied cannot understand. He fears the blood lust of the mob:

> . . . . one stroke struck,
> And the mere instinct of the first-born Cain,
> Which ever lurks somewhere in human hearts,
> Though circumstance may keep it in abeyance,
> Will urge the rest on like to wolves . . .[26]

Although his aims are to restore freedom and inaugurate a "bright millennium," he grieves as he takes the eternal view of his actions:

> . . . . but oh! by what means?
> The noble end must justify them. . . . .
> . . . . Oh world!
> Oh men! What are ye, and our best designs,
> That we must work by crime to punish crime?
> And slay as if Death had but this one gate,
> When a few years would make the sword superfluous? [27]

Ultimately the plot fails, not through the doge but because one of the conspirators, more softhearted than the rest, cannot bring himself to kill the innocent with the guilty.

Such qualms as Byron himself may have felt about nocturnal assignations with lowborn Italian conspirators were doubtless counterbalanced by the picturesque charm of the cabalistic rituals of the Carbonari, and did not prevent him from compromising himself with them in a way that Manzoni, the future author of *I Promessi Sposi,* hesitated to do. Soon Byron's house in Ravenna was a veritable armory, and the love of risk took command: "I suppose that they consider me as a depôt, to be sacrificed, in case of accidents," he wrote. "It is no great matter, supposing that Italy could be liberated, who or what is sacrificed. It is a grand object—the very *poetry* of politics." [28] To the romance of risk and the poetry of politics would be added a belief in the unique power of revolution to achieve universal purification, a feeling

> . . . . that revolution
> Alone can save the earth from hell's pollution . . .[29]

as he expressed it in *Don Juan.* How had he come to see revolution as the only means of salvation for himself and the world at large?

For Byron, the revolutionary cause meant a refuge from the hated self, an activity that might help him to lose his own "wretched identity," as he had sought in vain to do amid the grandiose torrents and avalanches of the Swiss Alps. He suffered from constitutional ennui, the malady of the age, in acute form around the age of nineteen, though, he thought, to a somewhat lesser degree in later years. Only some form of activity—travel to exotic lands (as Spain, Greece, and Turkey were then), the thrill of adventure in swimming the Hellespont, the excitement of gambling, the risk involved in womanizing—diverted him from boredom and brooding. Revolutionary activity had one obvious advantage over these diversions: the grand altruistic end of freedom for the oppressed.

In *The Deformed Transformed,* the crippled hero is told that

> In life *commotion* is the extremest point
> Of life.[30]

As Byron had confessed to Annabella Milbanke: "The great object of life is sensation—to feel that we exist, even though in pain. It is this 'craving void' which drives us to gaming—to battle—to travel—to intemperate, but keenly felt pursuits of any description whose principal attraction is the agitation inseparable from their accomplishment." [31] (One is reminded of Keats, writing of war, high deeds, the stresses of life as the subtle food to make us "feel existence.") In his journal, Byron added revolution to the forms of agitation that help us to feel we exist: ". . . . a little *tumult,* now and then, is an agreeable quickener of sensation; such as a revolution, a battle, or an *adventure* of any lively description." [32] Revolution, then, was one form of adventure in Byron's eyes, one release from emptiness and ennui, at a time when the astonishing dramatic episodes of the French Revolution and the meteoric career of Napoleon had aroused a universal taste for strong excitement.

Speaking of Napoleon in the third canto of *Childe Harold's Pilgrimage,* published in 1816, Byron wrote:

> But quiet to quick bosoms is a hell,
>   . . . . there is a fire
> And motion of the soul, which will not dwell
> In its own narrow being, but aspire
> Beyond the fitting medium of desire;
> And, but once kindled, quenchless evermore,
> Preys upon high adventure, nor can tire
> Of aught but rest . . .[33]

With Napoleon he associated, among others, revolutionaries and poets—including, presumably, himself:

> This makes the madmen who have made men mad
> By their contagion! Conquerors and Kings,

> Founders of sects and systems, to whom add
> Sophists, Bards, Statesmen, all unquiet things
> Which stir too strongly the soul's secret springs . . .
>
> Their breath is agitation, and their life
> A storm whereon they ride, to sink at last,
> And yet so nursed and bigoted to strife,
> That should their days, surviving perils past,
> Melt to calm twilight, they feel overcast
> With sorrow and supineness, and so die . . .[34]

At the other extreme from agitation and self-assertion lie rest, oblivion, self-forgetfulness, which some of his heroes so ardently seek.

Yet if rest is from some points of view highly desirable, from others (as his verses show) it is dreaded. Anything rather than stagnation: it is better to do something than nothing; it is better to live, to "snatch the life of life" than to exist; it is better that one's life's blood should flow than that it should creep in lazy channels. If Byron stopped for a moment, he became conscious of life slipping away, of opportunities gone forever, of potentialities unfulfilled. For him, as he takes stock of himself, the best is over at twenty-three. He is the supreme singer of youth, played out after thirty, a poet in terror of idiocy, sterility, and old age. He should have been able to shape the course of his life into an artistic pattern, he felt; he should have been "a pasha," for instance, by such and such an age; but destiny, though it showered him with gifts and energies, failed to comply. In the end, he hoped for death in action, "for that would be a good finish to a very *triste* existence," [35] a noble rounding-off that fate denied him.

Byron reveals, perhaps more clearly than any other poet before or since, the sheer thrill of agitation and commotion. Where formerly writers might have expressed dread at violent storms, the romantics desired them ("Swiftly arise, you longed-for storms," exclaimed Chateaubriand in *René*). Byron went further than longing: he was thrilled by the beauty and power of a storm at night in the mountains, by the electric excitement of the awe-inspiring spectacle. He wrote in *Childe Harold's Pilgrimage:*

> The sky is changed!—and such a change! O night,
> And storm, and darkness, ye are wondrous strong,
> Yet lovely in your strength, as is the light
> Of a dark eye in woman! Far along,
> From peak to peak, the rattling crags among,
> Leaps the live thunder! Not from one lone cloud,
> But every mountain now hath found a tongue:
> And Jura answers, through her misty shroud,
> Back to the joyous Alps, who call to her aloud!
>
> And this is in the night:—Most glorious night!
> Thou wert not sent for slumber! let me be
> A sharer in thy fierce and far delight—
> A portion of the tempest and of thee!
> How the lit lake shines, a phosphoric sea,
> And the big rain comes dancing to the earth!
> And now again 'tis black,—and now, the glee
> Of the loud hills shakes with its mountain-mirth,
> As if they did rejoice o'er a young earthquake's birth.[36]

Not content with witnessing the upheaval of the tempest, undeterred by the destruction it must cause, Byron yearns to share in its fierce delight, longs to be part of it. In the final simile, the birth of an earthquake appears as a theme of rejoicing, not of terror; as an inspiriting phenomenon, not as a disaster. By analogy, since tempests and earthquakes are traditional metaphors for revolution, the sentiment of exaltation and the desire for participation can be aroused by revolutionary as well as by natural catastrophe.

A stanza that follows shortly after these is among the most remarkable and revealing that Byron ever wrote:

> Could I embody and unbosom now
> That which is most within me,—could I wreak

My thoughts upon expression, and thus throw
Soul, heart, mind, passions, feelings, strong or weak,
All that I would have sought, and all I seek,
Bear, know, feel, and yet breathe—into one word,
And that one word were Lightning, I would speak:
But as it is, I live and die unheard,
With a most voiceless thought, sheathing it as a sword.[37]

Here is an attempt to express the inexpressible: all the frustration and all the suppressed inner violence that help to explain the passion for movement and the need for excitement and high drama. The revolutionary cause would provide an outlet for that repressed inner lightning. The hitherto sheathed sword could be drawn at last, and the unuttered thought made manifest, despite the avowed hatred of bloodshed.

Throughout his life, Byron tended to flee from complications. Whenever things became intolerable to him, as not surprisingly they often did, he felt the urge to move, to get out, to emigrate to South America (with letters of recommendation to Bolívar), to offer his services to some revolutionary junta, to have a finger in any "row" that was brewing, as he liked to put it. The young, beautiful, disinterested Countess Guiccioli rescued him from his plebeian Venetian Medeas, and he was attached to her, but it was not long before he became bored with inactivity. Besides, he felt the role of *cicisbeo,* of accredited bearer of shawl and fan, was degrading. The Italian cause in which he joined the countess' father and brother at least prevented him from yawning for a couple of days, just as the Greek cause would give him "something to *think* of at least, . . . "[38] Like the humane but indolent Assyrian monarch Sardanapalus in the tragedy he dedicated to Goethe, he must be "roused"; for all is not lost, "even yet he may redeem/His sloth and shame."[39] In the end, Sardanapalus and his devoted Greek mistress mount the funeral pyre—"This leap through flame into the future . . ."—prefiguring Byron's redemptive sacrifice.[40]

Goethe, who was fascinated by Byron and by his end, declared to Eckermann that the author of *Don Juan* was finished anyway, that he had reached the summit of his creative power and would not have been able to extend the boundaries of his talent. No less than the high Tory, Sir Walter Scott, the fundamentally apolitical Goethe considered that Byron's revolutionary turn was not really the result of principle. Lady Blessington, who talked with Byron when he was preparing for the Greek expedition, remarked upon his lack of enthusiasm for so chivalrous an enterprise. Indeed, just before sailing to Greece, Byron told his banker that he would have turned back but was afraid his friends would laugh at him. If he lived, he hoped to return with something better and higher than the reputation of a poet; and he hoped the glory of action might change public opinion about him at home. If he died, and he had constant premonitions of his death in Greece, there would be "a sort of demi-poetic and demi-heroic *renommée* attached to my memory." [41] He was right.

It was Goethe who selected Byron as the only possible representative of the modern poetical era. What Byron handed down to future generations was the adventure and romance, the glamor and exoticism of conspiracy and revolutionary action, not only for one's fellow citizens but on behalf of strangers, the replacement of narrow patriotism by a devotion to humanity that acknowledged no frontiers. He did not invent the estranged hero, at war with himself and the world, but colored him indelibly with his own self-tormenting and self-destructive personality. Many who followed, right down to our own day, would be able to say after him, "I have not loved the world, nor the world me." [42] He showed all these unhappy spirits what looked like a way out of the impasse of boredom, dissatisfaction, self-loathing, and an intractable world, a path to purification and redemption of a kind through commitment to the revolutionary cause.

chapter **6**

*literary revolutionism,
despotism, and outlawry*

One of the most perplexing attachments to be found among proponents of the high cause of liberty, humanity, and a new world of peace, justice, and love, is the admiration for absolute power and grandeur in the shape of the leader, hero, or conqueror. That French writers as divergent in their declared political sympathies as Stendhal and Balzac should look back with nostalgia upon Napoleonic glories during the mediocre, materialistic reign of Louis-Philippe is readily understandable. But that English poets and men of letters should identify themselves with Napoleon, as did Byron, Hazlitt, and Godwin, at a time when their country was engaged in war with France, seems at first far more strange.

When Madame de Staël, who defiantly condemned Napoleon as the assassin of revolutionary liberty, was in London in 1813, she had an argument with Godwin about another self-made despot, Oliver Cromwell, and perspicaciously remarked, "It is curious to see how naturally Jacobins become the advocates of tyrants." [1] The paradox upon which she commented, and which appeared in particularly striking form during the Napoleonic era, has proved an enduring one. How is it that farseeing thinkers and poets who declare their loathing for despotism, whose professed ideal remains libertarian and humanitarian, can manage to accommodate themselves to authoritarian rule—and, indeed, can fail to observe anything odd in that accommodation? How is it that they can sometimes even interpret authoritarianism as a form of freedom?

Clearly, for some, the radiance of the very idea of revolution and of the ideals they thought it embodied proved so powerful that it permanently dazzled them. Once they had seen the light, no matter what protean form the revolution assumed, it remained for them the dominating creed. This was certainly true in the strange case of William Hazlitt, a "Jacobin" who was not attached to any party, who defined love of liberty as the hatred of tyrants, but to whom Bonaparte figured always as the revolutionary enemy of hateful courts and monarchs and of the detested principle of the divine right of kings.

Hazlitt, we know, understood the immense attraction of power. He brilliantly perceived that the poetic imagination tends to be aristocratic in its tastes. Consequently, a lion hunting a flock of sheep appears a more poetic object than its victims, "and we even take part with the lordly beast, because our vanity or some other feeling makes us disposed to place ourselves in the situation of the strongest party." [2] That is why, he contends, we incline toward Coriolanus in all the insolence of pride and power rather than toward the starving citizens of Rome in Shakespeare's play. He was fond of repeating that the admiration of power in others is as common and natural as the love of it in ourselves: the one makes a man a tyrant; the other, a slave. "Power is the grim idol that the world adores; . . . that dazzles the senses, haunts the imagination, confounds the understanding, and tames the will, . . ." [3] But when Hazlitt affirmed that he could not sit down quietly under the claims of barefaced power, he failed to extend his dislike of monarchy to the person of the

Corsican upstart who had obliged the Pope to crown him emperor and had installed his relatives and generals as monarchs throughout Europe.

For Hazlitt there was only one question: whether men are born slaves or free. In a scriptural turn of phrase, that was "the one thing necessary" to know and rectify, the one theme that mattered. Men could not be anything but slaves under kingly rule, or anything but free under Napoleon, he seems to have felt, despite a system of centralization, censorship, and police spies more efficient than that of the old regime. For here, as his contemporaries observed, emotion took command, and reason and logic fled. There were people, Hazlitt declared, who failed to understand his viewpoint, rooted in principle, and who could not perceive "how a cause can be connected with an individual, even in spite of himself, nor how the salvation of mankind can be bound up with the success of one man." [4] Once Napoleon was associated with the idea of the salvation of mankind inherent in the revolutionary ideal, he was clearly unassailable.

Passionately affirming that Napoleon was the savior of humanity, the being who saved men from falling into deepest despair, Hazlitt became more personal and his words tumbled out in emphatic enthusiasm: "He who did this for me, and for the rest of the world, and who alone could do it, was Buonaparte. . . . He, one man, did this, and as long as he did this, (how, or for what end, is nothing to the magnitude of this mighty question) he saved the human race from the last ignominy. . . ." [5] Thus the manner and purpose, the wars of conquest and self-aggrandizement, do not count where the salvation of mankind is supposed to be at stake. As for the allied crusade against Napoleon, which Hazlitt called the shameful alliance between kings and people, it was a mockery, since the true cause of liberty and humanity lay on the other side, with the French.

For it was Napoleon who was the true heir of Jacobinism: "Did any of the Princes of Europe ever regard Buonaparte as any thing more than the child and champion of Jacobinism? Why then should I: . . . If Buonaparte was a conqueror, he conquered the grand conspiracy of kings against the abstract right of the human race to be free; and I, as a man, could not be indifferent which side to take. If he was ambitious, his greatness was not founded on the unconditional, avowed surrender of the rights of human nature. But with him, the state of man rose exalted too. . . ." [6] Hazlitt appears to feel that the greatness of Napoleon somehow elevates humanity, that the glory of his achievements somehow reflects upon all human beings, and especially upon the individual who, by appreciating that greatness, is able in some small measure to participate in it.

But for this to happen, it is essential to realize that Napoleon's absolutism differs from all other forms of absolutism. This is doubtless because of its revolutionary origins, because he rose in the service of the revolutionary armies. If Napoleon was a tyrant, says Hazlitt, tyranny in him was not founded on divine right, it was not eternal, and would end with the temporary causes which gave it birth "and of which it was only the too necessary reaction." [7] Thus Hazlitt tries to justify the absolute rule of Napoleon as temporary and necessary, just as so many others from Wordsworth to Byron justified the crimes of the Terror as a distressing but inevitable response to oppression, and as a passing phase.

The defeat of Napoleon at Waterloo left Hazlitt prostrate. For weeks on end, wrote the painter Haydon, he went about unwashed, unshaven, in a drunken stupor. The light of the world had gone out for this embittered, independent radical who found it hard to forgive his own countrymen for being victorious. Early in life, Hazlitt had discovered the abstract "metaphysical" principle of revolutionary liberty, and continued to worship at its shrine. The ambivalence of the changing image of Napoleon, which he glimpsed but out of pride or loyalty refused to recognize, confused him as it did so many others. He denied the evidence of his eyes and reason because he did not want to abjure his faith in the abstract principle he had adopted. And he misguidedly saw Napoleon as the embodiment of that principle because of his own secret need for a savior, his own secret yearning to be raised to greatness through the great hero, his own secret adoration of the grim idol, power, whose magnetic attraction he described so well, even though passion blinded him to some of its ramifications.

There is no doubt that the complex figure of Bonaparte in his various roles presented a problem for many besides Hazlitt who sympathized with the revolutionary ideal and saw it as the hope and salvation of humanity.

On the one hand, Bonaparte appeared as the great revolutionary hero who carried the ideals of the French Revolution with the eagles of his victorious armies into the lands he conquered. Yet if the partisans of freedom in Italy welcomed the victor of Lodi and Marengo as their deliverer from the Austrian yoke, in Spain Napoleon—through his brother Joseph—came to figure as the foreign oppressor. He himself, during his exile on St. Helena, sedulously fostered the legend that he was the true heir of the revolution, the new Prometheus bringing benefits to mankind. However, the more percipient saw through the Napoleonic mystique, perhaps not always at once, but after a while.

If for some the daring of the revolutionary officer and the glamor of the First Consul obscured the sinister aspect of the coup d'état of 18th Brumaire 1799, for others the conqueror's determination to achieve his aims regardless of the cost in human lives, together with the emperor's dynastic pretensions, eventually revealed the less attractive side of his grandeur. The republican Wordsworth (to Hazlitt's disgust) became so convinced that the world would be reduced to utter slavery if Bonaparte prevailed that he modified his antimonarchist opinions, and from pacifist and internationalist turned nationalist, in a move that would be widespread. Coleridge, who had originally hoped Bonaparte would prove another Washington, eventually looked forward to the death of "the great fiend" as a blessing. Keats believed that Napoleon had done more harm than good to liberty, despite the attachment of his friends, Leigh Hunt and Hazlitt, to the Napoleonic cause. Shelley, though fascinated by Napoleon's energy, disliked and distrusted him, and thought his actions differed from those of pirates only in the numbers of men and the variety of resources under his command.

But for Byron, whose views on Bonaparte likewise offended Hazlitt, the questions raised by the Corsican military genius were not so easily resolved. Where Hazlitt stuck to his principles, Byron was affected primarily by Napoleon's heroic greatness. The hero whose bust Byron had defended against all comers when a schoolboy at Harrow, the triumphant ruler whom he described as *"a Héros de Roman* of mine,"* though prudently adding "on the Continent; I don't want him here," [8] had proved an idol with feet of clay, a flawed imperial diamond. Byron, who had hoped for Napoleon's victory, was shaken by the "crouching catastrophe" of his hero's abdication in 1814. His despair was that of a self-confessed disappointed lover when Napoleon, in defeat, failed to live up to the expected heroic standard: the erstwhile conqueror did not commit suicide.

In the years after Waterloo, Napoleon became for Byron a haunting puzzle. Why, he inquired in "The Age of Bronze," did Napoleon-Prometheus change from sustaining man's awakened rights to associate with kings and courtiers? Why (through court and concordat) did he renew the very fetters he himself had helped to break? Napoleon could have been the Washington of Europe; why, then, was he distracted by mere personal ambition from fulfilling so lofty and beneficent a role? Byron was fond of asking provocative questions to which he suggested no answers.

The clue to his response lies elsewhere, in his rueful image of Napoleon's decline from an all-powerful Tamburlaine to a caged Bajazet. The fact is that Byron, who with most of his fellow poets loathed war, liked to identify himself with Napoleon Bonaparte, the ruthless man of action and man of power, even to the point of having his coach modeled on the emperor's and adopting the same monogram, N.B. (Noel Byron) on the death of his estranged wife's mother, Lady Noel. Although Byron was a genuinely humane and magnanimous man who did not always please his fellow activists by his remarkable generosity to opponents, he told Lady Blessington that what he liked best in Napoleon was the emperor's lack of sympathy for others.

But Byron, who in *Don Juan* called himself humorously the "grand Napoleon of the realms of rhyme," was far from being the only writer to identify himself with the great hero; Balzac would be perfectly serious when he frequently compared his form of creativity with that of Napoleon. Regardless of their political tendency, Byron the patrician rebel and after him the bourgeois novelists, Balzac the legitimist and Stendhal the equivocal liberal, all admired Napoleon as the incarnation of ruthless energy and grandeur, the embodiment of the force that secretly, with one part of their being, they would have loved to be.

Still, it is only in those who professed revolutionary sympathies or adherence to revolutionary ideals, like Hazlitt, Byron, and Stendhal, that this admiration might seem rather inconsistent. Coleridge called the attitude of the English radical supporters of the despot "an inward prostration of the soul before enormous power." [9] Yet the same might be said of all those, including Heine, who, while flirting dangerously with revolutionary liberty, admired Bonaparte. To what private inadequacies and secret needs that position of inward prostration responded can only be guessed. Clearly, the writer who, like Hazlitt, sympathizes with revolutionary liberty or who, like Byron, conspires on behalf of it, is concerned with power insofar as he desires to replace the existing regime with that of his own side. Clearly, to profess libertarian, humanitarian, radical, or revolutionary ideals by no means precluded or precludes fascination with vast power and humble submission before it. A high revolutionary line could and can accord quite well with support for despotism and blatant dictatorship.

While some saw in Napoleon the unchanging embodiment of the revolutionary ideal or the flawed but still awesome incarnation of heroic greatness and energy, for others he provided a superb precedent and inspiration. Bonaparte was the successful conspirator after the 18th Brumaire, the conspirator who becomes Caesar as opposed to the unsuccessful conspirator who is a mere Catiline, the savior as distinct from the traitor or conspirator who fails. In this role he fascinated generations of plotters and would-be plotters of all shades. He was, too, the most remarkable instance of self-creation; he rose from nothing to be lord of the earth and to make and unmake kings, a figure who relied on his talent, not his birth, to shape his destiny and who offered a similar opportunity to his trusted followers. If he could do it, why not others? All one needed, it seemed, was daring and yet more daring.

Greatness is not necessarily to be found in what is moral, observed Goethe in connection with Byron, thus continuing the long conflict between Christian virtue and pagan *virtus* which is by no means concluded. The same may be said of energy. Energy, like greatness, may manifest itself in good or evil forms, but it remains awe-inspiring whatever form it assumes. "I like energy—even animal energy—of all kinds," wrote Byron.[10] Already for Godwin—in his novel *Caleb Williams,* published in 1794—energy is praiseworthy, and the idea of exerting oneself with energy in opposing omnipresent tyrannous authority appears as a potential source of consolation to the persecuted eponymous hero.

At the same time energy is associated in Godwin's novel with ferocity and crime. Captain Raymond, the noble leader of the robber-outlaws who befriends Caleb, proclaims: "We, who are thieves without a licence, are at open war with another set of men, who are thieves according to law." [11] His men "frequently displayed an energy, which from every impartial observer would have extorted veneration. Energy is perhaps of all qualities the most valuable; and a just political system would possess the means of extracting from it thus circumstanced its beneficial qualities, instead of consigning it as now to indiscriminate destruction." [12] But if Godwin, philosophical anarchist and later Napoleonist, cannot resist indicating how the energy of these outlaws is misapplied, his own reverence for this quality is plain. One is reminded of Keats, hating a street brawl yet admiring the energies displayed in it.

The most provocative and influential exponent of the cult of energy was Stendhal, whom Hazlitt met in Paris in 1825 while working on his four-volume life of Napoleon—a theme to which the French novelist also devoted many years of reflection. With such an interest in common, it is small wonder that Hazlitt afterward often referred to him as "my friend Mr. Beyle." Underrated in his own day, Stendhal came into his own toward the end of the last century, at the same time as the anarchists and nihilists.

With Stendhal, energy is admirable wherever it is found, even in crime. Indeed, for him anything is preferable to bourgeois mediocrity, selfishness, materialism, and money-grubbing. The outlaw-criminal, like a strong human plant, manifests energy and risks his life; whereas modern cultivated man, dependent on material comforts, risks nothing, droops, and grows etiolated. Modern society is so base, despicable, and destructive of true values and positive living that revolt is the only response. Stendhal's criminal-outlaw Valbayre, in the unfinished novel *Lamiel,* was to take a step further than Godwin's Captain Raymond or Byron's Childe Harold (who said, "I have not loved the world, nor the world me") when he proclaimed in words that ring down the years: "I make war on society which makes war on me." [13]

In hatred of mediocrity and love of energy, Stendhal the professed liberal differed little from the avowed legitimist Balzac (whose reactionary opinions, according to the malicious, were attributable to his fondness for titled mistresses). The creator of the superhuman criminal Vautrin, the embodiment of power and Satanic energy, could not fail to admire in Stendhal's *The Charterhouse of Parma* the figure of Ferrante Palla, doctor-poet, devotee of Napoleon, sublime and disinterested robber-outlaw whom he thought superior to Byron's Corsair.

And if nowadays the attitudinizing of rebellious heroes modeled on Schilleresque robbers and Byronic pirates looks like mere romantic cliché, nevertheless something of the shocking glamor that those romantic outlaws, the Captain Raymonds and Ferrante Pallas, then had for their readers, rubbed off on the revolutionary outlaws in real life—on the Carbonaro and later on the conspiratorial anarchist, the nihilist, the terrorist, the underground Bolshevik or Trotskyite revolutionary, the guerrillero. They could all echo Valbayre's justification that they make war on a society that makes war on them. They would all produce the authentic romantic shudder of fascinated horror and awed admiration at their energetic and ruthless ability to act regardless of moral considerations and no matter what the risk or the consequences to others or themselves.

That fearful thrill is felt by the eccentric aristocrat Mathilde de la Mole, in *The Red and the Black,* as she hovers hypnotized on the fringe of the febrile conversation between the frustrated plebeian hero, Julien Sorel, and the failed Spanish conspirator, Count Altamira, at the Parisian ball. Julien is obsessed with Danton (to whom is ascribed the book's epigraph, "the truth, the bitter truth"), the Danton who dirtied his hands and did not draw back from ruthless action to save his country. Altamira attributes the failure of his conspiracy to his reluctance to cut off three heads and to distribute rewards in the right places. In the face of the fastidiousness of Altamira, Julien asserts that in similar circumstances he would not hesitate to kill three if it would save four. Haunted by the notion that the safety of the people is the supreme law, Julien roundly declares that the end justifies the means. The next day Mathilde disturbs him in her father's library, where he is still darkly brooding on whether unscrupulousness and dishonorable conduct are essential to the success of lofty enterprises. Must the man who seeks to banish ignorance and crime from the earth sweep through it like a whirlwind and do evil as if at random? Julien demands fiercely. And Mathilde feels deliciously afraid and yet ashamed of her fear—sentiments that such an air of ruthless commitment would continue to inspire among the privileged and protected.

The irony of the situation is that Julien has neither the temperament nor the opportunity to put into effect his dreams of stern revolutionary republican virtue, and that is probably the point of the discussion. On the contrary, he is drawn into intrigues on behalf of the ultras, though action in any cause, so it would appear, is preferable to none. Yet Julien's dreams were also those of Stendhal himself, who remained the Roman republican (in the style of Robespierre and Saint-Just and the "energetic government of 1793") that he had been as a boy in Grenoble.[14] The boy who rejoiced when the execution of Louis XVI took place could be found in middle age dreaming of assassinating Louis XVIII. *"I am* encore *in* 1835 *the man of* 1794," the bored consul at Civitavecchia admitted in the *franglais* he reserved for some of his innumerable jottings.[15]

Like Julien, Stendhal did not become involved in the kind of revolutionary action that haunted his imagination. As the former dragoon in the Grande Armée and the Napoleonic official who claimed to have shaken the dust of France off his feet in Napoleon's downfall in 1814, Stendhal in fact solicited office under Louis XVIII. In Italy he did not assist the Carbonari. Neither did he play any part in the revolution of July 1830. He was a liberal who thought the liberals were fools, and he despised them as much as the legitimists and ultras. He went on dreaming ruthless revolutionary dreams, but while he might express distaste for Napoleon as a tyrant, nevertheless he declared that "whoever says tyrant says superior being."[16] And Stendhal differed not at all from Balzac in longing for some great leader, savior, and deliverer: "Till one greater man restore us and regain the blissful state. But where is the greater man?" Stendhal inquired in his idiosyncratic English.[17]

What he conveys through his novels is the exciting dream of energy, greatness, risk, ruthless action, conspiracy, ambition, and power. Yet he had quailed when his carriage passed over the corpses on the Napoleonic battlefield, and his heroes turn out to be contemplatives who despise in the end the active role they thought they wanted (although without that illusion they would have forfeited the author's esteem). The sympathies of his heroes appear to be in the right place—with the oppressed. Lucien Leuwen remains unresponsive to the advances of Madame Grandet because he cannot forgive her coldness toward the sufferings of the workers and their families. But ultimately Stendhal's protagonists are no more concerned with actually achieving social and political ends than he was himself.

Stendhal's heroic vision of ruthless revolutionary action, ostensibly frustrated by the mediocrity, self-interest, and baseness of the age, in reality indicates little more than the disguised yearning for power in one who professed to scorn power. The fascination of criminal rebel outlaws and revolutionary conspirators represents the reverse side of the fascination of Napoleon. It is another aspect of the attraction of power: power in its daring, potential, and secret form, and that is the source of its enduring thrill.

From the varied archetypes of literary revolutionism we now pass to the period of the most intense wishful and active radical commitment on the part of poets and novelists to occur before the thirties of our own century. We must therefore follow the vicissitudes of a generation of ardently idealistic European writers, would-be guides and leaders of suffering humanity, in their heady encounter with the new Christianity, the religion of social revolution. What savage ironies lay hidden in the souls of literary dreamers who longed to reconcile thought and action would soon be revealed—and not for the last time—under the mounting pressures of revolutionary ruthlessness and violence.

part *2*

the religion of revolution

The religion of revolution, of the great social transformation, is the only religion I bequeath to you. It is a religion without a paradise, without rewards, without consciousness of itself, without a conscience.

ALEXANDER HERZEN *to his son*

There is something else than. the mere alternative of abstract destruction, or unreformed existence.

EDMUND BURKE

Revolution . . . it's such fun.

GEORGE SAND

He . . . always seemed ready to turn the world upside down for the fun of it.

ALEXIS DE TOCQUEVILLE *on Lamartine*

chapter 7

revolutionary desires and
fears: Heine

In the cold spring of 1827, *a keen-eyed visitor from Germany with a talent for* making enemies strolled along the streets of London and was horrified by what he perceived. For the first time it seemed as if the hidden secrets of modern social harmony, or rather disharmony, were being revealed to him. So many Londoners, automata-like, were in an acquisitive hurry, indifferent to their fellow creatures who fell by the wayside. The costly goods in the shop windows beckoned invitingly, but in the dark back alleys there existed a world of indescribable wretchedness. The sinister contrast between suffering want and self-satisfied surfeit impressed itself on Heinrich Heine's memory, and thereafter he rarely managed to speak of England without distaste.

How much more pleasant it was in our dear Germany, he exclaimed with heavy irony, how calm and subservient! And what a trick of fate it seemed that a dreamer like himself should feel destined to whip his fellow Germans out of their complacency, "to excite revolutionary desires, . . ." [1] When the atmosphere of Germany (with its petty oppression, censorship, and threat of prison) became unbearable and he was considering whither to go, it was not England that he chose, despite the fact that he felt an affinity with the dead Byron. Indeed, it was Byron's mantle that he inherited, Byron's banner of freedom, torn but flying, that he carried, and Byron's weapon of satire and sarcasm he wielded in the war against "ancient wrong, domineering folly and wickedness," declaring (like Byron) that poetry was but a secondary consideration. [2] Where Heine differed from the martyr of Missolonghi was that he fought not in the realm of action but in that of ideas. And for him the power of ideas was paramount, since he thought men of action were but the instruments of thinkers, and Robespierre merely the hand of Rousseau.

Just as there are birds who have a presentiment of revolution in the physical world, by storm, earthquake, or flood, so there are men who sense the coming of social revolutions, wrote Heine to his friend, the diplomat Varnhagen von Ense—rightly including himself among these, for his prophetic insight was uncanny. The secret of his illegitimacy (he was born before his parents' marriage), and the pressure of his Jewish origin at the moment when Jews were emerging from centuries of confinement in the ghetto, made of him the epitome of social and religious disorientation. Heine's sensitive antennae were as responsive to the contradictory movements of the age as to the contradictory moods of his own heart.

Swept away by an enthusiasm, seized by an idea, he would later perceive its lacunae and move into its opposite. He resembled Kitzler, the scholar who had to destroy his magnum opus, *The Splendour of Christianity,* because when he exhausted the proofs of his thesis he felt impelled to develop all the objections to it. Heine has been proposed as the Hegelian poet *par excellence,* and it is as a recalcitrant pupil of Hegel that he anticipates some of the insights of Hegelians like Feuerbach and the young Marx. Heine would characterize Feuerbach, for whom God was a mere projection of the human imagination, as the most logical of the *en-*

fants terribles of German philosophy. Marx he called his friend, at one time contributing revolutionary poetry to the cause, at others expressing reservations. A self-styled moderate who half admires, half distrusts the new men and the single-minded extremists whose eventual triumph he foretells and prepares; a radical revolutionary spirit who professes to be a constitutional monarchist; a lyric poet whose work is often inextricably mixed with politics yet who proclaims that art is an end in itself; a proponent of free thought thirsting for spiritual succor—Heine seems as elusive today as ever he did to his contemporaries. Some, like Marx, were prepared to make excuses for him as a poet; others were not.

At times Heine appears to be trying out various positions to see if they truly suit him, because he does not feel quite at home in any of them. The disconcerting contradictoriness and confusion of his attitudes cannot be eluded or resolved. Indeed, it is this very confusion which reveals his dilemma, a dilemma that he was the first to convey in so acute a form. For one so keenly aware of the tangled skein of the old world, revolution might prove one possible way of cutting through or consuming it.

When the news of the French Revolution of July 1830 reached him in Heligoland, he went wild with joy: "Lafayette, the tricolour, the Marseillaise. . . . I know now what I ought to do, what I must do. . . . I am the son of the Revolution and I take up the charmed weapons upon which my mother has breathed her magic words of blessing. . . . Flowers! Flowers! . . . Words like flaming stars that have shot from the Heavens to burn palaces and illumine hovels. . . . I am all joy and song, all sword and flame!" (adding with the deflatory turn characteristic of his poetry that perhaps he was mad, too).[3] Once again, as for Wordsworth and his generation, it was bliss to be alive; once again revolutionary hopes ran high after the reactionary twenties which the Russian publicist Alexander Herzen called one of the most oppressive periods in European history. This time the poor people are the victors, thought Heine mistakenly. Like Aurore, Baroness Dudevant, on the threshold of her literary career as George Sand, he too was awaiting some great renovation of society.

In Russia, in August 1830, the young Alexander Herzen heard the news delivered by a postilion covered with dust and sweat. "It was a glorious time," he wrote in his memoirs. "At that time we knew nothing of the artificial stage-setting of the Revolution in France, and we took it all for honest cash. Anyone who cares to see how strongly the news of the July Revolution affected the younger generation should read Heine's description of how he heard in Heligoland 'that the great pagan Pan was dead.' There was no sham ardour there: Heine at thirty [actually he was thirty-two] was as enthusiastic, as childishly excited, as we were at eighteen." [4] Revolutionary excitement would be short-lived.

By the end of October 1830, George Sand could see that little had changed: the great social improvement was not going to take place. The harsh suppression of the uprising in Poland, the renewal of tsarist oppression, the reaction in Germany and elsewhere, confirmed the worst fears. Stung by the maddeningly petty restrictions imposed by a German principality, Georg Büchner—the medical student who subsequently would write *Danton's Death,* the most forceful drama ever composed by a twenty-one-year-old revolutionary on the fatality and futility of revolution—prayed every evening for hemp to string up those who were driving the wretched people hard. But by then, Heine had gone into voluntary exile which, with brief intervals, was to last until his death nearly a quarter of a century later. He had packed his box and left for Paris, as he said, in order to breathe fresh air and to devote himself to his new religion, Saint-Simonism. Count Claude-Henri de Saint-Simon, its founder and prophet, had died shortly after finishing *Le nouveau christianisme* (1825), and his views had been systematized by his followers. Not yet torn by schism, they were still actively proselytizing when Heine arrived in Paris in May 1831.

Paris appeared to Heine as no mere city of bricks and mortar; it was holy ground, hallowed by the redemptive suffering of two revolutions. The sight of the controversial painting, "Liberty guiding the People on the barricades of 28th July 1830"—exhibited in the Salon of 1831 by the great colorist Delacroix (who was soon thereafter permanently disillusioned by revolutionary politics)—made Heine invoke those "sacred days of July" which he himself had not witnessed. In Delacroix's painting, the eye does not linger on the corpses in the foreground; it rises to the pistol-waving, working-class youth and the determined top-hatted citizen with gun in hand (Delacroix himself) united across the barriers of age and class by the fierce allegorical figure of revolutionary Liberty. Heine saw not the romantic appeal of this painting, which epitomizes the enduring popular heroic myth of the barricades, but its realism, its portrayal of the reawakened natural dignity of what he called the dregs of the people. After those sacred days, Heine wrote, man can believe in the resurrection of all peoples.

For Heine in his early enthusiasm, Paris was not the capital of France alone but of the civilized world. It was the rendezvous of noted intellectuals and political exiles from all over Europe, the Pantheon of the living, where he met the Saint-Simonist leaders and enjoyed the friendship of well-known figures in the world of letters like Balzac and George Sand, with whom he would conduct an intellectual flirtation.

In Paris, he wrote excitedly, a new art is being created: "Our present art must perish because its principles are rooted in the old régime . . . The new age will beget a new art, which will be in spiritual union with itself, which will not need to borrow its symbols from the dead past, and must produce a new technique altogether different from what has been. . . ." [5] Moreover, besides a new art, a new religion and a new life were being created in Paris; here the creators of an entirely new world were active. It seemed as if new gods were about to reveal themselves. The French were the chosen race of the new religion, whose first gospels were penned in French, and Paris was the new Jerusalem, the city of redemption.

His task as a journalist writing for both French and German periodicals was henceforward clear. On the one hand, he would interpret German thought to France. The French would then be able to understand how daring philosophers like Kant and Hegel were far more revolutionary and destructive of the old order than Robespierre, since the former dethroned God whereas the latter merely disposed of a king. Consequently the German political revolution, when it finally erupted, would be so terrible that it would make the French Revolution of 1789 look like a mere idyll. (In hair-raising visions of apocalyptic doom, Heine showed himself a true heir of his Hebrew ancestors.) On the other hand, he would interpret France to the Germans in the hope of rousing his compatriots from their lethargy and hastening the dread yet desired day.

When Heine called himself a child of the Revolution he was not being entirely figurative. As a boy he had enjoyed French liberties when the Grand Duchy of Berg was under French occupation from 1806 to 1813. For him the French Revolution and the Napoleonic era meant a time when a free fresh wind blew through Germany, when progressive French laws embracing the emancipation of the Jews were in force. The emperor, whom the fourteen-year-old Heine saw riding in the park and whose downfall he sang as poignantly as any Frenchman in his poem *The Two Grenadiers* (*Mein Kaiser, mein Kaiser gefangen!*), remained for him the son of the revolution, a son who had betrayed his awe-inspiring mother, it is true, but whose betrayal could never tarnish his immortal luster as the incarnation of the great cause of liberty and humanity.

After the restoration, careers were open solely to Christian talents, and under pressure Heine shamefacedly (and profitlessly) became a Lutheran. Both attracted and repelled by Judaism (which one of his characters called a misfortune, not a religion), attracted and repelled by Protestantism and Catholicism (he would marry his midinette mistress in a Catholic church), Heine was singularly well placed to feel the longing for some new spiritual force which would answer more closely contemporary emotional and social needs. For a while he thought he had found this in Saint-Simonism, along with a number of French Jewish disciples of the master.

Yet if recently emancipated Jews through their exposed position and social sensitivity were particularly responsive to the call of a new faith, many of the leading poets and writers of the day, whatever the religion of their birth, were equally dissatisfied with existing orthodoxies and were eagerly awaiting some new revelation—they knew not what, only that it must be in harmony with the spirit of the gospel rather than the letter of the Church. There was a widespread feeling that the old-established forms of religion had failed from a social point of view, and especially since the clergy after the restoration again appeared to be allied with the aristocracy and the monarchy in preserving social structures that perpetuated inequality and wretchedness.

Religious natures yearned for some total social-cum-spiritual solution to the problems of mankind. A spiritual answer that took no account of social misery, a social answer that did not embrace the spiritual needs of humanity would not satisfy them. This was an age which saw the rise of social doctrines, systems, and programs which offered an immediate universal cure for the diseases of society and were preached in mystical language by impassioned men conscious of their apostolic mission. A renewed religious impetus was given to the idea of revolutionary change at a time when many felt that the old world was at last in its death throes and a bright new world was struggling to be born. Already they could catch the faint glimmer of the beautiful new dawn through the pall of oppressive clouds.

Heine was among the leading spokesmen of this viewpoint in the eighteen-thirties and -forties. For him Christianity, despite its beauty and its contribution to civilization, had failed: it was "too sublime" in its emphasis on pure spirituality and asceticism. The abortive attempt to realize its unrealizable demands had cost humanity countless sacrifices "whose calamitous effects are visible in the social distemper that afflicts all Europe at the present day." [6] After the long reign of the sad Galilean, what was needed now was a return to joyous health, an idea that would delight Nietzsche, who deeply admired the poet. Or, in Saint-Simonist terms, there must be a rehabilitation of the flesh, of matter, a vindication of the rights of the senses, without thereby denying the value of the spirit. The aim of all modern institutions should be the religious sanctification of matter and its reconciliation with the spirit.

For Heine, God no longer reveals himself through an individual messiah but through collective humanity. Collective humanity is thus an incarnation of the divine. Poverty debases God's image in humanity as a whole as well as in the individual. "We are fighting not for the human rights of the people, but for the divine rights of humanity," Heine declared, insisting on the difference between this view and that of the French materialist thinkers. [7]

Echoing the Saint-Simonists, Heine believed that the advance of industry had at last made it possible to free men from material misery and grant them earthly equality and earthly blessedness. The existence of evil would not interfere with this agreeable prospect, for evil is partly the spiritualists' misconception of the world and partly the result of their mismanagement of affairs. One day, wrote Heine, men will no longer be able to understand the Christian opposition between soul and body. "Happier and fairer generations, born of free unions, and nurtured in a religion of joy, will smile with pity when thinking of their poor ancestors . . . Yes! I declare it with full conviction: our descendants will be a fairer and happier race than we are. For I believe in progress; I believe that happiness is the goal of humanity, and I cherish a higher idea of the Divine Being than those pious folk who suppose that man was created only to suffer. Even here on earth I would strive, through the blessings of free political and industrial institutions, to bring about that reign of felicity which, in the opinion of the pious, is to be postponed till heaven is reached after the day of judgment." [8]

Yet Heine could not rest there; he added a sentence which undermined his own affirmations. It expressed doubts about whether there might really be a resurrection of humanity in either a political or a religious sense. Hedging of a similar nature would lead politically committed activists like Börne, Herzen, or the poet Herwegh (with his straightforward query "Are you for or against?") to charge him with frivolity, vacillation, and irresponsibility.

Rather like the medieval heretical millenarians and their heirs, who anticipated the innocent sensual bliss of the Joachite third age, Heine could speak in a Saint-Simonist poem about building the Church's third foundation under a new dispensation that would eliminate the dualism of flesh and spirit. God is in our embraces, he wrote, buoyed by his Parisian amours. He foretold the coming of a "third emancipator," in golden armor and imperial purple, to complete the revolution begun by Luther and continued by Lessing in his struggle against the bondage of the letter of Christianity. Heine called Lessing a prophet pointing the way from the second or New Testament to the "Third Testament," or new revelation. This was an allusion to Lessing's secularization of the Joachite third age in his *The Education of the Human Race,* where he had proclaimed the certain advent of a "new eternal Gospel" as promised in the New Testament itself and glimpsed by medieval millenarians. Lessing's book, translated into French by Olinde Rodrigues, one of Saint-Simon's leading Jewish disciples, was to be found in the library of George Sand, who was as keenly interested as Heine in such heretical Joachite millenarian sects as the radical Hussites.

It was not long before Heine's enthusiasm for Saint-Simonism began to wane. The Saint-Simonist doctrine of the social mission of art struck him as absurd. He could see the comedy of the position of those Saint-Simonist opponents of the marriage yoke who were now married, and of the onetime martyrs who had become railway millionaires, like Olinde's brother Eugène Rodrigues. The quest for the Mother-Messiah (a role declined by George Sand) to reign alongside Enfantin, the Father-Messiah, could not fail to amuse the poet who was once named the First Father of the Church of the Germans.

What Heine went on struggling for was a very large, ill-defined cause: the liberation and emancipation of humanity from all forms of social, political, economic, and religious oppression, from all those tangible and intangible burdens which weighed so heavily on his own spirit. He saw himself as the *enfant perdu,* as the soldier who fought desperately, with the weapons of protest and defiance, in the forefront of what he called the cause of humanity and the democratic idea of the revolution. He was the sword, he was the flame; he brought light where there was darkness. He believed that his long Parisian exile earned him a martyr's crown in this cause.

But when Heine spoke of his liberal and democratic principles, what precisely did he mean? He was not averse to referring to his revolutionary spirit (directed, so he said, to converting the powers that be, not to inflaming the vulgar), and he once observed that he was "perhaps the most decided of all revolutionaries." [9]

Although his revolutionary zeal fluctuated, there was a sense in which the views of this professed moderate were essentially revolutionary. For one thing, he was opposed to reform. In justification, he quoted the parable of Jesus that said it was useless to mend old garments with new cloth and that new wine must be put in new bottles. Reform such as was being attempted in England was "a miserable patching up which cannot last long." [10] After Jesus, the Jacobins in the Convention preached a "tri-coloured gospel, according to which not merely the form of the State, but all social life should be, not patched, but formed anew, and be not only newly founded, but newly born." [11] Rebirth, as we have seen, is the basic need of the revolutionary spirit.

Moreover, the French Revolution, with its doctrines of freedom and equality, was an "unceasing revelation," preferable to the gospel. It was, in short, unfinished. The revolution could not be declared victorious "until the work is perfected." [12] By revolution, he does not mean endless upheaval, he declares. But, he continues, when the intellectual culture of a people, and the customs and needs resulting from it, are no longer in harmony with the old political institutions, a necessary struggle arises against the latter which brings about a change in these institutions: this is called revolution. As long as the revolution is not complete, as long as this transformation of the institutions does not absolutely accord with the intellectual culture of the people and its customs and needs, the sickness of the social body is not fully cured. In such a case, the fevered patient will tear off the bandage tied by the most kindly hands, and will throw out the noblest of nurses, continuing to suffer until he eventually attains the institutions that best suit him. Plainly, in such a view, even generous measures are insufficient. And who is to say when the revolution is complete?

It was not the French Revolution alone that was not yet finished; another vaster universal revolution had only just begun. According to Heine, the revolution is one and indivisible. There is no such thing as the old revolution, he wrote in 1840; there is only the same revolution. We have seen only its beginning, and many of us will not live to see the middle of it, let alone the end. For it is the people (as distinct from the bourgeoisie) which now claims its right not just to equal laws but to equal enjoyments, and demands "a radical transformation of society." [13]

For a self-confessed moderate who as a youth had wept over the death of the Gracchi, Jesus, Robespierre, and Saint-Just, in that order, Heine's language could be extreme. On one occasion he called the guillotine a most excellent and wholesome machine with which the stupidest heads are separated from evil hearts. Only applied in cases of incurable disease (for instance, treachery), at least the guillotine had the advantage over the *auto-da-fé* in that the patient was not tortured first. The satirical poems of this self-styled monarchist on the headless court of the headless Marie Antoinette, on the submissive Germans one day submissively executing their king, are savage and merciless. Yet Heine could be found criticizing the French republicans for their "guillotinomania"; he suggested it might have originated with writers and orators, who were the first to employ the phrase "the system of the terror" in connection with the extreme measures instituted by the government of 1793. On the contrary, he maintained, the terrorism of that time was less a system than a passing phase or a necessary medicine. Much as he admired Robespierre and Saint-Just, he owned that he would not have liked to live under their rule, which bled the First Republic to death, nor indeed under any republic.

Forms of government, however, were not really a matter of importance in Heine's view. Whether the political machinery be that of a monarchy, an aristocracy, or a republic is secondary. Whether there are democratic institutions is a small matter, "so long as the fight is for the first principles of life, while the idea of life itself is not yet decided. Only later comes the question as to the means by which this idea can best be realised in life. . . ." [14] Nor was Heine keen on democratic processes; he poured ridicule on elections as horse races where only well-trained mediocrity wins. Elections spelled egoism, sordid interests, torrents of words, and fear of action. Even the most resolute innovator in the Chamber of Deputies, he complained, did not seek the violent overthrow of the established order, but merely desired to exploit for his own profit the fears of the upper stratum of society and the appetites of the lower.

No less than Stendhal or Balzac, Heine stigmatized the repulsive new rich under Louis-Philippe. No less than they he was awaiting the bridegroom, the right man, the Caesar who would slay mediocrity and inaugurate the reign of greatness and genius. When he spoke of democracy, he had in mind a democracy of terrestrial gods: he dreamed of "nectar and ambrosia, purple mantles, costly perfumes, luxury and splendour, dances of laughing nymphs, music and comedies," not the austere Roman virtues advocated by the republicans.[15] He desired a way of life that would be free, beautiful, witty, and gay, a lovely dream such as Nietzsche could appreciate.

Through his antiliberal attitudes and his exposure of the nullity of the ruling bourgeoisie, Heine helped to prepare the way for the rough beast he half desired and half dreaded. "Like me you have helped to bury the old times," wrote Heine to Varnhagen von Ense, introducing the formidable young German-Jewish socialist Ferdinand Lassalle, "and have acted as wet nurse to the new—aye, we have brought them up and are afraid— . . ."[16] Heine foretold the coming of a European and universal revolution, a struggle between the possessing classes and the disinherited, after which there might well be one shepherd with an iron crook and one single flock of men, all equally shorn and equally bleating. The prophet writing a new Apocalypse, he said, would have to invent new and fearful monsters beside which those of St. John would seem gentleness personified. To him, the future smelled of Russian leather, blood, atheism, and violence, and he advised later generations to acquire thick skins. This gloomy and by no means inaccurate prophecy was penned in July 1842.

The poet who had once remarked that to destroy the past in the spirit of the people is "a praiseworthy preparatory task, without which no radical revolution is possible," [17] came to fear the iconoclastic fury of the proletarians because he believed it would destroy the humanist civilization of which he felt a part. He who, as a Hegelian divine biped (so he ironically named himself), had described with warmth the advance of free thought culminating in the end of deism and the divinization of collective humanity—regardless of the power of free thought to destroy the old order and himself along with it—now quailed before the alliance of atheism and communism among the Left Hegelians, and turned, a sick man condemned to spend painful years on his mattress-grave, toward a personal God.

While subversive ideas remained the province of an aristocracy of men of letters, he subscribed to them; but it was a different matter when these dangerous advanced ideas were taken up by the ignorant populace. If in theory Heine was on the side of the people—the suffering, disinherited, exploited masses—he nonetheless disliked and avoided contact with members of the plebs and their tribunes, like the communist tailor Weitling. Revolutions were all very fine in books, but shabby and mean in actuality. Men are born equal, but some have aristocratic tastes, he observed.

All the same, the future belonged to the communists in the catacombs of a decaying society that would collapse just as the decadent ancient world crumbled before Christianity; he acknowledged this time and again, with increasing anguish at the indifference of the new men toward the beautiful and the socially useless. Yet their doctrines, so inimical to all he loved as an artist, exerted an irresistible attraction. For not only did he hope the communists would put an end to the Prussian nationalism he loathed; he also recognized the justice of the idea that all men have a right to eat.

Besides, the old social order did not deserve to be saved: "It has been judged and condemned for long, the old social order, let it meet its due! Let it be destroyed, the old world, where cynicism flourished, and man was exploited by man! Let them be utterly destroyed, these whited sepulchres, where lies and injustice dwelt! . . .—*fiat justitia, pereat mundus.*" [18] Another form of this tag is: let justice be done though the heavens fall. Heine is more precise: let justice be done though the world perish. That cry would be echoed by poets in the years to come, though frequently with less reluctance and more relish.

At last the ambiguous Heine had ceased to be ambiguous. He had unequivocally revealed the consuming progress of the death wish that moves from the individual to society as a whole, the agonized yet not unpleasurable acquiescence of the confused and disoriented intellectual in the crash of his imperfect world. If weary consent to revolutionary self-destruction and world destruction was Heine's temptation, that of George Sand would be the sheer excitement of revolutionary activity.

chapter **8**

revolutionary violence:
George Sand and Lamartine

"the revolutionary conception of woman"

Heine ventured to call George Sand the greatest writer in France; Turgenev modestly thought himself inferior to her. But it was not only as a novelist that she was admired; it was her life style, too, that won her notoriety and acclaim. In 1831, she left her husband, Baron Dudevant, who preferred hunting and other women, in possession of her country estate of Nohant and came to Paris to join her lover, Jules Sandeau, and try to earn her living by her pen. For a while she divided her year between lover and husband.

In order to economize and to be able to move freely, she often dressed as a man. Dark-haired, with large dark eyes, she had the forthrightness of a man, and her conduct frequently mystified male observers. In old age, looking back on this period, she said: "We despised paddling in the shallows. What we wanted was to swim far out above unsounded depths . . . To get away from the ruck of our fellows, to put an ever greater distance between ourselves and the safety of dry land, to strike out onward and ever onward—that was what we longed for!" [1] In her novels she dared to speak about the sexual frustrations of women, about their unjust subordination to men in the eyes of the law and society, about the ideal of equality between the sexes in love, at a time when the Saint-Simonists were preaching the emancipation of woman and the rehabilitation of the flesh. In literature and life, she stood for protest against social conventions and for freedom from worldly prejudice, as she acquired, usually but not always one after the other, a train of eminent lovers in the name of the sacred rights of passion.

For the jaundiced aristocrat Vigny, she was a lesbian Don Juan, but for many others throughout Europe her writings and her example made her "the highest authority on all that pertains to woman." [2] Herzen wanted to consult her about the much-publicized liaison between his wife Natalie and his former friend, the poet Herwegh. For Herzen, George Sand "resumes in her person the revolutionary conception of woman." [3] Small wonder that she turned the heads of highly strung women as far afield as Russia; not only Natalie Herzen, who confided to her diary that George Sand had carried the soul unscathed through sin, but the first wife of Herzen's lifelong friend the poet Ogarëv was among the countless ladies who took to living the part of the new emancipated female, often with disastrous consequences. As for the Russian critic V. P. Botkin, he called George Sand a female Christ, and broke with his French bride because she did not share his high regard for George Sand's *Jacques.*

Independent spinsters who wrote admiringly to the successful novelist from the provinces, or militant female followers of the handsome Enfantin, who found the emancipation of women rather convenient for his roving tastes, were often surprised to learn from her replies that she did not go nearly as far as they expected. She wished to see the institution of marriage preserved, though as a sacred bond with equal rights and duties instead of a form of tyranny. During the revolution of 1848, in which she herself played so notable a part, she refused to stand as a candidate, and she opposed political action by women for the present, on the ground that society must be radically transformed first.

She was indeed a great deceiver, and the first person she deceived was herself. The Rousseau-inspired religion of love that she lived by cast a purifying veil over her own amours, yet for her, as for Shelley or Herzen or so many more, the reality never turned out to be quite so noble and undamaging as in the case of Julie and Saint-Preux.

Through her friends and her succession of famous lovers in the field of poetry, music, philosophy, and politics, George Sand became acquainted with almost everyone who was anyone in the world of art, thought, and action in the Europe of her day. As prolix and indefatigable a letter writer as she was a fluent novelist, she numbered among her correspondents Delacroix and Liszt and Flaubert, Mazzini and Louis Blanc and Bakunin. Moreover, she was able to preserve the lifelong friendship of those who did not share her own opinions. The center of ever-widening circles, this spirited woman was the uncrowned queen of her epoch. Eventually she would become known, in Heine's words, as the daring "champion of social revolution." [4]

Of aristocratic descent on her father's side, plebeian on her mother's, she felt that she understood the people. She liked to contrast the peasants and the workers with the selfish bourgeoisie (and Herzen could think of no greater insult than to compare Herwegh with the eponymous bourgeois protagonist of her novel *Horace*). If the people behaved badly, it was always the moral responsibility of the bourgeoisie. She would have liked to sweep away everything that was imbued with the bourgeois spirit, and only in later, calmer years could she bring herself to admit that, for all its faults, the old bourgeoisie had its uses as a counterbalance.

Apart from a sentimental attachment to the people and to Bonapartism, originally she was not much concerned with public affairs until her husband began to dabble in local politics. She never really became interested in the machinery of politics, the replacement of one government by another. As she once told Mazzini, she had political feelings, not a political mind. The deepest experience of her youth had occurred when she was still at convent school. Mystical in nature, this experience made her long to take the veil, but she was dissuaded by her confessor. As with so many of her contemporaries, concern for social justice and equality would assume the form of a substitute faith and would be expressed *ad nauseam* in religious vocabulary, in terms of Church, priests, martyrs, dogmas, beliefs. The implementation of social justice would be seen as the fulfillment of the true spirit of Christianity, exemplified (she felt) by the Gospel of St. John. A faithful disciple of Rousseau, she believed in the natural goodness of man, and rejected with horror the idea of original sin or eternal damnation. Following the inner light that guided Rousseau's Savoyard Vicar, she would seek a "purified" egalitarian form of Christianity outside the Church.

Not long after she arrived in Paris, early in 1831, she saw the archbishop's palace being plundered by the discontented populace—a nice little revolution, she called it, because there was no bloodshed. Her confidence in the people was such that she felt the great revolution which was bound to come would be harmful solely to the ill intentioned. "I like noise, storm, even danger, and if I were selfish I'd like to see a revolution every day, it's such fun," she wrote half facetiously.[5] Contact with the tragic consequences of revolutionary violence in the following year would make her change her opinion. But for a long while she would veer between the fascination and exhilarating fun of revolution and a distaste for blood that did honor to her native good sense.

The incident (one among many attempts to overthrow Louis-Philippe) which inspired her with revulsion was the insurrection of June 5 and 6, 1832, following the funeral of General Lamarque. For the benefit of his German readers, Heine described the last stand of the ardent young republicans, mostly students, artists, journalists, and a few workers, in heroic terms, comparing their self-sacrifice with that of the Greeks at Thermopylae. He wrote of the heart-rending scenes he witnessed at the morgue, where relatives queued to identify their dead. At this time George Sand was living in a fifth-floor apartment on the Quai Saint-Michel, close by the morgue, and from her window she could see fighting in the street below, the Seine red with blood, the carts laden with corpses.

Her reaction was one of horror at the savage acts of men blinded by political partisanship. For you and me (she wrote to her friend Laure Decerfz), a soldier, a student, a worker, even a gendarme represent living beings with feelings like our own who ought to go on living. For the committed, there are only murderers and victims: "They do not understand that all of them are victims and murderers in turn." [6] For such people, an enemy is not a man. She felt disgusted with all men, with life itself. "I hate kings and the equally sanguinary heroes who want liberty *at any price*. I am going to try and forget them both at Nohant." [7]

Consequently for a while she remained horror-stricken and withdrawn, skeptical about systems aiming to improve society. What can be done about evil, about man when he yields to his instincts? she inquired. Her love affair with Alfred de Musset, and its celebrated lengthy, ink-stained postmortem, left little time for public concerns. As the final break with the poet approached, she began to search vainly for a spiritual prop, a religion of some kind: God, love, friendship, the public weal. Like so many romantics, loathing her self-absorption and immersion in her own unhappiness, she yearned for self-oblivion in devotion to humanity. Then opportunely she fell in love with a "genius" who appeared to understand her needs. He initiated her into the cause of revolution, in whose service she felt she could be done with herself and for the first time could be of some use, giving her life in blind obedience to an idea.

"my dear executioner—Robespierre in person"

The genius in question was a noted provincial lawyer, Louis-Chrysostome Michel, known as Michel de Bourges. The posthumous son of a woodcutter massacred by royalists in 1797, he became a fiercely vengeful republican, a devotee of those followers of Robespierre—the blood-curdling, authoritarian, egalitarian communist "Gracchus" Babeuf and his disciple, the dedicated archconspirator Buonarroti—who would not have hesitated to impose their theories by force. Prematurely aged at thirty-seven and decidedly unprepossessing in appearance compared with the handsome, dissipated Musset, Michel fascinated George Sand with his feverish exaltation, his dominating plebeian personality, his incendiary oratory and fanatical logic. She longed "to share this political passion, this faith in universal salvation, these invigorating hopes of a forthcoming social renovation which should transform even the humblest of us into apostles." [8] For his part, Michel was eager to win so illustrious a recruit to his cause of militant revolution. In a marathon of perambulatory eloquence lasting from seven at night to four in the morning, he impressed the novelist and her friends Planet and Fleury as they walked through the deserted streets of Bourges. She called him "my dear executioner," "Robespierre in person." [9]

Yet she put up a spirited resistance, using her sense of humor as a weapon, against "the humanitarian arguments of the guillotine" urged by this fevered apostle, firm in his faith, who could make politics so thrilling to her. She and her friends were always talking of the need to come to grips with the social problem that oppressed their consciences. However, she interpreted equality of goods metaphorically; she did not intend that property should be carved up (a process which would make men happy at the cost of turning them into barbarians) but that all should have a share in the general happiness. She certainly did not mean something as "old hat" as Babouvism.

One balmy spring night in 1835, as they were returning home from the Théâtre Français, Michel de Bourges showed his hand and expounded his system unequivocally to George Sand and Planet. They had paused on the Carrousel Bridge, and could hear music coming from the illuminated palace of the Tuileries. George Sand was torn from her reverie by the word "Babouvism." Earlier, Michel had given her Buonarroti's history of Babeuf's conspiracy and she admired it, but she could not approve of the means employed by men in despair after the fall of Robespierre. Such methods "would be folly to-day, and it is not by those paths that a civilized age can wish to proceed," she told him. [10]

"Civilization!" exclaimed Michel de Bourges angrily, striking the balustrade with his cane. "That's the artists' catchword! Civilization! I tell you that this corrupt society of yours will never be rejuvenated and renewed until this fine river runs red with blood, until that cursed palace is reduced to ashes, until the whole vast city you are gazing at has become a bare waste, where the poor man's family will drive the plough and build its cottage." [11]

Thereupon Michel launched into what she called a "horrible and magnificent" tirade against the corruption of large cities, the enervating effect of the arts, of industry, in short of civilization. "It was an appeal for dagger and torch, a curse upon Jerusalem the impure, and apocalyptic prophecies; then, after these gloomy images, he conjured up the world of the future as he was dreaming of it at that time, the ideal of rustic life, the manners of the golden age, the earthly paradise flourishing upon the smoking ruins of the old world through some fairy magic." [12] At the same time as he dreamed of colossal destruction and evoked the brave new world of innocence and purity, he accepted the claims of political necessity, the need for ruses, lies, broken promises, believing that the end justifies the means.

Saddened by what she called Michel's antisocial and antihumane rhetoric, George Sand intended to break with him. She felt that his passion for action could only have impractical or disastrous results. Wisdom must come before action. With her countrywoman's common sense, she wanted to know what concrete plans he proposed, what "solution" he offered. To effect the desired social renovation by some fairy magic was much too vague to impress her. Michel fought back in an effort to retain his disciple. He had no secret key, he admitted, and she was wrong to expect one. But certainly the answer would never be found by withdrawal. In order to discover the truth applicable to societies in their birth pangs, men must consult together. Whatever formula they reached would represent man's aspiration to the truth, not absolute truth itself. She was demanding the impossible: not only absolute truth but perfect harmony between sensibility and the requirements of action, between individual liberty and public duty.

Writing long after the event, and after the revolution of 1848,

George Sand probably emphasized her reservations. At the time her conversion seemed complete. If anyone could steal from God the ray of light that illumines the world, she had written, it was the children of Prometheus, the "lovers of cruel Truth and inflexible Justice." [13] No matter what the colors of their banner, so long as they marched along the road to the ultimate republic, she—though but a poor drummer-boy—wanted to be taken along with them in the name of Jesus, Washington, Franklin, and Saint-Simon. The man of conviction had, for the moment at least, won over the defender of art and civilization who wanted nothing so much as to be convinced.

Michel de Bourges may not have converted her to the use of dagger and torch, but his fierce republican views did color hers. The idea of dying with him on the scaffold appealed to her imagination. She who had felt she would rather be a dog than a member of the human race after the blood-stained barricades of June 1832, now refused to judge the Terror and began to defend Robespierre's "sublime inflexibility." Robespierre was the most humane of the terrorists, the greatest man of the French Revolution, of modern times. Indeed, the only truly republican leaders of the revolution were Robespierre, Saint-Just, and the public prosecutor Fouquier-Tinville.

Why the sudden cult of the Incorruptible? Robespierre believed in the salvation of the world. With his religion of the Supreme Being he had tried to unite the spiritual and the temporal in one symbol, but neither he nor Saint-Just was capable of carrying through so mighty a task. They were sullied by their era. That task had devolved upon the present generation. The revolution, which only became "meaningful, efficacious, . . . and sublime" with the Jacobins, ended with Robespierre's execution, she told Louise Colet—a writer with a gift for acquiring eminent lovers second only to her own, and who resisted her arguments as vigorously as she herself had once resisted those of Michel de Bourges. [14] "You are fond of Charlotte Corday, you would not be sickened by a little blood," wrote George Sand to Louise Colet; ". . . you would have knifed Marat without turning a hair." [15] George Sand had taken to defending political assassination; Alibaud, who attempted to kill Louis-Philippe, was a hero in her eyes. She had come to respect fanatics because they were so logical and acted in accordance with their convictions. After all, she asserted, St. Matthew in his fierce purity was an ancestor of Robespierre and the Jacobins.

The moment came when, in her new enthusiasm, she found others too lukewarm, too peace-loving for her taste. The Saint-Simonists, for instance, were milk-and-water republicans, decent enough but much too gentle and patient. Like Heine, she prophesied the advent of a race of violent proletarians, ready to seize human rights by force. She told the Saint-Simonists that the republicans would carry out the work of destruction while the followers of Saint-Simon would have to see to the process of rebuilding. You are long-suffering priests, she informed them; we are impatient soldiers, "swords of extermination." [16] Both would work toward regeneration, toward the salvation of the world, but it is plain she preferred the militant party at this time. Eventually even the authoritarian "pasha" Michel, who once locked her in her room, began to mellow somewhat and was left behind.

the new Christ

If Michel de Bourges introduced George Sand to the passion of revolutionary politics, Pierre Leroux, the mystagogic socialist philosopher, inspired her total commitment. According to Heine (and his view was shared by the condemned priest Lamennais, whom she adored), Leroux's influence on her novels was unfortunate. A gifted, grubby-looking plebeian, a former follower of Saint-Simon, Leroux had the astonishing power to arouse the most intense devotion among the intellectuals of the age. George Sand saw him as nothing less than the new Christ, and so did the Russian critic Belinsky: "Red-headed Peter . . . is becoming my Christ," he wrote to Herzen, whose love for Leroux's philosophy lasted some thirty years until he eventually wearied of its religio-political brew. [17] To George Sand, Leroux seemed indeed the savior she had been looking for: his philosophy, she believed enthusiastically, rehabilitated the Christian doctrine of equality and was the only one to speak to the heart like the Gospel. It gave her everything she had dreamed of in Catholicism without the disadvantages of an outworn form of worship. It was a religion at once old and new, familiar and forward-looking.

Here at last was the end of the quest, the new revelation which combined religious truth and social truth in an indivisible whole, replacing Christian charity by human solidarity. Leroux, who preached human perfectibility, preferred his own term, "communionism" (meaning a social doctrine founded on fraternity and the communion of souls), to "communism" (which he understood as tending to the practical goal of a republic where equality would actually be the rule). But he did not see any reason to reject the appellation "communist," already a term of abuse in the forties. Criticized for preaching communism in her novels, George Sand was not even sure if what she believed could be called communism: "I dream of ideal fraternity as the first Christians desired it. . . ." [18] Later, without adhering to any particular definition of communism, all too dictatorial for her, she was to own that she considered herself a communist now much as she might have been a Christian in 50 A.D., since in her view communism represented the ideal goal, the religion of the future.

In her passionate proselytism, George Sand bombarded her correspondents with Leroux's gospel. Today, why are we stirred by a need for action and by fanatical zeal, without knowing where to start? she asked rhetorically. And she replied at once that what makes us full of ardor for a moral revolution in humanity is the religious and philosophical consciousness of equality, of a divine law, understood by men from the beginning, then acknowledged and won in principle but considered impossible in fact, rejected by the nobles, the priests, the sovereign, and the democratic bourgeoisie, too. Where Michel de Bourges and his republican friends wanted to make a revolution and see afterward what would have to be done, she and her new associates thought differently: they agreed in wanting to make a revolution, but they believed they should consider straightway what would have to be dealt with afterward. The masses would be inspired by the revolutionary moment, but only if they were enlightened as to their rights and duties beforehand.

With this aim in view, George Sand, along with Leroux and Louis Viardot, founded *La Revue indépendante;* it failed. Leroux the sponger and "sharposopher" (or "filousophe"), as Victor Hugo called him, was incapable of completing any of his grandiose projects for a brave new world, and he and his numerous dependents proved a considerable drain on the novelist's financial resources. The feet of clay of the socialist savior began to be visible to his formerly adoring disciple.

Soon she placed Leroux in his turn among those insufficiently concerned with action. Like the Saint-Simonists, he was too peace-loving; he forgot that "the ideal is a conquest, and that humanity has now reached the stage where every conquest requires our blood." [19] She was suspicious of systems, she told Mazzini, who concurred. That is why he, Mazzini, fostered insurrection while Leroux put his hopes in preaching: "He seeks the goal; and we the instrument to attain it," Mazzini told her.[20] They were corresponding in the first weeks of 1848, and George Sand would be swayed by Mazzini's activism. Poetry was now to be found in action, she would instruct one of the proletarian poets she had met through Leroux.

the man of the hour—Lamartine

Scarcely anyone expected revolution in February 1848, though a great many people had been talking and planning revolution for years. When it came, nobody knew quite what to do with it. The February Revolution was the most literary of all such manifestations, not only because it was trying to imitate and reproduce the awe-inspiring grandeur of the revolution of 1789, not only because it affected so many literary talents, from Baudelaire and Flaubert to Turgenev—who were present and some of whom have left enough detailed eyewitness accounts to enable posterity to draw a literary map—but because an elegiac poet, Lamartine, was among its leaders, and a novelist, George Sand, was one of its chief propagandists. This is not the place to relate the events of 1848; instead, we shall try to see how they appeared to these literary protagonists.

The February Revolution provided an opportunity for literary figures who had felt the Byronic lure of action to put themselves to the test. All those who shared Coleridge's belief (significantly expressed in a lecture on *Hamlet*) that "Action . . . is the great end of all" were irresistibly drawn to the arena. Some years before, Lamartine had asked, "What is the good of having been the first poet of one's country, if one does not become its first man of action?" [21] With his handsome profile, his aristocratic elegance, his gift of oratory, he was sure that he was the man France was waiting for and that in the hour of danger the country would be his. Not for nothing did Louis-Philippe name him "le vain de Mâcon," after the wine-growing district of his birth.

No revolutionary, Lamartine had once, in an ode, counselled the people to abandon the bloody revolutionary furrow, and had moved from legitimist monarchism to self-appointed leadership of the liberal opposition in the name of "Christianity made law." Nevertheless he was among the first to recognize the urgency of the problem of the wage-earning class, and believed that one leaves it to others to make the revolutions one does not make oneself. In a France supposedly bored to tears, he yearned for "a storm or nothing." [22] The regime of Louis-Philippe, while scarcely ideal, was far from being the most repressive tyranny ever known. Yet, as Heine observed, a weak government encourages the first comer to try his strength, and inspires in him a demonic impulse to overturn it.

With his history of the Girondins, which caused a sensation when it appeared in 1847 and was even named as one of the causes of the revolution by the journalist Arsène Houssaye, Lamartine aimed to show the sacred democratic principles of the revolution of 1789 purified of their bloodstains, so that if there were another revolution the people would understand how a policy of terror means the death of liberty. Thus instructed, the people would behave in an exemplary manner in any future revolution. Guided by Lamartine, the revolution would assume its ideal form.

It was said that Lamartine discussed revolutionary ideas as if he knew how to apply them without crime, violence, and storms. At the same time he was unable to withhold his admiration for Robespierre, and the former *émigré* Chateaubriand, now approaching death, said the poet had gilded the guillotine. George Sand observed that the book was a maddening continual yes and no, as if the author did not know what he believed or wanted. He appeared all things to all men: "Besides, that's M. de Lamartine to a t. He has never reached a conclusion in his life." [23] Meanwhile Lamartine convinced himself that without his history of the Girondins the February Revolution would have meant terror and anarchy, that he had not only awakened but had actually controlled and purified the revolution.

When Louis-Philippe suddenly abdicated on February 24, there was the possibility that a regency might be established in the name of his grandson. A mightier egoist than Lamartine, Victor Hugo, who also had vague political ambitions and who had been elevated to the peerage in 1845, favored this constitutional solution; he earned cries of "Down with the peer of France!" for his pains. Lamartine was opposed to a regency and in the Chamber he urged a provisional government as a means of transition to a definitive government that would be set up when the nation had cast its vote. When militants of the political clubs invaded the Chamber, George Sand's friend, the actor Bocage, cried, "Long live Lamartine! Everybody to the Hôtel de Ville!" where the pseudo-Danton Ledru-Rollin insisted on the immediate proclamation of the republic.

Victor Hugo came to the Hôtel de Ville to congratulate Lamartine on his new post as Minister of Foreign Affairs. The author of *Notre-Dame de Paris*—he had not yet found his role as the conscience of humanity and would not urge the people to take up arms until the coup d'état of Napoleon the Little in December 1851—admitted to Lamartine that a republic was the only rational form of government, but was this the right moment? Lamartine confided in him: how onerous this revolutionary power was! One had such unexpected responsibilities. He did not know how he had managed to live through the last two days. Yesterday he had some grey hairs; tomorrow they would all be white.

An armed demonstration appeared demanding the red flag as the symbol of a socialist revolution. Louis Blanc would agree; Lamartine would not—and won a victory for the tricolor. "The new, pure, holy, immortal, popular and transcendental, peace-loving and great Republic is founded," he wrote.[24] He was at the peak of his popularity. Everywhere he went, there was "a riot of love," he said complacently.

Among the members of the provisional government were several besides Lamartine who were known to George Sand. Believing that the reign of social equality had dawned at last, that the dream of her life was being realized, she arrived in Paris from Nohant on March 1 and was soon in contact with "everybody," including Louis Blanc and Ledru-Rollin. The latter engaged her to write articles for the *Bulletin de la République*. Of one thing she was sure—the new men would do better than their revolutionary predecessors: "We are plunging headlong into the unknown with faith and hope. I say the unknown because this republic will not repeat the errors and aberrations of the one you witnessed," she wrote to a conservative cousin who had lived through the revolution of 1789.[25]

On the morning of March 4, chatting with Lamartine, she watched the funeral procession of the victims of February: it was orderly and admirable, and the people of Paris were the finest in the world. Personal sorrows—the end of her liaison with Chopin, the pain caused by her daughter's conduct, even grief at the death of her granddaughter—were submerged in public activity. (High on her list was the discomfiture of the "renegade" Michel de Bourges.) "What a dream, what enthusiasm . . . !" she told one of her proletarian protégés. "One is mad, one is intoxicated, one is happy to have gone to sleep in the mire and to awake in the heavens. . . . My heart is full and my head is on fire. . . . I am alive, I am strong, I feel no more than twenty."[26] (She was, in fact, in her early forties.)

Revolutionary euphoria lasted several weeks, during which she felt that progress toward equality would be steady, swift, and even easy. If doubts arose, they were brushed aside: the members of the provisional government were not quite equal to a task demanding the genius of Napoleon and the heart of Jesus, but their intentions were noble. A grave financial crisis clouded the new republic's future. The material they had to work on was recalcitrant; the bourgeoisie were obstructive, the peasantry ignorant, and the workers as yet unable to understand. She herself was ready to die on the barricades if the republic failed—but of course it would not fail.

Meanwhile she was stirred by revolutionary festivals modeled on those of the First Republic, by processions of workers with drums and flags, and by the planting of trees of liberty. Above all, she was enjoying being at the center of affairs and not having two minutes to herself. ". . . Here I am already doing a statesman's work. I have drawn up two government circulars to-day. . . . I do not know whether I am standing on my head or my heels. There is somebody at me all the time. But this kind of life suits me," she told her son Maurice, the new mayor of Nohant.[27]

Action went to her head as it did to Lamartine's, though in a rather different way. With her it took the form of impatience for the immediate realization of the ideal. She was not averse to a little fanaticism to prosper the cause. Never a parliamentarian, she despised the liberal bourgeoisie and its "so-called democracy."[28] She had no faith in elections, since the only sector to gain from them was the middle class. It was a problem to get the people to vote for the "right" candidates, those who would indubitably look after the interests of the underprivileged. The will of the people, as demonstrated inside or *outside* the National Assembly, counted for more than the majority decisions of the provisional government if these went against her own ideas and wishes and her own eagerness to mold experience as she could shape it in her novels.

In Bulletin No. 16 of April 15, George Sand wrote: ". . . if elections do not assure the triumph of social truth, if they express only the interests of a caste, and if the trusting loyalty of the people is by violence deceived, then beyond all doubt, instead of being, as they ought to be, the salvation of the Republic, they will sound its death knell. Should that happen, there can be but one road to salvation for those who built the barricades, and that will be for them to manifest their will a second time, and defer the decisions of a false national representation. Does France wish to force Paris to have recourse to this extreme and deplorable remedy? God forbid!"[29] These words were understood as inciting the people to take to the streets and the barricades once again, and some held her responsible for the troubles of April 16, when the clubs of the extreme Left under Blanqui, Raspail, and the utopian communist Cabet attempted a coup d'état which failed.

George Sand was shocked; she would have preferred exile to living under the rule of such men, but bourgeois cries of "Down with the communists, hang the Cabétists, death to Cabet!" destroyed the fraternal atmosphere of her ideal republic. However, others also were plotting against the provisional government because they feared the result of the elections. She herself favored the plot of Ledru-Rollin and Louis Blanc to eliminate most of the moderates. This group, she believed, would have solved the financial crisis and changed the electoral law, thus obtaining a National Assembly that would not have to be overturned by force. Present at the workers' demonstration on April 16 outside the Hôtel de Ville, she was not at all favorably inclined toward Lamartine, who congratulated those who suppressed it; this was his last triumph.

From that time forward, George Sand's tone began to darken. She did not blame the ignorance of the people or the immaturity of current ideas, but human nature; with the exception of the chivalrous Barbès and of Etienne Arago, "Men are false, ambitious, vain, selfish, . . ." [30] Fear took command of Paris as rumors of plot and counterplot spread, though not a mouse was stirring; each group or club was trying to frighten its rival, and succeeded so well that all were petrified. "It is a proper comedy," she remarked. [31] Her paper, *La Cause du peuple,* died after three numbers. She attempted to revive her spirits with the thought that there would be no great merit in being a revolutionary if everything passed off smoothly. She wondered how she and her associates had been able to think that three days of fighting would lead to the untroubled reign of their philosophy.

On May 15, George Sand followed the workers' demonstration led by Barbès and Blanqui—ostensibly to present a petition in support of suffering Poland, in reality to assert popular force. The National Assembly was invaded, pronounced dissolved, and a socialist government proclaimed. The coup was quickly suppressed. This was the day which Herzen said "had swung a scythe across the second shoots of our hopes," after he had perceived the deadly hatred on both sides that burst into bloodshed a month later. On May 17, fearing reprisals, sickened by bourgeois reaction, and believing her fraternal socialist republic to be dead, George

Sand left Paris for Nohant. She was tired and not a little disgusted at the way revolutions stir up evil passions as well as good. Besides, she had had enough of politics.

"One must not play with *action*," she now observed,[32] acknowledging the "lure" of gunshot, expressing reawakened scruples, and feeling less ill disposed toward Lamartine. He had yearned for a revolutionary storm without violence, trusting Canute-like in his own person and honeyed tongue to still the waves and save the country; she had thought it possible to transform society into an ideal brotherly union without class war or civil strife, which she dreaded as much as he did. But, as Herzen saw on May 15, both sides wanted victory, wanted to have their own way—just as she had seen it long before, in June 1832, when her humanitarian feelings revolted against blind political partisanship. "I knew nothing, I understood nothing of what was going on," she wrote miserably to the imprisoned Barbès.[33]

For George Sand and a good many others, General Cavaignac's savage repression of the riots during the terrible June days wrote a blood-stained finis to committed literary revolutionism. As for Lamartine, he lost his position and his popularity. Until his death he remained a broken man, burdened with debts, disgusted with politics: "That nerve is shattered." [34] George Sand found solace in Nohant and in her family. But after the June days she felt ashamed to be French. Besides, even the "people" were no longer stainless; they were not ready to govern. The majority of the French people were blind, ungrateful, wicked, stupid—in a word, bourgeois, because they endorsed bourgeois policies. Only a sublime minority, the people of the future, the urban proletariat, survived in her esteem. She would remain a socialist, but she now wrote that no conceivable revolution could eliminate the deep causes of human suffering.

George Sand's finest hour came when she appealed to the president, Prince Louis-Napoleon, for clemency for the proscribed and persecuted victims of the new regime, and worked tirelessly on their behalf. Twenty years after, at the time of the Commune of 1871, when she was quite an old lady, she had so far forgotten her earlier revolutionary self that, like most of her celebrated literary colleagues (with the notable exception of

Victor Hugo, who pitied the defeated insurgents), she condemned the Communards as a criminal mob.

By instinct a woman of genuine humanitarian sympathies, George Sand was swept by her literary imagination to admiration for inflexible tribunes and condonation of senseless crimes. She had once seen the man in the enemy. She feared violence, she did not desire it, she counseled moderation; but in the hour of revolution her love of activity and eagerness for the ideal made her play with fire. To such aberrations can devout impatience for the immediate reign of human solidarity lead the most generous heart.

chapter *9*

the parting of the ways

In the years after the revolution of 1848 *and the coup d'état of Louis-Napoleon* in December 1851, the European exiles who had gathered in Paris, believing that only there could the revolution be consecrated, moved elsewhere, their numbers increased by Frenchmen who had managed to evade persecution and imprisonment. Alexander Herzen was admirably situated to observe the multifarious exiles who were waiting or working for the second coming of the revolution, for he himself was one of them and could appreciate the comedy and the tragedy of their position in limbo. He takes his place here less as a creative writer, the author of the novel *Who Is Guilty?* than as a brilliant chronicler and man of letters.

A freethinker himself, Herzen derived from the same religious-political atmosphere as did Heine and George Sand, from the world influenced by the Saint-Simonists and Pierre Leroux. The example of the gradual and checkered rise of Christianity as a revolutionary movement in the decaying ancient world seemed to provide a precedent for the slow advance of modern revolutionary idealism, for the modern stalemate. But after 1848 he could say that "the redemption by revolution has been proved insolvent. . . ." [1] Would there indeed be victory for the revolutionary cause of egalitarian social justice, as there had been for Christianity?

Herzen was no longer sure, and he half envied, half scorned all those who felt no doubts and who disregarded hard truth. Gifted with keen critical intelligence, he would not take the desire for the fact, as so many of his fellow exiles did. He felt that chance, stupidity, and confusion vied with justice and perfection in the workings of nature and history. Above all, one had to consider "the complex, intricate process of balancing the ideal with the real," [2] which was overlooked by the impatient activists and the doctrinaire disciplinarian disciples of Babeuf or Cabet.

The illegitimate son of a Russian nobleman and a middle-class German girl, at fourteen Herzen sympathized with the unsuccessful Russian conspirators of December 1825. At twenty-two he participated eagerly in radical student discussions in Moscow, was accused of complicity in a student "plot," imprisoned, and then banished. Some years later, having rashly criticized the police in a letter to his father, he was again exiled. In 1847 he left Russia, never to return. On his arrival in Paris, he at once sought out his friends among the Russian exiles, including the tempestuous arch-romantic Bakunin. Bakunin had become a great friend of the anarchosocialist philosopher Proudhon; they used to sit up all night talking about Hegel in Bakunin's lodgings in the Rue de Bourgogne. There Herzen met this French thinker, whose journal, *La Voix du peuple,* he later financed. It is vis-à-vis Proudhon and Bakunin that Herzen's evolving attitude toward the question of the necessity of revolutionary destruction and revolutionary violence can be seen most clearly.

The debate on violence and destruction had been going on with varying intensity in Europe at least since the revolution of 1789, as men now sought to stimulate a phenomenon that had then arisen, as it were by itself, like a force of nature. Should one seek to destroy utterly the old forms of society and start again with a fresh slate? Should the forms of the future be left to arise spontaneously from the ashes, or should one try to make plans beforehand? Such themes had been adumbrated in the observations of Heine and in the discussions between Michel de Bourges, George Sand, and other members of her circle. While Bakunin was studying in Germany in the early eighteen-forties, these questions were being raised by intellectuals like Bruno Bauer, who was heard to advocate total destruction. Bakunin was permanently marked by this milieu, whose destructive views were always frowned upon by Marx, believing as he did that it was folly to destroy without knowing how to build.

As for Proudhon, he was fond of the epigraph *"Destruam et aedificabo,"* based on the words of Jesus in Mark 14:85: "I will destroy this temple made with hands, and within three days I will build another made without hands." But Herzen finally saw the French thinker as a destroyer rather than a creator. He came to regard Proudhon's views, which were to shape both revolutionaries and counterrevolutionaries, as the "apotheosis of an inhuman *pereat mundus, fiat justitia!"* [3]

Nevertheless, at the time of their projected collaboration in 1850, Herzen himself was far from averse to destruction. The way the revolutionaries had contributed to their own downfall, the sight of the corpses of June 1848 had made him call down vengeance on the criminal old world that was standing in the way of the new man. He had shouted then: "Long live chaos and destruction! Long live death!" He told Proudhon that "like a true Scythian, I saw with joy that the old world was falling into ruins. . . . I know one liberal Frenchman—that is you. Your revolutionaries are conservatives. They are Christians without knowing it. . . . You alone have raised the question of negation and revolution to a scientific level, and you have been the first to tell France that there is no salvation for an edifice that is crumbling from within, and that there is nothing worth saving from it; that its very conceptions of freedom and revolution are saturated with conservatism and reaction." [4]

Thus there were moments when, like Heine, Herzen acquiesced in destruction, even if at others he regretted having to march forward over the ruins of his ancestral heritage, and feared for the treasures of past civilizations he knew and loved. Sometimes, when suggesting that decayed forms can only be restored by "a complete rebirth," the awful thought struck him: what if there was not going to be any rebirth?

Proudhon himself had reached the conclusion that a peaceful advance by scarcely perceptible transitions was no longer feasible. Those who wanted revolution must make "fearful leaps." But he felt, too, that "as journalists announcing the coming catastrophe, it is not for us to present it as something inevitable and just, or we shall be hated and kicked out. . . ." [5] This relatively humane note can be found from time to time in Bakunin also, at least before his fatal subservience to the sinister Nechaev.

Bakunin, who (with Proudhon) once enjoyed greater fame than Marx and who has recently come into his own again, was a colossal figure of a man whose impotence channeled his untiring energies into activity and action. For Bakunin, revolution meant instinct rather than thought. It is scarcely surprising that he has more frequently served as a model for imaginative writers than has the author of *Capital*. The Russian revolutionary astounded his contemporaries by the scale of his misfortunes: by his fateful imprisonment (when he was chained like the Prisoner of Chillon) after the failure of the 1849 Dresden rising, in which he had been associated with Richard Wagner; by his escape from Siberia; and by his ceaseless imprudent attempts at insurrection, however unsuccessful these might prove. The indomitable legendary anarchist seemed the living embodiment of the fierce Schilleresque brigand or fascinating Byronic corsair, a being created to flourish in storms, who could hypnotize his hearers by his personality and eloquence.

One of those who heard Bakunin speak described the effect he produced: "I no longer remember what Bakunin said, and it would in any case scarcely be possible to reproduce it. His speech had neither logical sequence nor richness in ideas, but consisted of thrilling phrases and rousing appeals. It was something elemental and incandescent—a raging storm with lightning flashes and thunderclaps, and a roaring as of lions. The man was a born speaker made for the revolution. The revolution was his natural being. His speech made a tremendous impression. If he had asked his hearers to cut each other's throats, they would have cheerfully obeyed him." [6] The connection between this scene and the poetic imagery of Shelley and Byron is evident.

It was Bakunin, aiming at the abolition of state and church, who emphasized the creative element in destruction. "Let us put our trust in the eternal spirit which destroys and annihilates only because it is the unsearchable and eternally creative source of all life. The urge to destroy is also a creative urge." [7] Destruction as the ineluctable harbinger of creation and resurrection: that was the theme of Shelley's "Ode to the West Wind." As Bakunin expressed it, ". . . there can be no revolution without a sweeping and passionate destruction, a salutary and fruitful destruction, since by means of such destruction new worlds are born and come into existence." [8] The idea of the fruitfulness of destruction is a pagan one, doubtless deriving from primitive animal sacrifice, where the blood of the victim or incarnate god seeps into the ground and renders it fertile.

Yet at the same time as he owed something to this pagan view, Bakunin knew perfectly well what was involved in revolution: "Revolutions are not child's play," he wrote, "nor are they academic debates in which only vanities are hurt in furious clashes, nor literary jousts wherein only ink is spilled profusely. Revolution means war, and that implies the destruction of men and things. Of course it is a pity that humanity has not yet invented a more peaceful means of progress, but until now every forward step in history has been achieved only after it has been baptised in blood." [9] A hint of regret may be found in these words, along with complacent acceptance of baptism in blood; and Bakunin certainly differed from a number of his successors in urging humanity and magnanimity toward the enemy in the hour of victory.

Notwithstanding this humane touch, Bakunin justified the righteous avenger, reproaching Herzen, who disapproved of political assassination. Herzen had grown to dislike Bakunin's methods, and toward the end of his life he was severe on the anarchist's "blind stumbling after the Unknown God of Destruction." [10] He told Bakunin that he preferred compromise and gradual progress (despite the shortcomings and mistakes of reformers) to an ill-considered, impatient, headlong dash forward that would do more harm than good: "You tear along, as before, filled with the passion of destruction which you take for a creative passion. . . . I do not believe in the former revolutionary paths. . . ." [11] And Herzen went on, "I do not believe that people who prefer destruction and brute force to evolution and amicable agreements are really serious." [12] One should seek to enlighten the enemy, who ought to be pitied.

Meanwhile, Bakunin had fallen under the spell of the young student terrorist Nechaev, an admirer of Marat and Babeuf. However, it is now believed that, for all his impetuosity, Bakunin did not collaborate with Nechaev in producing the notorious *Revolutionary Catechism,* where the new revolutionary is described as a doomed man, for whom everything that helps the triumph of the revolution is moral, and everything that stands in its way is immoral. The revolutionary subordinates to the cause all feelings of friendship, love, and honor. He must be without pity for himself or others, and must be ready to die or to kill with his own hands. He should have one exclusive interest, one thought, one passion: the revolution. He has only one purpose: merciless destruction. Between him and society there is war to the death.

This is the religion of revolution in the garb of romantic Satanism, where the revolutionary appears not only as gloomy outlaw but as perverted martyr, leaving his father and mother in order to devote himself to his "faith." As Nechaev told Herzen's daughter Natalie (who was fascinated by him rather as Mlle de la Mole was hypnotized by Julien Sorel in his would-be Danton pose), one should follow all the rules of the Jesuits, "changing the aim, of course." [13] His respect for the Jesuits was shared by Bakunin and later by Trotsky. Natalie Herzen, finally undeceived, warned a friend: "Be very cautious with all these Russians who have recently arrived. . . . A new type of man *à la* Nechaev is forming among them, a kind of revolutionary Jesuit, who is ready for every vileness in order to achieve his goal, *i.e.,* the revolution in Russia." [14] The *Revolutionary Catechism,* often considered an aberration, was in some respects prophetic.

The single-minded revolutionary anarchist, nihilist, or terrorist who henceforward takes the stage and attracts the interest of poets and novelists had no appeal for Herzen. The great publicist had already observed with increasing distaste the new ruthlessness, the narrowing of horizons, the extremism he hated. Moreover, the new generation accused him and his associates of being the dilettanti of revolution, and rejected them as dreamers—those who had endured prison and exile and had sacrificed so much for the cause. Like Heine, like George Sand, Herzen lived to be outstripped by the militant monks of revolution and learned to count its cost, while the new men thought it would be cheap at any price.

It was the parting of the ways. With the rise of the nihilists and later of the dedicated Bolsheviks, a more consistently relentless note will be heard in the response of many writers to revolution. But before approaching the great literary haters and destroyers of the twentieth century, we must first consider how some of the major poets and novelists of the second half of the nineteenth century—witnesses, sympathizers, or participants in the great upheaval of 1848–1849—faced the challenge of the failure that Herzen so tellingly characterized as the bankruptcy of the idea of salvation through revolution. Their eloquent reactions to revolutionary faith and tradition may help us to discern the shape of a conflict that has yet to be resolved.

part *3*

confrontations and
reactions

The cannon thunders, human limbs fly in all directions . . . groans of sacred victims and yells of sacrificial priests are heard . . . . It is Humanity in quest of happiness.

BAUDELAIRE

Above all, get rid of evil passions, which have not lost their loathsome sway over the human heart, despite the liberal and fraternal slogans of our age!

DELACROIX

chapter *10*

salvation through art:
Baudelaire

"Great works of art carry more weight than five hundred million democratic and social almanacs. The work of Homer will count for rather more than that of Blanqui in the sum total of humanity's moral efforts," wrote Leconte de Lisle, ex-disciple of the utopian socialist Fourier, in 1849.[1] The Parnassian poet had moved from a firm belief in universal revolution to a single-minded devotion to art. A similar path was to be taken by many who, like Baudelaire (two and a half years Leconte de Lisle's junior), were confirmed in the religion of art and beauty after the collapse of revolutionary hopes in 1848. The Keatsian dilemma between the poles of action and poetry was resolved by Baudelaire, the Byronic Satanist, first by following (though less deliberately and spectacularly) Byron's course into revolutionary action, then by adopting the opposite extreme, the rejection of revolution in the name of a higher reality.

As the garrulous champion of social revolution who tended to subordinate art to political or social ends, George Sand became an obvious target; Baudelaire in his maturity amiably called her "this latrine." [2] One possible source of his aggressive dislike of the advocate of sexual equality was his obsessive tormented relationship with his mother. She, widowed when he was a cherished six-year-old, married shortly afterward the promising Captain Aupick, with whom Baudelaire failed to get on. For feminine company, artists should associate with prostitutes or stupid creatures, advised Baudelaire, who often followed his own advice and who did not warm to the idea of the newly emancipated female.

Indeed, he was opposed to all that George Sand stood for. This "theologian of feeling," as he called her,[3] who resisted the notion of original sin and who did away with hell out of love for humanity, represented the obverse of his own medal. George Sand, the disciple of Jean-Jacques Rousseau, with his cult of nature and trust in the natural goodness of man, could not but offend Baudelaire. The poet of *Les Fleurs du Mal* had become an admirer of the gloomy and potent counterrevolutionary philosopher Joseph de Maistre, who saw man in the deadly grip of sin and who thundered against Rousseau and against nature.

Echoing Joseph de Maistre (and the Marquis de Sade), Baudelaire found that everything "natural" is vicious and appalling. Crime is natural, virtue supernatural. Nature produces nothing but monsters. All creatures feed on each other. Woman is natural, hence abominable. Man is depraved, the supreme beast of prey. Life is little but a catalogue of unspeakable horrors, bearing witness to "indestructible, eternal, universal and ingenious human ferocity." [4] There is love for blood, intoxication with blood, intoxication with the crowd, wrote Baudelaire.

Joseph de Maistre himself had noted in the soldier the co-existence of an *enthusiasm for carnage* (his italics) with tender feelings of humanity, and had decided that war is a divine scourge: "The whole earth, continually steeped in blood, is nothing but an immense altar on which every living thing must be sacrificed without end, without restraint, without respite until the consummation of the world, the extinction of evil, the death of death." [5] Over this earth of savagery and sacrifice reigns Providence. For

Baudelaire, too, every being, the executioner as much as the victim, is a blind instrument of Providence. Man may yearn for grace, but that does not mean it will be vouchsafed to him.

So grimly Jansenist a view of damnation and grace left little room for interest in the possibility or desirability of social change or amelioration. When Victor Hugo declared that his novel *Les Misérables* would prove useful "as long as" there existed a legally consecrated form of social damnation artificially creating hells in the midst of civilization, "as long as" there was ignorance and poverty—Baudelaire sighed, " 'As long as . . . !' Alas! You might just as well say ALWAYS!" [6] With his complex, ambivalent reaction toward his dominating predecessor, he regarded Hugo as both a genius and a fool, and told his friend the painter Manet: "I don't give a damn for the human race, and he hasn't even realized it." [7]

Although Baudelaire lacked religious faith, he had a nostalgia for faith, an insatiable thirst for everything beyond the purely material and visible. He had been molded by his Catholic upbringing to believe in the value of the individual human soul, in sin and damnation. For him, progress and civilization did not mean gas, electricity, and steamships but the diminution of original sin.

It offended him to hear revolution described as the modern church, the modern form of sainthood and martyrdom. "Revolution is not a religion," he declared, "since it has no prophets, saints or miracles, and since its aim is to deny all that." [8] The great modern error lay in confusing the spiritual and the material order. Could one say that the obsession with fornication revealed by an eighteenth-century writer like Choderlos de Laclos, the author of *Les Liaisons Dangereuses,* was more immoral than the way nineteenth-century writers loved to mix the sacred with the profane? Clearly, Baudelaire did not think so. He loathed this tendency, with its talk of the true revolutionary Jesus, and in opposing it he was battling against the current flowing from Saint-Simonism and against all those leaders, thinkers, and writers swimming with it, including Heine (to whose art-criticism he was otherwise indebted) as well as George Sand.

Yet Baudelaire did not always profess indifference to the social fate of his fellow creatures, nor did he always paradoxically advocate whipping the poor for their own good, in order to stiffen their resistance. In his middle twenties he had known a phase of keen social idealism. This was in the years immediately preceding the revolution of 1848, in which he unexpectedly played a wildly theatrical and hysterical role. The impetus for his participation in the revolution, one of the most bizarre episodes of that drama, lay in the consequences of his own youthful extravagance, the strict measures adopted by his mother and stepfather, and his bitter personal experience of failure, humiliation, and poverty.

As a rebellious young dandy indulging his fastidious tastes and the aristocratic pleasure of causing displeasure, Baudelaire consumed his inheritance at a rate that alarmed his parents, who decided to have the family lawyer appointed as his financial guardian. The poet who gave tongue to the anguished sensibility of modern man, shaped by political and industrial revolution, was to remain in tutelage to the end of his days. Conscious of his true worth, proud, hypersensitive, Baudelaire was deeply wounded by this misguided measure, which did nothing to cure his inability to cope with his financial affairs, ever more inextricable.

Often in dire straits, he began to frequent the cafés in the Latin Quarter, where the impoverished bohemians sentimentalized by Murger (whom he knew personally) used to meet and expound socialist or revolutionary ideas. Here he would have encountered those "perpetual suitors of the revolutionary Penelope," as Herzen called them, the unappreciated artists, unsuccessful literary men, students, actors, "persons of great vanity but small capability" who tended to drift into the milieu of rhetorical revolutionism.[9] Those whose talents went (rightly or wrongly) unacknowledged naturally longed to be rid of a society that had no place for them.

If the dandy could feel nothing for the people but contempt, and could see in the republican or anarchist only the iconoclastic enemy of the fine arts who deserves a good drubbing, the friend of the bohemians with his new awareness of the real misery of the underdog believed that criticism must be passionate and political, that social equilibrium was a possibility, even that the bourgeoisie had a contribution to make. He was not as yet consumed by hatred for his own class.

About this time, in 1846–1847, Baudelaire had long talks with the working-class poet Pierre Dupont (and spoke kindly of him even after their views diverged). In his poems Baudelaire began to write compassionately about the exhausted workman, his pitiable dwelling, and about the wretched workhouse poor, many of whom died without ever knowing the comfort of home and without ever having really lived. He was moved by the sight of the laboring multitudes, their health undermined by breathing the dust of workshops. And he became the poet who hauntingly expressed the sordid beauty of cities echoing to the sound of human lamentations.

Besides Dupont, among Baudelaire's companions in the years before the February Revolution was the socialist painter Courbet (who would become a member of the Commune in 1871). Courbet introduced Baudelaire to Proudhon, whose economic views (as distinct from his opinions on art) the poet still esteemed in later years. With Courbet and other bohemian friends, Baudelaire followed the crowds sweeping along the boulevards on February 22, 1848. As evening fell, they were obliged to seek refuge from the advancing soldiery on a garden parapet bordering the Place de la Concorde. Horrified, they saw that as one of the fleeing insurgents stumbled, the soldier pursuing him thrust a bayonet through his chest. Baudelaire and Courbet hastened to denounce this act of savagery to the newspaper editor Emile de Girardin, founder of the popular press.

On the following day, Baudelaire, with the realist novelist Champfleury and other friends, tried to reach the barricades on the right bank, and arrived only to find the fighting over. Baudelaire was disappointed that the curtain had fallen so early; but a friend said he had never seen the poet of ennui, spleen, and melancholy so gay: his eyes were sparkling. On the 24th, Baudelaire was glimpsed in the midst of a crowd that had just looted a gunsmith's. He was carrying a new, unused gun. "I've just fired my first shot," he claimed, and kept shouting hysterically, "We must go and shoot General Aupick!" [10] The high drama of the revolution had become an opportunity to settle scores with his stepfather. Afterward he would speak of the ignoble passions aroused by the February Revolution, and with cause.

Political clubs and newspapers were sprouting in the dew of the revolutionary dawn. The *Société Républicaine Centrale,* a club founded on February 26 by the emaciated conspirator Blanqui (who, de Tocqueville would say, looked as if he had just emerged from the sewers), included Baudelaire among its members, though he is only known to have attended the second meeting on the 27th. Together with Champfleury and Toubin, Baudelaire had founded a revolutionary paper with the resonant Jacobin title *Le Salut Public,* which he chose himself. In revolutionary times, he said, one must raise one's voice to be heard. He "loved the revolution like everything violent and abnormal." [11] Only two issues of *Le Salut Public* appeared: the second, with a vignette by Courbet, was sold on the streets of Paris by the poet himself, wearing a white smock.

During the June days, Baudelaire sided with the insurgent workers. A friend encountered Pierre Dupont and Baudelaire in the Palais-Royal; the latter was in a state of feverish excitement. He was wildly holding forth about his desire to be a revolutionary martyr, and kept shouting socialist slogans and demanding the end of the existing order. Dupont could not get him to calm down. At a time when people were being shot in the streets simply because they looked like workers, Baudelaire's behavior naturally aroused the apprehension of his friends. The poet who, according to Sartre, should be counted a rebel not a revolutionary, almost succeeded in getting himself killed on the revolutionary side.

the revolution of 1848 in retrospect

Baudelaire was profoundly shocked by the coup d'état of December 1851 ("Another Bonaparte! What a disgrace!"), which he said had effectively cured him of politics. If he had voted, he candidly averred, it could only have been for himself. As for political convictions, he had none. They were good for "brigands" whose sole interest was getting on in the world.

Among the numerous works he planned but never completed was the sketch for a prose poem that conveys his serious feelings about revolution, as distinct from his more jaunty ironical comments on the revolution of 1848, seen in retrospect as "amusing" and "charming." He wrote: "The cannon thunders, human limbs fly in all directions . . . groans of sacred victims and yells of sacrificial priests are heard. . . . It is Humanity in quest of happiness." [12] Those few lines convey with bitter discernment the tragic paradox that man's path to earthly happiness so often runs through cruelty and bloodshed. The subtle disciple of Sade, familiar with the union of cruelty, shame, and pleasure, observed: "In every change there is something at once infamous and pleasant, something connected with faithlessness and moving house. That is enough to explain the French Revolution." [13] The poet's insight into himself may not suffice to explain the French Revolution, but it does help to illuminate one aspect of the attraction of revolutionary change.

In later years, Baudelaire reflected on his conduct during the Revolution of 1848 and suggested various penetrating explanations, though all of them underestimated his zeal for revolutionary martyrdom and his awareness of social and economic problems at that time (as revealed by the way he coolly heckled ill-prepared candidates in April 1848 on such subjects as small shopkeepers and free trade, "perhaps the keystone of the social edifice").[14] He wondered about the origin of the sudden burst of energy and courage which impelled lazy, contemplative beings like himself, who normally procrastinated the most trivial daily actions, to perform absurd and even dangerous deeds. Such contemplative natures, unsuited to action, were driven into activity by some irresistible force. They risked their lives "in order *to see, to know, to tempt fate.*" [15] They wanted to test themselves, to experience the pleasurable thrill of anxiety, or else they were moved to action by a whim or simply for want of something better to do. Their sudden energy was of a type that sprang from ennui and dreaming.

What was the nature of his own intoxication in 1848? he asked himself. And he suggested that it embraced a taste for vengeance ("Down with General Aupick!") as well as *natural* pleasure in demolition." To this he added "Literary intoxication; reminiscences of books." And, recalling the abortive coup d'état of May 15, 1848, he wrote: "Always the taste for destruction. A legitimate taste if everything natural is legitimate." The horror of the June days, the madness of both the people and the bourgeoisie, merely revealed a "natural love of crime." [16] So Baudelaire conceived his youthful ardor as yet another manifestation of human depravity.

Toward the end of his life, in notes made after the unsuccessful Belgian lecture tour which preceded his final breakdown from syphilis, Baudelaire again returned to the theme of revolution and destruction. His reflections were inspired by people who were always talking of revolution in sentimental platitudes but were scared of the real thing. Such people did not know themselves. In this they resembled George Sand, who, in Baudelaire's view, represented evil unaware of itself and who was therefore inferior to the Marquis de Sade, the exponent of evil aware of itself and therefore easier to cure. "When *I* agree to be a Republican, *I do evil, knowingly,*" wrote Baudelaire, adding:

> Yes! *Long live Revolution!*
> Always! Despite everything!
> But I'm not taken in, I've never been taken in! I say *Long live Revolution!* as I'd say *Long live Destruction! Long live Expiation! Long live Punishment! Long live Death!* Not only would I be happy to be a victim, but I would not exactly hate being an executioner,—so as to experience Revolution both ways!" [17]

These words recall the celebrated poem on his own inner divisions in *Les Fleurs du Mal* in which he sadomasochistically proclaims that he is both wound and knife, victim and executioner. The revolutionary spirit had become for him another virus with which modern man was universally infected.

Baudelaire was convinced that a storm, a political and social revolution, would bring nothing new, since man was eternally depraved. He felt that the modern belief in material progress was a delusion, since technical advancement (or "Americanization") led to the atrophy of man's spiritual nature and to the debasement of the finer feelings. Nothing in the "sanguinary, sacrilegious or anti-natural dreams of the Utopians" might be compared to the consequences of mechanization, which he prophesied would end in universal ruin.[18] Yet there was another sphere, that of art, where he allowed man greater liberty.

the revolution in art

For while he denied the possibility of the new in the ordering of human affairs, he insisted upon it in art. Art must be unexpected, unusual, original. One must be ready to plunge into the metaphysical abyss of the Unknown—heaven or hell, what does it matter?—in search of the new. There could be change, progress, and revolution in art, as demonstrated by painters like Delacroix, composers like Wagner, poets like Victor Hugo. Of course, progress in art was not to be understood in the literal sense; it implied in the artist himself a greater degree of imaginative force than he had hitherto displayed. Where a great artist like Delacroix, the object of Baudelaire's lifelong admiration, is concerned, revolutions take place in the mind. The new, the revolutionary in art recur as terms of approval and praise in Baudelaire's influential art and literary criticism.

One of the great modern heresies, according to Baudelaire, is the belief that political revolution favors artistic revolution. Perhaps he himself may have momentarily subscribed to it in 1847–1848. The neglected, misunderstood artist is inclined to imagine that a new regime will prove more kindly disposed toward his aspirations. Certainly this was Wagner's error, said Baudelaire, who commented on it with a sympathy born of understanding that he rarely showed toward other modern heresies. He could not fail to respond to the composer who felt that the man born without the spirit of universal discontent would never discover anything new. It was to the artist's capacity for suffering at the sight of ugliness and injustice, all the greater because his instinct for beauty and justice is more intense, that Baudelaire attributed Wagner's revolutionary theories.

Wagner, who desired revolution more for artistic than for political ends, believed the new art of his dreams required a new humanity that could only come into being through political revolution. Embittered by lack of recognition, the highly sensitive Wagner, through an "excusable" mistake, said Baudelaire, associated bad music with bad government. Out of a longing to see the triumph of his artistic ideal, the composer of *Tannhäuser* came to hope that revolution in the political sphere would favor the cause of revolution in art. Yet by a revealing irony, observed the poet, it was under a "despot," the Emperor Napoleon III, that Wagner's music, the work of a revolutionary, was performed in Paris. Baudelaire drew the conclusion that there existed no connection between art and the kind of regime in power: all forms of government, with democracy in the lead (though with the possible exception of aristocratic rule), were inimical to art.

This was one of the many aesthetic views of Baudelaire which remained influential down to our own day. One current of the modern aesthetic that runs from Baudelaire to Ezra Pound and T. S. Eliot accomplished artistic revolution while remaining either counter-revolutionary or conservative in politics. Another—leading from Baudelaire and Flaubert, with their conception of the artist's vocation as a priesthood or martyrdom, and culminating in Proust, cloistered in his cork-lined room—found salvation nowhere but in art itself as the supreme reality.

For Baudelaire proclaimed that "Poetry is what is most real, it is what is completely true only in *another world.*" [19] True reality, he observed in his writings on the artificial paradises induced by drugs, is to be found only in dreams. The poetic imagination (whose value he stressed à la Coleridge, filtered largely through Edgar Allan Poe) was the queen of faculties, almost divine, a means of perceiving the secret connections between things, and therefore far more important than mere mundane "reality" as treated by inferior artists like his old companion Champfleury or manipulated by those "brigands," the despised politicians on the make.

In one of his poems he showed the poet ignoring revolutionary action in a comfortable image of secluded dedication vis-à-vis external uproar. He spoke of insurrection thundering outside his window; it would not make him raise his eyes from his desk, where he was deep in the pleasure of conjuring spring and drawing a sun from his heart. This image would trouble the conscience of some of his heirs.

The trust in the higher reality of poetry and great art, in the sacred nature of the word, in the worth of literature as an end in itself, though it may on occasion impel the unrecognized artist to seek recognition through political revolution, usually tends to militate against the pursuit of change and improvement in a world strangely less "real" than the world of imagination and dreams. Life as it is lived became less "real," less important than the life of art for Baudelaire and Flaubert; they were drawn to each other, both having suffered prosecution because their work allegedly offended public morals.

If a certain dissatisfaction with the world of the creative imagination or lack of confidence in the value of art encouraged Byron and many of his imitators to take to the field of action and revolutionary action, confidence in literature as a value sometimes subdues the artist's urge for revolutionary change in any other field than that of art. While such confidence may fluctuate, or may be a question of degree, nevertheless the writer's attitude toward revolution is often largely dependent upon his attitude to his art and on the extent of his faith in its worth. For Baudelaire and Flaubert, salvation lay through art, not revolution; and the single-minded artist, not the single-minded revolutionary, was the martyr in the tormented quest for the new.

chapter 11

literary commitment versus
revolutionary tradition: Flaubert

While Flaubert shares Baudelaire's views on the place of art (before he was twenty he proclaimed: "Superior to everything is—Art"),[1] he presents an even more extreme example of literary as opposed to political commitment. It was as the dedicated exponent of literary commitment that he launched in his masterpiece, *L'Éducation sentimentale,* a devastating critique of the revolutionary myth, dogma, and tradition. That critique has never been equaled, let alone surpassed. The title, *Sentimental Education,* to which Flaubert was so attached that he used it twice and ignored Turgenev's advice to change it, gives only a partial idea of what the book is about. When the novel first appeared, it went largely unappreciated, and perhaps its full implications have only become apparent in our own day.

By the revolutionary tradition is meant the whole mystique of revolution as handed down from the French Revolution of 1789: the intoxication of the crowd storming the Bastille, the spontaneous heroism of the barricades, the self-denying courage of the victorious volunteers of 1792, the "Roman" patriotic ideals of the government of 1793, the stirring revolutionary phraseology and rhetoric, the exciting revolutionary festivals with their processions and the planting of trees of liberty, the whole atmosphere of living outside ordinary time in a supreme moment when everything suddenly becomes possible, the feeling of playing a vital part in a heightened drama. There existed a tradition of violent action. Boys brought up on the legendary deeds performed on the barricades looked forward to the day when they too could show their mettle like the youth in Delacroix's picture. Some would give their lives with exemplary valor for this new chivalry, this dream of revolutionary heroism.

One of the revolutionary figures of 1848 who chose death on the barricades in the last days of the Commune was the elderly Jacobin journalist Charles Delescluze. In May 1871 he drew on a treasure-house of imagery with his cry: "Make way for the people, the fighters, the bare arms! The hour of revolutionary warfare has struck! The people knows nothing of scientific manœuvres, but when it has a musket in its hand, paving-stones under its feet, it fears not all the strategists of the monarchist schools. To arms! citizens, to arms!" [2] Such rhetoric could always be guaranteed to arouse a stock response.

When Flaubert in his novel undertook to question this revolutionary mystique as revealed in the revolution of 1848, he was attempting to analyze the psychology of revolutions in general. As a novelist, his prime concern was with "the eternal element," the portrayal of general human principles through particular instances. [3] One of these principles, Flaubert had perceived, was revolutionary imitation, the way the men of 1789 modeled themselves on their conception of republican Rome or austere Sparta, while those of 1848 modeled themselves on their conception of 1789 or 1793. What did it matter if the men of 1793 did not really understand Sparta, when the very act of imitation was the important thing? Concepts produce facts, or so thought Jules, the devoted novelist and

Flaubert's other self, in the first version of *L'Éducation sentimentale* (begun in 1843 at twenty-one, completed in 1845, and unpublished in the author's lifetime), as he commented on revolutionary imitation years before Marx did so in *The Eighteenth Brumaire of Louis Bonaparte.* Of course Marx, unlike Flaubert, thought this bourgeois phase of revolutionary imitation would eventually be overcome by the proletariat. So far, it is not the German philosopher who has been proved correct.

Flaubert, who was scarcely kinder to the bourgeoisie than Marx, did not expect the proletariat of the future to behave otherwise than in accordance with general human laws. The novelist was sufficiently swayed by the positivism of his age as well as by its respect for science to feel that what was needed was scientific inquiry in place of dogma. Instead of credulous affirmation and belief, there should be Voltairean doubt, questioning, and discussion. "The Revolution must cease to be a dogma and must be restored to the realm of Science, like the rest of human affairs," he would tell George Sand during the Commune in 1871. "If people had been more knowledgeable, they would not have believed that a mystic formula can create armies and that the word 'Republic' is enough to conquer a million well-disciplined men." They would have known that the victory of the volunteers in 1792 was not all it was cracked up to be. "But no, always the same old refrain, the same old humbug!" [4] Instead of invoking God and the saints, people now swore by the Republic and 1792; they foolishly wanted to re-create a legendary heroic situation although circumstances had completely changed, "but what does that matter, it's tradition." [5]

His friends, those sharp-tongued gossips the brothers Edmond and Jules de Goncourt, in their journal also criticized the revolutionary myth. After reading pamphlets published during the French Revolution for a play they were writing, they decided that were it not for its bloodshed, the revolution and its great men would be regarded as merely stupid. "And what hypocrisy, what lies, this Revolution was made up of! The mottoes, the walls, the speeches, the stories—everything was then a lie. *The Humbug of the Revolution:* there is a book to be written! . . . Is there one fact about the Revolution that patriotism and party passions and journalism have not turned into legend?. . . . And out of all the gulls and simpletons in society and in the streets who have their catechism of the Bastille by heart, how many know the number of prisoners that these horrible and devouring dungeons actually released to the light of day? Three, wasn't it? or was it four?" [6] While there is some truth in this sour view, it does overlook the fact that the Bastille was the symbol of a hated tyranny.

Flaubert had no more intention of being duped than had the Goncourt brothers. Still, unattractive as the modern age of revolutions in which he knew he was living might be, it was nonetheless fascinating to Flaubert the artist. At least, so he had felt when younger, and he had enough of the romantic in him to find storm more interesting than calm. His Jules wondered whether an artist did not enjoy more freedom in a period when there had been "a revolution to change the world and a hero to conquer it," when monarchies crumbled and peoples were born, than in an era of stability. [7] He could not but feel that this was a difficult yet fruitful subject for art. It all came down to art.

Of all the great nineteenth-century novelists, Flaubert stands as the most complete and confident representative of European literary culture for its own sake. (Not until shattered by the Franco-Prussian War did he voice grave doubts about the value and importance of literature). That confidence in literature is doubtless one reason why later writers, from Proust to Sartre, have been so preoccupied with the challenge he presents. True, when Flaubert speaks of taking ten hours to produce three unsatisfactory lines, and of the labor pangs of style, allowance has to be made for exaggeration (Edmond de Goncourt remarked, in a note, on Flaubert's penchant for magnifying things). Moreover, Flaubert wrote to friends describing his creative struggles when he was tired after many hours of toil in pursuit of the right word. Nevertheless, in modern eyes, he appears the literary saint incarnate. He quite deliberately stressed the opposition of art and life. Literature became for this son of a Rouen surgeon a means of evading a confined, shabby bourgeois reality that was permanently repugnant to his limitless imagination; it offered also the agreeable possibility of commanding and castigating the world he rejected.

His pessimism was temperamental. He was only thirteen when he spoke of life as a grotesque joke. The nervous attacks he suffered as a young man have been qualified as psychosomatic, an attempt to elude any other career than the literary one he desired to pursue. The isolated style of life the novelist would adopt (but for his travels and his emergence for Magny dinners and attendance in Princess Mathilde's salon during the years of fame) is foreshadowed in that of the writer Jules in the first version of *L'Éducation sentimentale.* Jules withdraws from the world into obscurity, into a manner of life called at once "sterile" and "rich," in contrast with Henry who frequents political salons and progresses from republicanism and socialism to support of the regime. Not that Jules was spared misgivings: "Occasionally he still experienced the temptation to live and act," but irony prevented him from accomplishing any action, and analysis undermined feeling.[8] Besides, Jules could perceive the "nothingness" of all human endeavor which made action vain.

Of feminine temperament (a hysterical old woman, his doctor called him) if not of homosexual inclination, Flaubert dreamed a lifelong impossible love for Madame Schlésinger, whom he first glimpsed when he was fourteen at Trouville. He found the muse gave less trouble than ties with any demanding flesh-and-blood female. During his liaison with the authoress Louise Colet, it has been estimated that he met her only six times in two years, and then was careful to arrange their rendezvous when he was not likely to be in the middle of writing a chapter. Years later he told George Sand that he had been afraid of life.

The writings of the Marquis de Sade haunted his imagination and encouraged him to dream of "limitless mastery and magnificent power." [9] One could have the illusion of attaining power through the word, the literary imagination seeming godlike in its capacity to embrace all things. Unlike the literary activists, Flaubert appeared content with power in the imaginative world (where, as in *Salammbô,* for instance, he could pile on the pagan atrocities to his heart's content).

He possessed the anarchist inclinations so common to the literary temperament, veering between thoughts of self-destruction and world destruction. In his notebook, written in 1840–1841, when he was between the ages of eighteen and nineteen, he envisaged the political future as an era of barbarism: "I wouldn't mind a bit seeing all civilization crumble like a mason's scaffolding before the building was finished—too bad! . . . I'd enjoy being at the gates of Paris with five hundred thousand barbarians, and burning the whole city. What flames! What a ruin of ruins!" [10] (The imaginings of his Nero complex would become reality sooner than he knew, with the siege of Paris by the Prussians, their occupation of his home in Normandy, and the destruction wrought during the Commune—disasters he conceived as the end of his world.)

It was quite early, then, that Flaubert took to expressing disdain and disgust with life. Life was meaningless. The attempt to attain a true and complete assessment in any field of endeavor was impossible. The novelist Jules, hearing historians express contradictory views on the French Revolution, on Robespierre (a blood-thirsty tiger or the gentlest of legislators), on the Mountain (a sacred host or a den of brigands), gave up talking about history. The history of the world is a farce, the young Flaubert had written in his notebook, adding, "Too bad that conservatives should be so despicable and republicans so stupid." [11] Partisanship is absurd. Opposing views and parties cancel each other out: they are roughly equivalent.

This attitude is not very different from the total impression conveyed by *L'Éducation sentimentale* (begun in 1864 when Flaubert was forty-three and completed in 1869). The feeling of disillusionment it exudes was therefore neither the result of his personal experiences during the revolution of 1848 nor the consequence of his meticulous documentation for that novel. These merely confirmed his opinion. In Rouen, Flaubert had attended one of the reform banquets that preceded the February Revolution and sat with frigid disgust amid the patriotic enthusiasm. With his intimate friend, the poet Louis Bouilhet, he visited Paris to find out what was going on "from the artistic point of view." [12] He saw the fighting in the streets and the sack of the Tuileries, and returned to Normandy the day after the proclamation of the Second Republic. What particularly pleased him about the revolution was the downfall of the bourgeois supporters of Louis-Philippe. Would the new government and social conditions be favorable to art? Could the new men possibly be more stupid than their predecessors?

In Rouen he briefly joined the National Guard and paraded when a tree of liberty was planted. A further visit to Paris before the June days elicited the opinion that all parties were equally inept and that it was enough to make a decent person vomit. And he was in Paris during the coup d'état of December 1851, saw people killed before his eyes, and was almost killed himself.

By the time Flaubert came to write his novel, which covers the period from 1840 to 1851 and beyond, he realized that while these experiences contributed a skeleton framework, they were insufficient. Not only did he read or reread the socialist thinkers and study the newspapers of the period, but he consulted his friends, including George Sand, who put him in touch with Barbès, the only revolutionary for whom Flaubert expressed esteem. (Barbès risked his life for liberty in the streets while I was phrase-making in my study, wrote the author of *Madame Bovary,* voicing a contrast that later writers were to find more oppressive.) Other correspondents were asked about methods of transport in 1848 and about the posts of the National Guard. His care was such that the book has been judged historically accurate in all but a few minute particulars.

The much-vaunted impartiality of Flaubert is another matter. He prided himself on impersonality: the novelist has no right to express his opinion on anything whatever, he told George Sand. Has God ever expressed his opinion? Great art should be scientific and impersonal. It should be as majestically just and impartial as science. This was an exhortation to a godlike indifference he wished to, but could not, feel. He often spoke of his ivory tower, but he remained passionately interested in what was going on outside. It was this which kept his anger on the boil.

He was permanently infuriated by baseness, pettiness, and folly. Indignant at eighteen, he savored his indignation and went on being angry all through life. This impotent rage fell indiscriminately upon all. What remained constant, in his view, was "a depth of stupidity in humanity which is as eternal as humanity itself." [13] He did not entirely exempt himself from that censure, and the fury of self-laceration is one of the sources of the novel's power.

To Frédéric Moreau, the passive, ineffectual, flaccid protagonist of *L'Éducation sentimentale,* with his hopeless love for Madame Arnoux, Flaubert gave the ideal love he himself cherished for Madame Schlésinger; but the novelist savaged his antihero, through whom he portrayed his own short-comings without the compensating factor of his genius. Frédéric has only the vast dreams of artistic fame, the ambitious plans for writing a series of plays on the French Revolution; he is far too weak willed to accomplish anything. He belongs to the generation of Flaubert's provincial school friends, molded by romantic revolt, dreaming of dramatic love affairs or conspiratorial glory; one of them penned an apology for Robespierre, while two others committed suicide. Instead of fulfilling the high hopes entertained of him, Frédéric fritters time away and becomes involved with women he does not really love: the plebeian courtesan Rosanette and the frigid, wealthy bourgeoise, Madame Dambreuse.

At first the sensitive Frédéric's friendship with the coarse-grained Deslauriers seems inexplicable. Despite the harm the latter occasionally does Frédéric, their union is indissoluble. They are in fact two faces of the same bourgeois phenomenon. In their old age, they both look back to a boyhood escapade, when they took some flowers to a local prostitute and fled, as the best moment of their lives. This is Flaubert's final comment on the ineffectualness of his generation, and on the bourgeois society he loathed, though he was inescapably a part of it.

Besides aiming to undermine bourgeois values and leave the bourgeoisie "stupefied," Flaubert sought to expose the nature of revolutionary attitudes and sympathies. This is how it was then, and how it always will be, he proposes. When the February Revolution erupts, Frédéric enjoys himself hugely, probably as Flaubert himself had done roaming the streets with Louis Bouilhet and Maxime du Camp. At the barricades, Frédéric was fascinated. The wounded and dead did not look real. He felt he was watching a play. Then he was gripped by the magnetism of the enthusiastic crowds. He sniffed "voluptuously" the stormy air that reeked of powder. However, like his creator, Frédéric did nothing. The idea of standing for election appealed to him. He thought of the great men of the Convention, of the new dawn, how he should throw himself into the revolutionary movement and even hasten its progress; and besides he was attracted by the deputy's uniform, which he understood would be a waistcoat with lapels and a tricolor sash.

As for the republican lawyer Deslauriers, he had dreamed beforehand of the coming cataclysm, of how he would shatter the foolish tranquility of the bourgeois who were unaware that a new 1789 was on the way. "Oh! how much more splendid it was when Camille Desmoulins . . . urged the people onwards to the Bastille! They lived in those days, they could make their mark, prove their mettle! Mere lawyers gave orders to generals. . . ." [14] Something of Flaubert's destructive urge, his satisfaction at the overthrow of the complacent ruling bourgeoisie, has passed into Deslauriers. But Deslauriers reveals, too, an ambitious envy, an impatience for an upheaval through which he could climb to a position of importance—feelings that Flaubert regarded as forming a considerable part of revolutionary psychology.

It was to the vulgar Deslauriers, however, that Flaubert gave his own views on Socialism. Deslauriers says of Saint-Simon "and his church" and of Fourier that they are "a lot of humbugs who would like to give us Catholicism all over again." [15] For Deslauriers, "modern reformers (I can prove it) all believe in Revelation." [16] This was the conclusion that Flaubert had reached as a result of reading Saint-Simon, Fourier, Leroux, and Proudhon for the novel. All these pedantic and despotic utopian socialist reformers, thought Flaubert, not only derived from religious revelation but were united by hatred of freedom and philosophical inquiry. Their outlook was medieval, dogmatic, Jesuitical, "Catholic" in a word. They had taken the wrong turn in following the path of Rousseau, sentimental father of envious and tyrannical democracy, instead of the major highway of Voltaire with his emphasis on justice and law. "I believe our ills partly derive from Republican neo-Catholicism," wrote Flaubert to the historian of the French Revolution, Michelet. [17] This was one of the novelist's favorite themes in his letters.

The true revolutionary of *L'Éducation sentimentale,* the future Saint-

Just according to Deslauriers, is the mathematics teacher Sénécal, and it is plain from the first moment that the author detests him as much as Frédéric does. Disinterested the austere Sénécal may seem to be, but he is described as pedantic and clerical in appearance, with something hard and cold about his gaze. His view that art should serve an educational purpose would have been enough to give the game away. After work, Sénécal annotated Rousseau's *Social Contract* and out of his reading of Mably, Morelly, Fourier, Saint-Simon, Comte, Cabet he had evolved "a sort of American Sparta where the individual would exist solely in order to serve the State, which was more omnipotent, absolute, infallible and divine than the Dalai Lama or Nebuchadnezzar." [18] (In Flaubert's eyes, the state was "hateful".) Sénécal employed "the good faith of an inquisitor" to demolish everything opposed to his view. And—an outlook particularly offensive to artists—he hated any sign of preeminence.

As foreman in the pottery factory of the thoughtless and shady Arnoux, he proves a petty tyrant to the girls who work there. Frédéric finds Sénécal's behavior cruelly harsh, but Madame Arnoux observes that there is such a thing as necessary severity. It is a revealing moment. At a first reading, one tends to see Madame Arnoux through Frédéric's eyes, in a soft, beautifying haze. On closer scrutiny, she appears an ordinary bourgeoise (as indeed she qualifies herself), with the ideas and ideals of her class.

All the same, when Sénécal is arrested for complicity in a terrorist plot, Frédéric, despite his dislike for the pedagogue, feels an all-too-human sympathy for the terrorist, "that admiration inspired by any man who sacrifices himself for an idea." [19] More enthusiastic toward Sénécal is Dussardier, with whom he is contrasted. Dussardier—the trusting, idealistic, simple man of the people—sees in Sénécal the victim of authority to be helped whether guilty or not, and regardless of whether his intended act was odious. When only fifteen, Dussardier had witnessed in the Rue Transnonain the 1834 massacre of defenseless workers and their families immortalized by Daumier's lithograph, and since then he had hated government as the embodiment of injustice and evil. (This attitude Flaubert calls naïve, but it has something in common with his own.)

Unlike Frédéric, Dussardier fought on the February barricades, and believed implicitly in all the revolutionary ideals. He thought that with the proclamation of the Second Republic there would be universal happiness and the whole world would be free. Recruited into the National Guard, he kills a youth on the barricades; thenceforward his conscience troubles him, for the boy had draped himself in the tricolor and cried, "Are you going to fire on your brothers?" So shaken is he by the betrayal of his ideals, and so disillusioned by the workers (whom he finds no better than the bourgeoisie) that he wishes to get himself killed. He is last seen shouting "Long live the Republic!", cut down by a policeman whom Frédéric recognizes as Sénécal.

This astonishing climax is one of the best sign-posted in all fiction: it has the satisfaction of surprise joined with the fulfillment of the reader's suspicions. The transformation of Sénécal into the instrument of tyranny follows implacably from the deepening authoritarian nature of his views: "The end justifies the means. Dictatorship is sometimes necessary. Provided the tyrant does good—long live tyranny!" [20] From the first, Flaubert makes it plain that Sénécal stands for tyranny under another name; ultimately there is no difference between his form of tyranny and that of the reactionaries. Both work to the same end. A decent, honest, simpleminded fellow like Dussardier, the only worthy character in the book, suffers for all the dupes and victims.

Besides its powerful strain of tragic irony, the novel presents a sustained satire on revolutionary conduct and attitudes. Here are the bands of students in revolt. Newly arrived in Paris, Frédéric asks the reason for the disorders in the university quarter and is told, "I don't know . . . and neither do they! It's their fashion of the moment!" [21] Here are the ritual cries, slogans, and rhetoric. The revolutionary myth of the sovereign people is mocked when the sack of the Tuileries culminates in a prostitute's adopting the stance of a statue of Liberty.

Flaubert ridicules, too, the sense of unlimited possibility awakened by revolution, long before the slogan "Be realistic, ask for the impossible" was written on the walls of the Sorbonne in 1968. For Mademoiselle Vatnaz, the emancipation of the proletariat cannot be accomplished without the emancipation of woman, and she puts forward an extensive program summed up as "everything for women." Indeed, if rights for women are not granted, they should be seized forcibly by a female army. The artists demand an arts forum or exchange where masterpieces would be produced by pooling talent.

As for the students, their cry is simple enough:

> "No more academies! No more Institute!"
>
> . . . "No more matriculation!"
>
> "Down with university degrees!"
>
> "Let's keep them," said Sénécal, "but let them be conferred by universal suffrage, by the People, the sole true judge!" [22]

These students form part of the audience of the ironically named Club of Intelligence. Frédéric hopes to obtain its support for his candidacy, but he is shouted down in favor of a Spaniard whom nobody can understand, in one of the most savagely comic scenes in the novel. Everyone was imitating a model. Some were copying Saint-Just, others Danton or Marat, while Sénécal "was trying to be like Blanqui, who imitated Robespierre." [23] The words, gestures, images of the French Revolution are all there, but the great passions are lacking. Along with Heine and Herzen, Flaubert perceived that there existed a revolutionary conservatism.

However, if Flaubert is not kind to the revolutionaries, he does not spare the reactionaries either. In a few telling paragraphs he evokes the imprisonment of Sénécal below the Orangerie terrace, where hundreds of men, sick, dying, and dead, lie in their own excrement. From time to time, bayonets are thrust haphazardly through the railings into the mass. When a prisoner begs for bread, Monsieur Roque fires; then returns home to be coddled by his daughter: "Oh! these revolutions! . . . ," he moans. "I'm too sensitive!" [24] The bourgeoisie are frightened, cowardly, cynical, vicious, and vengeful. Their leading representative, the banker Dambreuse, is acidly characterized as one who changed his coat so often and loved power so much that "he would have paid to sell himself." [25] Flaubert told George Sand that the reactionaries in the novel seemed to him more "criminal" than the rest.

He came to hate the bourgeoisie less as a class than as a mentality—a mentality shared by the workers as much as by the property owners, for "the bourgeoisie now *is* all of humanity, including the people." [26] Upon this humanity he wished to "vomit" his disgust. He detested the masses, who seemed to him irredeemably stupid; the herd; equality; democracy; universal suffrage (as silly as divine right, though a little less hateful). He would say of the Communards that he did not hate them because he did not hate "mad dogs." But he thought these "bloody imbeciles" should have been forced to clear the ruins of Paris with chains round their necks, like common convicts. However, because of romantic sentimentality, "people feel compassion for mad dogs, instead of for those they have bitten." [27]

Ideally, what Flaubert would have liked was government by the mandarins, an aristocracy of men of letters and men of science, the sole true representatives and torchbearers of humanity. Only then, he felt, would it be possible to avoid the crimes committed as a result of pursuing ideals in politics.

It is not difficult to see what is missing from this choleric indictment uttered by one who loftily declined to participate in the shaping of events, and who knew little and cared less about the day-to-day workings of politics or the deeper economic causes of unrest. The equally pessimistic but liberal Russian novelist Turgenev, to whom he was devoted, revealed a more sympathetic understanding of the forces of conservatism and change.

Flaubert was like a man sawing away at the branch he was perched on. The supreme bourgeois-hating bourgeois artist, the epitome of nineteenth-century bourgeois literary culture in its withdrawal from, and distaste for, modern life, the critic of the revolutionary tradition—Flaubert worked to undermine the basis and values of that culture as surely as did any revolutionary. He was one of a long line of nineteenth-century bourgeois writers who helped to make the word "bourgeois" a term of opprobrium, and whose antibourgeois strictures would eventually decline into the destructive commonplaces of revolutionary and counterrevolutionary alike.

chapter *12*

the liberal dilemma:
Turgenev

Paris in the eighteen-seventies. Deep in an armchair, Turgenev, the urbane,
witty, cosmopolitan charmer, would be speaking in a rather hesitant
manner, and Flaubert, after listening devoutly, would boom his reply.
Two prematurely elderly hypochondriac bachelors, both "born observers," [1] they rarely discussed current topics, occasionally skirted politics
(where a difference of emphasis can sometimes be discerned between Flaubert the aristocratic spirit and Turgenev the liberal nobleman), and confined themselves chiefly to the general awfulness and to literature.
Turgenev, elegant writer though he was, could not understand Flaubert's
fussing about relative pronouns. Simple things should be said simply, felt
the author of *Fathers and Sons*. And he once observed to George Sand, to

whom they were both personally attached, that Flaubert had been abraded by a free and easy life.

The Russian, who had known police surveillance, imprisonment, and banishment to Spasskoye, his country estate, may well have been thinking of his own youth, which was neither easy nor free. His mother ruled her vast lands and her household imperiously—an image, in little, of the cruel absolutism of Tsar Nicholas I. For a caprice, her serfs would be flogged or exiled to Siberia; families were separated, maids not allowed to marry and have children. Her own sons could be thrashed for no reason, and they suffered her tyrannical persecution until she died (when Turgenev was over thirty). Out of this bitter personal experience of monstrous tyranny was born Turgenev's hatred for serfdom (and it was generally agreed that his tales, A Sportsman's Sketches, played a considerable part in preparing the ground for emancipation). His upbringing may have encouraged his pessimistic fatalism as well as that weakness of will which made him replace his mother's domination with subservience to the opera singer Pauline Viardot, and which led Flaubert to call him a "soft mark." [2]

Turgenev has left a searing account of the difficulties encountered by the Russian intellectual in the early eighteen-forties, when there was no appeal against the often inexplicable and stupid decisions of the censor, when "bribery was rampant, serfdom remained as firm as a rock, the barracks were in the forefront of everything, no courts of justice, rumours about the impending closure of the universities, . . . journeys abroad were becoming impossible, no decent book could be ordered from abroad, a sort of dark cloud was constantly hanging over the whole of the so-called department of learning and literature and, to cap it all, denunciations whispered and spread on all sides; . . . everyone afraid and grovelling. . . ." [3] No wonder Turgenev's lifelong ideal remained free debate!

In such a situation as existed in Russia, change was imperative. But what degree of change and how to achieve it? Should it be fast or slow? In such conditions, where to start, and with what? These questions in varying forms would preoccupy Turgenev throughout his life. He saw the forces of stagnation and movement, of conservatism and progress as the basic urges of everything that exists. He understood the claims of conservatism, saw in it what was decayed and what worthy of respect, just as he perceived the merits and shortcomings of the challenging side.

Turgenev had studied Hegelian philosophy at the University of Berlin, sharing lodgings with Bakunin, who had not yet become converted to political activism. Complex, uncertain, as a novelist Turgenev tended to propose the tension of opposites without resolving it. He would say later (of Tolstoy) that "An artist who is incapable of seeing the *white* and the *black*—of looking both to the right and to the left—already stands on the brink of perdition." [4] According to Herzen, Hegelianism penetrated Russia like a battering ram, and, though often misunderstood, it "vaporised everything that existed and dissipated everything that was a check on reason." [5]

It was in 1843 that Turgenev met the ardent critic Belinsky, who shone like a comforting light in the surrounding gloom. Belinsky was shy, consumptive, but a fighter, said Herzen, who also fell under his sway. "The subjects of our talks were mostly of such a nature that no censor would in those days have passed them in print," wrote Turgenev, "but actually we never discussed politics: the utter uselessness of such discussions was clear to anyone. The general complexion of our talks was philosophic-literary, critical-aesthetic, and, I suppose, social, but rarely historical." [6] At that time, it was chiefly through literature and literary criticism that the existing order could be obliquely questioned.

Belinsky, regarded by his opponents as dangerous and destructive, not to say revolutionary, once wrote to a friend: "To make even a small fraction of mankind happy, I am perhaps ready to destroy the rest by fire and sword." [7] (Turgenev would never go so far.) All the same, Belinsky was devoted to truth, and demanded truth in art. He stood for reason, science, progress, humanism, civilization, the West. These "Westernizing" ideals were shared by Turgenev, who remained "an inveterate and incorrigible" Westernizer all his life. [8] Indeed, Turgenev's friendship with Herzen was to founder when, disillusioned after the failure of the revolution of 1848, the exiled publicist excoriated the West and drew closer to the Slavophile position, placing his hopes in the Russian agricultural commune. Turgenev would have none of this, and some years passed before they were reconciled.

Like Belinsky and Herzen, Turgenev was a skeptic in religion. "There is neither God nor Devil, and the advent of Man is still remote," he told Pauline Viardot in December 1847, also expressing deep admiration for Feuerbach.[9] He was under the influence of Feuerbach when he wrote to her that in Calderón's Catholic drama, man, in declaring his nothingness, rises to the level of the divinity whose plaything he acknowledges himself to be; yet this same divinity is man's own creation. As for himself, he preferred Prometheus or Satan, the prototype of revolt and individuality: "Mere atom though I am, I am my own master; I want truth and not salvation, . . ." and he expected to attain truth through his own reason, not through grace.[10]

Yet whatever ideal Turgenev proposed was undermined by his profound pessimism. Nature is breathtakingly beautiful but unheeding, and man's place in nature resembles that of the bird, the ant, the butterfly. This does not mean that ephemeral man should not seek generously to give life meaning, but in his novels activity usually ends not with triumph but with a query or an erasure.

Turgenev was in a Brussels hotel when he heard someone shouting on February 26, 1848, that the republic had been proclaimed, and he left for Paris immediately. More than thirty years later, in "The Man in the Grey Spectacles," he told the compelling story of his meetings with a mysteriously percipient Frenchman who turns into a murderous instrument of reaction, somewhat after the pattern of Flaubert's Sénécal. Turgenev maintained that the man really existed, though details (such as those concerning Herzen) have been judged inexact. It is curious that Turgenev had been rereading *L'Éducation sentimentale* with delight at the time he submitted the proofs of his story to Flaubert, urging him to correct, change, or cut whatever he pleased.

Much as he was fascinated by action, Turgenev did not think very highly of the poet Herwegh's ill-fated expedition to promote revolution in the Grand Duchy of Baden in April 1848, a romantic exploit which ended in "complete fiasco." [11] Herwegh should not have undertaken it, or should have got himself killed like his second in command. So much for the poet as unsuccessful revolutionary. By May, Turgenev was living in the same house as Herwegh in Paris. He spent several hours observing the procession of May 15, which ended in an abortive coup d'état, and at one stage went back to fetch Herwegh, who was not at home. After speaking to a number of workers who simply stood about waiting, he found it impossible to determine what the people really wanted or feared, if they were reactionary, revolutionary, or supporters of order. "What is history then? . . . Providence, chance, irony, or fate?" he asked.[12] In his opinion, order and the bourgeoisie had triumphed, with reason, on this occasion.

Turgenev witnessed the beginning of the fighting at the barricades on June 23, but he hastened away as firing began. Years later the novelist recalled a touching incident: A dignified old workman, at the risk of his life, had carried to Herwegh a message that the poet's son was safe in another part of the city. However, "My Mates Sent Me!" published after the Commune, ends by emphasizing the contradiction between the workers of 1848, who showed such consideration for a mere bourgeois, and those of 1871, who ruthlessly shot hostages; "but he who has even a little knowledge of the human heart will not be shocked by these contradictions."[13]

The better he understood his own nature, the more he was fascinated by its antitype—the single-minded, even fanatical and ruthless man of action, however clearly he perceived the limitations of this figure. (He can even be found telling Flaubert of his admiration for Robespierre's qualities.) His important essay on Hamlet and Don Quixote reveals the inner split between his temperament and his ideal. He reads himself into Hamlet and sees Don Quixote as the crusading spirit he would like to be if only he were not so lucid.

Hamlet and Don Quixote are the two opposing aspects of human nature, said Turgenev, and all men belong to one type or the other. They are two ways of conceiving the ideal; the former gives first place to the ego, while the latter proposes something outside the ego. And he added significantly that both aspects may be found at different times in the same man. For Turgenev, Don Quixote represents the self-sacrificing faith of the visionary social reformer: the aim of his quest is the triumph of truth and justice on this earth. The Knight of the Doleful Countenance lives for his fellowmen, to extirpate evil, to combat the forces hostile to man—giants, enchanters, indeed all those who oppress the weak. He is an enthusiast, a fanatic, the servant of an idea, unmoved by doubts, of unshakable will, albeit somewhat narrow as well as absurd.

On the other hand, Hamlet is all egoism, introspection, analysis, doubt, and negation. He does not believe in himself, nor can he find anything in the world to which he can cling with his whole soul. Certainly, when seeking to redress wrongs, Don Quixote often makes things worse, but whoever tries to foresee the possible consequences of his action will never do anything. One thing alone matters: sincere, strong conviction. As for the result of one's efforts, it lies in the hand of fate. One's duty is to take up arms and fight.

A Hamlet is useless to the people. He despises the crowd. It is coarse and dirty, and Hamlet is an aristocrat in spirit as well as a prince by birth. The crowd may at first reject a Don Quixote, but in the end it follows those who do not give up and who eventually make a discovery. A Hamlet discovers nothing and leaves no spiritual legacy. All the same, Hamlet's skepticism is not indifference; though he has no faith in the immediate realization of justice, he fights injustice and becomes one of the principal champions of a truth in which he cannot entirely believe.

The problem for Turgenev is how to keep the destructive power of negation within limits, to tell it what it should destroy and what it should respect. Here lies the tragedy of human nature as he conceives it: both thought and will are essential for action, but the modern divorce between them grows ever more marked. Thus the Hamlets who are endowed with such keen penetration and understanding are condemned by their nature to inaction, while the Don Quixotes are useful to humanity only because they see a single point on the horizon, a point which often does not in reality exist as they see it.

This essay, which betrays so vividly the conflicts and veerings in Turgenev's reflective and irresolute nature, appeared at the moment when his urge to stress the value of action seemed at its maximum intensity. In *Rudin* (1855) he had depicted a fascinating Hamlet-like character who is said to be based on Bakunin but who (apart from impotence, eloquence, and borrowing habits) bears a closer affinity with the author than with the founder of the political anarchist movement. The idealistic Rudin longs to be useful, but he has no firm convictions and his fine words do not result in deeds.

One of the curious aspects of the novel is the way Lezhnev, who was once a fellow student of Rudin's, as Turgenev was of Bakunin's, changes in his response to the dominating figure. He cuts Rudin down to size as shallow, lazy, a sponger, and a *poseur*. Yet later Lezhnev suggests that Rudin, despite failure, has possibly sown the good seed where it may fructify into action. Lezhnev veers from a position of attack to one of defense. But Turgenev was not content with this. In 1860, the year his essay on Hamlet and Don Quixote was published, he added an epilogue to the novel. There Rudin fulfills his own prophecy and sacrifices himself for something he does not believe in, by getting himself killed romantically on the barricades in Paris on June 26, 1848, those very barricades which Turgenev himself had witnessed on June 23 and which he had left under fire. "It was not my business to fight either on one side or the other: I went back home," said Turgenev.[14] Rudin's heroic death looks like a form of belated wish-fulfillment or compensation.

Why does Russia produce failures like Rudin? asks Lezhnev. Why are there no heroic men of action? In 1860, Turgenev published *On the Eve,* whose hero is Rudin's opposite, a young man of inflexible will who has "done things." But Insarov is not Russian; he is a Bulgarian whose cause is not the complex one of initiating reforms at home but the more straightforward one of liberating his land from Turkish occupation. In his sacrifice and dedication, Insarov is held up as a mirror to Russians. It is implied that there are "no real people" in Russia, only little Hamlets.

> "Why is it, Uvar Ivanovich? When is our time coming? When are we going to produce some real people?"
> "Wait a bit," Uvar Ivanovich replied, "they'll come." [15]

And this note of expectation is heard again in the last words of the novel.

Although the character of the Bulgarian revolutionary was based on a person who really existed (Turgenev had learned about him from a neighbor), yet the figure is so romanticized in the novel that it seems unlikely Turgenev could have met anyone of that type. There was something sinister and dangerous in Insarov's expression, we are told, when he impressively subdued the drunken German. "When he picked up that gigantic fellow and threw him into the water like a stone—no, *that* didn't frighten me, but *he* frightened me. And afterwards—how sinister his expression was, almost cruel . . . perhaps you can't be a man and a fighter and still be mild and gentle," Elena confided to her diary.[16] Not for nothing had Turgenev made his literary début with an imitation of Byron's *Manfred*.

As soon as Insarov falls in love with Elena, thus ceasing to be selflessly single-minded, he is doomed. It is surely revealing that Turgenev could not envisage a successful man of action. No less than his Hamlets, his Don Quixotes are cut off in their prime. As he had declared in his essay, the result lies in the hand of fate. Still, as novelist, Turgenev himself was fate, felling Insarov in his mysterious strength or fatally injecting Bazarov with typhus before these strong-willed characters could fulfill their promise.

Between *On the Eve* and his finest book, *Fathers and Sons* (1862), dedicated to his dead friend and mentor Belinsky, came the emancipation of the serfs and a subtle change of tone. As already noted, in *Rudin* the attitude toward the weak hero fluctuates, though in a fairly simple way, moving through fascination and criticism to sympathy; but in *Fathers and Sons* the treatment of the dominating strong-willed protagonist, who begins by arousing distrust and ends by inspiring pity, is far more complex and ambivalent. Bazarov embodies Turgenev's presentiment of the coming new man, a type he developed partly through acquaintance with two matter-of-fact doctors and partly from instinctive awareness of a new trend or mentality that would soon become widespread: nihilism. The nihilist is defined in the novel as one who refuses to submit to authority or to accept any principle on trust, however sacrosanct it may be. Such an attitude, it is assumed, may produce good or evil results, depending on the individual.

When Arkady brings home his friend, the young doctor Bazarov, they confront two members of Turgenev's generation: Arkady's father Nikolay and his uncle Pavel, who hold cultivated, liberal, progressive views. Nikolay Kirsanov (according to Turgenev a portrait of himself) has done everything possible to keep up with the times. His brother Pavel is a man who believes (with Turgenev) that principles are an essential basis for action and that civilization is the chief value. Though portrayed with affection, they are both faintly ridiculous. On the other hand, Bazarov has all the brash rudeness of youth in his contemptuous indifference toward the conditions that shaped the Kirsanov brothers and toward their cherished ideals; he utters a sustained indictment of their ineffectual chatter and inaction, which to his mind betray the vanity of their high-sounding pretensions. The shortcomings as well as the merits of the "fathers" stand revealed in what must surely be accounted a form of ironically oblique self-criticism. It stems from Turgenev's sense of social guilt at having failed to free all his serfs on his mother's death, his feeling that he had taken only half-measures toward their betterment before emancipation.

While Bazarov is not overtly revolutionary in the political sense (though at one stage Turgenev did say "nihilist" meant "revolutionary"), the implications of the young man's criticism of the existing order, with its dishonesty, injustice, superstition, and lack of freedom, are revolutionary—since he blandly aims to deny and destroy everything, including poetry and art, in the name of what is useful. The site must be cleared first: to construct is not his affair. Bazarov disapproves of discussions about parliamentarianism and legal niceties when "it is the bread of subsistence alone that matters." [17] He is not interested in the individual, and believes that moral disorders are the result of irregularities in the social body. Once the social body is correctly organized, there will be no more moral sickness. Whether men are good or evil will become unimportant. He is sufficiently arrogant to regard himself as a god vis-à-vis lesser mortals.

While it is evident that Turgenev's attitude is critical, he is plainly awed and fascinated by Bazarov's single-mindedness. There is surely a hint of liberal self-flagellation as well as of reluctant admiration when Bazarov parts (however sternly and cruelly) from the infatuated Arkady. As a member of the gentry, Arkady is told, he was not meant for the hard, bitter, solitary life of the nihilist fighter, since he lacks the necessary audacity and anger. In Bazarov's eyes, Arkady remains a fastidious, privileged, liberal softie, condemned for well-meaning inadequacy. (Ironically enough, Bazarov himself, though not nobly born, is regarded by the peasants as a member of the privileged class.)

It is not a simple matter to deduce Turgenev's attitude toward Bazarov in the novel because it seems to be modified in midstream, after the young man falls hopelessly in love and mellows somewhat when observed in the setting of his parental home. Certainly there is a tragic sense of waste in the manner of his death. Nor is it possible to determine what the novelist's view was from his own comments, for these are contradictory. He said that he felt for Bazarov "an involuntary attachment" while writing the novel; [18] that he shared all Bazarov's views except those on art (which is manifestly unlikely); that he loved Bazarov and, more convincingly, that he did not know whether he loved the character or not. The editor Mikhail Katkov, who had been Turgenev's fellow student in Berlin, wrote perceptively to the novelist that he seemed not so much to dislike Bazarov as to be afraid of him.

Fathers and Sons aroused heated controversy in Russia. Turgenev lost radical sympathy and did not regain a measure of it until his last years. Old friends whose progressive views he shared began to treat him coldly. Besides, there were now committed revolutionary activists among the writers, like the didactic utilitarian Chernyshevsky, men who despised Turgenev's aesthetic ideas and his shilly-shallying. For the lowly born extremists, upper-class liberals like Turgenev were no better than reactionaries. The novelist was accused of having travestied radical youth and betrayed the radical cause. On the other hand, conservative opponents held him responsible for nihilist outrages or, more embarrassingly, took him to their bosom. He was in the vulnerable position of those who remain true to their own inner divisions, however disconcerting these may be, and who succeed in pleasing scarcely anybody, perhaps least of all themselves.

As a result of his sense of isolation, his pessimism was reinforced. Although some live by the great ideas—democracy, justice, liberty, humanity, art (he wrote between 1862 and 1864 in *Enough!*), nevertheless everything remains the same: "The same gullibility and cruelty, the same urge for blood, for gold, for filth, the same trumpery enjoyments, the same senseless sufferings in the name of . . . in the name of just the same rubbish that Aristophanes laughed to scorn two thousand years ago, the same crude baits for which that oft-trapped animal—the human crowd—will fall just as easily, the same seizures of power, the same habits of servitude, the same kind of lies—in a word, the same busy jumping of the squirrel in the same old wheel. . . ." [19] This was the mood of *Smoke* (1867), which aroused chauvinist ire by satirizing Russian progressives as well as reactionaries: ". . . it all seemed as smoke to him [Litvinov], his own life, Russian life—everything human, especially everything Russian." [20]

The fact that Turgenev lived abroad in Germany and France, with occasional visits home, led to the accusation that he no longer understood the situation in Russia. In *Virgin Soil* (1877) he tried to show how the actions of a group of militant young populists—idealists, hotheads, and blunderers controlled by a distant leader who is thought to represent Nechaev—were bound to end in fiasco. A Hamlet trying to be a Don Quixote, the tragic romantic revolutionary Nezhdanov works for a cause in which he does not really believe, and commits suicide. He and his associates are seen struggling with inadequate means and understanding on behalf of a people that does not want them. They encounter intractable reality in the shape of blind reaction, absurd but genuinely Russian conservatism, hypocritical pseudo-liberalism, or the hostile stupidity of the peasants. This does not mean that the self-sacrificing new woman and the dependable realist will abandon the struggle. Turgenev was torn between desire for change, distaste for those on whose behalf the sacrifice is being made, and qualified esteem for the character of some revolutionary idealists, if not for their methods.

In his own eyes he was an independent moderate, not politically minded at all, or so he had submissively claimed when accused of complicity with the London exiles, with his old companions Herzen and Bakunin. The charge had put him in a panic, and he did not behave well. That he had been exonerated while Chernyshevsky was sent to Siberia did not exactly raise his standing with the radicals. However, this did not prevent him from secretly giving financial support to Russian radicals and revolutionary journals abroad.

Yet he desired gradual change and reforms from above. He could not really believe in a movement of change from below. It was an enlightened constitutional monarchy that he had in mind, one where there would be a free press and individual liberty. There was a point beyond which he did not wish to go, being "on principle opposed to revolutions." [21] Violence and terrorism appalled him, though he is said to have kept on his desk portraits of executed terrorists. While fascinated by revolution, he was afraid of it. He was haunted by the nightmare that one day the peasants would rise and kill all the landowners, whether these had behaved decently or not.

Despite his pessimism and his fears, Turgenev never took refuge in the religion of art, like Flaubert. He never tried to evade the writer's social responsibility, impressed upon him by Belinsky and the formative conditions of his intellectual milieu. But neither did he find any cause that commanded total allegiance; he could perceive only too well "the *white* and the *black*" in all tendencies. He saw the limitations of the young radicals, yearned for their admiration and sometimes curried favor with them; he advanced and he stepped gingerly back; he withdrew and he gave his support. Because he wanted truth, not salvation, he became the very embodiment of the liberal writer's dilemma. His attitude aroused the detestation of the formidable genius who stands opposed to him on almost every count and with whom he is locked in eternal argument.

chapter **13**

*spiritual versus revolutionary
salvation: Dostoevsky*

The proud, difficult, touchy Dostoevsky, who was at first dazzled by Turgenev's charm and talent, published one of the most damaging attacks ever made by one novelist upon another in *The Possessed* (or *The Devils*). There he caricatured his colleague as the "Great Writer" Karmazinov, the affected fellow traveler of revolutionary youth, the rat who would leave the sinking ship in time of revolution. It was not just that Turgenev was more smooth, received higher fees, lent the heavy gambler Dostoevsky money which he could not repay. Their differences were not merely those of temperament but of world-view. For Dostoevsky, Turgenev came to figure as a leading spokesman for those ideals of the intellectuals of the forties that had captivated him in his youth, those dreams for which he had suffered years of mental anguish and physical torment and which experience led him eventually to reject with horror.

Not only Turgenev in his own person, but the liberal historian Granovsky, Herzen, and Belinsky are present in *The Possessed* as the spiritual fathers of monstrous children. Dostoevsky had read Belinsky's work with admiration before the critic welcomed the manuscript of his first novel, *Poor Folk,* with exceptional warmth. No sooner had they met than Belinsky sought to convert Dostoevsky to socialism and atheism. The budding novelist was "initiated by Belinsky into the whole *truth* of that future 'regenerated world' and into the whole *holiness* of the forthcoming communistic society." [1] Belinsky "knew that the revolution must necessarily begin with atheism," wrote Dostoevsky. "He had to dethrone that religion whence the moral foundations of the society rejected by him had sprung up".[2] From what followed, it appears that the critic was successful in winning over the young engineer who had been brought up in traditional piety.

In his youth Dostoevsky was a lofty idealist, exalted by the sublimities of Schiller's Posa and by George Sand's religiose humanitarianism. (He could still speak warmly of "what that name has meant in my life" when he learned of her death.) [3] The son of a dissipated, tyrannical doctor who was castrated and murdered by his own serfs, Dostoevsky, the patriotic reformer, gravitated toward the progressive circle of an official named Petrashevsky. This circle was imbued with the ideas of the French utopian socialists, Saint-Simon and particularly Fourier, whose works the writer borrowed from Petrashevsky's private lending library. At Petrashevsky's he heard much talk of phalansteries, of future world harmony and happiness after the destruction of the existing order, and some incendiary rhetoric.

Tiring of speeches, Dostoevsky wanted action. He joined a more activist-minded group whose members frequented Petrashevsky's gatherings and whose leader was the poet Durov. It included the compelling romantic figure Speshnyov, whom Dostoevsky once referred to as his Mephistopheles and who aimed at violent seizure of power and peasant revolution. On more than one occasion, Dostoevsky read to both circles Belinsky's letter to Gogol attacking religion, a document the authorities regarded as criminal. The members of the Durov circle were planning to set up a clandestine press to propagate their views when the blow fell.

In April 1849 Dostoevsky and his companions were arrested. The government was extremely nervous as a result of the revolutionary upheavals in France and other countries of Western Europe, and reacted with harsh severity. At his interrogation the young novelist behaved with outspoken courage and dignity. "Who has looked into my soul? Who can define the degree of disloyalty, harm and insurrection of which I am accused?" he cried. "Let them prove that I am guilty of desiring changes and upheavals by force, by a revolution, . . ." [4]

His chief crimes were thinking, talking, and studying, he asserted. "What exactly am I accused of? That I talked about politics, the West, the censorship, etc.? But who did not talk or did not think of these questions in our time? . . . In the West terrible events are taking place, an unprecedented drama is being played out there. The century-old order is cracking and collapsing. The most basic principles of society threaten to crash down and carry a whole nation with them in their fall. . . . Am I really to be accused . . . of perhaps considering this crisis as historically necessary in the life of the French people as a transitory phase (who can now say it isn't?) that will bring better times at last? My freethinking about the West and the revolution did not go further than that opinion and these ideas." Reforms would have to be introduced in Russia, or else "the thing will have to be put through in a revolutionary way." [5]

In the eyes of the authorities, even as he insisted on his faith in Russian autocracy, Dostoevsky condemned himself out of his own mouth. He observed that despite its errors socialism was a science in chaos; it was alchemy before the advent of chemistry, "though I cannot help feeling that out of the present chaos something harmonious, sensible and beneficial will eventually emerge for the good of mankind. . . ." [6] This trust in man's future welfare as deriving from socialism was hardly likely to reassure his interrogators. Throughout his life, revolution would be associated in Dostoevsky's mind with French utopian socialism.

There followed one of the most sinister jokes ever conceived by a tyranny. All but two of the accused were sentenced to be shot, but the authorities had no intention of carrying out the death sentences, merely aiming to frighten the prisoners and their sympathizers. Dostoevsky and his companions were led to the scaffold, to be reprieved at the very last moment. One of them went mad. In after years, Dostoevsky sometimes spoke of those terrible moments of waiting for death. He maintained that the condemned would not have renounced their faith and thought of themselves as martyrs. His sentence was commuted to four years' hard labor followed by four years as a soldier in the ranks.

The Siberian prison to which he was taken in chains was a shattering experience for Dostoevsky, already subject to epileptic fits. Apart from physical toil, he had to endure the close proximity of felons and murderers whose suspicion and hatred increased his sense of isolation. Buried alive among bestial criminals in the place he called the "House of the Dead," he observed what human nature was capable of. How different from the optimistic expectations of the French utopian socialists, who thought that they could mold humanity to their rational pattern, that so long as men were shown the good, they would desire it. He became convinced that the evil in mankind is buried deeper than the utopian socialists imagined, that reason has no power over some human beings. Indeed, in the grim and grating mockery of his *Notes from the Underground,* he emphasized that men often prefer risk and difficulty to their own best interests and out of sheer perversity will act against those interests, choosing the harmful rather than the beneficial, the mire rather than the beautiful. Henceforward, for Dostoevsky, pride and willfulness will play a more important role than reason in his assessment of human conduct.

The change that came over Dostoevsky was a very slow and gradual process, extending over many years. While still in the army in Semipalatinsk, he petitioned the influential General Totleben, a former fellow student: "I was guilty, and am very conscious of it. I was convicted of the intention (but only the intention) of acting against the Government; I was lawfully and quite justly condemned; the hard and painful experiences of the ensuing years have sobered me, and altered my views in many respects. But then, while I was still blind, I believed in all the theories and utopias." [7] Afterward, Dostoevsky found it difficult to give an account of the "regeneration" of his convictions which, by an oversimplification, he sometimes attributed to contact with humble people in adversity and to the long-term effects of his pious upbringing. That he went to visit Bakunin as well as Herzen when in London in 1862 would indicate that his views had not yet hardened into the antiliberalism and antirevolutionism of his last period. As late as 1866 he was still urging freedom of speech, even for nihilists.

However, Dostoevsky was in Geneva in September 1867 when the First Congress of the League of Peace and Freedom, attended by Garibaldi and Bakunin, took place. He heard in the flesh some of the celebrated European radicals—republicans, socialists, and anarchists with whose works he was familiar—and he was astounded by "the nonsense these socialists and revolutionaries talked," by their feebleness and mutual contradictions. "They began with the argument that for the achievement of peace on earth one must destroy the Christian faith. . . . And, above all, fire and sword, and after everything has been destroyed, then in their opinion there will be peace." [8] Dostoevsky worried about the influence of such ideas on impressionable minds.

His critique of revolutionism gains immeasurably because he knew the revolutionary ideal from within: he had dreamed its dreams, and had paid dearly and disproportionately for his youthful convictions. Indeed, had he been executed in 1849, he would be remembered today as a minor literary revolutionary. He wrote as one who felt he had been led astray by his finer feelings and aspirations, and he wanted to utter a warning to others.

That is why his novels are not just an ever-pressing reply to Belinsky, Turgenev, and Herzen and to their less sensitive successors, the radicals Chernyshevsky, Dobrolyubov, and Pisarev; they are also a dialogue with a part of himself that acknowledged the fascination of the revolutionary dream. Hence the excitement they generate. Like Coleridge, Dostoevsky disputed the reactionary opinion that revolutionaries must be idlers, idiots, or fanatics; they were often diligent, enthusiastic youths, good but misdirected souls like his younger self. If these idealists wanted to overthrow society, it was in the name of something sublime: magnanimity, love of mankind, universal brotherhood. They were tempted by the very loftiness of the ideal.

Dostoevsky's argument with his early self forms part of the deeper theme of his major novels: the tension between belief and unbelief. He could speak of the force of negation which he experienced in contact with atheistic ideas in the forties. The question of the existence of God, he owned, worried him consciously and unconsciously throughout his life. In November 1854 he wrote to Natalya Fonvisina, the devout wife of a convicted Decembrist: ". . . I am a child of this age, a child of unbelief and doubts to this day and shall be (I know it) to the very day when I am laid in my grave. This longing to believe has cost and still does cost me terrible torments; it is a longing that is all the stronger in my heart the more arguments I have against it." Only belief in the beauty and perfection of the person of Christ gave him some quietude. And he added strangely: "Moreover, if anyone were to prove to me that Christ was outside truth and that truth really was outside Christ, I would still rather remain with Christ than with truth." [9] That claim, reechoed in *The Possessed* in the unfortunate Shatov's impassioned reminder to the mysterious Stavrogin, significantly reverses Turgenev's desire for truth, not salvation.

For Dostoevsky, revolution was intimately linked with religion. Gide was surely not mistaken in seeing a kinship between Dostoevsky and Blake: apocalyptic spirits dominated by the Revelation of St. John, both conceived religion and politics to be interdependent. In Dostoevsky as in Blake, the social, political, and economic aspects of revolution were secondary effects, and its true significance was metaphysical. The cause of revolution lay in the human spirit itself, thought Dostoevsky, in man's rejection of God, not in the world. If only all would follow Christ in true humility, problems of politics and economics would virtually solve themselves.

Where Edmund Burke at the start of the French Revolution had feared that if Christianity were cast aside, "some uncouth, pernicious and degrading superstition" would take its place,[10] Dostoevsky believed that this disaster had indeed occurred but that the superstition in question assumed the attractive shape of an alternative religion. He recalled that some of the founding fathers of French socialism compared their scheme of human betterment to Christianity and regarded it as an improvement on the Christian faith. What was being offered in the vision of ultimate human happiness on earth was a false religion, a false salvation, and Dostoevsky spoke of "this chimerical frenzy, all this gloom and horror which is being prepared for humankind under the guise of regeneration and resurrection." [11]

In this false religion, this Satanic enterprise, man, after dispensing with God, seeks to usurp the place of God. Denying the Savior, man presents himself as a pseudo-savior, often doing so in the name of a compassion greater than Christ's, since he proposes the elimination of human suffering on earth. This notion of man's compassion being greater than that of the divinity was already mooted in Shelley, and in Byron's *Marino Faliero* and *Cain* (which may well have been known to Dostoevsky; though not always enthusiastic about Byron, he once called him a mighty genius and passionate poet). It is the powerfully sincere "unanswerable position" of Ivan Karamazov returning his entrance ticket to God and rejecting the divine order if it requires the suffering of a single child. [12] And it is the standpoint of Ivan's Grand Inquisitor, who condemns the reincarnated Christ in the name of humanity, offering earthly bread or material well-being for all. Dostoevsky regarded the denial of God's creation and its meaning as the great blasphemy of Russian anarchism.

With a prophetic gift whose insights have since been startlingly confirmed, the novelist maintained that the Grand Inquisitor's sincere professions of humanity led to inhumanity, his liberty to despotism, and his equality to slavery. Similarly, the system of world organization proposed by Shigalov in *The Possessed* starts from unlimited freedom and arrives at unlimited despotism. Under Shigalovism, one-tenth of the population will enjoy undisputed power over the remaining nine-tenths. As expounded by one of the characters through Dostoevsky's inimitable ingenuous-seeming irony, Shigalov's theory postulates that the majority "have to give up all individuality and become, so to speak, a herd, and, through boundless submission, will by a series of regenerations attain primeval innocence, something like the Garden of Eden. They'll have to work, however." [13]

Dostoevsky made fun of such constructions in the firm belief that individual responsibility must be supreme. The idea that society was responsible for everything infuriated him. Without belief in individual responsibility, society can be blamed for all ills, and crime thus becomes a form of noble protest. People grow convinced that "Since society is wickedly organized, it is impossible to struggle out of it without a knife in hand." [14] Such a view debases man by denying his moral independence and reduces him to slavery; whereas the Christian faith insists upon man's freedom to choose good or evil, to feel guilt and suffer, to humble himself before God and men and thus discover the spiritual path to rebirth. In recognizing his moral responsibility, man paradoxically finds his real freedom. It is this unendurable burden of freedom of choice that men long to resign to the authority which would give them earthly instead of spiritual bread, and would reduce them to ants in the future universal anthill. People look forward to the future anthill "and meanwhile the world will be stained with blood." [15] Systems of earthly regeneration rooted in Rousseau are a snare and a delusion, since Dostoevsky believed that only in Christ can man find true renewal.

In his penultimate major work of fiction, *The Possessed*—written in Dresden during the Franco-Prussian War and the Commune, when he was overwhelmed by debts and subject to increasingly frequent fits—Dostoevsky created the greatest novel ever penned as a critique of the revolutionary spirit in the name of religious revelation. In the tendentious, satirical treatment of some of the scoundrelly characters involved in Peter Verkhovensky's political intrigue, Dostoevsky was inclined to forget a fact he emphasized elsewhere: that revolutionaries are often high-minded dreamers captivated by sublime-seeming ideas. But (as his sizable notebooks reveal) gradually, after much cogitation, the center of the book shifted from the impudent intriguer Peter Verkhovensky to the Byronic figure of Stavrogin; that is, from political terrorism to metaphysical revolt. Or rather, in Dostoevsky's mind, the two characters and the two elements became intimately connected. Political and spiritual revolt were twin facets of the same phenomenon: the denial of God. He saw the perverse assertion of the individual will as leading either to despotism or to self-destruction, either to the sunless system of Shigalov or the suicide of rootless figures like Kirillov and Stavrogin.

The *donnée* of the novel was a notorious political crime—the murder of a student named Ivanov by Nechaev, leader of the revolutionary cell to which he belonged. Aiming to discourage disobedience and to cement its members by blood, Nechaev lured the recalcitrant Ivanov to a secluded place, strangled and then shot him. With the help of his panicstricken accomplices, he threw the body into a pond, just as Peter Verkhovensky and his dupes dispose of Shatov. Dostoevsky followed the details of the Ivanov case in the newspapers, and in his preliminary notes he refers to Verkhovensky as "Nechaev." He later stressed that his nihilist was not like the actual Nechaev: "still, I believe that my imagination has created that person, that type, which corresponds to the crime." [16] The fact that all the revolutionaries of the sixties did not resemble Nechaev seems beside the point; Nechaev existed, a being who would have many heirs down to our own day.

How was it possible that people like Nechaev were able to recruit followers in modern society? This was the question Dostoevsky tried to answer. In an extraordinary page of *The Diary of a Writer* he confessed that in a sense, as a former member of the Petrashevsky circle, he was once himself a potential terrorist: "probably I could never have become a *Nechaev,* but a follower of Nechaev, I am not certain; it may be that I could have . . . in the days of my youth." [17] In his opinion there existed a direct spiritual link between the idealistic socialists and atheists of the forties and the revolutionary terrorists of the sixties, a connection between noble theory and criminal act which he sensed in the depths of his own being. And for him, the unspoken thought, the intention, or the idea could betoken as much guilt as the actual deed. The "Belinskys and Granovskys would not believe it if you told them that they were the direct fathers of the Nechaevs. It is precisely the close development of this thought, going from fathers to children, that I want to express in my work," he declared. [18]

Turgenev's image of fathers and sons becomes a key metaphor of *The Possessed.* Peter Verkhovensky is the son and Stavrogin the former pupil of the unworldly liberal phrase-monger Stepan Trofimovich, who is modeled on the Westernizer Granovsky. Because he judged Granovsky to be a pure idealist, Dostoevsky could write "I love Stepan Trofimovich and profoundly respect him." [19] A self-deceiver of the first order, who lives for years on the glamor of once having incurred the suspicion of the police, Stepan Trofimovich finally remorsefully recognizes his guilt, and as he does so the reader is made to feel that the devils leave him. To some extent at least he resembles in death the figure of the healed man in St. Luke's parable of the Gadarene swine, to which the book and its title allude.

In the repulsive buffoon Peter Verkhovensky, the novelist depicted the grotesque aspect of the sinister. Stavrogin calls him "my clown," and he calls Stavrogin his better half. Indeed, Verkhovensky appears to be an aspect of Stavrogin, as do both Shatov and Kirillov, and all of them serve as potentialities for Dostoevsky's inner being if carried to an extreme. The character of Verkhovensky, for instance, is constructed on the basis of a desire for immediate action, the impulse which had led Dostoevsky into the Durov circle. The novel is thus a kind of battlefield of the human soul, the soul of mankind as well as that of the writer himself.

Verkhovensky secretly dreams of Stavrogin as the "one magnificent, despotic will," the future savior-dictator whom he surprises with the words, "You are my idol! . . . You are the leader, you are the sun and I am your worm." [20] When society and received values have been cast into disrepute and overthrown by his nihilistic campaign, ruthlessly carried out after the style of the Revolutionary Catechism attributed to Nechaev, the agitator hopes to impose his idol in the person of Stavrogin. Thus Stavrogin, "our Prince," is greeted as a usurper by the doomed, crazed cripple he has made his wife.

What exactly is Stavrogin meant to be? A deliberate enigma. Dostoevsky said he had long wanted to portray this character, whom he found in his own heart. Some have thought Stavrogin was modeled on Speshnyov or Bakunin, but his most evident ancestor is the fascinating, alienated, and frustrated Byronic demonic rebel—the handsome, sardonic perpetrator of a thousand crimes to whom salvation is denied. Indeed, in his notebook Dostoevsky associated him with Byron's Corsair. Stavrogin commits his insufferable inconsequential acts and engages in debauchery à la Sade out of sheer boredom, out of the desire to assert his freedom and test his will to the utmost limit. He shares the Byronic hero's impulse to plunge into the abyss. One of the novel's projected pseudo-saviors, Stavrogin is revealed as a frigid and sterile monster of moral indifference.

Toward the end of his life, Dostoevsky could still speak with deep sympathy about the Russian Byronists Pushkin and Lermontov, and of Byronism as "a great, sacred and necessary" phenomenon in the history of European mankind and possibly of the whole human race.[21] Byronism arose, he said, at a moment of despair and disillusion, when the ideals of the French Revolution failed to turn out as so many had expected: "there has never perhaps been a sadder moment in the history of Western Europe," he declared.[22] This moment was associated in his mind with ideological as well as political bankruptcy, with frustrated gifts and powers and the repressed urge for action on a scale commensurate with those gifts.

In his youth, when a Byronic or Mephistophelean pose was widely fashionable, Dostoevsky had been particularly affected by Lermontov, whom he saw as one of the dominating "demons" of the age, and he responded deeply to Lermontov's Pechorin, the ironically named "hero of our time." Pechorin had been interpreted by Belinsky as "a link in the process of the emergence of the type of revolutionary fighting for new ideals." [23] Inevitably, Dostoevsky came to see Lermontov as embodying the movement of negation. The Byronic element in Stavrogin is thus related to a contemporary political malaise as well as denoting a psychological and spiritual impasse, though the latter appears more evident in the development of the character.

Originally planned as the protagonist of a novel concerning modern man's quest for God (entitled *Atheism,* or *The Life of a Great Sinner*), "our Prince" was to be "alternately an atheist and a believer, a fanatic and sectist and then again an atheist." [24] Something of this intention is left in Stavrogin's relations with Shatov and Kirillov: we learn that he formerly converted Shatov, once Stepan Trofimovich's student and a convinced socialist, to faith in Russia's sacred redemptive world mission (that is, to Dostoevsky's mystic messianic nationalism); yet at virtually the same time he was guiding the crazed engineer Kirillov toward atheism.

Kirillov is perhaps the most impressive of Dostoevsky's presumptuous pseudo-saviors. He dreams of the man-god, the "new man" who will conquer pain and fear, and thus become a god:

> "Then there will be a new life, a new man; everything will be new . . . then they will divide history into two parts: from the gorilla to the annihilation of God, and from the annihilation of God to . . ."
>
> "To the gorilla?"
>
> ". . . To the transformation of the earth and of man physically." [25]

Kirillov, like his twentieth-century descendants, lays great emphasis on this physical transformation of man, because he believes that man in his present physical state cannot do without God. Yet he does not believe in God. Foreshadowing modern man's urge to self-deification, he proposes himself as the new blasphemous savior whose self-inflicted death "will save mankind and will recreate the next generation physically," that is, will open the path to earthly resurrection. Kirillov, in his mad logic, represents self-will carried to the point of the usurpation of God's throne, the quest for a deceptive freedom that can only end in self-destruction. Insane as he is, it cannot be said that he violates certain enduring anarchic tendencies in modern thought and art.

While condemning the false perspectives of unlimited freedom, renewal, and salvation temptingly offered to modern man, Dostoevsky himself became trapped in a form of messianic nationalism which was supposedly to save the world and was no less hollow than the revolutionary salvationist positions he attacked and ridiculed. But what concerns us here is not the anti-Semite adapting to Russian ends the spiritual concept of the chosen people, nor the defender of the therapeutic effects of war, the aggressive expansionist, the man Turgenev could call "the most vicious Christian" he had ever known.[26] It is the writer who, by penetrating into his own yearnings and inner conflicts, discovered that the spirit of revolution can also lie within.

A founding father of the modern literature of existential anxiety and absurdity pursued by the revolution-haunted Malraux, Sartre, and Camus, the author of *Crime and Punishment* in his maturity strove against the modern revolutionary current. A psychologist who, in his understanding of the power drive, not only anticipated Nietzsche but foresaw the procedures and the society of the Bolsheviks, he regarded the revolutionary urge as the gravest malady of the age—a disease with which he himself had been infected. However strange his particular form of religion may appear, he seeks to present the salvation of the soul in constant battle with the earthly salvation claimed by the spirit of revolution. To whom the victory? He knew which side he prayed for, but he did not say who would win. The responsibility of choice and decision, he insisted, lay with man himself.

part *4*

*the phase of aesthetic
nihilism*

It is only strong passions which can produce great men . . . are not laws dangerous which inhibit the passions? Compare the centuries of anarchy with those of the strongest legalism in any country you like and you will see that it is only when the laws are silent that the greatest actions appear.

DE SADE

Elegance, science, violence! . . . Here is the age of the ASSASSINS.

RIMBAUD

The magic spell that fights for us, the eye of Venus that ensnares and blinds our opponents themselves—it is the spell of the extreme, the seduction exerted by every extreme.

NIETZSCHE

I cannot find harsh enough words to reproach those who try to prove something with bullets, bayonets, or a fist in the face.

GORKY

. . . the aim must be the total ruin of the caste to which we belong despite ourselves, and we shall only be able to work to abolish it outside us when we have succeeded in abolishing it within us.

ANDRÉ BRETON

chapter 14

literary decadence and revolutionary anarchism

"Oh, for excess, for crime!" sighed the Francophile Irish novelist George Moore, weaned from Christianity by Shelley. How he longed in sated weariness to watch gladiators in combat: "to hold the thumb down, to see the blood flow, to fill the languid hours with the agonies of poisoned slaves!" [1] A gift to parodists, this fondness for Roman decadence nonetheless betokens a deep psychological malaise which has subtly left its imprint on modern sensibility. The last decades of the nineteenth century witnessed in Europe a recrudescence of such frenetic romanticism. The aesthetic of "decadence" (a label poets adopted with perverse pride) often mingled with Satanic metaphysical revolt and sympathy with political anarchism, which was then at the peak of its notoriety through widespread bomb

outrages and assassinations fostered by the terrorist policy of propaganda by the deed.

The world of the rebellious artist, defying the conventions of bourgeois society and the ordering of the cosmos, merged in imagination with that of the outlaw warring with society—the criminal or the terrorist who in some instances were one and the same. Hypertrophy of the ego, the cult of destructive Satanism, the reversal of values, the pretension to deify man could be found not only in poets but in a number of anarchist terrorists. If, as Stendhal had proposed, living meant the experience of strong sensations, then the manner in which strong sensations were achieved became immaterial. Together with complacent sadistic satisfaction in barbaric rites and bloodshed, in exquisite refinements of torture, perverse eroticism, and violent crime, there existed among writers and artists a climate of dread and expectation of earth-shattering change, an apocalyptic sense of the imminent death and birth of worlds. Traces of the apocalyptic system of Joachim di Fiore have been found in French decadent literature.

In an atmosphere of imaginative Neronic excess, crime had acquired aesthetic possibilities and overtones: George Moore could even say he was prepared to sacrifice many lives to save one sonnet by Baudelaire, and this strained aestheticism was not just pose but a sign of deadening sensibility. Crime (like art) could be a way of reshaping the universe according to human logic and human desires. Dostoevsky, who derived in part from the frenzied romanticism of the eighteen-thirties and who in his turn influenced *fin de siècle* literature, proved how farseeing he was when he created Raskolnikov, the poor student who commits the aesthetic crime. In theory Raskolnikov intends to rid society of an old woman, a wretched pawnbroker whom he considers no better than vermin. In reality he is impelled by the urge to conduct an experiment, to discover whether he is indeed an exceptional Napoleonic being with a right to act above the laws, ostensibly in the service of humanity. Violence and murder appear in this way as a dare, an essential test, trial, or initiation rite for those who secretly seek power.

As for Kirillov, who yearns to enthrone man, physically transformed, as God and who appears to some as a mere figment of Dostoevsky's tortured imagination, he grew from the novelist's profound understanding of anarchist metaphysical revolt, from Sade to Bakunin. Sade combined advocacy of political anarchy with vengeful rage at the injustice and evil of the divine order. And the activist Bakunin, reversing Voltaire's dictum, declared that if God existed he would have to be destroyed.

It was the anarchists, including the gentle optimist Kropotkin, who took as their slogan Blanqui's cry, "Neither God nor Master!" At the very time that Dostoevsky was writing *The Possessed,* in the revolutionary clubs in Paris people were shouting their hatred of God and were absurdly proclaiming their Titanic longing to scale the heavens and stab God to death. The libertarian Swinburne, disciple of Sade, Blake, and Shelley, had written of the deity in hypnotic cadences:

> Him would I reach, him smite, him desecrate,
> Pierce the cold lips of God with human breath,
> And mix his immortality with death.[2]

Rimbaud, a mere schoolboy, with his wild anarchical antagonism to all forms of religious, political, legal, moral and family constraint, scrawled *"Merde à Dieu"* on the walls of Charleville. Less is known about Isidore Ducasse, self-styled Count of Lautréamont, admirer of Shelley and Byron—was he murdered at twenty-four as a social revolutionary? But he made his mouthpiece, Maldoror, attack and vie with that "wily bandit," God, and give lessons on how to win fame by a program of theft, assassination, and wading in blood.[3] Rimbaud and Lautréamont would be crowned saints and martyrs by the Surrealists, and would remain until today among the major cult figures of modern art and literature.

Of French descent, the aristocratic republican Swinburne was not so fortunate in his admirers and failed to achieve such legendary status. But before he dwindled into suburban respectability under the protective wing of Watts-Dunton, he had succeeded in thoroughly shocking his

Victorian contemporaries. He enjoyed the reputation of the most wickedly daring English poetic revolutionary of the age. It was he who expressed those very tendencies which Dostoevsky came to stigmatize as the greatest evils of atheist anarchism. For Swinburne not only proposed that man's compassion is greater than that of a cruel deity who made all creatures subject to time and suffering—"The supreme evil, God." [4] He also proposed to substitute man for God.

United in Swinburne are Promethean revolt against divine injustice, the romantically decadent aesthetic-erotic pleasure in the infliction and experience of pain, together with strong republican and anarchist sympathies (as an undergraduate he approved of Orsini's attempted assassination of Napoleon III and some twenty years later signed a petition to the French president on behalf of the imprisoned Kropotkin). These elements are basically aspects of the same phenomenon expounded by Sade: God is unjust, therefore man may imitate divine injustice (while bemoaning it) and demand unlimited freedom in all spheres—moral, sexual, and political. As Swinburne paraphrased Sade's view of the natural order: Nature wishes man to do evil, "that she might create a world of new things . . . ; she would fain create afresh, and cannot, except it be by destroying: . . . And what are the worst sins we can do—we who live for a day and die in a night? a few murders, . . ." [5] In this light, crimes committed by transient humans are therefore small stuff in comparison with those committed by the system (however defined). It is an argument which would be frequently used by anarchist terrorists.

Swinburne found a close parallel between the cold perverse logic of Sade and the visionary paradoxes of Blake, who (with Shelley) struck him as a noble precursor in the sphere of unbounded freedom from the moral laws. Those aspects of Blake which share the ambiguity common to mystics of a certain type were clarified by Swinburne, who seized on them for his own ends with undisguised delight. Thus he interpreted Blake's conception of "the Divine Humanity" as meaning no salvation outside man: " 'God is no more than man; *because* man is no less than God': there is Blake's Pantheistic Iliad in a nutshell." [6] The essence of Blake's belief, Swinburne maintained, was "not the assumed humanity of God, but the achieved divinity of Man." [7] Man through self-perfection makes himself God.

This theme runs through Swinburne's *Songs Before Sunrise,* poems presaging revolution and dedicated to the Italian patriot Mazzini. His poem "The Eve of Revolution," invoking "Swift Revolution," concludes with the hope of heaven reconquered, and man seated there. In another poem, the People—depicted (after Mazzini) as suffering Christ, with "labour-wounded," nail-pierced hands and feet—is urged to rise up as a republican savior whose gift of freedom must be independent of "that rotting tree," Christianity. [8] The poet sings of revolutionary resurrection as he constructs his incantatory blasphemies: "Glory to Man in the highest; for Man is the master of things," he cries. [9] And in "To Walt Whitman in America" he writes:

> The earth-god Freedom, the lonely
>   Face lightening, the footprint unshod,
> Not as one man crucified only,
>   Nor scourged with but one life's rod;
> The soul that is substance of nations,
> Reincarnate with fresh generations;
>   The great god Man, which is God. [10]

It is not the individual man but the essence of humanity in general which is God.

Some regard Swinburne's political poems as simply the logical outcome of his early libertarian sympathies. However, it has been suggested that his friends arranged for the German revolutionary exile Karl Blind to introduce him to Mazzini—an occasion Swinburne later called "the highest honour and purest happiness of my whole life" [11]—in order that the poet might sublimate in the Risorgimento his singular obsession with flagellation. His beautiful vision of freedom and regeneration certainly has something in common with his concept of lovely, pleasurable pain. Both are seen as imperious females beneath whose feet he is content to lie; and the republican spirit is also invited not to spare the rod:

Ay, with red cautery and a burning brand
Purge thou the leprous leaven of the land; . . .
. . . Smite, we will shrink not; strike, we will not weep;
Let the heart feel thee; let thy wound go deep; . . . [12]

In the final apocalyptic apotheosis, it is not God's name that will be one, but Man's. Yet as the poet expresses it in his epilogue through the superb image of the lone swimmer, if there is to be no mighty sunrise of universal boundless freedom and redemption, then he would prefer to see the world itself destroyed. It must be all or nothing.

Rather like Swinburne, Rimbaud seems to have hoped to bring about a new era, a new wisdom, the end of superstition, "Christmas on earth" through the magic power of the poetic word. In Rimbaud's brief poetic trajectory from imitation of Victor Hugo to mutism as a trader in Abyssinia, Christ appears as the thief of human energies. Man, scorning all the yokes of the past imposed upon him, will be resurrected, free of all his gods. Besides, "Man is god." [13] With Swinburne, Rimbaud prefers the free sensuality of paganism, but in the hallucinatory visions of the truculent prodigy there was perhaps an even more intense, exasperated effort to storm the heavens that ends inevitably in frustration. The silence of Harrar was more complete than that of The Pines.

Rimbaud's moments of tenderness were reserved for the exploited victims of church and state. However, the great new age which would see the removal of exploitation, the establishment of a simple life and reign of love, could be ushered in only by violence and guarded by guns. Robespierre, Saint-Just, the young await you, he wrote while still at school. Greatness can be experienced in Terror. There is to be no question of reform in his poem where the revolutionary blacksmith addresses Louis XVI, telling the king that the workers will no longer be duped by such bourgeois subterfuge. Eventually man shall be victorious and tame everything to his will. Although the myth that Rimbaud fought for the Commune has been exploded, all his sympathies lay with the Communards.

The victors' savage repression of the vanquished inspired a wild anarchist cry for vengeance and blood, terror and destruction.

As a child, Rimbaud admitted in *A Season in Hell,* he admired the incorrigible convict, the hardened criminal who "had more strength than a saint." [14] For the poet, crime was even proposed as a source of metaphysical discovery. In his much-quoted letter describing how the poet can make himself a seer through the derangement of all his senses, Rimbaud included in his recipe the ingredient of criminality as well as that of sickness: the poet also becomes "the great criminal." Crime may be one stage on the path to experience of the unknown. The visionary experience is considered to be worth any price, including madness. Here the metaphysical ambition and hubris of the poet embrace (in imagination at least) the experience of the criminal, just as the ambition of the revolutionary terrorist embraces it in reality. With Rimbaud, poetry has become potentially a form of terror, a disruptive and explosive force, an attempt to blast through all barriers, within and without.

Did Rimbaud, in his role of demonic bridegroom, possess any secrets that would "change life"? [15] Through the reply of the infatuated bride he denied it, suggesting rather that he was in quest of such secrets. The method for bringing about the psychological revolution of which he dreamed might lie beyond good and evil; it could be destructive and self-destructive, but that would not deter those poets, from the Symbolists onward, for whom Rimbaud with his violent yearnings had become precursor, model, and guide.

Rimbaud sang the union of grace and violence, aestheticism and destructiveness, and prophetically announced the advent of "the age of the ASSASSINS." [16] During the period of his stormy liaison with Verlaine, the two poets associated with exiled Communards in London. Verlaine had warmly supported the Commune. Like Rimbaud, he wanted a bloody revenge and yearned for action, readily accepting the idea that a new life and a new society might have to be won by force of arms.

The climate of violence after the atrocities committed by both sides in 1871 was such that few escaped being affected by it, even those who did not form part of "decadent" artistic circles. Victor Hugo, then aged sixty-eight, succumbed to it. Returning to Paris in triumph from his island exile, he expected to be made head of government, even dictator. With his apocalyptic imagination, obsessed by dark and light, he had brooded repeatedly on the Terror of 1793. Where once he regarded it as a stain on the revolutionary ideal, he came to justify the Terror as the inevitable consequence of the evils of the old regime. The savage reprisals carried out against the workers and their families by the victors during "Bloody Week" 1871 (he learned the details from refugees whom he sheltered in his Luxembourg home) shattered him. As a result, he now interpreted revolutionary terror, whether of the Convention or the recent Commune, in the light of the vengeful acts of the enemies of change.

The great humanitarian opponent of the death penalty urged that the defeated Communards should not be executed. Theirs were "the crimes of the dawn," he told the judges in a poem entitled "The Revolution on Trial." It seemed to him that in such extraordinary times of crisis traversed by the Convention of 1793 and the Commune of 1871, actions are inevitably complex and ambivalent; therefore, the grim deeds of revolutionaries should not be judged as if they were ordinary crimes. The pregnant revolutionary crisis suspends the moral law.

In Hugo's novel about the French Revolution, *Quatre-vingt-treize,* published in 1874, Cimourdain, the austere emissary of the Convention, a sort of mature Saint-Just, confronts his adored protégé Gauvain, the sublime revolutionary idealist whom he has had to condemn to the guillotine. Gauvain declares with exaltation: "What the revolution does at this moment is mysterious. Behind the visible work is the invisible work. One conceals the other. The visible work is savage, the invisible sublime. . . . Beneath a scaffolding of barbarism a temple of civilization is being built." [17] This is an excuse for the necessity of present barbarism in the name of a future that has to be taken on trust.

Gauvain "absolves" the present with all its bloodshed, including his own approaching execution: "Because it is a storm. A storm always knows what it is doing. As against one blasted oak, numberless forests are purified! Civilization was in the grip of plague; this gale comes to the rescue.

Perhaps it is not selective enough. Can it act otherwise? It is entrusted with the arduous task of sweeping away disease! In face of the horrible infection, I understand the fury of the blast." [18] Gauvain goes to his death sustained by the dream that one day man will be free of the yoke and "transfigured"—no longer a grub but a lovely butterfly. His harangue spells out in passionate prose the meaning of Shelley's poetic storm-image of purification and transformation through destruction.

The same idea would later enjoy the immense prestige given it by Nietzsche, who repeatedly affirmed that destruction was necessary for creation, and particularly for the birth of his Higher Man. The Nietzschean Superman would stand in the same relation to man as man to beast. But for Nietzsche there were two aspects of the desire for destruction and change: one positive and fruitful, the other negative and unproductive, the result of mere hatred. It seemed to him that the negative type could be found among the anarchists. However, the influence of Nietzsche would not be felt in French and English literature before the eighteen-nineties.

In the eighteen-eighties and -nineties the bond between literature, art, and political anarchism became marked. An entire literary generation was impregnated with anarchist thought. When novelists wrote about revolution, they usually meant conspiracy, terror, and revolutionary anarchism. Political anarchism provided the social philosophy of the Decadent movement, the forerunner of Symbolism and Dada. Libertinarianism in all fields—religion, morality, art—was accompanied by an urge for violence and destruction. In a society where everything was disintegrating, the mission of the Decadents was not to lay new foundations, it was to destroy, proclaimed *Le Décadent* in April 1886.

It comes as no surprise that writers and artists were fascinated by the numerous bomb-throwing episodes which grew in intensity in the eighteen-nineties. The Symbolist writer Paul Adam, who was associated with a literary circle interested in the occult and who favored novelistic scenes of barbaric gore and suffering, regarded Ravachol as a saint (thus continuing the parallel between saint and criminal envisaged by Rimbaud). Perhaps the most haunting and enigmatic of exponents of propaganda by the deed, Ravachol committed a series of vicious murders for money before taking to bomb-throwing, and was canonized as an anarchist martyr after his execution. He was greeted by Paul Adam as a kind of savior who renewed the ritual of necessary sacrifice. Another paradoxically viewed Ravachol as a violent Christ, possibly blending the stern avenger of the Last Judgment with the self-sacrificing redeemer. For the novelist Octave Mirbeau, author of *The Garden of Tortures,* with its decadent eroticism, Ravachol symbolized the storm before the dawn. In this novel, a woman inquires: ". . . in the act of love, for instance, have you never thought of committing a splendid crime? That is, to raise your self above all social prejudices and all laws, indeed, above everything?" [19]

Perhaps the most celebrated of French Decadent poets associated (like Paul Adam) with occultism and political anarchism was Laurent Tailhade, who invented the well-known line suggesting preference for the beautiful gesture rather than for human beings. It was Tailhade (later wounded in an anarchist explosion in a restaurant) who welcomed as a beautiful gesture the bomb thrown in the Chamber of Deputies by the bohemian anarchist Vaillant.

What drew the writers of this period to the deeds of these "saints," as Swinburne's friend Mallarmé called them? (Mallarmé was one poet among many who subscribed and contributed to anarchist journals.) The demand for total freedom from constraint, uttered by Friedrich Schlegel, led in a straight line to this point, as did the yearning for the full realization of all potentialities which, it will be remembered, was voiced by Schiller. The artist recognized the criminal or the revolutionary anarchist-terrorist as the romantic individual rebel who set himself proudly and defiantly against, above, and beyond the laws and who embodied one of the possibilities of which the artist and particularly the poet dreamed: that of going to the limit of his being, regardless of the consequences.

The revolutionary terrorist committed the supreme act of human will and human power in killing indiscriminately, in the belief that there are no innocent people in a corrupt society and that there must be a clean sweep before the pure white world of redemption can appear. His "gesture" was "beautiful" because many artists had become accustomed to finding erotic stimulus and beauty in bloodshed and savagery, in the sick, the diseased, the sinister, the agonized. Above all, in death, in his heroic self-sacrifice, the revolutionary terrorist figured as violent redeemer, a paradoxical notion that greatly appealed to the Satanist rebel. Nor, apparently, did Decadent apologists for revolutionary terrorism (any more than their heirs) find a contradiction between the high-sounding humanitarian pretensions of the violent activist and the consequences of his blood-stained deed. Just as they did not seem to perceive any contradiction between their own ideal of a better life for the suffering poor and their aesthetic gloating over human suffering and violence in their works.

The supreme anarchist aesthete of the *fin de siècle* was Maurice Barrès, whose brilliant, destructive nihilist début, with its rejection of the past and of the poison of the dead, became overshadowed by his later nationalist role as patriotic high priest of the cult of the dead and of roots. In the trilogy of didactic novels entitled *The Cult of the Ego,* he united a strain of decadent eroticism with a résumé of attitudes of anarchic romantic revolt. The immense influence of his works, which was out of all proportion to their novelistic merit, doubtless derived as much from his rich fusion of French, English, and German romantic tendencies as from the charm and the ironic elegance of his manner. Indeed, his influence as spiritual director extended far beyond his contemporaries to the threshold of the present day.

At eighteen, the dazzling young dandy from Lorraine, molded by the French defeat of 1870, was (as he put it) gorged with the most daring paradoxes of human thought. In a world where everything—morality, religion, the sense of nationhood—has crumbled, the ego is the sole reality, wrote Barrès, after Fichte. (He would deny close acquaintance with the tortuous writings of the egocentric anarchist philosopher Stirner, which became widely known in the last years of the century.) But like many of his romantic predecessors, Barrès was obsessed with the relationship between the individual and society. The Barrésian hero, pure in his lofty solitude, leans out of his tower to see the feared and despised "barbarians," who are hostile to his ego, swarming below. Although his sole obligation is to cultivate his own ego, he nonetheless feels at times the need for someone or something outside himself: "You alone, master, if you exist somewhere, be you principle, religion or prince of men." [20]

What Barrès meant by the cultivation of the ego was once described as the anarchism of millionaires. Indeed, he himself admitted that his "free man" required a private income. "Deeds do not count: the only thing that matters is my inner *self!* the God I construct," he wrote in *Un Homme libre.* "I give birth to all the possibilities struggling within me." [21] The Barrésian "free man" perceives that he would "become God" if only he could be granted unlimited time to pursue all the potentialities and the experiences that occur to his imagination. Here is the full expression of that development envisaged and dreaded by Dostoevsky: that if God is denied, then everything is allowed. The "free man" of Barrès, in his pursuit of authenticity and a life lived in conformity with his spontaneous instincts, drives toward domination and godhead—no matter how studied the irony with which he tries to forestall criticism.

Barrès felt a nostalgia for action, energy, heroism in order to assert his will. He dreamed of risking his life generously, regardless of the goal, but it never came to that. (Instead he inspired others to risk theirs.) In an essay of 1891 he tried to resolve the dilemma of thought and action. Since only the ego exists, the external world is a vulgar illusion: therefore one cannot act upon the world but only upon one's own ego. As his hero Sturel, in *Les Déracinés,* would define this view in a celebrated phrase: "To act is to annex to our thought wider fields of experience." [22] However, all the goals suggested for one's activity are stupid and pointless; one must remain fully aware of this fact while pursuing them. Can men of thought prove useful in the sphere of action? Significantly, Barrès turns to Keats for assistance. And he concludes that, in the state of anarchy free from antiquated notions of duty and obligations of belief in some kind of system, man can be guided to help his fellows only through love. Here is enunciated that Barrésian romanticism of generous heroic action that he himself could not put into practice, but which would govern the dreams and the acts of his disciples, like Malraux and Drieu la Rochelle.

The extreme formulation of Barrès's aristocratic anarchism lies in his didactic novel, *L'Ennemi des lois* (1892). A bomb outrage has occurred. At his trial a young anarchist lecturer, André Maltère, is accused of urging revolution in an article. "Urge revolution!" he cries. "It sweeps us along like wisps of straw!" [23] The force of revolution is always present in different forms: its eruptions are manifestations of the future in embryo. His desire to question established moral principles André Maltère sees less as an intellectual process than as an instinct of revolt which brings about an unceasing necessary revolution in the world. "I am guilty of wanting the free development of all my faculties and of giving the verb 'to exist' its complete meaning. As a man, and a free man, may I fulfill my destiny, heed and encourage my inner impetus, without regard to anything external!" [24] And, admitting that he wishes to destroy everything as it then exists, André Maltère does not know exactly what would replace the established order. He compares his dilemma to that of the man whose shoes are too tight and who only knows he must take them off.

André's views are not taken seriously in political circles because he adheres to no political doctrine. Without seeking violent change, he desires the reshaping of the social order. If only each individual would repudiate those aspects of contemporary society that wound his sensibility, the whole world would be "transformed." Still, André clearly envisages this forthcoming transformation as the work of an elite. The dominant role of Lassalle and Marx in the approaching psychological revolution is recognized, but their emphasis on economic revolution is distasteful. There must be something more inspiring.

A full stomach, in André's view, has nothing to do with interior perfection. As he frankly admits, "Those of us who never lacked the necessities of life, require something more than that human beings should not die of starvation. Once material needs are satisfied, our sensibility still has to be given the spiritual satisfactions it demands." [25] For André, the economic reforms of the German socialists, while necessary, are secondary: he demands nothing less than a complete change of mental outlook. All members of society, not just the working class, should be the object of concern. He admits the value of Marxist criticism, but rejects all systems and laws imposed upon the individual. His intention is to keep the criticism but not the plans of the reformers.

Barrès himself became afraid of the consequences of so negative a stance. Previously, even in his most egocentric works, he had suggested the connection between the individual and his "race," and had already envisaged politics as fuel for his sensibility. He grew to see the masses less as "barbarians" than as representing creative energy, the unconscious, the secret springs of spontaneity at which he longed to refresh himself. Above all, he yearned to join with something that would survive him.

Winning votes as a supporter of the would-be man of destiny, General Boulanger, after the Boulangist fiasco he progressed to nationalism combined with socialism (which he understood as the material betterment of the poorest and most numerous class). His nationalism predisposed him to belief in the guilt of the unprepossessing Dreyfus, which he deduced from his "race." In his account of how Dreyfus was publicly stripped of military rank, Barrès recalled his own deep fellow-feeling when he saw the fanatical anarchist intellectual Émile Henry (who had thrown a bomb into a station café and regretted he had not killed more victims) being dragged to the guillotine; whereas he felt nothing for Dreyfus, who was desperately protesting his innocence, and suggested the Judas should hang himself. But then Barrès could hardly resist the romantic association of the Byronic bandit-criminal with generous self-sacrifice.

Aesthetic anarchism of the Barrésian type left artists singularly open and available. Each individual has to discover his own personal truth, without intermediaries, without masters, without conventions of any sort. Each one must find his own moral law and idea of happiness. Barrès himself took refuge in the narrow nationalist mystique of the land, the dead, and roots. But those who imbibed his spiritual directives could move in any direction: toward religion or withdrawal, or, if they followed Barrès's own radical expectancy, toward socialism or nationalism of varying types. What Barrès taught was that the cause itself was subordinate to noble self-realization, and that political commitment and action could be desirable forms of self-fulfillment. It was a lesson that would not be lost on writers in the coming era of conflict between radical ideologies.

chapter *15*

*from Prometheus to
the hooligan*

*As the nineteenth century yielded to the twentieth, voices converged from all direc-*tions to blend in a great cry: the old world must be destroyed. Not only the followers of Marx and Bakunin but apolitical aesthetes were united in despising the society they lived in and yearning for its end. Huysmans's narcissistic exquisite, Des Esseintes, who regarded politics as a base diversion for the mediocre, was moved by indignation at universal ignominy to exclaim, "Well, crumble then, society! perish, old world!" [1] It was said at the time that there was nothing left for the author of *À Rebours* but a bullet or the Church. Huysmans chose the Church. Equally horrified by total nothingness, some of his heirs would choose suicide, while others (among them the Surrealist pope, André Breton) would find temporary or permanent refuge in a church of another color. Meanwhile aristocrats and lowborn but aristocratic souls, plebeians, bourgeois writers and intellectuals frequently agreed on one thing: the despicable bourgeoisie and the materialistic, ugly, soul-destroying world it had engendered and ruled must go. The bourgeoisie was no longer a collection of individual human beings, endowed with the usual mixture of faults and virtues, but an abstract entity signifying criminal responsibility.

There must be not only a new world, but a totally new kind of ethic, a new life, and a new physically and morally "transformed" man to live it. If a number of poets, envisaging man as God's rival, as another Prometheus or atheist savior, were agreed on this, so were philosophers like Renan who expected such a transformation to be brought about by science. The young Marx even saw man as his own creator, and (after Schiller) conceived of man-the-artist, the fully harmonious being. For Marx thought that communism would resolve all conflicts "between man and nature and between man and man; . . . between existence and essence, objectification and self-affirmation, freedom and necessity, individual and species." [2] Engels believed that by a revolution man would leap from the realm of necessity to that of liberty. For Nietzsche, it was by self-overcoming that his Superman would be born; the Nietzschean new being would be the magnificent blond beast, greedily prowling after prey and victory. Each in his different way was expecting the new man, whether member of the collectivity or of the elite, to be not only distinct from the old but vastly superior. What happened was something tragically different from their dreams.

With the collapse of the old values came bold revision and reversal. An idiosyncratic self-taught thinker like Georges Sorel, who believed that the general attitude to violence was modified after 1871, would distinguish between bourgeois force and proletarian violence. He could declare that the latter was not barbaric, as the bourgeois establishment liked to believe. On the contrary—shades of Stendhal!—it was a means of recovering energy lost through soft humanitarianism. It was fine and heroic. Though the reverse of a man of action, Sorel (who influenced writers on the radical Left and Right) shared with the anarchist propagandists-by-the-deed a belief in the renovating and purifying effect of violence. For him the myth of revolution, satirized by Flaubert, was a potent force to be utilized. His views, deriving in part from Proudhon, Marx, and Nietzsche, contributed to form a climate where violence or destruction could be seen as something positive, necessary, noble, creative, revitalizing.

However, not everyone was swept along by this current. Some resisted it, with aesthetic or compassionate arguments, on philosophical or temperamental grounds.

What seems to have struck some major novelists with particular force between 1880 and 1914 was the way in which the potential victims of the new destroyers were actually collaborating in their own approaching ruin. Henry James, for instance, in his novel *The Princess Casamassima,* showed the charitable Lady Aurora being informed by the objects of her kindness that despite her good deeds on behalf of the poor she will not be "let off" in the inevitable forthcoming cataclysm. Instead of being put out, Lady Aurora is gratified at "seeing her friends at last as free and familiar as she wished them to be." [3] As for the Princess Casamassima herself, she is fascinated by the glamorous idea of an all-pervasive underground conspiracy about which she imagines she knows far more than she does. She sees English society "before we blow it up" as resembling the old regime before the whirlwind of the French Revolution, or the Roman decadence when men were living in expectation of the coming of the barbarians. "You and I are the barbarians, you know," she tells the pathetic hero, Hyacinth Robinson. [4]

It looks as if Henry James gave the princess his own passionate disgust with the misery, vice, and squalor of London as he himself directly observed them in the first year of his stay, when he walked through the city's streets. But clearly this was only one pole to which his reactions tended.

The other pole was his sense of the beauty and value of the life and civilization to be destroyed. What would happen, he wondered, if someone had sworn a solemn vow to destroy existing society and had then suddenly become aware of the values that would be cast down? So the novelist created the none-too-convincing conflict in Hyacinth, a sensitive young working-class orphan whose plebeian French mother had murdered his father, an English nobleman, and whose heredity and situation therefore inclined him to be torn between his rash anarchist revolutionary vow and the beauty of the life to which he had been introduced when the capricious princess took him up. The aesthetic argument triumphs when Hyacinth nobly prefers to sacrifice himself rather than others. And it is this aesthetic argument, rather than the deliberately vague anarchist conspiracy, which predominates in the book that Henry James may have seen as his bid to rival such works as *L'Éducation sentimentale* and *Virgin Soil,* by authors he admired and knew personally.

With Joseph Conrad, another outsider who had walked alone through the London streets like James, it was not just ironical disapproval but sheer contempt and disgust for those members of the upper class or the educated elite who sympathized with and abetted anarchist revolutionaries. Conrad knew that Edward Garnett and his wife Constance, the translator of Tolstoy and Dostoevsky, were on friendly terms with Kropotkin and other revolutionary refugees. Through Ford Madox Ford he was aware of the involvement of Ford's aunt and cousins, the Rossettis, with anarchism. In *The Secret Agent* Conrad satirized the great "lady patroness" who graciously receives the celebrated anarchist apostle, Michaelis, in her salon. The social intercourse of this ill-assorted pair forms part of the great misunderstanding which culminates in the grotesque scene of cross-purposes between Winnie Verloc and her vain, lazy, murderous husband, the *agent provocateur* whom she murders. In *The Secret Agent* Conrad produced a harsh, dehumanizing caricature of those sham revolutionists who called "madness and despair to the regeneration of the world," [5] their pitiful victims and their opponents.

Conrad's bitter hostility to revolutionary action may have derived in part from his early childhood experiences and from the tragic fate of his father, an ardent Polish patriot and man of letters whose political agitation on behalf of the liberation of Poland earned him exile with his wife and son in Russia. There Conrad's mother died. Other members of his family perished in a later uprising against Russian domination. Yet Conrad did not warm to dreamers, idealists, and activists. Later he wrote: "At a time when nothing which is not revolutionary in some way or other can expect to attract much attention I have not been revolutionary in my writings. The revolutionary spirit is mighty convenient in this, that it frees one from all scruples as regards ideas. Its hard, absolute optimism is repulsive to my mind by the menace of fanaticism and intolerance it contains. No doubt one should smile at these things; but . . . all claim to specious righteousness awakens in me that scorn and anger from which a philosophical mind should be free. . . ." [6]

This feeling of indignant contempt for revolution brings about the downfall of the Russian student Razumov in *Under Western Eyes.* Without family and friends, decent, hard-working Razumov is enraged when his trusting fellow student Haldin takes refuge in his lodging after participating in a political assassination. Razumov, who believes in evolution not revolution, decides to betray Haldin to the police, who then force the betrayer into the role of their cat's-paw. Despite the satire of the Russian political exiles in Geneva, whither Razumov is sent as police spy, and especially of Peter Ivanovitch, "the Russian Mazzini," the novel aims at, and achieves, a finer balance than its predecessor.

Conrad blames the corrupting effects of Russian despotism for forcing generous and idealistic young men toward utopian revolutionism. In such a situation, where one form of lawlessness confronts another, "virtues themselves fester into crimes in the cynicism of oppression and revolt." [7] In a real revolution, the best do not come to the fore: noble and humane spirits may begin a revolutionary movement, but they become its victims, "the victims of disgust, of disenchantment—often of remorse," as it passes into the hands of fanatics, says the English teacher of languages who serves as commentator and whose opinions largely reflect the author's. "Hopes grotesquely betrayed, ideals caricatured—that is the definition of revolutionary success," he adds. [8] Once again, failure to perceive the true character and intentions of others falls under the lash of Conrad's irony. But one is made to feel that in betraying Haldin, Razumov betrayed his better self. Thus the novel seems ultimately less concerned with the Scylla and Charybdis of despotism and revolutionism than with personal honor and atonement. Deeply pessimistic, Conrad frequently stressed the uselessness of all political action.

Equally pessimistic was the Basque novelist Pío Baroja, though more reticent about showing his hand, in his novel *Aurora Roja*. The "Red Dawn" of the title represents both the name adopted by a group of Spanish anarchists and the "bloody dawn," the fire of the necessary revolution that would consume utterly the old social order.[9] This is what Juan, the antireligious, idealistic sculptor, ultimately envisages as he becomes involved in propaganda by the deed—only to die a broken man. Set in Madrid, the novel exposes the sordid conditions of the city's poor, at a time when Bakunin's ideas had taken root in the country and when Spanish artists and bohemians were attracted by revolutionary anarchism like their French counterparts.

In contrast with Juan, his brother Manuel puts the humane non-violent case, rejecting the sacrifice of innocent people for the sake of future happiness. Pío Baroja—a timid man who, though much traveled, led an outwardly uneventful life—veers between anarchist sympathies and belief in the futility of militant anarchism. Another of his mouthpieces, the Nietzschean Roberto, expresses the view that what Spain really needs is enlightened despotism and that anarchism should be regarded as a sport. Life is a perpetual struggle, thinks Roberto, adding that man can change and re-create himself but the conditions of modern life cannot really be radically changed. These three figures speak for the author's contradictory moods and impulses. His novel, with its lengthy discussions and confrontations, is the forerunner of the episodic political novels of activists drawn to Spain, like Victor Serge and André Malraux, though it lacks their shaping hand and their dramatic intensity.

Whether writers had been urging destruction, whether they felt a secret complicity with it, or whether they deprecated it, destruction took place on a scale beyond their wildest dreams or fears. The inferno and holocaust of the 1914–1918 war, the colossal upheaval of the revolution in

Russia, with its toll in human lives, confirmed the ruin of the old humanist values. This collapse, which had been anticipated by exceptional spirits in the nineteenth century, was now visible to all.

In Russia, perhaps the most powerfully violent poem about the Russian Revolution, "The Twelve," was written by a noted Symbolist—gentle, restrained, dignified in manner. Alexander Blok had sung ecstatically of his spiritual experience of the "Beautiful Lady" who made her first appearance in a poem entitled "I Seek Salvation" in 1900. Apparently she failed him as a path to salvation. In the years following the 1905 Revolution he grew anxious to free himself from the remote tower of poetic subjectivity in which he felt immured. He would have liked closer contacts between the artist and the people. However, after visiting Italy, he was repelled not only by the state of contemporary society but by Western civilization and European humanism. "Nothing can be changed now—no revolution will change it," he wrote gloomily from Milan.[10] Meanwhile he was oppressed with foreboding about the future. In a poem of 1910 he foretold the darkness of the days ahead, the imminent apocalypse, the descent of "the last, worst age." [11]

With the revolution of February 1917 it seemed to him that a miracle had occurred. Like so many of his poetic forebears in a similar situation, from Wordsworth and Heine, he could feel that everything was now possible. When the Bolsheviks seized power in October, he welcomed their doctrine as the repository of a "terrible truth," much to the surprise of his friends. "It seemed to him that the old world was really destroyed and that in its place must appear something new and beautiful. He went about, young, cheerful, fresh, with shining eyes. . . ." [12] Like the romantic poets who were passionately stirred by elemental upheaval, he yielded to the revolution as to a sublime, elemental force, despite the destruction it inevitably wrought: "A revolution, like a violent whirlwind or snowstorm, always brings new and unexpected things and cruelly disappoints many people. Its whirlpools devour the good and save the worthless, but that is in the nature of revolutions and changes neither the total direction of the current nor the terrible deafening tumult which accompanies it. The roaring noise is an expression of its sublimity." [13] For him, the revolution seemed a manifestation of the Spirit of Music, of vitality, renewal, and creativity.

Humanism, an earlier offspring of the Spirit of Music, was outworn, Blok thought. Man as hitherto known, ethical and humane, would be replaced by man the artist. Mankind would be able to live at the pitch he (Blok himself) had experienced only in moments of intense creativity. The notion of humanity rising through revolution to heights attained in the past only by rare creative genius can be found some twenty years later in the document put out in Mexico by André Breton, with Trotsky's collaboration. The artist is too readily inclined to confuse aesthetic notions with others that have nothing to do with them. But Marx had done the same.

The Twelve, written in January 1918, opens with elemental force as the revolutionary wind sweeps over the snow. Various representatives of the old order are seen, including a worried old woman who does not know what is going on, a bourgeois standing disconsolately at the crossroads, a doubting writer, a priest. Then twelve blasphemous Red Guards on the march appear like violent revolutionary apostles or like vital toughs, firing and looting:

> Hell and damnation,
> life is such fun
> with a ragged greatcoat
> and a Jerry gun!
>
> To smoke the nobs out of their holes
> we'll light a fire through all the world,
> a bloody fire through all the world—[14]

A whore is shot and for a while the revolutionary who killed her is downcast, but he soon recovers. Nothing can stop the inexorable onward march. Once again the bourgeois is glimpsed with a mongrel cur, representing the old world. The old mongrel world is told to "clear off." So the revolutionaries advance, with the cur trailing behind, and before them, carrying a blood-red flag, goes Jesus Christ.

The Christ with the bloody ensign at the head of the twelve revolutionaries who deny him appears less as the Christian Savior than as the immortal symbol of redemption by blood. He personifies the elemental spirit of regeneration, a new vital, creative force, no matter what the cost. We are not far from the French Symbolists who greeted Ravachol and his like as violent Christs or as redeemers who renewed the ritual of necessary sacrifice. Blok actually consents to the end of the old order to which he himself and his work inexorably belong. Survivors of the old way of life, like himself, have somehow to tag along like the mongrel cur. According to Trotsky, it was because Blok needed to convince himself that "he expressed his acceptance of the Revolution in the most extreme imagery, so as to burn his boats." [15] This psychological mechanism will recur.

Two years afterward, in 1920, the disillusioned poet declared that *The Twelve* was written in harmony with the elemental, "in that exceptional and always very brief period when the passing revolutionary cyclone raises a storm in every sea—nature, life and art; . . ." [16] Blok composed only one more major poem, "The Scythians," where the Asiatic barbarians wait to embrace the West in love and loathing—and then little else in the way of poetry. Though helped by Gorky, Blok fell into a despairing decline, and died a year later at the age of forty-one.

Some years before Blok exalted the revolutionary thug, Gorky had published an essay originally entitled "From Prometheus to the Hooligan," conveying his revulsion at the wild toughs who figure in his early stories. In the months before *The Twelve* appeared, Gorky had known his finest hour, struggling to resist revolutionary anarchy, terror, and violence. He warned against the dark instincts, and defended free speech, the freedom of the individual, and all those democratic rights in whose name he thought the revolutionary struggle, in which he shared, had been fought.

When he heard rumors that the Bolsheviks were conspiring to seize power, he was outraged. He accused Lenin and Trotsky of being corrupted by power, of committing crimes and restoring despotic authority that differed not at all from the abominations and the despotism of the tsarist regime. He thought the workers would soon wake up to "the utter impossibility of realizing Lenin's promises, to all the depth of his madness, and to his Nechaev and Bakunin brand of anarchism." [17] It was Gorky's belief that Lenin, whom he called "a cold-blooded trickster," was leading Russia to bloody slaughter and ruin for which the Russian people would have to pay. In his opinion, Lenin possessed all the qualities of a "leader"—the amorality necessary for the role and an aristocràtic, pitiless attitude toward the lives of ordinary people, lives which he was ready to sacrifice for the purpose of conducting a cruel experiment. Only later was Gorky uneasily reconciled with the regime. Only later did he come to praise the virtues of the labor camp.

But the exaltation of virile violence so forcefully expressed in *The Twelve,* and countered by Gorky's courageous journalism between 1917 and 1918, was by no means confined to Blok. The Futurist Mayakovsky (who later killed himself) favored rhetorical violence. The Futurist ideal, whether in Italy or Russia, meant a complete rejection of the past and the cultivation of inhuman, violent beauty. The Manifesto of Futurism, published by Marinetti (afterward a fascist) in 1909, had declared that beauty could only be found in struggle. There could be no masterpiece without an aggressive character. Henceforward, for many, the artistic keynote would be aggression and assault.

Meanwhile in Zurich in 1916, a European movement which, like Symbolism, embraced writers and artists, had been founded to vie in brutal lunacy with the destructiveness of nation-states locked in war. Dada arose out of Symbolism, Expressionism, Cubism, and Futurism, and in its unswerving and despairing nihilism was aiming to destroy all order, all values, an entire civilization, not merely art and literature. "Let each man cry: there is a great labour of destruction and negation to perform. We must sweep and clean." [18] Dada proclaimed total anarchy and carried it to the point of the absurd, the point of its own self-destruction: "No more painters, no more writers, no more sculptors, no more religions, no more republicans, no more royalists, no more imperialists, no more anarchists, no more socialists, no more Bolsheviks, no more politicians, no more proletarians, no more democrats, no more armies, no more police, no more nations, no more of these idiocies, no more, no more, NOTHING, NOTHING, NOTHING." [19]

It became the fashion to insult the audience, which came back for more. At a Parisian première in 1917, the dandy Jacques Vaché could be seen in one of his numerous disguises, dressed as a British officer, brandishing a revolver, and threatening to fire into the audience. Vaché, a bored nihilist, disgusted with the joyless futility of everything, thought of assassination as an amusing experience. As an opium addict, he must have known what he was doing when he killed himself by taking an overdose, having first administered the same amount to an innocent companion as a practical joke. This hero of the supposedly "humorous" gratuitous act was to join Sade, Rimbaud, Lautréamont, and the overrated Jarry in the Surrealist pantheon. André Breton, who knew Vaché personally and never faltered in his admiration for him, would be echoing his master when he proclaimed in the second Surrealist manifesto that "the simplest surrealist act consists of going out into the street revolver in hand and firing into the crowd as often as possible. A man who has not had, at least once, the longing to be finished in this fashion with the petty system of corruption and cretinization now rampant has his place reserved for him in that crowd, belly at pistol-point. . . ." [20] Surrealism, said Breton, whose personal magnetism won many adherents, looked forward to nothing but violence.

Already in May 1921 at the mock trial of Maurice Barrès, who was accused of betraying his early anarchist views, Breton and the founding father of Dada, Tristan Tzara, had exchanged words. At the première of Tzara's play *Cœur à gaz* in 1923, they came to blows and parted company. Surrealism, officially founded in 1924, inherited from Dada a partiality for fisticuffs. To punch a café proprietor on the jaw for no apparent reason was to give proof of acting "with *violence* and *disdain*," of performing "an *arbitrary* and *significant gesture*," and thus to win admiration.[21] The poet no longer merely sang of the thug or hooligan; he often behaved like one. The Surrealists thought nothing of breaking up a lecture or gathering of which they disapproved. At a banquet in honor of the Symbolist poet

Saint-Pol-Roux (whom they admired) they created an uproar. One poet swung from a chandelier, overturning plates and bottles; another put his head out of the window shouting "Down with France!" An attack was made on a nightclub whose proprietor had dared to name it the Maldoror, after the sacred text of Lautréamont. The poet Louis Aragon went to an editor's home to give him a hiding. Breton slapped Ilya Ehrenburg . . . This catalogue by no means exhausts the Surrealists' acts of personal violence, which sometimes involved broken bones.

To match their bullying and blows, intemperance of language frequently marred their utterances. Surrealist poets like Robert Desnos or Antonin Artaud (who suffered a long history of mental illness) were fond of issuing an invitation to the Asiatic barbarians, close cousins of Blok's Scythian hordes, the great savage, primitive destroyers. The elegant, charming Aragon told his student audience in Madrid in 1925: "Western world, you are condemned to death. . . . Let the Orient, your terror, answer our voice at last! . . . We are the mind's agitators. All barricades are valid, all shackles to your happiness damned. . . . And let the drug-merchants fling themselves upon our terrified nations! . . . Rise, O world! See how dry the earth is, and ready, like so much straw, for every conflagration." [22]

Aragon, who had once put the spirit of revolt far above politics and had shrugged off the Russian Revolution as a trivial "ministerial crisis," later became converted to Communism, simply carrying his anarchism into the Party. In his notorious poem, "Red Front," which caused him to be prosecuted for anarchist propaganda and incitement to murder, he urged his readers to "kill the cops," to assassinate politicians, especially "the trained bears of social democracy."

How sweet it is how sweet it is that groaning that rises from the ruins.
I am here at the elimination of a useless world
Here with intoxication at the destruction of the bourgeois
Has there ever been a finer hunt than the pursuit
of this vermin huddling in every corner of the cities
I sing the violent domination of the Proletariat over the bourgeoisie

for the annihilation of this bourgeoisie
for the total annihilation of this bourgeoisie.[23]

No Heine-like regrets are sounded here: the note is one of intoxication with destruction. The call for dynamite recalls the old French anarchist refrain quoted in *Aurora Roja*, "Let us dynamite."

> The blue eyes of the Revolution
> gleam with a necessary cruelty [24]

wrote Aragon in this excited paean to the magnificence of violence, this exaltation of the red of the dawn, of wrath, of blood.

The word "revolution" thrilled the Surrealists as the word "new," which it replaced, had thrilled the generation of the *fin de siècle*. Revolution is ecstasy, orgasm, mystic rapture, sacred insanity of madman-lover-poet, true reality, life at its most authentic and intense: "There is no total revolution, there is only perpetual *Revolution,* real life, like love, dazzling at every moment. There is no revolutionary order, there is only disorder and madness," wrote dithyrambically the poet Paul Éluard (later a Communist and eulogist of Stalin's "loving heart"), one of the early leaders of Surrealism.[25] The revolutionary word at its most wild orgastic extreme (joined with personal violence) was passing currency for the revolutionary act. To call loudly for blood and pitilessness was to give proof of the intransigence of one's revolutionary intent and commitment. From the work of demoralization consciously pursued there would arise "a bloody and pitiless Hope," affirmed Roger Vailland. Impressed by Fascist successes, the anti-Fascist Surrealists thought there was no reason why Fascist weapons should not be adopted: these libertarian poets (fulfilling Dostoevsky's prophecy) called for disciplined fanatical forces which would be able to exercise "a pitiless authority." [26]

For the most part, the Surrealists were young bourgeois intellectuals of good family in revolt against their origins and against everything expected of them in the way of family loyalty, piety, or patriotic sentiment.

They experienced the sense of utter futility and nothingness which Dada had carried to the point of farce and beyond; but they were not able to rest content with the destructive nihilism of Dada. They were seeking something more positive: Surrealist revolution or total liberation of the spirit. They wanted a revolution in every sphere: morality, sex, aesthetics, society. "Surrealism is not a new means of expression. . . . It is a means of total liberation of the mind. . . . We are determined to create a Revolution. . . . Surrealism . . . is a cry of the mind turning toward itself and determined in desperation to crush its fetters. And, if need be, by material hammers." [27]

But as poets Breton and his friends were (as he himself said in the second Surrealist manifesto) "the tail" of romanticism, part of the long romantic agony. Breton had made his debut as a Symbolist poet, drawn to Symbolists of known anarchist leanings. Not only did the Surrealists inherit the tradition of Satanic Promethean revolt, the militant anarchist antireligious stance which made Breton denounce "the exploitation of man by the so-called 'God' of absurd and irritating memory"; [28] they also inherited the urge to voyage in the uncharted lands of "the unknown," whether this meant heaven or hell, whether it implied sickness, madness, criminality, self-destruction, or the destruction of others. Somehow, out of the work of demoralization and destruction, out of the deliberate ruin of the processes of reason and logic, out of reliance on the sole promptings of the subconscious, chance, and "the unknown," a new type of man would arise.

However, the new totally liberated being was in no haste to reveal himself. Instead, the quest for total liberation, which had brought Rimbaud to despair and virtual suicide, now too frequently led others to actual suicide. The longing for some new atheist mysticism did not seem enough. Amid the dangerous precipices of the unknown or the subconscious, the writer was still locked in his private inner landscape. No matter what startling creative discoveries he might make, they were still part of "being," not "doing." And besides, the ambitions of the Surrealists extended far beyond the realms of art and literature: they wanted to be more than just a literary and artistic movement (though in vain). How to act upon the world outside themselves? How to find a path out of the despairing nothingness of the self? This was the old poetic dilemma, the very riddle that Marx's communism professed to solve.

After reading Trotsky's *Lenin* in 1925, André Breton thought he had found the answer. The Satanic Prometheans, Sade and Rimbaud, faded somewhat in the light of the titans of bolshevism. Having consulted Marx, Breton confessed himself converted to "dialectical materialism," which has itself been qualified as a myth. But in common with the rejected master, Barrès, he could not be satisfied with purely economic and social change. So he grafted the ideal of Marx onto that of Rimbaud. Marx had sought not to interpret the world, like other philosophers, but to change it; Breton intended to do both. " 'Transform the world,' Marx said; 'change life,' Rimbaud said—these two watchwords are for us one and the same," Breton announced.[29]

Today it seems clear how far Marx was affected by romantic literature, and to what extent he was a great myth-maker. However, Breton thought that he himself as a poet was adding a new Surrealist dimension (love, dream, madness) to the Marxist ideal, a dimension that he was certainly not ready to renounce. Marx had conceived communism as the resolution of all human contradictions, the solution to the riddle of history. Breton would pursue the quest for the "spiritual point" where all antinomies are resolved, where life and death, the real and the imaginary, past and future, construction and destruction cease to be seen as contradictions.[30] This was the object of the Great Work of the alchemists, and Breton would remain more lastingly faithful to the occult and the apocalyptic (he too discovered Joachim di Fiore) than to dialectical materialism. What he shared with Fourier and Marx was an enduring irrational belief in progress toward an Edenic future.

This is not the place to relate the misunderstandings that followed Breton's decision to put Surrealism at the service of the revolution and the Third International—misunderstandings that reached grotesque proportions. The Communist party was suspicious of Surrealism as a bourgeois diversion; Breton could not understand why the members of a revolutionary movement should favor reactionary positions in art. Where some of his Surrealist friends became, and remained, pillars of the French Communist party, he withdrew. He retained an emotional attachment to the black flag of anarchism. He worshipped the outcast Trotsky (somewhat to the mighty exile's embarrassment), not Stalin. Toward the end of his life, Breton expressed sympathy for Robespierre, not Marx. There, perhaps, he revealed the true model for his revolutionary ideal.

The Surrealist poets, writers, artists of bourgeois origin, inheritors of romantic revolt and romantic agony, were busy digging their own graves at the same time that they were helping to dig the grave of Western civilization. The poetic tradition of Rimbaud and Lautréamont, which they carried to the extreme of irrationalism, made them uncertain as to where "reality" lay: if it was not in the banal everyday world they hated and rejected, then it must be in the world of the subconscious, of dreams and nightmares, of "surreality," where there ceased to be frontiers between dreaming and living, madness and nonmadness, death and life; where truth even seemed to be hidden in madness and death. Either they pursued this line to its logical end, suicide, or else they drew back in dread, seeking some other issue. The extremism of the religion of art advocated by Baudelaire and his heirs—with its emphasis on the uselessness, amorality, and subjectivity of the work of art, and their own consequent frustration, guilt, and sense of all-pervading futility—impelled some to turn outward in an effort to escape.

The opposition of the Surrealists to forms of religious orthodoxy was too strong for them to accept Huysmans's solution: the Church. At first the communist faith seemed to offer a way out of nihilism and anarchism; in some instances this solution proved more lasting than in others where anarchist inclinations were more pressing and could not be resisted. In such cases, the flirtation with communism was based on a misapprehension.

The total revolution of spirit and body, mind and sex that Breton and his friends envisaged, the elevation of revolution into a transcendental value, had little to do with the more mundane objectives of the French Communist party hierarchy; all they shared was the vocabulary of revolution and a desire to destroy the existing order. Breton and his followers anticipated the so-called counter-culture of today, many of whose proponents have more in common with him and with Artaud than with Marx. It was Artaud who told Breton: "With society and its public, there is no longer any other language than that of bombs, barricades, and all that follows." [31]

chapter **16**

revolutionary resurrection:
D. H. Lawrence

D. H. Lawrence's commitment to revolution was more lasting than might be supposed. He has aptly been called a "moral terrorist." [1] The author of *The Rainbow* believed that a new age, a new ethic and metaphysic, a new mode of being "must" be brought about by a destructive revolution, or else the world would be enveloped in total ruin: "One must try to save the quick, to send up the new shoots of a new era: a great, utter revolution, and the dawn of a new historical epoch: either that, or the vast amorphous dust." [2] The word "must" was one of the favorites in the apocalyptic vocabulary of this former schoolmaster. It was as if emphatic reiteration not only silenced his doubts but forced his dream nearer reality. The alternatives of revolutionary destruction or utter ruin, which might well appear equally disastrous, seemed to Lawrence quite distinct because he firmly believed in the fruitfulness of destruction—indeed, that it was only through destruction that new creativity could come into being, that rebirth and resurrection could occur.

As firmly as the Symbolists of the *fin de siècle* (with whose procedures he had much in common), Lawrence believed in the irredeemable decay and degeneration of a dying world. The dread events of the 1914–1918 war were so many signs and portents confirming this belief. He loathed the supporters of the war above all for their hypocrisy, for the gap between their professed ideals and their deeds. His liaison and marriage to Frieda Weekley (née von Richthofen, a distant relative of the German war ace) strengthened his attitude as an outsider amid the general frenzy. The personal humiliations he suffered at the hands of the military convinced him that the old world had come to an end in 1915. But after the end of the world as it was now, there must be a new heaven and a new earth. Quite as much as André Breton (some ten years his junior), who shared many of his views on the central importance of the relationship between man and woman, he intended "to smash the frame" of existence in order to achieve his goal: an entirely new and authentic way of living.

The young Lawrence, brought up amid the contrast between the grim coal mines of the Midlands and the radiant countryside, was a charismatic figure of striking duality. He appeared as a mixture of faun (Katherine Mansfield would say black devil) and fiery prophet. Lawrence regarded himself as "primarily . . . a passionately religious man." [3] But he had made up his mind that Christianity was done for, that the cycle of Christian civilization had come to an end. Another cycle, another religion must take its place, and who better to found it and expound it than he himself? "It is not *I* who matter—it is what is said through me," he remarked, draped in the mantle of inspired prophet of a new faith.[4]

Lawrence took himself quite seriously as hierophant and unacknowledged legislator of mankind. And others have only too often taken him at his own valuation, despite his advice to heed the tale rather than the teller. Both directly and indirectly, where attitudes to life and culture are concerned, his action upon successive generations—even among those who seek to separate wheat from chaff—has been profound.

But however questionable his preaching may be, his marvelous gift for expressing his fugitive responses with unaffected directness provides an invaluable key to the modern apocalyptic mentality.

What precisely was the wonderful new religion which required for its birth so mighty a destruction? "My great religion is a belief in the blood, the flesh, as being wiser than the intellect. We can go wrong in our minds. But what our blood feels and believes and says, is always true," he told an artist friend as early as 1913.[5] The new religion, as so often happens, turns out to be less an innovation than the development of a familiar poetic theme: a return to the pre-Judaeo-Christian era, to the supposed vital consciousness of the true pagans, with whose death the Christian era began. Lawrence took his stand with Heine—he was acquainted with Heine's poetry—on the side of the vanquished old gods. He echoed Swinburne's grandiose "Hymn to Proserpine," with its paean to the dethroned unknown gods conquered by the pale Galilean whose grey kingdom, in its turn, would pass away. What Lawrence wanted was virile potency, the primacy of the senses and the passions, the fullness of being and the spontaneity which flourished (so he thought) "before the pale Galilean . . . conquered." [6]

The anti-intellectual religion of Lawrence is rooted, then, in willed rejection of Christianity and weary disgust with humanity. Self-loathing (in the shape of detestation of the private inadequacies of a man who idolized strength and vitality but suffered from perennial ill-health) turns into hatred of humanity and of human weakness and imperfection. Lawrence was fond of quoting Nietzsche's epithet, "all-too-human." He was attracted by the nonhuman element in Futurist art, and longed for a new, superior, nonhuman race of beings.

Yet ironically, if Lawrence was preaching the supercession of Christianity, he was doing so while retaining Christian terminology, for he was steeped in the Bible. He might reject the intellect in favor of "blood-consciousness," but he preserved sufficient intellectual command to engage in self-criticism. The criticism built into his best novels—for instance, Ursula's adverse judgment on the views of Birkin, Lawrence's alter ego, in his role of Savior of the World in *Women in Love*—helps to rescue them from the crude brutality that disfigures the works of his decline, notably *The Plumed Serpent*. Lawrence once remarked of Melville that he preached in *Moby Dick* because he was unsure of himself, and the same might be said of the novelist from Eastwood, whom Galsworthy patronizingly called "that provincial genius." [7] No less than the visionary Blake (whom he discussed with his first love, Jessie Chambers, in his youth and whose apocalyptic, prophetic manner prefigures his own), Lawrence was preaching his own new word, his personal "everlasting gospel," with its elect and its new dispensation, where warring social and sexual elements are to be reconciled in blissful harmony.

Like Blake, Lawrence was deeply affected by the imagery of the Revelation of St. John, familiar to him from the chapel and Sunday school he attended in his Nottinghamshire childhood. Lawrence thought its influence upon uneducated working people greater than that of the gospels, and called it the hidden side of Christianity. Though later in life Lawrence rejected the Apocalypse as a horrible travesty of some pre-Christian work, he never denied the mysterious enduring power of its symbols. Such symbols could "arouse the deep emotional self, and the dynamic self, beyond comprehension. Many ages of accumulated experience still throb within a symbol. And we throb in response." [8] The visions and phraseology of the Book of Revelation haunted him throughout his life.

It has been suggested by Frank Kermode that Lawrence's Joachitism may have derived from the esoteric sources in which he was interested, along with Blake, or from the writers and poets of the French decadence with whom he was familiar. For Lawrence, too, there were three epochs: an epoch of the Law and an epoch of Love, both of which were to be transcended in the epoch of the Holy Spirit. The Holy Ghost was conceived by Lawrence traditionally as the comforter, balancer, reconciler of opposites. In the epoch of the Holy Spirit would be achieved the harmonious relationship between man and woman in which both would remain poles of individuality yet at the same time in perfect balance. And this proper balance between man and woman was essential for harmony and vitality in the individual, in art, in social relations, in the nation or the "race." So Lawrence could maintain that "only through readjustment between men and women . . . will she [England] get out of her present atrophy." [9] He believed that "a vision of a better life must include a revolution of society. . . . And the drama shall be between individual men and women, not between nations and classes." [10]

This was the Lawrentian gospel expounded in his essay on Thomas Hardy, in his two best novels, *The Rainbow* and its sequel, *Women in Love.* Yet the conclusion of *Women in Love,* where it is implied that the fulfillment of the man-woman relationship is insufficient for Birkin, hints at a sense of failure to inaugurate the third epoch. Lawrence's furious battles with Frieda, the neglect or prosecution of his work, together with increasing ill-health and frustration, doubtless contributed to the eventual darkening and coarsening of his vision.

But for Lawrence there could be no dark without light, no hell without paradise. In the encompassing gloom, he insisted upon the resurrection of the body, upon a new life here and now. "Shall I not see those who have risen again walk here among men perfect in body and spirit, whole and glad in the flesh, . . . arrived at last to wholeness, perfect without scar or blemish, healthy without fear of ill-health?" [11] In this visionary passage from *The Rainbow* there is an echo of Shelley's *Prometheus Unbound,* whose imagery, with that of the "Ode to the West Wind," constantly comes into Lawrence's mind. One of the two poems that most profoundly stirred the young Tom Brangwen in *The Rainbow* was Shelley's ode, and its very substance was absorbed into Lawrence's poetic vision.

Lawrence thought Shelley and Swinburne the greatest English poets, admiring them for their philosophic and spiritual revelation. Both invoked revolutionary resurrection; Swinburne's presaging red, tempestuous, revolutionary resurrection echoed the trumpet of Shelley's prophecy. Bertrand Russell noted the resemblance between Lawrence and Shelley: "Lawrence is very like Shelley—just as fine, but with a similar impatience of fact." [12] It seemed to Russell that Lawrence's idea of revolution had much in common with Shelley's. However, while yearning for a revolution in sexual relations, Lawrence (like Breton) never flirted with free love as did Shelley in theory. Certainly both dreamed of escaping from a base, artificial, hypocritical, and detested world to some lovely island paradise where a new elite community, a nucleus of rare like-minded souls, would be established. In Lawrence's "Rananim" there would flourish a band of free, spontaneous beings living fully in perfect harmony: "We will found an order, and we will all be Princes, as the angels are," he informed Lady Ottoline Morrell.[13] His efforts to found this paradise in various parts of the world from Cornwall to Taos came to nothing, but he liked to believe the idea was right and only the people were wrong.

Common to both Shelley and Lawrence is the nature-image of destruction as a prerequisite for creation and renewal, one of the most ancient patterns of change. "Except a seed die, it bringeth not forth." If winter comes, can spring be far behind? Decaying woods, dead leaves, hibernation, spring, new buds, new birth—these images frequently recur in Lawrence's poems, stories, and letters. To the New Testament and Shelley he added not only the vegetation myths described in Frazer's *The Golden Bough* but a personal, distorting emphasis.

In Lawrence's view, some people, indeed most, are dead just as the leaves are dead: "Old leaves have got to fall, old forms must die. And if men must at certain periods fall into death in millions, why, so must the leaves fall every single autumn. And dead leaves make good mould. And so dead men." [14] In spelling out his acceptance, Lawrence succeeds in making it horrible. Men are more than leaf-mold or fertilizer. It is characteristic of Lawrence that the best and the worst lie so closely juxtaposed. From his extraordinary empathy with nature, one source of the sense of throbbing life communicated by his best passages, there springs also this distasteful indifference. Meanwhile, amid the rotting compost, some individuals (including naturally himself), even some nation (presumably England), must carry the fructifying seed through the winter of degeneration, darkness, and death, bearing through the general destruction the germ of the next, higher civilization.

However, although the leaves are rotting on the tree, they continue to cling to it. "There are myriads of human beings hanging on the bush—," says Birkin. They look nice enough, but they are Dead Sea fruit: ". . . mankind is a dead tree, covered with fine brilliant galls of people . . . they won't fall off the tree when they're ripe." [15] Birkin would like dirty humanity to be swept away, and although Ursula challenges him, she too finds the idea of a world cleansed of human beings attractive. Lawrence expressed similar views in his letters. The influence of the dead past and old dead forms is corrupting, poisonous, and it breeds flowers of evil. The portion of the self or the nation that lingers with these sterile elements must be eliminated. For in Lawrence's opinion, when an era ends, it turns into a force for evil. In this manner, he moves swiftly from the idea of natural decay to that of moral evil. There has to be a harrowing of hell before the beautiful new life can arise.

Accordingly, a poetic image which concerns the spiritual relation between the old self and the new, or the growth of the artist to new forms of creativity (a growth which, however, usually involves not just the rejection of past forms but a degree of continuity), becomes subtly transformed in Lawrence. The evolution of the natural process of the seasons is extended to embrace the seed of the elite, the nation (England), the white northern race (Lawrence prided himself on his "whiteness and Englishness"), all of which are doomed *unless* the harmful element is destroyed. So Birkin's near blood brother, the beloved Gerald in *Women in Love,* symbol of the white northern race in the deadly grip of ugly materialism and industrialism, is doomed to a sterile, icy end.

But once the harmful element is ravaged, then there comes a new dawn, a new day, a new germination or liberation. Consequently man, the secular savior, takes upon himself the function of a destructive force of nature. What was a natural process of decay and death becomes a deliberate, necessary act without which there can be no life-giving change.

The death of the initiate in the pagan fertility mysteries, of Persephone-Lawrence or the saving seed, is not an irrevocable death. The phoenix (once an emblem of Christ), adopted by Lawrence, is consumed in fire yet resurrected as the immortal eagle of St. John the Evangelist. Besides, the destruction of the mass is not a theme for unhappiness: "This world of ours has got to collapse now, in violence and injustice and destruction. . . . What is death, in the individual! I don't care if sixty million individuals die. The seed is not in the masses, it is elsewhere." [16] Let the present inadequate lot cease to be, let them all make way for a stronger people. Lawrence was writing in this vein during the slaughter in the trenches.

In his essay "The Whistling of Birds," written in 1919, Lawrence described with savage power the cruel death of innumerable birds in the winter frost. The singing survivor, the resurrected creature, has nothing to do with the mass of the destroyed. "There is no connexion. They are not to be referred the one to the other. . . . What is the past, those others, now he is tossed clean into the new, across the untranslatable difference?" [17] This ability to separate what is saved from what is condemned to perish (a separation formed by analogy with the imagery employed to convey the meaning of Christian resurrection in Scripture) is here carried to extreme lengths. It allows Lawrence and those of a similar turn of mind to envisage a holocaust without turning a hair, so long as it is to be followed by the miraculous transmutation of phoenix into eagle, by the rebirth in which they firmly believe.

Naturally no sympathy need be wasted on those whom Lawrence considers to be dead souls. Such a one is the sterile Skrebensky in *The Rainbow*, who stands for the upholders of established order and exhausted ideals and who would consider making improvements in the state merely in order to preserve it; or the avant-garde sewer rat, the decadent artist Loerke, "probably" a Jew, in *Women in Love*. Despite appearances, the beastly bourgeois of Lawrence's poem ("How Beastly the Bourgeois Is") is wormy like an old mushroom, and it is a pity he and his fellows cannot be kicked over like "sickening toadstools" to rot back into England's soil. But why despair, "so long as one has a hobnailed boot to kick with?" The urge to smash what he *knows* to be rotten (his italics) provides the basis of what Lawrence called his "revolutionary utterance." [18]

What Lawrence meant by revolution was the birth of a new idea, a new way of feeling, a new man. The old ways were indubitably finished, and somehow (with the help of a few kindred spirits) he had to force the transition to the new life. As for the upheavals to which historians gave the name of revolution, these were scarcely worth talking about. The French Revolution was "a brief inundation." The Russian Revolution of 1917 would momentarily arouse his hopes, and at one stage he talked of going to Russia. But he changed his mind, having reached the conclusion that the revolution in Russia was "nothing new." [19] The great Lawrentian revolution for life's sake, like all true revolutions, remained to be made.

At the beginning of 1915, he discussed revolution with E. M. Forster (soon found to be virtually moribund), and he expounded his revolutionary views in letters to friends, particularly Bertrand Russell. At first the philosopher was attracted by Lawrence's ardor and conviction that something fundamental was needed to right the world, while the novelist hoped for a notable addition to his band of rare souls. Lawrence believed that the whole way of life should be revolutionized: material and monetary standards should yield to considerations of actual living. "We must make it so at once," he urged Russell. "There must be a revolution in the state. It shall begin by the nationalising of all industries and means of communication, and of the land—in one fell blow." [20] Lawrence was voicing the sacred impatience for an immediate transformation.

Humanity (including Lawrence) is Prometheus "nailed" (like Christ) on the rock of modern industrial capitalism. Man must tear himself from the rock. Literature—"vain, irrelevant, impudent words"—seems shameful in the face of suffering Prometheus. Manhood requires action. For Lawrence social action is associated with virility: "If I cannot help Prometheus—and I am also Prometheus—how shall I be able to take a woman?" [21] The "real" sexual bond is a means to the self-discovery and self-knowledge that are essential for action on behalf of humanity. The present form of existence is a prison; therefore, the present shell, or frame of life, has to be smashed. "Then, and then only, shall we be able to *begin* living." [22] That is, real fullness of living will only be experienced after the revolution. There must be a social revolution after the war: "We must form a revolutionary party. . . . We must create an idea of a new, freer life, where men and women can really meet on natural terms, . . ." [23] Later this evolves into the grotesque idea of joint government by a dictator concerned with public life and a dictatrix whose realm is private life and looking after the "race."

Meantime, Lawrence was telling Russell that he cared only about the forthcoming revolution, "the great and happy revolution," as he called it when writing to Viola Meynell.[24] Then a black mood descended and he remarked that "It would do me so much good if I could kill a few people."[25] His visit to Russell in Cambridge had proved a disappointment; Keynes and the rest were all "sick." Contact with the legal profession when he refused to pay the costs of Frieda's divorce elicited the outburst: "I cannot tell you how this reinforces in me my utter hatred of the whole establishment—the whole constitution of England as it now stands. . . . But softly—softly. I will do my best to lay a mine under their foundations."[26]

It soon became clear that Lawrence's idea of a "real revolution" had nothing to do with democracy. Democracy is the enemy, the rule of the mob. The working man is not fit to elect the government. Some are born fit to govern, others only to be governed, observed this son of a miner married to a German aristocrat. Aristocracy may be more dead than democracy, but there must be real leaders, a body of wise patricians, a ruler, or else one would have "another French Revolution muddle."[27] Moreover, what was required was "a new unanimity among us, a new movement for the pure truth, an immediate destruction—and reconstructive revolution in actual life, England, now."[28] At this stage, relations with Russell were becoming strained, especially when the philosopher—"like Judas"—informed him that the spirit of unanimity in truth was an illusion. Russell found Lawrence undisciplined, muddleheaded, one who mistook wishes for facts: "He has not learnt the lesson of individual impotence. . . . When one gets a glimmer of the facts into his head, as I did at last, he gets discouraged, and says he will go to the South Sea Islands, and bask in the sun with 6 native wives."[29]

However, Russell's "betrayal," like that of other prospective apostles, did not deter Lawrence from persisting in his quest. In Lawrence's outlook there are two conflicting notions: one is that the old world is completely finished, and the other that it remains to be smashed. He wrote, "this order of life must go, this organization of humanity must be smashed. . . . One wants this which *is*, shattered, and the chance to reconstruct according to one's heart's desire."[30] To remold the world in accordance with the dictates of one's heart: this is one form of modern self-will stigmatized by Dostoevsky, whom Lawrence came to detest. It is curious that Lawrence should have been so sure that smashing was right, when he once admitted to Russell that his own sense of reality was insecure.

He yearns for the smash to come quickly because "the longer the old decency remains standing," the longer one will be kept in a state of uncertainty.[31] All reformers (including Russell and the socialists) are "our disease, not our hope," since what is needed is "a clean sweep, and a new start":[32] either a cleansing fire such as devoured the cities of the plain or another flood. At first, Lawrence was not sure if he wanted to be Noah, but later he declared that he would like another Deluge, provided he could stay in the ark until the waters subsided. He wrote to the painter Mark Gertler in 1918 that "nothing but a quite bloody, merciless, almost anarchistic revolution will be any good for this country; . . . And yet, somehow, I don't want to be in it."[33] By 1921, however, he no longer saw himself as Noah, the chosen survivor, but as an active participant in a revolutionary struggle: "If I knew how to, I'd really join myself to the revolutionary socialists now. I think the time has come for a real struggle. That's the only thing I care for: the death struggle. I don't care for politics. But I know there *must* and *should* be a deadly revolution very soon, and I would take part in it if I knew how."[34]

In his Australian novel, *Kangaroo,* Lawrence explored how it would be if, like Shelley's Laon, he were to become involved in a revolutionary movement. For the political background of his book he drew upon what he had seen of the clashes between Communists and Fascists in Italy. But there is a distinction between many of his own pronouncements in his letters and the impression conveyed by his novel, where the reactions of the writer Somers, a projection of himself, are countered by the skepticism of Somers's wife, Harriet. Moreover, Somers is presented as a hesitant figure. As a result, one is left with a strong hint of Lawrence's temptations.

The Australian Diggers movement is the dangerous, desperate cause to which Somers is attracted, convinced as he is that democratic liberty is an exhausted ideal. It resembles those militant organizations of European war veterans that would readily merge in fascism. Its members engage in athletics and military training; they are sworn to secrecy and must serve their leader (a Jew known as Kangaroo) with unquestioning obedience. Their aim is "a sort of revolution and a seizing of political power," and the establishment of a dictatorship.[35] Somers at once thrills to the cause and mistrusts it. He would like to be convinced; he would like to commit himself if he could, but he cannot. It is not quite what he is seeking; he prefers to listen to the dark gods. So he rejects Kangaroo, whom Lawrence has to transform into an all-too-human sloppy sentimentalist of the kind the militarist Diggers would not have stood for a moment.

Through Somers one perceives both the artist's quest for fellowship and the failure to achieve it, the return to private vision, the deepening obsession with pagan sensuality and violence, with "the great God, who enters us from below." [36] Basically the realm of political affairs was as alien to Somers as to Lawrence, and his concern, like that of Lawrence, was with "religion." But Lawrence was fascinated by the mystery of power. He had earlier rejected the Nietzschean will to power as destructive, while acknowledging his own urge to dominate. It seemed to him, modeling himself on Dostoevsky's Grand Inquisitor, that when leaders relieve their followers of responsibility, "the populace can again become free and happy and spontaneous, leaving matters to their superiors." [37] Or as he put it even more candidly: "I would like him [the working man] to give me back the responsibility for general affairs, . . ." [38] Homage to the hero makes one heroic, he wrote toward the end of his life in *Apocalypse*. Yet at about the same time he judged the hero and the leader of men to be obsolete. The tone of his remarks on leadership and "dear heroic Mussolini" tended to vary with his correspondents.[39]

Just as Somers-Lawrence is tempted by the leadership cult, so he is tempted by the call of pre-Christian blood sacrifice. Lawrence baldly declared (in his essay on Melville's *Typee*) that a cannibal feast seemed to him a more valid sacrament than the Eucharist. This is the line which led him directly to the ghastly ritual executions in *The Plumed Serpent*. Yet there was a side to Lawrence that loathed blood sacrifice for the ideal, or the image of being washed in the blood of the Lamb. The greatest irony of all lay in the way that the romantic quest for fullness of life, natural-ness, spontaneity, and primitive authenticity took him, via "the truth of blood-consciousness," to a savage near-fascist ethic of virile mastery and lordship that denied his own early ideals.

If Lawrence was for a while tempted by fascism, as he had been briefly attracted by bolshevism, it was because of his impatience for resurrection through destruction. This made him ready to welcome any instrument that seemed likely to hasten chaos, and thereby accession to the plane where one could start real, full living. His attitude, like that of so many poets, was quite irresponsible. In his poem "A Sane Revolution," he said the revolution should be made not for equality, the working class, or in-ternational labor, but for fun: it would be fun to upset the apple cart and see which way the apples would roll.

Lawrence's post-Nietzschean resistance to humane values in the name of a nonhuman race of men allows him paradoxically to hate mankind while advocating the glorious transmutation of human beings into the princes of the new order—the blissfully fulfilled, harmoniously balanced creatures of the third epoch of the Holy Spirit, creatures never seen on earth, which has only known struggling and aspiring men. "I believe in Paradise and Paradisal beings: but humanity, mankind—*crotte!*" he ex-claimed.[40] Yet there would be many who were still ready to sacrifice themselves generously for the religion of humanity which Lawrence wished to transcend.

chapter 17

literature or revolution?
Victor Serge and André Gide

On the eve of his departure for Russia in 1936, *André Gide received an open* letter, urging him to "have the courage to see clearly." [1] It came from one of the most determined and courageous members of a doomed generation, the revolutionary agitator and writer Victor Serge. How did these two authors, of totally differing background and upbringing, temperament and gifts, happen to find themselves on the same side? What ideals, illusions, needs, and pressures made such strange allies?

When Victor Serge, then in his prime, met André Gide in Brussels and Paris in the thirties, the celebrated author of *The Immoralist,* who had sat at the feet of Oscar Wilde and attended Mallarmé's Tuesday evening gatherings, was well past sixty. Both men were led to embrace the cause of revolutionary communism by different forms of spiritual quest. For the

Protestant André Gide (rather after the style of George Sand and her circle), it was part of his longing for some kind of austere "authentic" Christianity, unsullied by orthodoxies, churches, or, worst of all, crusading believers. For the agnostic Victor Serge, it was a purely secular faith, the religion of humanity and the future.

This religion of humanity served an unholy trinity that required human sacrifice: the abstract divinity, History; her daughter, the stern, majestic, demanding goddess Revolution; and the ruthless spirit, Necessity. There were men ready to sacrifice everything on this insatiable altar, men who believed that they were living in "a period of transition," and that their own blood might have to fertilize the soil for the future. Such a one was Victor Serge; he saw "the Revolution as a tremendous sacrifice that was required for the future's sake; . . ." [2] In his eyes, the revolution appeared as a living being. The concepts of philosophers like Hegel and historians like Michelet, the images of poets like Lamartine and Victor Hugo became translated into the motives and the justification for action.

The life of Victor Serge was selflessly devoted to the religion of humanity: he was an active revolutionary first, and a writer and novelist second. Indeed, he said he had given up writing when he "entered the Russian Revolution," rather as if he were a poet burning his secular poems on entering the Church. At that time he had found it difficult to reconcile his sensibility and his opinions. Later, circumstances forced him to take up the pen. He united unswerving revolutionary faith with the sharp eye and the critical sense of the born novelist. There were objective standards of truth and humane dealing that he was never prepared entirely to abandon. One of these was respect for the human being in the enemy. So he became quite consciously the witness, spokesman, and representative of an entire tragic generation, many of whose literary and political figures— from Blok to Lukács, and from Borodin (the Soviet emissary to the Kuomintang who figures in Malraux's *Les Conquérants*) to the luckless Spanish leader Andrés Nin—were personally known to him.

Serge was the embodiment of the modern cosmopolitan *déraciné*. His real name was Victor Lvovich Kibalchich, and he was born in Brussels in 1890, the son of Russian revolutionary exiles molded by Belinsky, Herzen, and Chernyshevsky. A distant relative of his father's was executed for his part in the assassination of Tsar Alexander II. Serge's parents and their friends, as he put it, "knew that the Revolution was advancing toward them, inexorably, out of the depths of the future. In simple words they taught me to have faith in mankind and to wait steadfastly for the necessary cataclysms." [3] Meanwhile they struggled on in dire poverty and often knew hunger.

The young Victor Serge fell under the influence of Kropotkin and went off to France (he never saw his father again). People who were complacently ensconced in society aroused his indignation and he determined to ally himself with the exploited and work for revolution to destroy injustice. In Paris he became involved in the second wave of the French anarchist movement, during which a number of wild adherents, followers of Stirner, perished either in gun battles or on the guillotine. Serge refused to inform against his comrades who had joined the desperate Bonnot gang, though he thoroughly disapproved of their terrorist methods; as editor of *L'Anarchie,* organ of the individualist faction, he was sentenced in 1912 to five years' imprisonment. This experience he finally exorcised by writing his first novel, *Men in Prison.*

Released in 1917, he traveled to Barcelona, where he worked as a printer and participated in the abortive workers' insurrection led by the revolutionary syndicalist Salvador Seguí, whom he depicted as Dario in his second novel, *Birth of Our Power.* This was Serge's first and only contact with a popular revolutionary upsurge of lyrical enthusiasm, directionless and undisciplined but never to be forgotten. Meanwhile the Russian Revolution had erupted, that "purifying tempest" to which he had looked forward for so long, dreaming that it "would be the beginning of everything, the prodigious first day of Creation." [4] Aiming to reach Russia by way of war-torn France, he found himself instead interned in a French camp with other flotsam. He finally arrived in Petrograd in 1919, to be welcomed by Gorky (who had formerly known his mother's family) and in time to experience the famine and the civil war.

As a convinced libertarian who had been swept along by the inchoate romantic forces in Barcelona, he was expecting something very different from what he found. He could not imagine that the idea of revolution could be distinct from that of freedom. From all he had read about the French Revolution and the Commune, he thought in legendary terms of popular excitement, lively discussions, clubs: "In Petrograd we expected to breathe the air of a liberty that would doubtless be harsh and even cruel to its enemies, but was still generous and bracing." [5] From this it would appear that some degree of ruthlessness was inherent in his revolutionary ideal.

Instead of heady freedom, he encountered a regime that would be cruel not only to its enemies but to its best servants, often scarcely distinguishing between the two; he found bureaucracy rampant, blinkered authoritarianism, intolerance, one-party rule, summary executions. Nevertheless, faced with "the ruthlessness of history," he became convinced that bolshevism was right and necessary, and he threw in his lot with the Bolsheviks, though fully intending to preserve his independence. It was at this time, after years of political agitation, that he was initiated into Marxism and joined the Party.

With mounting horror, he witnessed the elimination of his libertarian friends (foreshadowing the terrible suppression of the anarchists in Spain nearly twenty years later) and the silencing of critics and dissidents. Serge's volume of memoirs intones a litany of the names of friends and associates who committed suicide, were done to death, or who vanished in mysterious circumstances never to be heard of again.

All the same, despite his misgivings, Serge admitted the necessity of terror: "I am well aware that terror has been necessary up till now in all great revolutions, which do not happen according to the taste of well-intentioned men, but spontaneously, with the violence of tempests; and that it is our duty to employ the only weapons that history affords us if we are not to be overwhelmed through our own folly." [6] So, paradoxically, man fights for a revolution in order to be able to control his destiny in freedom; then calls it a spontaneous tempest over which he has no control, and to which he must submit willy-nilly. However, while admitting the inevitability of terror in certain extreme situations, Serge nonetheless objected to the deliberate choice of terror as a political weapon, and to its continued use when he thought it was no longer necessary, that is, after the end of the civil war.

Thus, although he believed that the Soviet regime would have been stronger if it had maintained faith in human rights, he also believed that it was possible to distinguish between necessary and unnecessary or arbitrary terror, between the needful and the "needless crime." In him there can be seen the conflict between humane feelings and the idea of a revolutionary ruthlessness, deemed indispensable for practical efficiency, that finds expression in the use of surgical metaphors.

When Serge returned to Russia, after a period of revolutionary activity in Berlin and Vienna, he militated outspokenly in the ranks of the Left opposition (though he was no blind admirer of Trotsky). As a result, he was arrested and sent to Orenburg, where he spent three years of misery and deprivation and where he might have remained to die with other political deportees. But his writings had made a name for him in France, and literary colleagues like André Gide and André Malraux mounted a campaign which obtained his release. After the fall of France, Serge escaped to Mexico, where he completed his fine novel of the purges, *The Case of Comrade Tulayev,* as well as his memoirs. He died there in poverty in 1947.

So ended a life of unceasing struggle and hardship, a life of mingled blindness and lucidity, of ruthlessness relieved by humanity and moral courage. He had cared nothing for personal comfort, possessions, literary fame. As he said of his generation, "All we lived for was activity integrated into history; we were interchangeable. . . . None of us had, in the bourgeois sense of the word, any personal existence. . . ." [7] Married three times, he left his second wife behind in Russia: she had lost her reason through the privation and persecution they had undergone. He spoke little about his personal concerns. For him the ego was hateful, a relic of bourgeois selfishness: human personality might be the supreme value, but it had to be viewed in the context of society and history. The existence of the individual took second place to the theme of human solidarity, the urge to share in a common fate, which he named as his principal motive for action.

Individual egoism was, he believed, a thing of the past; the meaning of life lay in "conscious participation in the making of history." [8] This sense of being the instrument of history, as once men had felt themselves to be instruments of Providence, gave him and his comrades a feeling of purpose and importance they would otherwise have lacked. The worst blow to human vanity is the awareness of *vanitas*. For him and for so many of his colleagues who perished, especially if they were tough old Bolshevik revolutionaries whom he could not help admiring when he saw them confronted by mediocre bureaucrats, there was no alternative. To give up their faith would mean admitting their own nothingness. So after many years of imprisonment, after working for revolution in several countries, after experiencing failure and defeat and even Communist persecution, Serge could still declare in his Mexican exile, "I have more confidence in mankind and in the future than ever before." [9]

Many of his writings were composed in the most adverse circumstances, when he could not always be sure whether his manuscripts might be destroyed—some were lost or confiscated. He could not linger over niceties of style. Indeed, his attitude toward literature was peremptory. He respected literary activity, but scorned "Literature." His novels were not written out of any love of art, but in order to bear witness to the age.

At first thought, no two men could seem further apart than Victor Serge, the self-suppressing revolutionary agitator, and André Gide, the hedonist aesthete, whose life was devoted to literature and to the pursuit of the authentic self. Yet the reflective, cautious Gide, who once said he would rather cause action than act himself, shared one quality with Serge: his moral courage.

Gide admitted to lacking a sense of reality—the external world seemed to him a spectacle to which he responded but from which he felt strangely detached—and recognized in himself a certain scorn for actuality that distinguished the literary heirs of Mallarmé. Nevertheless he would have liked literature to serve life, if it must serve anything at all. In 1897 in his highly influential *Fruits of the Earth,* he by inference urged each of his readers to cast the book aside and find his own true way for himself; each person must discover how to make himself unique. In *The Immoralist,* in 1902, Ménalque, the tempter and liberator, observes that poetry and philosophy are dead because they have grown separate from life. For Gide, the self-absorbed man of letters, in constant inner debate with Barrès, living in accordance with one's secret desires and instincts is the supreme obligation.

But by the time this aging Narcissus (as the Catholic novelist François Mauriac called him) reached the age of sixty in 1930, he was concerned about waning powers and loss of a sense of purpose. Three years earlier, he had published a travel diary condemning the horrors of colonial exploitation he witnessed in the Congo, and had dedicated the book to the memory of Conrad who, in *Heart of Darkness,* had exposed these abuses before him. Once Gide had seen what was going on, he felt he must speak out; to keep silent would have meant being an accomplice of the exploiters. Despite this first salvo against capitalism and imperialism (an effort which brought about tangible reforms), many were surprised when in the *Nouvelle Revue Française* of 1932 there appeared excerpts from Gide's journal of 1931 proclaiming his heartfelt hopes for the success of the Soviet regime. "So André Gide, who taught our youth that each one of us is unique, now seeks the triumph of the Bolshevik antheap where each person will be interchangeable," complained Mauriac.[10]

Gide was moved by the increasing sense of social guilt which assailed many middle-class writers in the thirties, at a time of loudly trumpeted ideological certainties. The course he took gives some idea of the intense pressure these were exerting. Having known solid comfort all his life, he began to feel a sense of inferiority because he had never been obliged to earn a living or forced to experience poverty. It upset him to realize that he was among the haves whenever his path crossed that of the have-nots.

The idea that there should be no change in this unjust state of affairs now seemed as unbearable to him as it had been to the young anarchist Victor Serge, starting out from the opposite extreme of poverty and hardship. Whatever criticism might be leveled at Soviet Communism, Gide thought, it was at least trying to redress injustice and do something for the betterment of the have-nots. As for himself, he would have liked to lay down his life for this cause.

It was not comfort and possessions he wanted, it was austerity, devotion, self-abnegation, heroism—in short, the path taken by men like Victor Serge. The advocate of unlimited freedom came to consider liberty a snare and a delusion, and he yearned for discipline. The ever-receptive being, the elusive Proteus who had once appreciated that to follow a particular course of action meant rejecting all the other possibilities open to him, now admired in the dedicated Communist, as in the dedicated Christian, the strength and single-mindedness to "leave father, mother, brothers and sisters, and possessions" and follow the chosen path.[11] The heroic revolutionary's ability to subordinate family ties could not fail to appeal to the author of *Fruits of the Earth,* who had shattered the complacency of middle-class dovecotes with his rousing cry of hatred for the family.

With his newfound faith (and he always thought of it as faith) he regained a sense of purpose. There were meetings to address, petitions to be sent, conferences to attend. On rare occasions, too, came the joy of communing with others, a new sensation for this egocentric individualist who had sacrificed his wife on the altar of self-fulfillment as the revolutionary Serge sacrificed his on the altar of history. Even as a child, Gide had wept when he realized that he was not like others, and it had distressed him to feel that he was a member of an elite, unable to communicate with the vast majority whose pleasures he despised. Gide was convinced that, in a hypocritical bourgeois society, with its false conventions, one could only feel "authentic" in opposition to other people. There was thus no way of avoiding individualism in a bourgeois society, particularly if (like Gide) one felt obliged to defy the world, both as an artist and a homosexual, in order to be one's true self.

But supposing there existed a society where the seeker for authenticity could feel at one with the mass of other human beings, a society from which hypocrisy would be banished? Gide seems to have imagined that in Soviet society there could exist none of the privileges and restrictions, none of the injustice and falsity of bourgeois society, and neither received religion nor the family counted any longer. He even thought it possible to reconcile individualism and communism; he did not envisage communist society as egalitarian but rather as one that would encourage the development of strong personalities. His attitude, as has been pointed out, presents much in common with that of the anarchist rebel.

What Gide found in his new faith, then, was an opportunity to intensify his war on all forms of bourgeois hypocrisy that stunted the growth of the personality. It was an extension of the war consistently waged by artists since the advent of romanticism. Now he could expose the way he thought Christianity, and especially the Catholic clergy, abetted capitalism. He could take a hearty swipe at the indifference and antagonism of Christian believers toward his new faith—so much more worthy, generous, and truly Christian than their own. Belief in a future life encouraged the acceptance of social evils and made revolution impossible. Get rid of the concept of eternal life, and you will have revolution, he noted, well aware of the lack of originality of this idea. A religion which did not fight the evils of bourgeois capitalist society seemed to him a betrayal of Christ greater than that of Judas. It was organized religion, not Christ, that he opposed. For whatever other doubts he might feel, there was no question in his mind that Christ was on the side of Soviet communism.

True, what had led him to communism was, he maintained, "not Marx but the Gospel." [12] (He had conscientiously made his way through the writings of Marx and found them stifling.) What also helped to bring him to support the cause of revolution (along with so many other writers who freely owned, as he did, that they were temperamentally unsuited to political affairs and did not understand them) was a profound contempt for politics. Disdain of this kind was doubtless reinforced by the scandals of the Third Republic. He saw politics as resembling one of Balzac's plots, full of lies and base maneuvers. Contempt for politics, among members of the literary fraternity who do not think politically, encourages a tendency to adopt extreme solutions.

So one is treated to the spectacle of the elderly Gide, one of the most highly regarded literary figures of his day, pondering on what was keeping him from being a revolutionary, or was making him only a reluctant one. Among the obstacles was his knowledge of the grim methods employed in Soviet Russia (though at first he saw these as a thing of the past). In public, however, he could be as forceful an advocate of necessity as Victor Serge. Thus, in his speech to the Association of Revolutionary Writers and Artists in March 1933, he distinguished between terror in Nazi Germany and Soviet Russia: the former was geared to the hateful past, the latter to the promising future, "and doubtless some distressing abuse of force was necessary to allow the establishment of a new society. . . ." [13] Yet despite his public asseverations, Gide was always conducting a debate within himself, as his *Journal,* probably his greatest work, shows. All the time secretly beset by doubts, he offered his sympathy, his collaboration, but did not join the Party.

The remedy Gide thought he had found for declining literary powers turned out to be worse than the disease, because preoccupation with social questions dried up the springs of literary creativity. Gide admitted to Mauriac and others in 1935 that since his conversion to communism he had not been able to write. Marxist orthodoxy was a danger to art, he told them. But at that time he was still prepared to sacrifice art in some degree if that was essential for creating a brave new world.

In the summer of 1936, Gide spent six weeks visiting the Soviet Union, where he was not at all pleased to be lavishly wined and dined and where he was grieved to discover privilege, authoritarian rule, disregard for free inquiry, a climate hostile to great art—in short, yet another dogma and orthodoxy of the sort he had always loathed and defied. For him, as for Serge, the truth came before the struggle against fascism. Against the advice of Malraux, and disregarding Communist pressure, he published his criticism of the Soviet system in *Return from the U.S.S.R.* When its sequel, *Afterthoughts on the U.S.S.R.,* was already on the press, one of his old sensual selves returned, restless and at a loss. "I should like to forget everything," he wrote in his journal, "spend a long time among naked negroes, people whose language would be unknown to me and who would have no idea who I am; and at night, fornicate furiously, silently with anybody at all, on the sand. . . ." [14] Having purged his despair with words, he began to feel better.

It was the end of the revolutionary phase of the future Nobel prize winner. Or rather, he went back to what he had always known: that in the independence, nonconformism, and originality of the great artist lay his revolutionary force. From the moment that Soviet communism presented to him, as it did to Serge, its "counterrevolutionary" aspect, he saw both inner Christianity and art reendowed with their revolutionary significance. For this was the age when, as Malraux's justification of his own metamorphoses would prove, it often appeared imperative for artists to be revolutionary in one way or another.

chapter *18*

revolutionary neo-romanticism:
Malraux and Drieu

It is customary to think of the writers who favored revolution in the twenties and thirties as being on the extreme Left, but D. H. Lawrence reveals the shallowness of this point of view. They could also be found on the extreme Right. This was the time when the creative intelligence was put to a severe test, perhaps the severest it had hitherto known though surely not the last.

The god of war or revolution reigns over the twentieth century, observed Drieu la Rochelle, and nobody could be above the struggle. Many, having rejected long-established values, were tempted by some form of totalitarian sleight-of-hand for private, temperamental, often high-minded, or even aesthetic reasons rather than strictly political ones. Many succumbed, to a greater or lesser degree. That powerful denigrator of humanity, Louis-Ferdinand Céline, for instance, who began as a lower-middle-class anarchist savaging every respected ideal of the establishment, was at first taken for a man of the Left. Despite his tendency, he never joined any fascist party; but as doctor to the members of the Vichy government in exile he found an apocalyptic atmosphere that exceeded the wildest prophecies he had uttered at the outset of his literary career, concerning the mad rush of the moderns into the maw of the Beast.

The resounding title of Céline's first and best novel, *Journey to the End of Night,* epitomizes the determination—shared by many of his colleagues—to go to the end of everything, whatever it might cost them. And it often cost them dear. In 1937, Céline too was calling for revolution, but it had nothing much to do with political revolution: "I've got a hunger! . . . an enormous hunger! . . . a real totalitarian hunger! . . . a world-wide hunger! . . . a hunger for Revolution! . . . a hunger for planetary conflagration! . . . for the mobilisation of all the charnel-houses in the World! An appetite which is surely divine! Biblical!" [1] This grating and gloating cry came from a man who hated modern life and who wanted destruction, without any nonsense about Utopia, dictatorship of the proletariat, redemption, or resurrection.

But with the anarchist writers who were yearning for the end, so as to have done with everything and themselves, and with those anarchist surrealist poets who, as we have seen, mistook revolutionary rhetoric for revolutionary act—came the heroic Nietzschean neo-romantics dominated by the idea of living dangerously, the urge for commitment, and the cult of action. In heroic revolutionary neo-romanticism, a writer who chose the Communist side, like Malraux, and one who chose the Fascist side, like Drieu, sometimes appear to be separated by a hair's breadth. Perhaps ultimately it was the nature of their respective temperaments which would lead the former to legendary self-creation and the latter to the all-too-real self-destruction—"the act of those who have never been able to commit any other" [2]—with which he had flirted throughout his life.

Where Malraux sought lyrically to affirm the positive element in mankind, in the face of every rational argument that would destroy it,

Drieu was submerged by the negative waves of his experience. But they were united in their unshakable hatred of bourgeois society and its values, especially liberal parliamentary democracy, a hatred which they inherited in particular from Maurras in their youth. And although both had passed beyond the narrow nationalism of the founder of Action Française, they retained a nostalgia for the nationalist ideal which would reassert itself in their maturity.

In their analysis of the ills of the twentieth century they showed themselves as would-be breakers of tablets after Zarathustra, radicals in quest of a new ethos, with a taste for dramatic apocalyptism and a penchant for violence. Whatever extreme ideology they might exalt, their roots lay entangled in the nineteenth-century romantic Stendhalian and Barrésian dilemmas of the frustrated ego and its power complex. They were, by the nature of their imagination, conscious descendants of Julien Sorel as he stood on the height contemplating the flight of the bird of prey and dreaming of a Napoleonic destiny. That dream was to bring one of them international adulation and the other obloquy.

Before Malraux was forty (an English critic claimed), he was "already an almost legendary figure, reaching the stature of a Byron in modern Europe's wars of liberation." [3] These words were written not so very long after Malraux's exploits in the early months of the Spanish Civil War, at a time when the Spanish Republican cause was widely viewed (so Orwell indicates) as a revolutionary one. Malraux had tirelessly built up a nucleus of planes and international pilots, and he took part in over sixty missions, being wounded twice. Yet this assessment of Malraux as the contemporary Byron, often reechoed since, was penned before the most astounding of his metamorphoses: his emergence as Colonel Berger, Resistance hero (rejoicing, according to an eyewitness, in the ferocity of his men), and eventually minister in the government of a lofty Barrésian leader.

Malraux appears as the twentieth-century Byron principally because he too touched, as did few others, a chord in the sensibility of his contemporaries, and appeared to fulfill their dreams of heroic revolutionary action and power. To one American critic, Alfred Kazin, "it looked as if the imagination of revolution and the imagination of literature were stirred by the same fiery depths. . . ." And he went on, describing in revealing terms the effect of Malraux's books upon susceptible readers in the thirties: "He was the novelist of the intellectuals' revolutionary *grandeur*. To those for whom society was a metaphor and the instrument of their newly exalted revolutionary will, Malraux was intoxicating, a breath of power." [4]

Literature alone could not satisfy Malraux any more than it could Byron. With the martyr of Missolonghi, Malraux came to see in revolutionary action a way out, a means of personal salvation, a sublimation of the insufferable ego. The only child of parents who separated when he was about four, he hated his childhood and generally seems to have disliked the cards of identity he had been dealt as the grandson of a Dunkirk ship chandler. Like the conspiratorial Byron, who had adopted Napoleon's monogram, he was haunted by the yearning for a shaped and mastered destiny. More successful than Byron, however, he became in time a "pasha" of sorts. In his own lifetime, therefore, Malraux contrived to transform man into myth, as he felt his heroes had done. One of these heroes was the hollow adventurer who said he wrote his "will across the sky in stars," Lawrence of Arabia, whom he supposedly met in London in 1935 just before the fatal motorcycle accident; the other was the spartan Saint-Just, who would speak of the life he had given himself "in the skies." [5] What does Malraux love about Saint-Just? It is that the Jacobin has no family, that his destiny is man-made, shaped by the revolutionary alone.

Slim, handsome, with a hypnotically intense gaze, a monologist who would be capable of intimidating Gide with his brilliance, Malraux made his Parisian debut in 1920 with an article on Cubist poetry and a review of the Decadent anarchist poet Laurent Tailhade, exponent of the beautiful gesture. He wrote literary essays for a periodical of anarchist tinge, to which Victor Serge also contributed. But before he went out to Cambodia in search of Khmer statuary (having gambled and lost on the Stock Exchange), there seemed to be nothing of the political animal, let alone the revolutionary, about him. However, the imagination of this admirer of artists of the romantic agony, like Lautréamont, was already haunted by fantastic scenes of massacre and sadistic torture that were to recur in his novels.

Two experiences were radically to alter the outlook of Malraux the dandy and dilettante. One was his glimpse of the abuses of colonialism in Djibouti in French East Africa on his first journey to the Far East in 1923. The other was his arrest and trial in Phnom-Penh, where he was accused of the theft of statues from the temple of Banteay Srei and sentenced to a term of imprisonment. As a result of this humiliation, he was to put his pen at the service of the exploited Cambodian subjects of the French empire. On his return to Saigon in 1925, he helped to revive the Young Annam movement, and in the paper *L'Indochine* (later *L'Indochine Enchaînée*), which he edited with Paul Monin, he flayed the injustices of capitalist imperialism with indignant sarcasm.

While he was active in Saigon, he joined a local branch of the Kuomintang, the Chinese Nationalist Party being at that time allied with the Comintern. From this period dates the beginning of his legendary reputation as a revolutionary, about which little is known in actual fact. It is thought that he may have attended some sessions of the Kuomintang when he was in Hong Kong to buy type for his paper, shortly after the principal revolutionary events in Canton which are described in his first novel, *The Conquerors*. Although he remarks in *Antimemoirs* that he was in Shanghai before 1930, according to his first wife, Clara, he did not set foot on the Chinese mainland (visiting Canton, Shanghai, and Peking) until 1931—that is, after the suppression of the Communist rising in Shanghai in 1927, portrayed in *Man's Fate*.

On the subject of what role (if any) he played in events in China, Malraux has remained deliberately vague, and when directly questioned on the matter by Janine Mossuz in 1968, he proved evasive. True, much is known, and can be substantiated, about his activities in Indochina, or as a communist sympathizer in the struggle against fascism between the wars, and his later exploits in Spain and during the 1939–1945 war. But his career as an active revolutionary, often suggested by biographical details he himself has furnished, belongs in the realm of speculation.

Of course it is the very vagueness which enhances his romantic allure: the possibility that so gifted an intellectual, so knowledgeable about art and archaeology, and a writer of a high order to boot, may have been involved in clandestine activities or, like his ruthless revolutionary adventurer Garine in *The Conquerors,* may have served as "deputy commissar for propaganda" with Borodin (as one version of Malraux's biography has it). All this adds as irresistibly to his aura as the image of the poet in the role of Carbonaro does to Byron's. In any case, here is a man who has not been content to live as the majority of writers do, pursuing their solitary task, often singing of arms and men, and dreaming of blood and barbarism, but condemned to suffer the Keatsian dilemma.

"The drama of the modern intellectual is that he would like to be a revolutionary, but cannot make it," wrote Malraux's friend Emmanuel Berl in 1929 in *Death of Bourgeois Thought.* This revealing study is dedicated admiringly to Malraux as a long defense of Garine, the character most frequently associated with Malraux himself because he too experienced the full force of nothingness and the absurd when on trial for a crime which he declined to recognize as one. Berl would have liked Garine for his chum. He and another of his friends, Drieu la Rochelle, actually regarded the weary Garine as a new type of man. (Garine, it will be remembered, shoots a prisoner allegedly for the purpose of expediency, after the style of T. E. Lawrence). Perhaps what was really significant about Garine (as indeed about T. E. Lawrence) was that such dubious figures could now command the unqualified esteem of men of letters, whose ideal once was to preserve humane values.

In its day, the impact made by *The Conquerors* was extraordinary, and bears witness to the novel's epoch-making character as regards theme and attitude, if not technique. Malraux himself later spoke rather scathingly of this early work, but the book is a remarkably powerful accomplishment for a young man of twenty-six. Not every author would be invited to participate in a debate on the problems raised by his first novel, or would find himself engaging in public controversy with the legendary Trotsky about its revolutionary import.

From the first, Malraux's contemporaries questioned the precise nature, meaning, and degree of his commitment to revolution—even if they did not go as far as Trotsky, who found Malraux's sympathies for the Chinese rising to be marred by aestheticism. Trotsky suggested that what Malraux needed was a good dose of Marxism, but eventually decided he was beyond Marxist cure. Meanwhile Malraux defended himself by declaring that he had written a novel, not a revolutionary tract. Only some years later, when Malraux expressed admiration for Stalin's contribution to human dignity and failed to denounce uncompromisingly the Russian purges, did the exile see him as a crypto-fascist. Whatever may have been meant by that (the word "fascist" was then and afterward bandied about as a meaningless term of abuse, applied to Trotsky and his followers as well), there was a sense in which the old revolutionary had hit upon Malraux's fundamental ambiguity. It was an ambiguity revealed in particular by those writers who, while defending humanist or heroic values, detested parliamentary democracy and rejected what Orwell could still call the spirit of liberalism.

But before discussing Malraux's attitude toward revolution in more detail, it will be necessary to speak of the intellectual and spiritual atmosphere in France when he made his mark, and of the disastrous career of his friend Drieu, who presents the reverse of his medal.

Malraux began to write during the years of postwar malaise, of Spenglerian pessimism, when Europe appeared to him as a cemetery. At that time, many had convinced themselves of the decadence and decay not only of their country but of Western civilization for the values and ideals which had guided the Western world for centuries seemed to have crumbled into dust with the corpses on the European battlefields. This attitude was in effect the continuation of the late nineteenth-century sense of gloom, catastrophe, and apocalyptism, but exacerbated by the horrors of modern mechanical warfare. It was the new *mal du siècle,* as Marcel Arland, one of Malraux's friends, called it—a social, moral, and metaphysical crisis. Many were struggling to find an outcome, they knew not what. Some of them passionately began to feel the "need for voluntary joining." [6]

To some extent, this state of mind resembled the frustration of the Byronic hero and his descendants after the Napoleonic wars. Only, where Byron cast his dramatic spotlight on the individual, Malraux could not bring himself to do so. In his early writings, with their critical assessment of Western civilization (an assessment he never disowned), Malraux declared the bankruptcy of nineteenth-century individualism, which had reached its culmination in the Barrésian cult of the ego. Somehow there had to be a new view of man which would replace all the attitudes and doctrines that exalt the self. This quest coincided with the proclaimed antiliberal intentions of totalitarian ideologies aiming to sublimate the ego in some collective identity, the proletariat or the nation-state.

It was the antiindividualist and antiliberal outlook which encouraged Malraux, at the height of his fellow-traveling period (he was never a Marxist nor a member of the Communist party), to laud bolshevism because "on the metaphysical plane" it maintained that "the highest human values are collective values." [7] Malraux, whose writings on art and literature tend to be more revealing of his own private obsessions than of his ostensible subject, would annex another Nietzschean, D. H. Lawrence, for thinking it more important to be a man than an individual. And he would insist that where the bourgeoisie elevated the individual, communism elevated "man." At the same time, this stress on man in general is paradoxically countered by his own enduring fascination with rare self-creating individuals who are incarnations of some collective myth—not only artists but those marked by the fever of power, an attitude symptomatic of the very tendencies he dislikes and condemns. His hypnotic rhetoric may serve to obscure the fundamental elitism of this view.

True, Christianity had insisted upon the worth of each individual soul, but it seemed to Malraux that the world after 1919 was left merely with the remains of the Christian heritage. While acknowledging the loftiness of Christianity, Malraux, speaking through his other self, A. D., in *The Temptation of the West,* could not accept it and declared that he would never do so. How to fill the "inner void left gaping by the power of centuries and instincts?" asked Marcel Arland; he added, "The absence of God is the denial of all morality. Can the political form of a country or economic and humanitarian problems replace that ancient foundation in us?" [8] Extremist violent political activity was one possible way of asserting one's existence for those who, like Malraux's terrorist Tchen, would inquire what to do with a soul if there is neither God nor Christ.

For clearly all that remains for the members of a gifted elite is a kind of latent power, a sense of dormant possibilities. Such men resemble "pitiful actors" who are reluctant to give up glorious roles, although they have seen through all the old ideals that sustain these roles. Fatherland, justice, truth merely arouse their melancholy irony. "There is no ideal for which we might sacrifice ourselves, . . . And yet, what sacrifices, what unjustified forms of heroism lie sleeping within us." [9] So broods A. D. in a letter to a Chinese friend in *The Temptation of the West,* written between 1921 and 1925 and published in 1926.

In that year Drieu la Rochelle began work on his book *Geneva or Moscow.* A disciple of Sorel, he was one of the early advocates of a supranational European federation; had written on the Decadent anarchist novelist, Paul Adam; frequented Surrealist circles, and was (then) friendly with Aragon. In *Geneva or Moscow,* published in 1928, he reiterated one of his basic ideas, the decadence of the West—nay, of the planet. "We only feel the strength and the beauty of the present day in the destructive and heinous," wrote Drieu. "God, aristocracy, bourgeoisie, property, country, proletariat no longer exist. On the right and the left everyone knows this in his heart. There are only men striving to create something else so as not to die." [10] The "new man" Drieu was to propose differed from Malraux's in that he would have to be a combination of warrior and ascetic, but he too must serve as a militant partisan in the modern wars of religion, a hero endowed with a political mystique in place of the lost mystique of the Church.

Both Drieu and Malraux sprang from the same despairing nihilism and shared the same desire to replace it with some positive affirmation or self-suppressing heroic ideal. Both also inherited that morbid strain in romanticism that blossomed into deadly flowers of sadistic eroticism and violent action. "Everything sang to me of violence," said Drieu. "No doubt I was born to respond to that call rather than another." [11] An inveterate womanizer and frequenter of bordellos, Drieu seemed even more afraid of sexual impotence than was Malraux, who once told the novelist Julien Green that he dreaded it as a token of death. And through sexual imagery Drieu projected his admiration for virile leadership. He acknowledged with rare candor the feminine, masochistic character of his own love of force, an aspect he rightly thought was common to certain communist intellectuals and fascists, and one which Orwell later harshly illuminated in his essay on Raffles and Miss Blandish.

Despite the opposite paths followed by Malraux, and Drieu, they remained friends—the writer who fought tirelessly against racism and the one who declined into a rabid racist. At any time between 1927 and 1943 (the period of Malraux's most intensive commitment to the Left, though before his emergence as Resistance hero; and of Drieu's collaboration with the Fascist leader Doriot and later with the Nazis under the Occupation), they might be found pacing the streets of Paris or the south late at night, deep in discussion. Doubtless they touched upon the figures they both admired so much: Saint-Just and Michelet, Dostoevsky, Nietzsche, and T. E. Lawrence. This association in itself perhaps serves as an indication of the nature of their respective commitment, with its element of role-playing.

What Drieu longed to do was to incite men to action, to destroy some empires and rebuild others. It was a dream he would finally embody in his novel set in a Bolivia of the imagination, *Man on Horseback*. There Felipe, a poet, and Jaime, an army officer (both aspects of the author's wish to reconcile thought and action), seek to restore the lost empire and religion of the Incas. This dream of Drieu's was distantly related to that of Malraux's adventurer Perken in *The Royal Way*, who aspires to leave a scar on the map; it doubtless owed something also to the gruesome Mexican revivalists of D. H. Lawrence, one of whose stories Drieu translated into French.

It is scarcely surprising, then, that Drieu saw the author of *The Conquerors* and *The Royal Way* as the embodiment of his ideal of the writer who does not live solely in order to write. Drieu had always preferred blood to ink, though ironically he was more a man of letters than of action. "Malraux has leapt into the heart of the adventure that comes from the union of thought and action," wrote Drieu.[12] Thought alone was insufficient: it was imperative to be prepared to stake one's life on one's "ideas." This was what Drieu eventually did when he decided to collaborate with the Nazis during the Occupation, against the advice of his friend Otto Abetz, the German ambassador. For he was well aware that he was risking his neck. When all was lost, he wrote that he had wanted to compromise himself. Anything, he said, was better than being taken for an intellectual in an ivory tower. The self-betrayal of the literary intellectual could go no further. In the end, by taking his own life in 1945 in order to avoid trial for collaboration, he would find what he sought: "a death worthy of the revolutionary and reactionary I am." [13]

For Drieu, too, spoke in terms of revolution. He recognized as "the new fact of the twentieth century" a Nietzschean reversal which occurred in 1903—when Lenin, having learned the totalitarian lessons of the Jacobins of 1792, rejected liberal values and created a totalitarian revolutionary party, determined to achieve and preserve power by ruse and force.[14] From this "new fact," according to Drieu, flowed the series of authoritarian or totalitarian revolutions that had occurred since 1917. Thus Nazi Germany represented a revolutionary force, not always recognized as such. Here Drieu finds strange confirmation in Orwell who, stressing the common element of oligarchical collectivism in both Nazism and Communism, wrote: "National Socialism *is* a form of Socialism, *is* emphatically revolutionary, . . ." [15]

Drieu had hoped for an antiparliamentary revolutionary movement, an alliance of Left and Right, after the events of February 6, 1934, when the Third Republic was almost overthrown. This was the moment when he flirted with Communism, but he told the Argentinian poetess Victoria Ocampo, another admirer of Lawrence of Arabia, that he could not accept Communism because he could not be a materialist. For his sickness was that he had no grasp of his own being or of existence in general. Instead of becoming a Communist, he joined the party of Doriot, the former Communist workman turned Fascist, and did not leave it until 1938.

All the same, Drieu always thought of himself as a socialist, and wrote a book entitled *Fascist Socialism* to explain his position. He expounded fascism as a form of socialism faithful to the spirit of the French pre-Marxist Socialists Saint-Simon, Fourier, and Proudhon—a system renewed in the revolutionary syndicalism of Sorel, through whom it passed to Mussolini. It seemed to Drieu that young Socialists and Communists were among those most likely to become Fascists. For him, the Jacobin and even Caesarian tradition, together with the socialist or syndicalist tendency, underlay all forms of fascism: "Fascism always starts on the Left," he declared.[16] One of the characters in his novel *Gilles,* fighting for Franco during the Spanish Civil War, sees fascism as "an immense salutary revolution." [17] Drieu became disillusioned with the Nazis during the Occupation because they were not revolutionary enough for his liking, and failed to foster in France the kind of "revolution" they had accomplished in Germany. When he knew they were bound to lose, he believed Communism would triumph, but felt too old to change his coat. In short, whatever solution he admitted, it had to be an extreme totalitarian one.

There is a curious moment in Malraux's *The Conquerors* when the former agent of the tsarist police, Nikolaieff, wonders whether Garine (who evidently knows his Pareto) may not end as an adherent of Mussolini. This query acquires a strange resonance when one recalls that Malraux in his youth wanted to be another d'Annunzio. Later, in his novel *Man's Hope,* Malraux has the Communist Manuel declare that "A man who is both active and pessimistic is or will be a Fascist, unless he has an allegiance behind him." [18] What precisely was Malraux's allegiance?

It lay in the instinctive refusal of a proud man who had suffered humiliation to accept the humiliation of others with indifference. Although Malraux could never find any rational explanation for doing so, he persisted in justifying human dignity and fraternity and positive human or transcendental values (as symbolized by the descent from the mountain in *Man's Hope* or the walnut trees of Altenburg). On the contrary, Drieu was ready to destroy existing society in order to restore the notion of aristocracy and fulfill his ideal of virile plenitude, because in reality he could affirm and justify nothing, least of all himself: "Mystery of humanity which gives itself for nothing, to nothing!" [19] His novel, *Straw Dogs,* ends in a furious blaze of destruction. Drieu could never extricate himself from the nihilism that threatened to overwhelm the period immediately after the 1914–1918 war. He was the self-confessed victim of the ills he denounced, those disintegrating factors that Malraux was determined at all costs to transcend.

We are now ready to consider Malraux's attitude toward revolution, essentially equivocal from the beginning. Revolution appeared to him as one possible means of transcending nothingness, one possible substitute for the lost absolute. It was less a historical phenomenon than a force and a mystique that captivated the imagination, as transmitted to him not only by Michelet but by Hugo's *Quatre-vingt-treize.* For Malraux, the French Revolution meant the Convention, Danton, Robespierre, Saint-Just, "the one and indivisible Republic." This aspect of revolution would always remain with him.

Many years after he showed Garine's imagination dominated by Saint-Just, Malraux wrote a prefatory essay on the austere, fanatical Jacobin— seeing him as the incarnation of the "revolutionary dream," a man whose "fixed star" was the Republic, considered not merely as a form of government but as "an Apocalypse, and the hope of an unknown world." Malraux shared the view that Saint-Just was "passionately totalitarian," the forerunner of Communists, Fascists, and the single all-powerful party—though this does not seem to lessen the writer's admiration. Moreover, Saint-Just, said Malraux, longed *"to change man,* by compelling him into a transfiguring epic." [20] The novelist even tried (apparently unsuccessfully) to convince General de Gaulle of Saint-Just's merits. And what was Saint-Just, after all? He was a creature of single-minded ruthlessness who used terror as an instrument of power.

Perhaps no twentieth-century novelist has expressed more passionately than Malraux the fascination of terror as an aspect of the will to power, omnipotence, and godhead. One of his most striking achievements was to penetrate into the mind of the "rather handsome" revolutionary terrorist in the person of Hong (and later, in *Man's Fate,* to even greater effect in the more developed character of Tchen). Of Hong, governed by hatred and the desire to avenge the wrongs of the Chinese poor, Malraux would say afterward: "I know what is engaging in this figure, in his resolve, in his savage purity; . . ." [21] If Garine thought Hong could be used, and was annoyed when Borodin had him executed, Malraux himself agreed that in order to win it was necessary to use Hong, and accused Trotsky of joining with Lenin to liquidate Hong's Russian equivalents. This wounded the proud and ruthless Bolshevik, and with unconscious irony he stigmatized Garine and Borodin as bureaucratic supermen whose policy bore "the mark of Cain." [22]

Was it Nietzsche's Zarathustra, asserting that the tablet inscribed "Thou shalt not kill" should be broken, who enabled Malraux to depict political assassination for the revolutionary cause with sustained excitement? Killing becomes simply another field of experience to be transformed into awareness. After the act of political assassination which opens *Man's Fate* in so stunning a fashion, Tchen can declare that those who have not killed are "virgins," to be despised.[23] For Tchen, therefore, killing resembles a sexual initiation rite, a proof of virility. In Malraux's cinematographic account of such deeds in his novels, or even in his obsession with corpses horribly mutilated by torture, the Dostoevskian sense of moral condemnation is lacking, through the deliberate rejection of remorse and the notion of crime. Malraux stands Dostoevsky on his head. What remains in the reader's memory is the author's intense fascination with the situation of intellectuals who are capable of taking life, and with cruelty as a mystery. This, however, is not the whole story, which depends on the balance of opposites. Tchen the terrorist has to be balanced with Kyo, who strives in prison to resist the fascination of cruelty and bestiality and to preserve human dignity.

The same kind of balance is preserved in the assertion and the denial of the will. Garine, who betrays a total absence of scruple in the service of something beyond his personal interest, is a gambler who seeks in the revolution a means of solving his own problems and uniting himself with "some great action." [24] The revolution is thus a pretext for the exertion of his energy and will. At the same time, the sense of nothingness—which, combined with hatred for the bourgeois class and its "stupid principles," led him to the revolution in the first place—never really leaves him. As a sick and possibly doomed man (here a direct projection of Malraux himself, who was then in the grip of illness), Garine is obliged to leave the scene of his activity and triumphs. What will remain? The impulse of Malraux's characters is to assert their will in the full knowledge of its limitations. This is illustrated in Garine's Goya-like recollection of the young soldier who boasted that he would bayonet anyone who tried to assault him, but was nonetheless raped in the most hideously grotesque way.

Already certain reservations are evident, even in Malraux's first novel, in the contrast between Garine and Borodin (whom Malraux conceived, wrongly in Trotsky's view, as a professional revolutionary and strict disciplinarian). Garine thoroughly dislikes discipline and dogmatism. Nor does he feel any great love for humanity, the poor, the people on whose behalf he fights. Indeed, he believes the masses will prove abject in the hour of victory. All he shares with them is the common struggle. The revolutionary need not be motivated by a preconceived doctrine or technique of revolution, thought Malraux, but his will is placed at the service of his brothers in the cause, and therefore he will always act in such a way as to benefit them. This notion strikes one as precarious.

The stress on the brotherhood of revolutionary fighters appears more clearly in Malraux's explanatory remarks than in the novel itself. It was in *Man's Fate* that the novelist exalted this ideal, in Katow's heroic self-sacrifice when he gives his cyanide to two of his comrades and faces a terrible death. The celebrated climax of *Man's Fate* fulfills, without Christian faith, the Christian ethic of noble self-sacrifice for the salvation of others, a consummation magnanimous spirits ardently sought in the revolutionary cause, if Silone is to be believed. It offers the highest expression of Malraux's ideal of salvation through heroic transcendence of self in revolutionary solidarity, that solidarity which Trotsky defined in virtually mystic terms as taking man out of "the dark night of the circumscribed I." [25]

The beginning of a revolutionary movement is characterized by the ecstatic upsurge of hopes and dreams and all that Malraux calls "the Apocalypse of fraternity." But this revelation, conveyed in the early pages of *Man's Hope,* entitled "The Lyrical Illusion," cannot endure: it has to be transformed into an instrument of victory. The growth of the Communist Manuel into a solitary revolutionary leader, becoming ever "less human" until he reaches the point where he refuses to listen to cries of mercy, underlines the insoluble tragic dilemma. "It might be said," observes García, "that the struggle, Apocalypse, hope, are the baits War employs to catch men. After all, syphilis begins with love." [26]

Earlier, in *The Conquerors,* Malraux had sketched out some of the problems raised by revolutionary commitment, but in *Man's Hope* these are worked into the dialectic of the novel itself. The impassioned discussions of the intellectuals in *Man's Hope,* embodying Malraux's inner arguments, return to the enduring conflict between the revolutionary dream and the means necessary to put it into effect; between the requirements of action which is seen as "Manichaean," concerned with clear-cut alternatives, and the nature of the intellectual, a man concerned with nuance, truth, complexity; between "being" and "doing," private moral perfection and the need to win.

These dilemmas are not resolved but are held in irreconcilable tension. Revolution no longer appears as a means of escaping from man's tragic destiny, but as yet another aspect of the human tragedy: "For a man who thinks, revolution is tragic. But for such a man, life also is tragic. And if he is counting on revolution to remove its tragedy, his thinking is all wrong," says García. [27] Nothing is changed, since even after victory man is still confronting his solitary death.

The writer who took the political stage after the Liberation in 1945 was opposed to communism, for in the course of the war he had "married France," as he embarrassingly expressed it. [28] In the tank corps and the maquis, not in a foreign cause, he had found his own true national brotherhood of arms. Moreover, the Russian Revolution had ceased to be an upsurge of hope and had become instead a weapon of Russian nationalism and imperialism. Consequently it was the Russians and their supporters in France and elsewhere who had changed, not himself. Where the revolution was concerned, he maintained, he had remained perfectly consistent.

In his role as propagandist he was thus at pains to prove that the Gaullist movement was a revolutionary one. It was the heir of the French Revolution and the First Republic of 1792, the republic of Robespierre and Saint-Just. His deep-seated hostility to parliamentary democracy remained unchanged. The guarantee of political liberty and intellectual freedom was not political liberalism but a strong state at the service of all its citizens, he declared in 1948. And in the following year he could proclaim: "There is ourselves, the Communists and nothing"—nothing being the legally elected government.[29] At this point he was not so far from Drieu and his extreme alternatives. His tone was similarly apocalyptic: the situation in France was that of a dying, decadent, prerevolutionary regime, resembling that of 1788. France, on the brink of catastrophe, was awaiting a man, a leader, a savior, the great one who was the incarnation of the national myth.

Malraux saw Gaullism as "a movement of public safety," and (unlike General de Gaulle himself) he expected it to seize power by force.[30] When the Gaullist movement became a political party like any other, he lost interest in it. His loyalty was to General de Gaulle alone, and when the great man withdrew, he retired. Decadence, the futility of parliamentarianism, the strong state, the cult of the savior-leader, the myth of national grandeur, the readiness to achieve power by coup d'état were themes common to fascism. All that saved him was his anti-fascist record: "General de Gaulle is not a Fascist: the proof is that I am with him, and I have been wounded fourteen times in the service of liberty." [31] That does not obscure the dangers inherent in his influential outlook.

One cannot help perceiving the fragility of such labels as Left and Right, Communist and Fascist in relation to a figure as unstable as Drieu or one as ambiguous and elusive as Malraux. They followed their aesthetic notions and the pull of their temperaments whither these led. Byron might have coined the phrase "the poetry of politics" for them. They were, in their different ways, actors yearning to be taken seriously, for whom the mask became the face. Malraux was alluding to opponents when he spoke of those who longed "to act in a heroic drama called Revolution," or when he saw revolutionary romanticism as a failure to distinguish political action from the theater; but these insights may equally be applied to himself.[32]

Some form of political or revolutionary commitment was also, for Drieu as well as Malraux, a substitute for a lost religious mysticism. To Sartre they stood as types of the committed artist, the one to be excoriated, the other admired, adventurers who made respectively the incorrect and the correct choice, though united in the virile romanticism of violence, dirty hands, and the extreme. With the benefit of hindsight, we may well feel that they and their heirs were too ready to accept the so-called "new fact of the twentieth century," the rejection of hard-won but despised and discredited safeguards.

chapter 19

dirty hands: Sartre,
Camus, Orwell

"What do Camus, Malraux, Koestler, Rousset, etc., write but a literature of extreme situations?" Sartre exclaimed in a note to *What Is Literature?* "Their characters are at the pinnacle of power or in prison cells, just about to die, to be tortured, or to kill; wars, coups d'état, revolutionary action, shellings, massacres are everyday occurrences. On every page, in every line, it is always man as a whole who is at issue." [1] Total man is the modern chimera. Besides, how can man be complete, entire, and real if he has not experienced everything, including dirt, mud, blood?

The romantic quest for the heights of power, authenticity, and wholeness leads paradoxically, like so many romantic quests, into the most murky depths, where hearts may be pure but hands are not. Sin (delicious thought) comes before redemption. Writers brood on the difficult moral

choices presented in extreme situations where the taking of life is involved, situations into which they themselves were thrown willingly or un-
willingly by the dread circumstances of war or revolution and which they
could not elude even if they did not actively participate. "There is only
one problem to-day," wrote Camus (who was discreetly modest about his
role in the French Resistance) in 1946, "and that is killing." [2] (He used
the French synonym for "murder.")

Among the modern heirs of the "romantic agony" who came to prom-
inence in the years immediately before, during, or just after the
1939–1945 war, the early Malraux still enjoyed immense prestige. It was
not only Sartre, less than four years his junior, who could often be found
quoting him with the respect of disciple for master. Briefly a Communist
at twenty-one, Camus, too, owed more to Malraux than his adaptation of
Days of Wrath into a play might suggest. Orwell, the new Hazlitt, in
Paris not long after the Liberation, called on Malraux to present him with
a copy of *Homage to Catalonia* but found the great man absent. "I'd like to
be another Malraux," Mailer candidly admitted; [3] he paid his hero the
tribute of imitation not only in his first novel, *The Naked and the Dead*
(in the central discussion between General Cummings and Lieutenant
Hearn on man's drive to omnipotence), but in his second, *Barbary Shore,*
on the theme of the revolutionary grail, a work begun when he was
studying at the Sorbonne in 1948.

Some writers appear to have felt that, in order to be great, complete,
or genuine, one must be on the side of political, economic, social, or sexual revolution. This attitude would evolve, with Sartre and his companion
Simone de Beauvoir, into a form of revolutionary snobbery, where it becomes imperative that one must be further to the Left, more concerned
for the oppressed, more uncompromising, and more revolutionary-
minded than everybody else. Always in the *beau rôle,* the writer then provides a "revolutionary" spectacle rather than promoting actual social
change. At the same time, neither Sartre nor Simone de Beauvoir proved
particularly revolutionary in their literary manner or in their free liaison,
(which permitted other attachments), in which the author of *The Second
Sex* figures as a rather subdued George Sand.

Above all, with the growing pressure of extraliterary considerations, and under the pervasive dominance of the revolutionary ideal, writers worried about what good they and their tribe could do for the world. The question of the writer's confidence in literature and in his own calling—a question which had been raised with urgency at times, since the moment when Keats queried the function of poetry compared with "real things" and Byron demanded "actions . . . and not writing"—now reached a crisis from which it has not recovered.

So there occurs the anomaly of authors who are endowed with great gifts and possess an indisputable literary vocation but are dissatisfied or ill at ease with literature and aspire to be something other than men of imagination—something more "real," authentic, uncomplicated. In the romantic yearning for true naturalness and simplicity, they no longer wish to see themselves, as their forebears did, innocently piping among Arcadian shepherds, but rather seek to be accepted and honored by depressed 'manual laborers and factory workers, the supposed harbingers and dictators of the future. The trouble is that, whatever efforts middle-class writers might make, they could never experience the authentic condition and sufferings of the underdog. This failure would be a source of immense frustration and self-reproach to a thinker like Sartre, another proof of inherited inauthenticity, or original sin (modern version). The cultivated intellectual's craving "to become single- and simple-minded" has been characterized by Koestler as a kind of intellectual self-castration. [4]

Doubtless an offshoot of the cult of the tough proletarian (heir of the noble savage) and his natural untaught virtues was Orwell's idealization of the illiterate young Italian militiaman whom he met briefly in Barcelona in the early days of the Spanish Civil War, and whom he transformed into the symbol of the martyred European working class. This Italian soldier, whom he never forgot, appeared to him as a superior being who was "born knowing what I had learned/Out of books and slowly." [5] In appearance "fierce" as well as innocent and pathetic, the Italian volunteer would (in Orwell's romanticizing imagination) readily "commit murder and throw away his life for a friend." [6] This aspect linked him with a familiar long-lived heroic tradition exalting the pathos and energy of outlawry—a tradition likely to appeal to the former imperial policeman with anarchist leanings who, despite his anti-fascist stand, sympathized with what he felt were the good aspects of fascism.

Orwell's Italian militiaman grew into the mighty incarnation of the crystal spirit that could never be broken. He embodied the common people, who had never learned to think and whose plebeian odors, moreover, could offend the nostrils of the author, struggling to quash the old Etonian in himself, but who would somehow, at least until the final despairing vision, save all. Among the obscure drives which impelled Orwell, descended from the impoverished lesser gentry, to immerse himself for months in the life of the down-and-outs in France and England, was a special kind of romanticism—the belief not only that the lower, grubbier, and more uncomfortable one gets, the closer one comes to salvation, but that salvation must come from below. This is a notion to which we shall have to return.

As the novelist and critic John Wain has observed, Orwell the compulsive writer glossed over the fact that he also had a literary aim in pursuing the strange fauna—the workmen, tramps, and outcasts—into the lower depths. They could prove a suitable theme for literature. One did not write to please (or, as Orwell expressed it some years before Sartre, to produce "the dope that a privileged minority demands"), nor even in order to influence the reading public. For, he declared in 1938, a few months before the Munich crisis, "at a moment like the present, writing books is not enough." [7] How could any thinking person go on living in society as then constituted without wanting to change it?

Two years later, in 1940, Orwell, in a telling image, saw the writer "sitting on a melting iceberg; he is merely an anachronism, a hangover from the bourgeois age, as surely doomed as the hippopotamus." And he prophesied: ". . . from now onwards the all-important fact for the creative writer is going to be that this is not a writer's world. That does not mean that he cannot help to bring the new society into being, but he can take no part in the process *as a writer*." [8] Such gloomy skepticism about the writer's role and mission would doubtless have shocked the George

Sands and Belinskys of a hundred years before. Yet there is a genuine crisis and conflict expressed here, since if the writer *as writer* may often be liberal in the sense of being open and disinterested, he is nonetheless committed to the destruction of liberal values as an advocate of violent revolution (such as Orwell was then). No wonder he feels disturbed and disoriented.

"Literature. Mistrust this word," noted a writer who differed from both Orwell and Sartre in springing from the working class.[9] Camus's widowed mother had worked as a charwoman. In his early years the author of *The Outsider* had known hunger and poverty in French Algeria, not as a voluntary form of exotic trial but as an inescapable condition. Through literature, he broke free of his disadvantages, but no less than Orwell he experienced loss of faith in literature: "The fact of writing implies a self-confidence which is beginning to desert me," Camus confessed during the war, foreseeing a future when he might no longer write.[10] Such moments were transitory; both Orwell and Camus continued writing until each met an untimely end, but these waverings reveal a failure of literary nerve that was not confined to them alone.

Where the writer's unease is concerned, however, the most commanding figure among the moderns is surely Sartre; he may, with some justification, claim to be the last major antiromantic romantic to be torn asunder by the irreconcilable orders and demands of literature and of social, political and economic revolution. Diminutive, squint-eyed, self-conscious, scathingly ironic, he is always moving between extremes. Sartre has long been haunted by the exponents of art for art's sake, by Baudelaire (whose childhood circumstances distantly resembled his own), and above all by Flaubert, incarnation of the writer as martyr and dedicated exponent of salvation through art. What Sartre apparently cannot forgive Flaubert, whom he projects as literary alter ego and whipping boy, is that the author of *Madame Bovary* did nothing to prevent the suppression of the Commune in 1871—for the existentialist philosopher has felt that he himself failed to do anything to prevent the disasters which overtook the Left in the thirties.

Sartre's disquiet about literature, and about the values and life style or "neurosis" it fosters, was already manifest in his first novel, *La Nausée*. Known in English as *The Diary of Antoine Roquentin*, this novel was written in 1934, though it was not published until 1938. The most important fact about Roquentin from our point of view is that he is a writer undergoing a crisis of consciousness which naturally affects his faith in literature. *"I was* Roquentin," Sartre would later admit (echoing Flaubert's "Madame Bovary, c'est moi") in *The Words*, his self-flagellating autobiography and avowed farewell to literature.[11] Yet when Sartre began his career as a writer he was convinced that only writers, artists, or thinkers can grasp reality. To the young Sartre, still in those days a true heir of Flaubert, nothing seemed more important than a book, and his pen served as an instrument not only for his own glory but for the redemption of mankind (or so the mature Sartre tells us). As early as his first novel, Sartre traced the disintegrating process which undermined this certitude and contributed to what he afterward called his "slow apprenticeship in reality."[12]

Roquentin, however, is not simply a writer engaged in a scholarly work on an obscure eighteenth-century adventurer, the Marquis de Rollebon. After the style of Malraux, Roquentin has also been involved in an adventurous enterprise concerning Khmer statues at Angkor. But while he writes about Rollebon, Roquentin begins to wonder whether he is more interested in the book or the man. As Roquentin comes to see it, in a characteristic Sartrean either/or, one must choose between living and telling a story. Sartre himself would say in his autobiography, "the urge to write embraces a refusal to live."[13]

In the crisis Roquentin undergoes, nothing seems real, not even his own existence. The doubts and horrors he feels are, he is sure, totally unknown to the self-satisfied ruling bourgeoisie whose portraits he examines in the provincial art gallery—the "swine" convinced not only of their right to exist but of their right to everything. Now the white sheets of paper on his desk obsess him. If he cannot write, what shall he do? Writing has allowed him to feel that he exists; it has warded off "nausea," the dread awareness of his own nothingness. Although he abandons the biography of Rollebon, he still intends to write a book. But this work will be of a different kind: it will contribute to social change by aiming to make people ashamed of the way they live. At the end of all, in some inexplicable way, literature is still to be a means of salvation for others as well as for himself.

The most violent passages in the book are those which scorn the self-righteousness of the bourgeois class into which Sartre was born, and those which envisage, in terms of anarcho-surrealist terror, the bourgeoisie's day of reckoning. Not for nothing was the novel's epigraph taken from the anarchist doctor Céline, who would come to view its author as Tartre, his renegade offspring. "I ask nothing better than that things should change a bit, so as to see what happens," notes Roquentin, the typical literary anarchist.[14] His antibourgeois frenzy would be rationalized by Sartre, speaking in his own name, in his essay "Materialism and Revolution." If an interview reported in December 1938 is to be believed, Sartre intended to write a sequel in which Roquentin, conscripted into the army during the Munich crisis, would discover his freedom in an act of surrealist violence.

Roquentin thus fades into the vacillating Leftist philosopher, Mathieu Delarue, whom Wyndham Lewis once acidly called "a very boring would-be Malraux." [15] Mathieu, in the notorious scene of the third volume of *The Roads to Freedom*, fires vengefully from the bell tower upon "man, Virtue and the World"; and this act prompts the cryptic aphorism, "Liberty is Terror." What precisely can that mean? (Those who were actually experiencing systematic terror in Stalin's Russia in the years when Sartre was meditating on being and nothingness—the ill-fated poet Osip Mandelstam and his wife, for instance—took a very different view of terror, finding nothing in it which resembled the liberty they dreamed of.) As Mathieu fired indiscriminately, though, he became "pure, all-powerful, free." [16] Not only power but purgation and liberty came out of the barrel of a gun.

The progress from Antoine to Mathieu—from literary blockage, doubt, and disarray to the imagined purity and omnipotence of the man behind the gun—is complete. Most readers believe that, after fifteen minutes of omnipotence, purity, and freedom, this is the end of the line for

Mathieu. Yet according to Sartre's plan, Mathieu would survive, and in Part Four (never completed) he was to become a hero of the Resistance. Mathieu's gratuitous violence (prefiguring Sartre's later endorsement of extreme revolutionary violence) appears as a form of imaginative compensation for Sartre the philosopher; his adventures are of the mind, much to his own fury, and in him there survives something of the small boy endlessly scribbling heroic adventure stories.

It was only a short step from the queries of the ingenuous self-taught humanist, curious about Roquentin's reasons for writing, to the celebrated manifesto on commitment in *What Is Literature?* There the writer's activity is described as useless, and the writer himself stigmatized as a parasite of the bourgeois elite. Equally sweepingly, it is announced that "a member of the clerisy is always on the side of the oppressors." [17] Nonetheless the writer can and should present a challenge to society's complacency. True, only in a classless society will the writer be able to transcend his subjectivity and the antinomy of thought and action. The writer, who in a bourgeois regime is yoked to a public of his own class, really needs a different public: one free to change everything, one that can ceaselessly overthrow established order as soon as this order tends to become fixed. A society "in permanent revolution" is thus envisaged. Only in such a revolutionary society, which admittedly is not for today, would literature flourish "in its plenitude and its purity." [18] Until that distant day dawns, one is left with an unsatisfactory situation.

Essentially Sartre's complaint against literature would be that it did not "save," as he had suggested it might at the end of *The Diary of Antoine Roquentin,* whatever the word "salvation" might mean to a professed atheist. Literature would follow God into the limbo of failed absolutes. As the disappointed literary apostate pungently told Simone de Beauvoir in a Strasbourg restaurant in 1954, not long after his first visit to the Soviet Union, "Literature . . . is shit." [19] The argument that Sartre eventually used to challenge literature recalls the one Dostoevsky put into the mouth of Ivan Karamazov, followed by Malraux and by Camus (in *The Plague*), when they reject the divine order which permits the suffering of a child. *The Diary of Antoine Roquentin* could not be weighed in the balance with a child dying of hunger, Sartre affirmed. But then, who would have supposed it (or any work of art) could? Here are two distinct orders.

In an attempt to clarify his position, Sartre declared: "One cannot write unless one regards literature as *everything*. I don't know any writer who has ever thought anything else. When I defended commitment, it was not in order to reduce the scope of literature, but on the contrary in order to allow it to conquer all the realms of human activity. At the same time, unless one assumes that hunger is merely a word, it is obvious that reality, all reality, challenges literature, and that literature, in a certain sense, is *nothing*. . . . To fight against hunger, the political and economic system must be changed, and literature can play only a very subordinate role in this struggle." [20] That did not mean literature had no part to play, but clearly the role of literature was very far from the all-embracing one which Sartre, ever straining after totality, would originally have wished for it.

Sartre grew reluctant to acknowledge that there may be a poetic truth of imagination and contemplation as distinct from the truth of visible reality and practical humanitarian or revolutionary concerns. Indeed, there exists an affinity between poetic and spiritual or religious perception. That anti-Sartrean dramatist Ionesco, a partisan of artistic revolution but a bitter opponent of other forms of revolutionary conformism, would go so far as to say that "only the imaginary is real." [21] Still, after having abandoned salvation by literature, for a long while Sartre thought man could be "saved" by politics and action; but these, too, he would discover, were not without their problems.

To be "saved" by politics and action, one has to risk dirtying one's hands. The idea of dirty hands fascinates those who could not bear the feeling that they might once have followed Pilate in washing theirs. The more they idolize purity (not least the purity of terror), the more meritorious dirty hands appear. Once having made up his mind that there is no reality except in action, the author of *Dirty Hands* liked to repeat that man is not what he thinks but what he *does*. (This reiterated belief would not prevent him from following Merleau-Ponty in maintaining that the

Soviet Union, "whatever its crimes," was superior to the bourgeois democracies in the nature of its revolutionary illusion, aim, or ideal).[22]

A brilliant caricature exists showing Sartre, in the style of his romantic actor Kean, as Hamlet. One cannot help being reminded of an earlier devotee of German philosophy, Coleridge. "Action . . . is the great end of all," said Coleridge, who was not noted for it. He was lecturing on Hamlet, the vacillating scholar-prince who haunted writers from Manzoni and Turgenev to Sartre and beyond; Hamlet, who wondered whether he was pigeon-livered and lacked gall to make oppression bitter; Hamlet, who was commanded to act, scrupled to do so, yet could dispatch his victims either on impulse or by ruse.

The theme of dirty hands and pure hands had been dear to the nineteenth-century romantics ever since the French Revolution and Napoleon had given them the taste for strong excitement, action, and power. If Stendhal's Julien Sorel brooded on Danton and other great leaders who dirtied their hands, his Lucien Leuwen, ingenuous and honorable, hesitated to cross the dung-stained threshold of action, convinced that action could no longer be pure in the modern world. Musset's Lorenzaccio, while taking a dirty road to reach the "sublime end" of tyrannicide, deeply respected the "pure hands" of the noble Strozzi, who in turn asked, "How can the heart remain great with hands like yours?" [23] Late in the line of scrupulous political assassins (who follow the high-principled Charlotte Corday in exclaiming with unfeigned astonishment, "He takes me for a murderer!") comes Sartre's young blood-intoxicated bourgeois idealist, Hugo: "What am I doing here? Am I right to want what I want? Aren't I playing a part?" [24] This dread of playacting, of reenacting, as it were, the scenes of Hamlet's assumed madness bothers the Sartrean protagonist—the actor, "bastard," or "traitor" for whom authenticity and the real seem ever out of reach.

More sharply in *Dirty Hands* than in his often arid, difficult scholarly and philosophical works, Sartre focused upon the secret temptations of a good many of the modern heirs of nineteenth-century romanticism. In this play, set in a mythical East European country named Illyria during World War II, the assassination of the Communist leader Hoederer by his secretary Hugo may have been inspired by the assassination of Trotsky, but what seems obliquely suggested is the dilemma of the dramatist and all who share it.

Hugo's loathing for his father and his father's class parallels Sartre's cruel lack of indulgence for his fond bourgeois grandfather, Charles Schweitzer, who brought him up—and for everything associated with the bourgeoisie. It is this loathing which has carried Hugo into the Communist party, where he bears the code name of Dostoevsky's power-driven gratuitous murderer, Raskolnikov. As a writer, Hugo does not want to be given tasks commensurate with his talents. He is sick of writing while his friends are being killed. What he wants is direct action, "real work" (the assumption being that writing is not "real" work). He looks forward to the title of Sartre's autobiography when he cries in frustration, "Words! Always words!" [25] It is worth noting, too, that Hugo shares Sartre's disapproval of Communist lies, expressed in the year before the play appeared, in *What Is Literature?* One of Hugo's declared motives for joining the revolutionary cause was the desire to escape from the lies of the bourgeoisie. But Hugo can no more find true acceptance among the proletarians who have joined the cause from necessity than Sartre can find a proletarian public.

Although Hugo is entrusted with the mission of assassinating Hoederer for deviationism, he feels drawn to the hardened leader as a man or as surrogate father. But the intransigent young intellectual resists Hoederer's plan to transform a revolutionary organization into a coalition government party (a plan that will later, ironically, become the party line). Hugo affirms purity of principle (to culminate, not surprisingly, in "a rule of iron") as against Hoederer, who accepts and even glories in his own dirty hands. "My hands are dirty. Filthy to the elbows. I've plunged them in shit and blood. So what? Do you fancy one can govern innocently?" Hoederer asks rhetorically, echoing Saint-Just's emphatic aphorism *"It is impossible to reign innocently . . ."*—words in fact uttered when the Jacobin was demanding Louis XVI's head. [26] In Sartre's view, the play's epigraph could be Saint-Just's cry, which he significantly misquoted as "Nobody rules innocently." [27]

Following in the steps of his hero, Corneille, Sartre affirmed that he allowed both Hoederer and Hugo to have right on their side; a good play should pose problems, not solve them. Yet to some degree the case is weighted against Hugo. Besides being unable to discard or overcome his bourgeois idealism, he retains the destructive anarchist traits common to rebels of his class and, in playacting the revolutionary for all he is worth, betrays the inescapable "bad faith" of the bourgeois. The self-punishing tendencies of the bourgeois dramatist are by no means concealed in the portrayal of Hugo.

Still, Simone de Beauvoir has said bluntly in her memoirs that Sartre's sympathies lay with Hoederer. "As for me," Sartre declared, "I think politics demand that 'hands should be dirtied,' and that it must be so." [28] Some sixteen years later, after a long and tortuous flirtation with the Communists at the height of which any anti-Communist was pronounced a cur, Sartre would proclaim: "I am embodied in Hoederer. Ideally, of course; . . . Hoederer is the person I should like to be if I were a revolutionary." [29] One cannot help wondering whether he would like to be Hoederer despite the revolutionary's stained hands or because of them. However, Sartre here clarifies what is obliquely suggested toward the end of the play itself, when Hugo confesses that he loved Hoederer, the man he had killed, more than anyone else. For, unlike himself, Hoederer belonged with the tough, the conquerors, the leaders. Together with the word "conqueror," with its echoes of Malraux's adventurers, the choice of the word "leader" (*chef*) is particularly instructive, since it is frequently used elsewhere by Sartre in his list of nasty bourgeois and even fascist attributes. One may draw the conclusion that it is all right to be a leader so long as you are a revolutionary one. It is all right to have dirty hands so long as they are not bourgeois hands.

The romantic fascination with dirty hands in an ostensibly just cause was by no means confined to Sartre, who simply popularized a metaphor with a long ancestry. Others, Camus and Orwell for instance, saw dirty hands as unavoidable. In a sense, for those who denied God dirty hands were the secular equivalent of sin, and shared the romantic aura pertaining to Satan and other fallen angels, the damned and their ineluctable suffering. In a twisted way, to undertake the dirty job, to be so committed to the ideal that one was ready to sully oneself for the good of others, could be seen even as a difficult path to redemption—rather as some theologians look on sin as a prerequisite for salvation. One has to experience the mire before one can transcend it. Something of this tormented notion is expressed by Norman Mailer's blood-stained ex-Stalinist revolutionary McLeod, for whom "the only path to absolution is to do more of the same so that you end up religious and climb to salvation on the steps of your crimes." [30] Dirty hands suggest a perverted way of losing one's soul to save it.

Underlying the theme of dirty hands is a preoccupation with power as the end of action. Sartre, in his continuing ruthless analysis of his literary self, which he insists on projecting as typical of the literary mind in general, has proposed that the writer sees himself in two antithetical roles: as the hero-martyr battling against tyranny—André Chénier perishing on the guillotine or Byron dying for Greece—and at the same time, through creative empathy, as the tyrant who knows all "the temptations of power." [31] Is it true that, as he has averred, he himself was not consumed by the canker of power? There was his short-lived experiment as founding father of a political movement, the R. D. R. (*Rassemblement Démocratique Révolutionnaire*), launched under the double aegis of Saint-Just and Marx shortly before the first performance of *Dirty Hands* in April 1948—an enterprise which presumably had power in view. The artist is always divided between power in the world and power over his work, wrote Mailer, the onetime self-styled Marxian anarchist, evidently torn and damaged by this very dilemma.

Central to the argument of *Dirty Hands* is the exchange between Hoederer and Hugo: ". . . how can one retain power?" asks the political animal, Hoederer. "Why take it?" asks Hugo, the reluctant *littérateur*. [32] If power corrupts, if to rule means the inevitable loss of purity and idealism, then power cannot be the aim of revolution and permanent violent revolution alone becomes an end in itself. Sartre's fundamental anarchism, characteristic of his early attitudes as described by Simone de Beauvoir, is conveyed through Hugo, as well as his determination to suppress the anarchist tendency.

The anarchist theme of the corruption inevitably wrought by power was one which had deeply troubled a writer who, as an underground Communist, had suffered and seen his friends suffer in the revolutionary cause. This was Arthur Koestler, briefly a member of Sartre's circle after the Liberation, though ultimately both the sage of Saint-Germain-des-Prés and Simone de Beauvoir resisted the blandishments of the Hungarian's charm. Sooner or later, Koestler had maintained in his first novel *The Gladiators,* about the slave revolt led by Spartacus, the quest for the just and perfect society or "Sun State" involves "the law of detours." Sooner or later, the idealist-in-power is tempted by "the very bloody and very unjust detour which alone could lead to salvation." [33] According to the old servant, Nicos, there can be no perfection on earth and all action is wicked: "even the action you think good throws a shadow which is wicked." [34] Ever since he had known something like a mystic experience in a death cell during the Spanish Civil War, Koestler was torn between nonaction and the urge to continue the struggle, between detachment and the thrill of the homemade bomb.

If there was one aspect of Koestler's writings to which Orwell frequently reverted (like Camus, he was not only influenced by the author of *Darkness at Noon,* but became his personal friend), it was the question of power. For as early as 1938 "the cynical thought" had crossed Orwell's mind that "men are only decent when they are powerless." [35] Orwell did not know how the problem of the abuse of power by successful revolutionaries could be resolved; whereas the more optimistic Koestler could envisage hopefully a synthesis between saint and revolutionary, a new order of revolutionary monks, "the creation of a new fraternity in a new spiritual climate, whose leaders are tied by a vow of poverty to share the life of the masses, and debarred by the laws of the fraternity from attaining unchecked power." [36] Such chimerical notions were not likely to appeal to those who, like Sartre and Madame de Beauvoir, chose to follow

Merleau-Ponty in subordinating morality to history, and who, without having entirely liberated themselves from moral considerations, decided that these moral considerations were the last refuge of bourgois idealism.

A double and contradictory movement may be discerned which, exemplified by the celebrated Sartre-Camus controversy, can still impel writers and critics to take sides. This controversy, once seen as a mere storm in a Parisian teacup, now assumes symbolic proportions. On the one hand are those who follow Sartre in moving toward an ever more emphatic demand for, and justification of, revolutionary violence as if to give proof of their revolutionary good faith. On the other stands the party which favors Orwell and Camus because, having once accepted the necessity of revolutionary violence, they strove to break free or (more thanklessly) to define its limits.

Reform would always seem too slow and unsatisfactory to Sartre and Simone de Beauvoir and their disciples. They were temperamentally opposed to it, believing that "society could only change globally, at one go, through a violent convulsion." [37] The total transformation to be accomplished by revolution had, as ever, to resemble St. Paul's concept of spiritual resurrection, accomplished "in the twinkling of an eye." At first Sartre, despite his native aggressiveness, sometimes hedged his remarks on violence with qualifications; but eventually the Manichaean in him took command, and he could be found defining the class enemy, in terms formerly applied to Satan, as "the enemy of men."

Thus he could visualize of "the contra-man, the anti-man, another species . . . our demonic double. We see that nothing, neither the great wild beasts nor microbes, can be more terrible for man than an intelligent flesh-eating cruel species, who understands and thwarts human intelligence, and whose end is the destruction of man." Moreover, "the imperative consequence of any attempt to destroy this inhumanity is that in destroying in the adversary the inhumanity of the contra-man, I can only destroy in him the humanity of man, and realize in me his inhumanity." [38] This concatenation of antitheses, which tends to stun the unwary, is nothing but the totalitarian's denial of freedom to a class of beings he dislikes, and the attempt to justify his own passionate self-disgust and rationalize his private irrationalism.

His play *The Prisoners of Altona* was likewise written under the impact of the Algerian war and in the realization that some of his fellow countrymen had employed torture. Yet Sartre could movingly have its protagonist, a German officer compromised by using torture in World War II, recognize that the enemy of man lies within his own heart. The doomed Frantz von Gerlach proclaims: "I surprised the beast, I struck, a man fell, in his dying gaze I saw the beast, still alive, myself." [39] The artist appears more subtle, ambivalent, and complex than the philosopher blandly expatiating on the revolutionary brotherhood united by terror.

The least attractive aspect of Sartre's writings is the way he clothes his avowed undying hatred of bourgeois humanism and its cultural ideals in a mantle of spurious humanity. For (so the argument runs, long after Rousseau), true, authentic, harmonious, total humanity has not yet been born. Man as he is now, miserable creature, is certainly not authentic. And as Sartre envisaged the birth of the new man at the end of his allegorical drama, *The Devil and the Good Lord,* it must be admitted that this specimen does not look very much more promising than the old. The German mercenary Goetz, having tried to impress God by a succession of flamboyant evil and good deeds, announces the kingdom of man with two killings, the second committed for the sake of expediency and military discipline. "Now the reign of man is beginning. Fine start . . .," Goetz comments savagely as he kicks the corpse of the peasant he has just slain. [40]

In his essays, Sartre can speak of "making the revolution, preparing Man and his reign," or of the aim of politics as the "advent" of the reign of man. [41] Nowadays, according to Sartre, the absolute is man (although he has yet "to be made"). Sartre can sound like a secular John the Baptist announcing the coming of a grim, blood-stained pseudo-redeemer: abstract, authentic, total Man, mythical in his attributes but all too human in his bloody acts.

Disappointed by the failure of the European proletariat to distinguish itself by a violent revindication of its rights, Sartre transferred his allegiance to those whom colonialism sought to render subhuman, the underdogs of the Third World. Such victims of imperialism, he wrote in his inflammatory preface to Fanon's *The Wretched of the Earth,* actually discover their humanity in the act of killing their oppressors: "shooting a European means killing two birds with one stone, doing away with oppressed and oppressor at one and the same time: there remain a dead man and a free man; . . ." [42] The oppressed colonial's resort to violence is defended as follows: "As the offspring of violence, he draws his humanity from it every minute: we were men at his expense, he becomes a man at ours. A different man: one of superior quality." [43] A glimpse of the devil's horns, the Nietzschean elitism of violence, is vouchsafed here as it was at the end of *The Devil and the Good Lord.* Violence can cauterize the wounds it has made, Sartre suggests, yet unfortunately the dead do not, like his Kean, stand up to take a bow.

The events of May–June 1968 in Paris have been called a Sartrean revolution, and certainly one of the dominant figures of the student rising, the anarchist Cohn-Bendit, said that many of the militants were familiar with Sartre's works. Nevertheless the abortive rising may well mark the high point of the active influence of Sartre (reduced afterward to seeking the martyrdom of arrest and imprisonment, but in vain). Violence, said Sartre at the time, is the only thing that remains for the young who reject the system made by their rotten fathers (among whom he included himself as unavoidably—like all true romantics—somewhat besmirched by society despite his many generous public protests against injustice). The young must "smash" the university, said this former teacher of philosophy, and the only way to do that is to take to the streets. At this point, Sartre indeed appears in the role he preferred to that of lackey—as literary "gravedigger of the West," the most self-abasing, perhaps, though not the last, of a long and distinguished line.

Of Sartre one might repeat what Orwell said of Auden when the poet spoke of "necessary murder" (a phrase later removed from the poem "Spain"), that he was one of those for whom "murder is at most a *word*" and who are "always somewhere else when the trigger is pulled." And

Orwell, the former assistant district superintendent in the Indian Imperial Police in Burma, explained: "It so happens that I have seen the bodies of numbers of murdered men—I don't mean killed in battle, I mean murdered. Therefore I have some conception of what murder means—the terror, the hatred, the howling relatives, the post-mortems, the blood, the smells. To me, murder is something to be avoided. . . . So much of left-wing thought is a kind of playing with fire by people who don't even know that fire is hot." [44]

Yet only a few months later, Orwell could adopt a tone which, when it was used by what he liked to call the pansy Left, aroused his anger: "Only revolution can save England. . . . I dare say the London gutters will have to run with blood. All right, let them, if it is necessary." [45] In the apostle of ordinary human decency there survived a conflict between realism and revolutionary romanticism on the theme of violence for the sake of the revolutionary cause. The very existence of such an inner struggle points to the enduring thrill of romantic revolutionary ruthlessness, whose course and development during two centuries we have charted here and whose end is not yet in sight. Moreover, that strange moment in *Nineteen Eighty-Four*—when the power-drunk torturer O'Brien convinces Winston that he, the pitiful would-be defender of the human spirit, is also morally compromised by his earlier willing acceptance of dirty hands—remains not only one of the most bitter passages in that somber and savage book but also one of the most challenging episodes in modern literature.

Like Orwell, Camus had originally hoped that World War II would lead directly to revolution. Thus at first he could justify the purges at the Liberation, against the protests of François Mauriac, in the name of a terrible law which obliged Frenchmen "to destroy a still living part of this country in order to save its very soul." [46] Soon, however, his tone changed. No longer ready to justify violence and terror so cursorily, Camus now spoke of those "who grant to each side the right to affirm its truth but refuse the right to impose it by murder, individual or collective." [47] Before writing his critique of revolutionary romanticism, *The*

Rebel, where he advocated reform rather than revolution, Camus had searched his own heart, his hidden motives and temptations, which he perceived were not his alone. He knew all about those who bring forth apocalypses in a garret. "I have lived nihilism, contradiction, violence and the vertigo of destruction," he confessed.[48]

However, just as in Orwell the strain of revolutionary romanticism associated with red flags and barricades cannot be entirely suppressed (even where one would least expect to find it, in the essay on Newspeak at the end of *Nineteen Eighty-Four*), in Camus, too, revolutionary romanticism lingered on. It was not only in September 1944 that Camus could say of France, "This country . . . needs a Saint-Just."[49] In *The Rebel* itself, written between 1947 and 1951, Saint-Just may be described as a dubious figure, but he is also handsome, mysterious, and grandiose.

Camus's romantic revolutionary tendency is particularly evident, despite all his efforts to overcome it, in his treatment of the Russian terrorists who assassinated Grand Duke Serge in 1905. "And then we are killing in order to build a world where no one will ever kill again! We consent to be criminals so that the earth should at last be peopled with innocent beings," says the idealistic poet Kaliayev in Camus's play *The Just,* voicing the revolutionary's immortal longing for the restoration of lost innocence. "Suppose that was not to be?" asks Dora, who frequently expresses doubts.[50] These "fastidious assassins" (as Camus called them) give utterance to the conflict in the artist between dream and sober skepticism.

Deeply troubled about killing children, these terrorists are portrayed as noble, self-sacrificing redeemers who take upon themselves the sufferings of the world. In doing so, they are shown to betray hubris, but also courage and magnanimity. And because they conceive of revolution-with-honor, and only take life on the understanding that their own is forfeit, their purity, their "grandeur and humanity" enjoy the dramatist's respect; indeed, "he who writes will never attain the elevation of those who die."[51] For Camus, a life for a life (or killing followed by suicide) was clearly in a different category altogether from killing carried out for the sake of revolutionary expediency, discipline, or rule, such as Sartre could exalt in the name of practical reality. Without personal responsibility, thought Camus, *"Violence has been made comfortable."* [52]

It was in his compelling novel *The Fall,* with its theological undertone, that Camus exposed with greater force and subtlety the self-searching which had prompted *The Rebel.* Through the sardonic, self-torturing, and accusing narrator, Jean-Baptiste Clamence, an enigmatic pseudo-prophet named after St. John the Baptist, Camus plumbed the depths of current humanitarian cant. In failing to rescue a drowning woman and perform an act of unpublicized charity, Jean-Baptiste discovered that his public parade of humanitarianism disguised a secret urge to sadistic domination. Every intellectual, in his opinion, dreams of ruling over society by violence alone. At the same time, he asserts, contemporary intellectuals are all really obsessed by religion: "Whether they are atheists or pious, Muscovites or Bostonians, they're all Christians, from father to son. Only there you are, there's no longer any father, any rule of conduct! One is free, so one has to shift for oneself, and as they certainly don't want either freedom or its judgments, they beg to be rapped on the knuckles, they devise dreadful rules, they rush to build stakes to replace churches. A lot of Savanarolas, in my opinion. But they believe only in sin, not grace." [53] Not for nothing was Camus working on his dramatic adaptation of Dostoevsky's *The Possessed,* with its prophetic pseudo-saviors, during this period.

As one listens to Jean-Baptiste, one cannot help being reminded of Sartre (often mentioned as one of the more obvious targets of Camus's irony), an unbeliever of mixed Protestant and Catholic ancestry who alludes, half seriously, half mockingly, to his minutest political veerings as if he were at the very least another Saul on the road to Damascus. "I believed, I knew, I saw the light," Sartre said of his "conversion" to the communist cause, echoing (with a slight rearrangement of words and tense) Corneille's Pauline after she had witnessed the martyrdom of her Christian husband Polyeucte and had been baptized in his blood. [54] The continued use of religious metaphors by professed unbelievers points to a genuine sense of frustration and even anguish. Drieu was among the earliest to perceive that Sartre belongs with those innumerable anti-Christians who cannot elude the heritage of their birth.

If romanticism is "spilt religion," as T. E. Hulme suggested, then so is its offshoot, romantic revolutionism. The great temptation lies in the area left arid by the decay of religion, in the thirst for the waters of faith of some kind, in the quest for a sustaining absolute without which men find it difficult to live. Abhorring the void, the human mind substitutes a fictitious absolute—Literature, Revolution, History, the Future, Mankind—for the one it has decided that it can no longer accept, while continuing to employ the language of the discarded faith. It is true, of course, that one cannot "prove" the traditional religious absolute, but one can certainly disprove the fictitious absolute; one knows from experience that man is not god.

Quite the most illuminating episode in this connection is the tragicomic parody of conversion and salvation at the end of *Nineteen Eighty-Four,* following the discussion of the "existence" of Big Brother. Broken, gin-sodden Winston is reconciled with a sordid and vacuous invented absolute or Satanic substitute for the Christian redeemer. This sinister yet grotesquely maudlin dénouement was the work of a metaphysical rebel who as a schoolboy had preferred Cain to Jesus (whom he said he "hated") but who came to realize how much had been lost by the decay of Christianity.

"No salvation outside revolution" is the great cry from Byron onward. But salvation belongs to the Lord. It seems that men in their folly actually prefer any road along which they are directed by innumerable would-be messiahs, rather than the hard path offered by traditional faith. Consequently they risk finding themselves not in Abraham's bosom but in Big Brother's. The oasis of salvation to which they are guided by false prophets crying in the desert is nothing but a mirage. There is only one promise that contemns power and defies the sword.

epilogue:

revolution as the modern shibboleth

There is complete continuity between the Romantics and contemporary literature.

MICHEL BUTOR

If there is a revolution, why shouldn't Julien Sorel play the part of Roland, and I that of Madame Roland?

(*Mathilde de la Mole in* STENDHAL'S
The Red and the Black.)

The idea of Revolution fascinated me.

SIMONE DE BEAUVOIR

The intelligentsia destroyed itself, burning out of itself . . . everything that conflicted with the cult of power. . . .

At such moments he [Osip Mandelstam] would say that he wanted to be with everybody else, and that he feared the Revolution might pass him by if, in his shortsightedness, he failed to notice all the great things happening before our eyes. It must be said that the same feeling was experienced by many of our contemporaries, including the most worthy of them, such as Pasternak. My brother Evgeni Yakovlevich used to say that the decisive part in the subjugation of the intelligentsia was played not by terror and bribery (though, God knows, there was enough of both) but by the word "Revolution," which none of them could bear to give up. It is a word to which whole nations have succumbed, and its force was such that one wonders why our rulers still needed prisons and capital punishment.

NADEZHDA MANDELSTAM

. . . contemporary history is so bloody only because the European mind, betraying its heritage and its calling, has chosen excess out of a predilection for pathos and excitement.

CAMUS

"Sooner or later," said Coleridge, *"the same causes, or their equivalents, will call* forth the same opposition of opinion and bring the same passions into play".[1] Our journey bears this out. Beginning with archetypal responses, subconscious attitudes, and dilemmas of the English Romantic poets; by way of the roused sensibility of many a nineteenth-century European writer in his encounter with successive revolutionary dramas, and the often enriched insight he provides into their dramatic motivation; right down to modern recapitulations of the original poetic patterns—we can observe a process of exacerbation. We see writers moving from a quasi-divine conception of their literary role and function in the world to one of total abdication, with Sartre, or one that resembles abdication, since it involves literature feeding cannibalistically upon itself and its own techniques.

We witness today, with an increasing sense of familiarity, the latest sudden conversion to "action" on the part of formerly apolitical young mandarins, the high-minded posturings, and wild rhetoric of yet another generation of writers, surrendering body and soul to the revolution, as if nobody had ever done so before; and we may well wonder whether they are partaking in some prescribed initiation rite or in a black comedy. The new literary advocates of violent revolution, deliberately seeking to undermine all that has been so gingerly built up, good with bad, seem to be naïvely caricaturing the gestures of their mighty forebears—and doing so with the indulgence and complicity of critics and public alike. The deep and enduring causes of that complicity are no longer far to seek.

For we can perceive that Baudelaire was mistaken when he said that revolution was not a religion because it lacked saints, prophets, and martyrs. (Indeed, since his day it has acquired many more). On the contrary, revolution is the religion of many atheists and nihilists, in what has been called the post-Christian era. It is a vast, universal, and all-embracing faith, far wider than Soviet communism, which merely represents one church, sect, or orthodoxy. Consequently the fact that a particular denomination, Soviet communism or anarchism with its extensive ramifications, may suffer defeat or setback is immaterial; Maoism or some other doctrine will take its place. For the religion of revolution is not affected by passing failures. It lives unsullied, while whatever goes wrong is due to the mistakes or betrayals of men, or can be ascribed to the work of the devil, who has supposedly outlived the deity.

We are therefore in a better position to appreciate why violent and total revolution appeals to the literary imagination, notwithstanding so many repeated failures and so many shattering personal tragedies. For the literary imagination is but the human imagination carried to the nth degree and endowed with masterly powers and charms of expression. The poet, the creative writer, the artist, men of more than usual sensibility, express what we do not always know we feel until they say it, directly or obliquely; then we recognize it as potentially our own.

In the religion of revolution, not only are the noblest, most generous, and worthy motives involved—compassion, hatred for injustice, determination to right wrongs, altruism, the desire that all should enjoy the same benefits and freedoms as oneself—but also the highest hopes for personal and universal rebirth, renewal and salvation, and the sweetest dreams of beauty, innocence, harmony, wholeness, heroism, power, and glory. Along with dreams and rational programs to implement them, however, there flourish at the same time primitive fears of the ever-wakeful spirit of darkness, archenemy of man's aspirations, together with secret aggressive and destructive urges, hidden instincts and irrational impulses (so deeply buried that they are not always fully recognized by the writers themselves, or discovered only late and at severe cost).

Hence the paradoxes which continue to puzzle the mind: the way in which tender and sensitive souls urge and condone cruelty out of compassion, or advise shedding a brother's blood in the name of the brotherhood of man, just as their forefathers did in the name of the love of God. It is the instinct of Cain, which Byron said was always lurking somewhere in human hearts.

No less astonishing is the way lofty moral indignation at abuses and evils leads by imperceptible degrees to justification of the same abuses, support for blatant terror, or admiring abasement before tyranny. Nor should we forget the strange conviction that it is possible to destroy everything and everybody yet remain unscathed oneself—to wade through oceans of blood and nonetheless emerge unstained onto the blissful shore of a pure, new, lovely, innocent world. We may well deduce from such paradoxes that men are always ready to find noble masks to disguise their primeval animal fascination with blood and bloodletting. Men are, as Blake perceived, double creatures. For that reason alone they should fear themselves.

Naturally, self-deception on this scale is not peculiar to the literary mind, but the writer's situation tends to throw it into relief. This situation is basically constant. The writer may "act" before or after, but not while he is writing. One or two may be able to work in the human warmth of crowded cafés or noisy rooms, but the majority have to withdraw into privacy and silence. It is not a question of the ivory tower, though this is an ever-present temptation. Solitude—with its anguished yearning as well as its tranquillity—is inescapably the writer's condition.

If our soundings have confirmed anything, it is the degree to which the literary temperament tends toward the anarchy whose other face is despotism. But the inner anarchic disorder of the writer finds true resolution only in the timeless order of art. All too often he inwardly adores power because he is powerless or because the kind of action he can hope to exert through his writings seems too leisurely, remote, intangible, and derisory for his dreams. In his dreams, he alone is the lord of immediate destruction and creation, a commanding aesthetic process he easily transfers from the world or art to that of affairs. Change often fascinates him because his own position as a writer is static. However far he roams in imagination, however Protean his fictional metamorphoses, he remains seated at his table, in all the grandeur and misery, ecstasy and frustration of the sedentary lot!

How can change be understood? While we know little about how it works, we ardently wish to explain it and thereby obtain some kind of control over it. Religion fulfilled this function by placing the cycle of human life in the divine hand, and drawing the sting from death. In its turn, revolution purports to offer an explanation of the secret workings of time and change and renewal, an explanation rooted in ancient analogies. Numerous nature metaphors give us the illusion that we have grasped the mechanism of change. Such metaphors, while deeply satisfying to the human mind, are too commonly treated as if they were blueprints rather than convenient fictions.

Whichever metaphor of change a person fancies probably depends partly upon cultural climate and mood and partly upon temperament, whether he is by disposition contented or discontented, submissive or rebellious; whether he belongs with those who strive to accept the world (as a wag suggested we had better) or with those who hasten to condemn it and reject it utterly; whether he is a yea-sayer or a nay-sayer. Despite the far-reaching influence of Nietzsche, the yea-sayers are now distinctly out of favor. Worse, in an age without morality, they alone are regarded as immoral, as upholders of an evil state of affairs. In Western societies enjoying democratic liberties (for I am not alluding here to military regimes or dictatorships) the attackers, or nay-sayers, are all too often assumed to be necessarily right and admirable. To subvert the established order because it permits abuses—instead of engaging in the slow, hard, often unrewarding task of working to remedy such abuses—is nowadays commonly thought to be the prerequisite of a humane, liberated world rather than a prelude to chaos.

Still, whether the past is regarded as a treasure-house to be cherished and preserved or as the clean slate on which one may write what one likes, both metaphors imply obvious disadvantages. The former fosters complacency or ossification, the latter blind self-sufficiency, the notion that nothing good is to be learned from one's forebears and their experience. As always, the difficulty is how to preserve what is good in the past without sinking under its weight, and how to accomplish change without throwing away the good with the bad. The very least one can ask of those seeking a better and more just society—or a new art—is an awareness that the difficulty exists.

The way in which so many writers have felt impelled to recommend revolution (and later permanent revolution) in literature, whether or not they approved of it in the political and social sphere, is founded upon a misapprehension, a mistaken analogy between literary and sociopolitical change, whose pace is quite different. The modern era since the French Revolution of 1789 has witnessed a strange confusion between the world of literature and that of political revolution, a confusion from which ultimately the latter has gained in cultural prestige what the former has lost. For while the writer at all times cannot help being concerned with new ways of saying, still literature and art (no less than other forms of human activity) are impossible without some continuity.

It was the impact of the mighty revolutionary upheaval itself which made writers use the analogy of political revolution when referring to literary developments. Thus Goethe could speak of "literary sansculottism." [2] In fun, Victor Hugo even associated literary change with political terror: his romantic melodrama *Hernani* served as a pretext for a notorious "battle" and consecrated the military notion of a daring, young, outrageous literary avant-garde. Replying wittily to his conservative critics, he saw poetry—before his own arrival on the scene in the role of bandit-outlaw—as the *ancien régime* before 1789. He was the one who caused a revolutionary hurricane in the ink pot and, placing the red Phrygian cap on the old dictionary, brought liberty and equality to the kingdom of words. The slate of the old literary order, he averred, was wiped clean. In the field of literature if nowhere else, Victor Hugo was quite happy to project himself as a poetic Robespierre, inaugurator of a literary reign of terror.[3] He humorously established the idea of the poetic innovator as the equivalent of the political revolutionary, an idea which, taken seriously, has come to bedevil literature.

All the same, the literary revolution of the eighteen-thirties, in which Victor Hugo gaily saw himself as the leading "terrorist," was a relatively minor affair in comparison with those which came afterward and whose path he prepared. Yet while the Symbolist movement, for instance, is credited with having established the idea of permanent revolution in literature, it was also distinguished by continuity with the remote past, especially with the decadent period of the Roman Empire or the cruel splendors of Byzantium. From the onetime revolutionary Wordsworth to the royalist T. S. Eliot, heir of the Symbolists through his debt to Jules Laforgue, the true literary innovators have rarely hesitated to acknowledge what they owe to the past. It is only the wild iconoclasts of Futurism and Dada, and their new barbarian descendants urging the demolition of museums and libraries and proclaiming death to the intellectual, who insist upon a clean slate. Ironically, even they still feel they have to write one of those despised and outmoded things, a book, in order to demand the burning of books.

Today not only young hotheads but distinguished novelists and critics of mature years are among those drawn to the most potent myth of the religion of revolution, the dream of a total human transformation to follow general destruction. On the clean slate of the new classless society, men continue to sketch the outline for the ideal moral revolution that is the concomitant of sociopolitical revolution. They still expect the arrival of an ideal new man, endowed with a new consciousness, capable of leading a completely free, new, full, harmonious life. Like the redeemed soul, the newborn man of the postrevolutionary future will mysteriously transcend human frailty, sickness, pain, and maybe even death. Human nature, the human condition are denied, since all ills are the result of the "system." One eminent literary critic goes so far as to suggest that so long as there exists any flaw in human arrangements, there must be a revolution to put an end to it.[4] The inevitable consequence of this trend has been a tragic loss of interest in the interior life.

As ever for some dreamers, the moral revolution could not be complete without total sexual revolution. This might take the form of complete sexual liberty or it might also assume another shape. The idea that political, social, and economic ills would find a solution once a perfect balance in sexual relations between men and women had been achieved runs from Blake through D. H. Lawrence to Mailer and after. This view of the sexual revolution has little to do with the reformist struggle for female rights and belongs essentially in a perfectionist metaphysical scheme.

"Be realistic, ask for the impossible," one of the liveliest and most telling slogans of the Parisian student rising of 1968, was coined by the novelist and playwright Marguerite Duras. When asked in 1971 how she pictured the outcome of the revolution, this ex-communist who still believed in the communist world-view replied: "A new state of the human being, man and woman. It is yet unforeseeable, but it will probably consist—for 80 per cent at least—in the destruction of conceit, of selfishness, of 'virility'. . . ."[5] By "virility" Marguerite Duras appears to mean the whole heroic warrior ethos; yet this ethos, which she hopes will be superseded, forms an essential part of the revolutionary outlook she cherishes.

For to participate in revolution is exciting and daring. It involves adventure, risk, a role in a great action, holy war, or crusade, and thus replaces the ancient values of fatherland, war, and glory which few would openly defend today. The fact that revolution is associated with what is manly was underlined long ago by Thucydides, speaking of extravagances of revolutionary zeal in his own day: ". . . to think of the future and wait was merely another way of saying one was a coward; any idea of moderation was just an attempt to disguise one's unmanly character; ability to understand a question from all sides meant that one was totally unfitted for action. Fanatical enthusiasm was the mark of a real man. . . ." [6] Here is described that enduring tendency which finds true virility and heroism in the extreme, whereas moderation and measure are regarded as cowardly and base.

The revolutionary hero is therefore one for whom moderation (or reform) must necessarily be excluded. His realm is the extreme, and he enjoys the prestige of that frenzied extremism commonly thought to distinguish the modern mentality, though in effect it is essential to the supererogatory nature of the heroic ethos. Whether he appears as the poetic and artistic revolutionary risking his health and his life in desperate pursuit of the unknown, or as the ruthless underground political revolutionary suffering untold hardships, he personifies the romantic rebel-outlaw and outsider, fighting against heavy odds, misunderstood and rejected by the common herd. It is this heroic-cum-pathetic theme which contributes so much to the force of the revolutionary drama in either its artistic or sociopolitical form. The attraction of such a heroic role also underlies much current incendiary rhetoric. One of Sartre's Maoist disciples, who saw himself outstripping his master in formulating a bloodcurdling philosophy of terror, dreamed aloud: "Life will be hard for us: . . . we are destined for mockery to-day and persecution tomorrow." [7] The figure of the Suffering Servant is not far off, but subtly transformed and perverted by politics.

Nineteenth-century admirers of the violent Christs who died upon the barricades exalted the heroic intermingling of ruthlessness, sacrifice of others, and self-sacrifice. This same exaltation has been expressed anew in the response to the charismatic revolutionary whom General de Gaulle saw as a character out of Malraux's novels: Che Guevara. For some, the Christlike aspect of Guevara was emphasized by his betrayal, "his passion and his death," conceived as transcending such evidently non-Christian characteristics as his hatred for his enemies, his readiness to kill, and his "dubious or inhuman" tactics. [8] More skillfully discriminating, the Leftist art critic and novelist John Berger contrived to eat his cake and have it too when he saw that Guevara was no Christ yet compared a photograph of the slain revolutionary with Mantegna's painting of the dead Savior.

Berger recognized, though, a "degree of emotional correspondence" between his own reactions to the photograph of the dead leader and the feelings he surmised that a Christian of the Renaissance might have had for Mantegna's painting of the dead Redeemer.[9] Equally revealing is Berger's related meditation on Saint-Just and the nature of revolutionary heroism, a meditation inspired by Guevara's death.

Such incongruities point to the unresolved conflict in the Western heritage between the Judaeo-Christian virtues of humility and long-suffering and the Greco-Roman values of manliness and heroism. At various times in the past, awkward or baroque attempts were made to reconcile these opposites. Today, through an unholy merger or sleight of hand, this conflict is seemingly eluded. The association of Christ's redemptive sacrifice with a purely secular, ruthless, and hubristic revolutionary heroism underlines the ambivalence of the general response toward any manifestation of violence or sacrificial bloodshed which involves personal risk, self-sacrifice, and service to a cause. Subconsciously, spiritual and Christian elements are adduced to gloss a pagan ideal.

During the last two centuries, then, many aesthetic, heroic, and religious currents have converged to help make the words "revolution" and "revolutionary" sacred, and not only in countries with a revolutionary tradition. Revolution has become "a good thing" in every sphere of human activity. Any sign of originality, novelty, or difference is characterized as revolutionary and receives thereby a seal of approval. The now common commercial use of "revolutionary" for "new" was arousing comment in France as long ago as the nineteen-twenties, when the latest silk stockings were named "Revolution."[10] This development infuriates *enragés* on both sides of the Atlantic, who see the holy word being debased: "A 'REVOLUTION' IN TOILET PAPER. . . . *Have the capitalists no respect?*"[11] A society where a shop can be called Che Guevara, and where commerce has stolen (among other things) the revolutionary's thunder, should give us pause.

It is surely significant that while in some contexts the words "revolution" and "revolutionary" have become drained of their force, the rhetoric of extremists grows more intense. This rhetoric is all too often quietly accepted by putative victims who buy the books of their would-be executioners and make their reputations. Middle-class readers tolerate the idea of a world in which they know they would not be tolerated, a world where the liberties slowly earned by their forefathers (however limited such liberties may still be in scope, and however far short of perfection) would be at an end. These readers, indeed, are almost won over in advance. Is it simply because they do not want to be left behind? Or is it because that world is also recognizably a thing of their own creation and dear to their innermost hearts?

Since the French Revolution of 1789, made principally by men of the middle class, revolution (whether affirmed or denied) has become an integral part of bourgeois civilization—that is, in effect, modern Western civilization, a house tragically divided against itself. Ever since revolution was declared the ideal or envisaged as the absolute, everything contributed to make the new party in power, the middle class, the enemy—the political, social, economic, moral, and artistic enemy. If it had remained faithful to the purity of the revolutionary ideal of liberty, equality, fraternity for all, in all spheres of endeavor, the argument went, it should not have been in power. The middle class built its own ruin into the very civilization it created; its best sons grew to despise, and worked to destroy, the civilization they themselves graced.

The revolutionary tradition, however—already a theme for mockery in the nineteenth century—has evolved into the tedious revolutionary conformism of today. Now the "new" in everything has to be (and is) accepted immediately, and because it is new or "revolutionary," not necessarily because it is good. Moderns can be satisfied with very little, if only it is, or looks, new. "It's time to move on to the next step in the psychedelic revolution," said the novelist Ken Kesey (who, if he thinks writing an old-fashioned or artificial form, goes on using it). "I don't know what this is going to be in any way I could just spell out, but I know we've reached a certain point but we're not moving any more, we're not creating anymore, and that's why we've got to move on to the next step—" [12] Here is aimless perpetual motion for its own sake.

Let us imagine that someone today queries whether revolution is such "a good thing," whether there may not be more economical ways of effecting social or artistic change, methods less damaging to the human and cultural fabric and less problematical in their outcome. (At an international conference of historians in Paris in 1948, a shabbily dressed elderly gentleman rose at the back of the hall to raise this kind of question, amid pitying smiles. Unfortunately, Daniel Halévy [for it was he] had been compromised by his support for Pétain.[13]) Let us imagine that this person has no ax to grind, boldly claims to be a moderate, an upholder of liberal values, and, moreover, ventures to find some good in the contribution of the contaminated bourgeoisie. He suggests that the bourgeoisie consisted of human beings of all shades and types, not just monsters, and that while its rule was guilty of much, nevertheless there had been far worse masters in the past and doubtless would be in the future. The poor creature will be lucky to escape being labeled a fuddy-duddy in an age when brinkmanship is so highly prized. And to make matters worse, he himself will be oppressed by scruples, lest he defend a system which permits shameful abuses. He will inevitably lack the self-righteous certainty of those who preach fire and sword and "creative" terror.

In an age when dread of technology has supplanted the nineteenth-century fear of mechanization, it may well be that we are witnessing the last thrashings of the romantic revolutionary beast before it is ignominiously hauled away like a bull from the arena. Yet might not this bull be replaced by another rougher beast, a kindred superstition under a different name? Meanwhile, whether the colorful sanguinary ritual is destined for survival or oblivion, the equivocal and irrational elements which occupy so profound a place in the cult of revolution can no longer be ignored. Nor can the element of humbug which invites revolutionary ruthlessness under the cloak of more justice, life, and love. This form of humbug is no less nauseating than that of which the establishment stands accused.

In modern times, the obsession with revolution has encouraged many to neglect that disinterested service to the truth which should be among the writer's highest concerns. (Those who would deny that truth exists, because they believe all truths are dependent on class interests, are merely playing the game of Pilate). The French critic who between the wars made famous the term "betrayal of the intellectuals" once declared: "The something for love of which I wrote this book [*The Treason of the Intellectuals*] is the disinterested activity of the mind, that which rejects subordination to any interest, including the most 'sacred,' which above all will not grant that the claims of those interests are necessarily identical with the truth." [14] More recently, Alexander Solzhenitsyn has movingly reaffirmed this ideal in the published version of the Nobel prize address which he could not deliver in person.

Doubtless it is hard for writers to acknowledge that their sphere of action is relatively limited, that all they can aspire to accomplish obliquely through the power of their art is a change in outlook, in standards, perhaps a change of heart. Otherwise, they make common cause with the new barbarians who will surely destroy them—and with them, the tender plant of which they are, or should be, the wary guardians.

notes

prologue: writers and salvation through revolution

1. Schiller, *The Robbers* (published 1781), Act I, scene ii. Mme de Staël, *De l'Allemagne,* 1813 (Garnier-Flammarion, 1948), Vol. I, Part 2, chapter xvii, p. 268; Coleridge, Letter to Southey, 3 November 1794, *Collected Letters,* ed. E. L. Griggs (Clarendon Press, 1956), Vol. I, p. 122.

2. Mme de Staël, *De la Littérature,* 1800, *Œuvres complètes* (Treuttel et Würtz, 1820), Vol. IV, Part I, chapter xx, p. 392.

3. Alexis de Tocqueville, *L'Ancien Régime et la Révolution,* 1856, trans. M. W. Patterson (Blackwell, 1956), Book 3, chapter i, pp. 149–150.

4. Edmund Burke, *Reflections on the French Revolution,* 1790, (Methuen, 1923), p. 77.

5. Schiller, Letter 11, *Letters on the Aesthetic Education of Man,* 1795, ed. and trans. E. M. Wilkinson and L. A. Willoughby (Clarendon Press, 1967), pp. 76–77.

6. F. Schlegel, quoted in Arthur O. Lovejoy, "Schiller and the Genesis of German Romanticism," 1920, *Essays in the History of Ideas* (John Hopkins University Press, 1948), p. 226.

7. Schiller, Letter 23, note 1, *Letters*, p. 167.

8. Jean-Jacques Rousseau, *Émile*, 1762, trans. Barbara Foxley (Everyman's Library), pp. 10, 46, 172. For Saint-Just, see J. L. Talmon, *The Origins of Totalitarian Democracy* (Secker and Warburg, 1952), p. 157, and P.-H. Simon, *Le Domaine héroïque des lettres françaises* (A. Colin, 1963), p. 291.

9. Schiller, Letter 6, *Letters*, p. 35.

10. *Ibid.*, Letter 27, p. 205. For Schiller and Marx, see David McLellan, *Marx Before Marxism* (Macmillan, 1970), pp. 187–189.

11. Isaiah Berlin on Schiller's "On Naïve and Sentimental Poetry," 1796, in "The Naïveté of Verdi," *The Hudson Review*, Vol. XXI, No. I, Spring 1968.

12. Mme de Staël, *De la Littérature*, Part I, chapter viii, p. 206.

13. *Ibid.*, Part II, chapter ix, p. 593.

14. Mme de Staël, *De l'Allemagne*, Vol. II, Part 3, chapter xii, pp. 188, 189, 191.

15. Quoted in Burke, *Reflections*, p. 138 note 1.

16. Louis de Saint-Just, "Rapport sur la nécessité de déclarer le gouvernement révolutionnaire jusqu'à la paix" (Report to the National Convention in the name of the Committee of Public Safety, 10 October 1793), *Œuvres choisies* (Collection Idées, Gallimard, 1968), p. 178.

17. Mme de Staël, *De l'Allemagne*, Vol. I, Part 2, chapter xv, p. 258. See also *De la Littérature*, Part II, chapter ii, pp. 413, 423.

18. E. L. Woodward, *French Revolutions*, 1934 (Oxford University Press, 1965), p. 28 and note 2.

19. De Tocqueville, *L'Ancien Régime*, p. 15.

20. André Chénier, "Réflexions sur l'esprit de parti," April 1791, *Œuvres en prose*, ed. L. Becq de Fouquières (Charpentier, n.d.), p. 61 and note 1, p. 62.

21. Rousseau, *Emile*, p. 199.

22. E. Benz, *Les Sources mystiques de la philosophie romantique allemande* (J. Vrin, 1968), p. 78.

chapter 1 the apocalyptic vision of William Blake

1. John Beer, *Blake's Humanism* (Manchester University Press, 1968), p. 96.

2. Blake, *Jerusalem*, III, 57, in *Complete Poetry and Prose*, ed. Geoffrey Keynes (Nonesuch, 1967), p. 505.

3. Edmund Burke, *Reflections on the French Revolution*, 1790 (Methuen, 1923), pp. 19, 60–61.

4. George Woodcock, *William Godwin* (Porcupine Press, 1946), pp. 27, 29.

5. *Milton,* II, 43, Keynes, p. 426.

6. A. L. Morton, *The Everlasting Gospel* (Lawrence and Wishart, 1958), p. 50, note 1.

7. Quoted in Morton, p. 46; also Norman Cohn, *The Pursuit of the Millennium* (Mercury Books, 1962), pp. 363, 371.

8. *A Descriptive Catalogue,* V, Keynes, p. 610. Also *Annotations to Watson's Apology,* 1798, Keynes, p. 765; *Jerusalem,* I, 27, Keynes, p. 463.

9. *Annotations to Watson's Apology,* Keynes, p. 761.

10. *Annotations to Bacon's Essays,* circa 1798, Keynes, p. 769.

11. "Auguries of Innocence," *Miscellaneous Poems,* or *Rossetti MSS,* Keynes, p. 118.

12. *Jerusalem,* I, 25, Keynes, p. 462.

13. *A Descriptive Catalogue,* V, Keynes, p. 610.

14. *America,* etched 1793, Keynes, p. 203. See also *The Song of Los,* etched 1795, *ibid.,* p. 250.

15. *Europe,* etched 1794, Keynes, p. 219.

16. *A Vision of the Last Judgment,* 1810, Keynes, pp. 646, 649.

17. *Vala, or the Four Zoas,* 1795–1804, "Night the Ninth Being the Last Judgment," Keynes, p. 348.

18. *Annotations to Lavater's Aphorisms,* circa 1788, Keynes, p. 707.

19. *Ibid.,* p. 714.

20. *A Vision of the Last Judgment,* Keynes, pp. 638–639. See also *The Book of Los, ibid.,* p. 242.

21. *Jerusalem,* I, 15, Keynes, p. 449.

22. *Visions of the Daughters of Albion,* etched 1793, Keynes, pp. 199–200.

23. Alexander Gilchrist, *The Life of William Blake,* ed. Ruthven Todd (Everyman's Library, 1945), p. 97. See also Morton, pp. 52–55, and Cohn, pp. 189–191.

24. "Then She Bore Pale Desire," before 1777, Keynes, p. 670; Gilchrist, p. 301.

25. *A Vision of the Last Judgment,* Keynes, p. 650.

26. *The Marriage of Heaven and Hell,* Keynes, p. 191, and *The Everlasting Gospel, ibid.,* pp. 142–143.

27. *The Everlasting Gospel,* Keynes, p. 133.

28. *Ibid.,* p. 143.

29. *The Marriage of Heaven and Hell,* Keynes, p. 182.

30. Preface to *Jerusalem,* Keynes, p. 433.

31. Gilchrist, pp. 301–302.

32. *The Marriage of Heaven and Hell,* Keynes, p. 181.

33. "The Grey Monk," *Miscellaneous Poems,* or *Rossetti MSS,* Keynes, p. 118.

34. *Public Address,* Keynes, p. 629.

35. *A Vision of the Last Judgment,* Keynes, p. 650.

36. *Jerusalem,* III, 55, Keynes, p. 503.

37. Henry Crabb Robinson, *Blake, Coleridge, Wordsworth, Lamb, etc.,* ed. E. J. Morley (Manchester University Press, 1922), p. 3.

chapter 2 the God that failed: Wordsworth and Coleridge

1. *The Prelude,* text of 1805, ed. E. de Selincourt, rev. S. Gill (Oxford University Press, 1970), Book VI, ll. 539–542, p. 100.

2. *Ibid.,* ll. 567–572.

3. Henry Crabb Robinson, *Blake, Coleridge, Wordsworth, Lamb, etc.,* ed. E. J. Morley (Manchester University Press, 1922), pp. 15–16.

4. Coleridge, Letter to J. Thelwall, 13 May 1796, *Select Poetry and Prose,* ed. Stephen Potter 1933 (Nonesuch, 1962), p. 562.

5. *The Recluse,* quoted in the Preface to *The Excursion* (1814), ll. 31–41, 47–55.

6. *The Prelude,* text of 1805, Book X, ll. 722–727, p. 197.

7. *Ibid.,* Book IX, ll. 289–293, p. 159.

8. *Ibid.,* Book IX, ll. 519–520, p. 165.

9. *Ibid.,* Book VIII, ll. 410–415, p. 137; ll. 761–764, p. 147; ll. 802–807, p. 148.

10. *Ibid.,* Book IX, ll. 328–333, p. 160; ll. 522–534, p. 165.

11. *Ibid.,* Book X, ll. 689–693, p. 196.

12. *Ibid.,* Book X, ll. 36–37, p. 178.

13. *Ibid.,* Book X, l. 82, p. 179.

14. *Ibid.,* Book X, l. 179, p. 182.

15. *Ibid.,* Book X, ll. 222–226, p. 183.

16. *Ibid.,* Book X, ll. 284–285, p. 185.

17. *Ibid.,* Book X, ll. 335–336, p. 186.

18. *Ibid.,* Book X, ll. 355–360, p. 187.

19. *Ibid.,* Book X, ll. 368–380, p. 187; Book XII, ll. 331–332, p. 227.

20. *Ibid.*, Book X, ll. 541–545, 551–552, 556, p. 192.

21. *Ibid.*, Book X, ll. 577–578, p. 193.

22. *Ibid.*, Book X, l. 585, p. 193.

23. *Ibid.*, Book X, ll. 819–829, pp. 199–200; ll. 834–839, p. 200; ll. 896–900, p. 202.

24. *Ibid.*, Book X, ll. 934–935, p. 203.

25. *Ibid.*, Book X, ll. 662–665, p. 195; Book XI, ll. 59–60, p. 207; "Lines Written in Early Spring," 1798 ("I heard a thousand blended notes").

26. *The Prelude*, text of 1805, Book XIII, l. 119, p. 232.

27. *The Friend*, Section the First ("On the Principles of Political Knowledge") Essay VI, *Collected Works*, Vol. I, ed. Barbara E. Rooke (Princeton University Press, 1969), p. 223.

28. Letter to Southey, 21 October 1794, *Collected Letters*, ed. E. L. Griggs (Clarendon Press, 1956), Vol. I, pp. 117–118.

29. "Apologetic Preface to *Fire, Famine, and Slaughter*," *Complete Poetical Works*, ed. E. H. Coleridge (Clarendon Press, 1912), Vol. II, p. 1100.

30. Letter to the Rev. J. H. Cary, 6 February 1818, *Select Poetry and Prose*, p. 674.

31. "Religious Musings," *Complete Poetical Works*, Vol. I, pp. 108–123.

32. Letter to Southey, 6 July 1794, *Collected Letters*, Vol. I, p. 83.

33. "To a Young Ass," *Complete Poetical Works*, Vol. I, pp. 74–75.

34. Letter to Southey, 21 October 1794, *Collected Letters*, Vol. I, p. 115.

35. Letter to Southey, 13 November 1795, *ibid.*, p. 163.

36. Letter to Southey, 21 October 1794, *ibid.*, p. 114.

37. Letter to Southey, early August 1795, *ibid.*, p. 158.

38. Letter to John Morgan, 17 March 1808, *Select Poetry and Prose*, p. 623; *The Friend*, p. 224.

39. "Reflections on Having Left a Place of Retirement," 1795, *Complete Poetical Works*, Vol. I, p. 108.

40. *The Friend*, pp. 223–224.

41. "A Moral and Political Lecture," *ibid.*, p. 327.

42. *Ibid.*, p. 328.

43. *Ibid.*

44. *Biographia Literaria*, 1817 (Everyman's Library, 1947), chapter x, p. 93; also "The Statesman's Manual," in *Political Tracts of Wordsworth, Coleridge and Shelley*, ed. R. J. White (Cambridge University Press, 1953), p. 14.

45. "A Moral and Political Lecture"; see *The Friend*, p. 331.

46. "A Moral and Political Lecture"; see *The Friend*, p. 332.

47. *The Friend*, Section the First ("On the Grounds of Government"), Essay IV, p. 187.

48. *Ibid.*, Essay VI, p. 226.

49. *Ibid.*, p. 227.

50. "France: An Ode," *Complete Poetical Works*, Vol. I, p. 247.

51. Letter to George Coleridge, circa 10 March 1798, *Collected Letters*, Vol. I, pp. 395–397.

52. Thomas De Quincey, *Recollections of the Lakes and the Lake Poets*, ed. David Wright (Penguin, 1970), pp. 172–173.

53. William Hazlitt, "On the Living Poets," *Lectures on the English Poets*, 1818, 1819, ed. C. M. Maclean (Everyman's Library, 1967), pp. 161–162.

54. Hazlitt, "Mr. Wordsworth," in *The Spirit of the Age*, 1825, ed. C. M. Maclean (Everyman's Library, 1967), p. 253.

55. Hazlitt, "My First Acquaintance with Poets," *Selected Writings*, ed. Ronald Blythe (Penguin, 1970), p. 62.

56. William Wordsworth, Preface to the second edition of the *Lyrical Ballads*, in *Poetical Works*, ed. T. Hutchinson, rev. E. de Selincourt 1904 (Oxford University Press, 1936), pp. 934, 935–936, 937.

57. *The Prelude*, text of 1805, Book XII, ll. 166–168, p. 222.

58. Samuel Taylor Coleridge, Letter to Southey, 29 July 1802, quoted by Mary Moorman in *William Wordsworth: A Biography* 1957, 1965 (Oxford University Press, 1968), Vol. I, pp. 492–493.

59. Coleridge, Letter to the Rev. J. P. Estlin, 18 May 1798, *Collected Letters*, Vol. I, p. 410.

60. Coleridge, Letter to Wordsworth, 30 May 1815, *Select Poetry and Prose*, p. 661.

61. William Wordsworth, *The Excursion*, 1814, *Poetical Works*, Book 4, ll. 260–265, p. 805.

62. *Ibid.*, Book 4, ll. 269–272, p. 805.

63. *Ibid.*, Book 4, ll. 307–309, pp. 805–806.

64. *Ibid.*, Book 4, ll. 317–319, p. 806.

65. Hazlitt, "Observations on Mr. Wordsworth's Poem *The Excursion*," in *The Round Table*, 1817, ed. C. M. Maclean (Everyman's Library, 1964), p. 119.

66. Hazlitt, "Mr. Southey," in *The Spirit of the Age*, p. 245.

67. Wordsworth, *Sonnets Dedicated to Liberty and Order*, Sonnet II, 1832, *Poetical Works*, p. 513; Sonnet VII, 1842, *ibid.*, p. 514.

68. Coleridge, *The Friend*, Essay VI, p. 223; Letter to T. J. Street, 22 March 1817, *Select Poetry and Prose*, p. 667; "Apologetic Preface to *Fire, Famine and Slaughter*," p. 1108.

69. Coleridge, "The Statesman's Manual," *Political Tracts of Wordsworth, Coleridge and Shelley*, pp. 28, 33.

chapter 3 the anarchist response: Shelley

1. William Hazlitt, "On Paradox and Commonplace," *Table Talk*, 1821–1822, 1824, ed. C. M. Maclean (Everyman's Library, 1967), p. 151.

2. *Queen Mab*, Canto 6, l. 105, *Poetical Works*, ed. Thomas Hutchinson, rev. G. M. Matthews (Oxford University Press, 1970), p. 785.

3. Preface to *Prometheus Unbound*, *ibid.*, p. 205.

4. *Julian and Maddalo*, ll. 449–450, *ibid.*, p. 199.

5. "Hymn to Intellectual Beauty," l. 53, *ibid.*, p. 531.

6. Letter to Thomas Jefferson Hogg, 20 December 1810, *Letters*, ed. Frederick L. Jones (Clarendon Press, 1964), Vol. I, p. 27.

7. Letter to Thomas Jefferson Hogg, 3 January 1811, *ibid.*, Vol. I, p. 35.

8. *The Revolt of Islam*, Canto 2, stanza xliii, l. 1045, *Poetical Works*, p. 63.

9. "A Philosophical View of Reform," in *Political Tracts of Wordsworth, Coleridge and Shelley*, ed. R. J. White (Cambridge University Press, 1953), p. 251.

10. *Ibid.*, p. 213.

11. *The Revolt of Islam*, Canto 8, stanza xvi, *Poetical Works*, p. 119.

12. "Note on *Prometheus Unbound*, by Mrs. Shelley," *ibid.*, p. 271.

13. Notes on *Hellas*, *ibid.*, p. 478.

14. *Ibid.*, p. 479.

15. *Queen Mab*, Canto 4, ll. 82–89, *ibid.*, p. 775.

16. *Prometheus Unbound*, Act 4, l. 364, *ibid.*, p. 262.

17. Preface to *Hellas*, *ibid.*, p. 448.

18. *Queen Mab*, Canto 3, ll. 239–240, *ibid.*, p. 774.

19. *Prometheus Unbound*, Act 3, scene 4, ll. 131–133, 193–201, *ibid.*, pp. 252–253.

20. "Essay on Christianity," *Selected Poetry, Prose and Letters*, ed. A. S. B. Glover (Nonesuch, 1951), p. 989.

21. "A Philosophical View of Reform," p. 249. See also "Essay on Christianity," pp. 1004–1005.

22. William Godwin, *An Enquiry Concerning Political Justice,* ed. and abr. Raymond A. Preston (Knopf, 1926), Vol. I, p. 120.

23. Preface to *Hellas, Poetical Works,* p. 448.

24. Fragmentary essay on parliamentary reform, quoted in Kenneth Neill Cameron, *The Young Shelley: Genesis of a Radical* (Collier Books, 1962), p. 287.

25. "A Philosophical View of Reform," pp. 222, 224. See also "Liberty," *Poetical Works,* p. 622.

26. Letter to Byron, 8 September 1816, *Letters,* ed. F. L. Jones (Clarendon Press, 1964), Vol. I, p. 504.

27. "Ode to Liberty," stanza xii, l. 175, *Poetical Works,* p. 607.

28. Preface to *The Revolt of Islam, ibid.,* p. 33.

29. *Ibid.*

30. Letter to a Publisher, 13 October 1817, *Selected Poetry, Prose and Letters,* p. 1074.

31. "A Defence of Poetry," in *Political Tracts of Wordsworth, Coleridge and Shelley,* p. 206.

32. Preface to *Prometheus Unbound,* p. 206; and "A Defence of Poetry," p. 206.

33. *Prometheus Unbound,* Act 4, ll. 570–574, p. 268.

34. *Julian and Maddalo,* ll. 182–191, *Poetical Works,* p. 194.

35. Letter to Mary Shelley, 16 August 1821, *Selected Poetry, Prose and Letters,* pp. 1100–1101.

36. Letter to Godwin, 8 March 1812, *Letters,* Vol. I, pp. 267–268; Godwin, Letter to Shelley, 14 March 1812, *ibid.,* p. 270; Shelley, Letter to Godwin, 18 March 1812, *ibid.,* p. 277; Jean Overton Fuller, *Shelley: A Biography* (Cape, 1968), p. 116.

37. *The Revolt of Islam,* Canto XI, stanza xx, ll. 4400–4401, *Poetical Works,* p. 145.

38. *The Mask of Anarchy,* stanza xci, ll. 368, 372 (compare stanzas lxxxiv–lxxxvi, ll. 340–351), *ibid.,* p. 344; and "Song to the Men of England," stanza vi, *ibid.,* p. 573.

39. *The Esdaile Notebook,* ed. Kenneth Neill Cameron (Faber, 1964), p. 40.

40. "On the Medusa. . . . ," l. 33, *Poetical Works,* p. 583; Mario Praz, *The Romantic Agony,* trans. Angus Davidson (Oxford University Press, 1970), pp. 25–26.

41. "Ode to the West Wind," *Poetical Works,* p. 579.

42. *Hellas, ibid.,* pp. 477–478.

chapter 4 the lure of action: Keats

1. H. W. Garrod, *Keats* (Clarendon Press, 1926), p. 28.

2. Letter to John Hamilton Reynolds, 9 April 1818, *Letters,* ed. H. E. Rollins (Cambridge University Press, 1958), Vol. I, p. 267.

3. "Sleep and Poetry," ll. 122–125, *Poetical Works,* ed. H. W. Garrod 1956 (Oxford University Press, 1967), p. 45.

4. Letter to Richard Woodhouse, 27 October 1818, *Letters,* Vol. I, pp. 387–388.

5. Quoted in H. W. Garrod, *Keats,* p. 23.

6. Letter to George and Georgiana Keats, 14 February 1819, *Letters,* Vol. II, p. 61.

7. "Sonnet Written in Disgust of Vulgar Superstition," *Poetical Works,* p. 421; "Sonnet to a Young Lady Who Sent Me a Laurel Crown," *ibid.,* p. 363; "Epistle to George Keats," August 1816, l. 76, *ibid.,* p. 27.

8. Letter to John Hamilton Reynolds, 3 February 1818, *Letters,* Vol. I, p. 223–224.

9. *Ibid.,* p. 225.

10. Letter to Shelley, 16 August 1820, *ibid.,* Vol. II, p. 323.

11. Letter to Benjamin Bailey, 22 November 1817, *ibid.,* Vol. I, p. 184.

12. Letter to George and Tom Keats, 21, 27 (?) December 1817, *ibid.,* pp. 193–194.

13. Letter to George and Georgiana Keats, 24 September 1819, *ibid.,* Vol. II, p. 213.

14. Letter to Richard Woodhouse, 27 October 1818, *ibid.,* Vol. I, pp. 386–387.

15. William Hazlitt, "A Letter to William Gifford Esq.," 1819, *Collected Works,* ed. A. R. Waller and A. Glover (Dent, 1902), Vol. I, p. 389; quoted by Keats in Letter to George and Georgiana Keats, 13 March 1819, *Letters,* Vol. II, pp. 74–75.

16. Hazlitt, "On the Pleasure of Hating," *Selected Writings,* ed. R. Blythe (Penguin, 1970), p. 398.

17. Letter to George and Georgiana Keats, 19 March 1819, *Letters,* Vol. II, p. 79.

18. "Epistle to John Hamilton Reynolds," 25 March 1818, ll. 92–97, 102–106, *Poetical Works,* p. 383, and *Letters,* Vol. I, pp. 262–263.

19. Letter to George and Georgiana Keats, 19 March 1819, *ibid.,* Vol. II, p. 79.

20. *Ibid.,* pp. 80–81.

21. Letter to same, 21 April 1819, *ibid.,* p. 101.

22. *Ibid.,* pp. 101–102.

23. Letter to same, 17 September 1819, *ibid.,* p. 193.

24. *Ibid.,* pp. 193–194.

25. H. W. Garrod, *Keats,* p. 69.

26. "Hyperion," Book 1, ll. 141–144, *Poetical Works,* p. 224.

27. *Ibid.,* Book 2, ll. 181–182, p. 234.

28. *Ibid.,* ll. 212–214, p. 235.

29. *Ibid.,* ll. 228–231, p. 235.

30. *Ibid.,* Book 3, ll. 114–116, p. 242.

31. "The Fall of Hyperion," Canto I, ll. 16–18, *ibid.,* p. 403.

32. *Ibid.,* ll. 145–149, p. 406.

33. *Ibid.,* ll. 167–169, p. 407.

34. See J. Middleton Murry, *Keats,* 4th ed. (Cape, 1955), p. 239.

chapter 5 revolution as personal salvation: Byron

1. Leslie A. Marchand, *Byron: A Portrait* (John Murray, 1970), p. 378.

2. Doris Langley Moore, *The Late Lord Byron: Posthumous Dramas* (John Murray, 1961), p. 297.

3. *Don Juan,* Canto 14, stanzas, v, vi, in *Poetry,* ed. E. H. Coleridge (John Murray, 1898–1904), Vol. VI, p. 517.

4. "Darkness," ll. 1, 69–71, *ibid.,* Vol. IV, pp. 42, 45; also *Don Juan,* Canto 9, stanzas xxxvii, xxxviii, *ibid.,* Vol. VI, p. 385.

5. *Childe Harold's Pilgrimage,* Canto 4, stanza cxxvi, *ibid.,* Vol. II, p. 422.

6. Quoted by Bertrand Russell, *History of Western Philosophy* 1946 (Allen and Unwin, 1961), p. 718. See also Byron, Letter to Thomas Moore, 14 May 1821, in *Byron: A Self-Portrait,* ed. Peter Quennell (John Murray, 1950), Vol. II, p. 653.

7. Shelley, Letter to Horace Smith, 11 April 1822, *Letters,* ed. F. L. Jones (Clarendon Press, 1964), Vol. II, p. 412.

8. To Dr. James Kennedy, quoted in *The Late Lord Byron,* pp. 345–346.

9. *Lara,* Canto I, xviii, l. 3, *Poetry,* Vol. III, p. 335.

10. Controversy between Byron and Bowles, Appendix III, *Letters and Journals,* ed. Rowland E. Prothero (John Murray, 1898–1901), Vol. V, p. 542.

11. Letter to John Murray, 9 October 1820, *Byron: A Self-Portrait,* Vol. II, p. 536; Lady Blessington, *Conversations of Lord Byron,* ed. E. J. Lovell (Princeton University Press, 1969), p. 220.

12. Letter to Annabella Milbanke, 10 November 1813, *Letters and Journals,* Vol. III, p. 405.

13. Journal, 24 November 1813, *Selections from Poetry, Letters and Journals,* ed. Peter Quennell (Nonesuch, 1949), p. 633.

14. Letter to Thomas Moore, 28 February 1817, *Letters,* ed. R. G. Howarth (Everyman's Library, 1962), p. 159.

15. Letter to Lord Holland, 25 February 1812, in Thomas Moore, *The Works of Lord Byron with His Letters and Journals, and His Life* (John Murray, 1832), Vol. II, pp. 123–124.

16. Letter to John Murray, 15 September 1817, *Letters,* ed. Howarth, p. 175.

17. Journal, 23 November 1813, *Selections from Poetry, Letters and Journals,* p. 630.

18. *The Corsair,* Canto I, ii, l. 63, and Canto I, viii, *Poetry,* Vol. III, pp. 229, 233; also *The Bride of Abydos,* Canto 2, xx, *ibid.,* Vol. III, pp. 194–195.

19. *Manfred,* Act 3, scene i, ll. 121–122, *ibid.,* Vol. IV, p. 125.

20. Letter to John Murray, 21 February 1820, *Letters,* ed. Howarth, p. 249; "My Dictionary," 1821, *Letters and Journals,* Vol. V, p. 406.

21. Quoted by Leslie A. Marchand, pp. 415–416.

22. Journal, 16 January 1814, *Selections from Poetry, Letters and Journals,* p. 655.

23. *Don Juan,* Canto 15, stanzas xxii–xxiii, *Poetry,* Vol. VI, p. 550.

24. Letter to John Cam Hobhouse, 29 March 1820, in *Byron: A Self-Portrait,* Vol. II, p. 507.

25. *Marino Faliero,* Act 3, scene ii, ll. 166–167, *Poetry,* Vol. IV, p. 398.

26. *Ibid.,* Act 4, scene ii, ll. 55–59, pp. 422–423.

27. *Ibid.,* ll. 160–161, 166–170, p. 426.

28. Diary, 18 February 1821, *Letters and Journals,* Vol. V, p. 205.

29. *Don Juan,* Canto 8, stanza li, *Poetry,* Vol. VI, p. 346.

30. *The Deformed Transformed,* Part I, scene 2, ll. 24–25, *ibid.,* Vol. V, p. 500.

31. Letter to Annabella Milbanke, 6 September 1813, *Letters,* ed. Howarth, p. 82.

32. Journal, 22 November 1813, *Selections from Poetry, Letters and Journals,* p. 626.

33. *Childe Harold's Pilgrimage,* Canto 3, stanza xlii, *Poetry,* Vol. II, p. 242.

34. *Ibid.,* stanzas xliii, xliv, pp. 242–243.

35. *Conversations of Lord Byron,* p. 221.

36. *Childe Harold's Pilgrimage,* Canto 3, stanzas xcii, xciii, pp. 273–274.

37. *Ibid.,* stanza xcvii, p. 276.

38. Letter to Augusta Leigh, 12 October 1823, *Letters,* ed. Howarth, p. 358; Diary, 8 January 1821, *Letters and Journals,* Vol. V, p. 160.

39. *Sardanapalus,* Act I, scene i, ll. 9, 18–19, *Poetry,* Vol. V, p. 14.

40. *Ibid.,* Act 5, scene i, l. 15, p. 109.

41. *Conversations of Lord Byron,* p. 101; also pp. 85, 181 note 60, 227.

42. *Childe Harold's Pilgrimage,* Canto 3, stanzas cxiii, cxiv, p. 286.

chapter 6 literary revolutionism, despotism, and outlawry

1. J. Christopher Herold, *Mistress to an Age: A Life of Mme de Staël* (Hamish Hamilton, 1959), p. 430.

2. William Hazlitt, "On Coriolanus," *Characters of Shakespeare's Plays,* ed. C. M. Maclean (Everyman's Library, 1964), p. 215.

3. Hazlitt, "On the Connexion between Toad-eaters and Tyrants," 12 January 1817, *Political Essays,* in *Collected Works,* ed. A. R. Waller and A. Glover (Dent, 1902), Vol. III, p. 173.

4. Hazlitt, Preface to *Political Essays, ibid.,* p. 33.

5. *Ibid.,* pp. 34–35.

6. *Ibid.,* p. 36.

7. *Ibid.*

8. Byron, Journal, 17 November 1813, *Selections from Poetry, Letters and Journals,* ed. Peter Quennell (Nonesuch, 1949), p. 622; also Journal, 9 April 1814, *ibid.,* p. 669; Letter to Thomas Moore, 9 April 1814, *Letters,* ed. R. G. Howarth (Everyman's Library, 1962), p. 97; *Don Juan,* Canto 11, stanza lv, *Poetry,* ed. E. H. Coleridge (John Murray, 1898–1901), Vol. VI, p. 444.

9. Quoted in E. Tangye Lean, *The Napoleonists: A Study in Political Disaffection 1760–1960* (Oxford University Press, 1970), p. 273.

10. Byron, Journal, 23 November 1813, *Selections from Poetry, Letters and Journals,* p. 629.

11. William Godwin, *Caleb Williams,* ed. David McCracken (Oxford University Press, 1970), p. 216.

12. *Ibid.,* pp. 218–219.

13. Stendhal, Plan, 25 November 1839, *Lamiel,* ed. Henri Martineau (Hazan, 1949), p. 411.

14. Stendhal, "Dernière Préface," *De l'Amour,* written 1842, ed. Henri Martineau (Cluny,

1938); *Vie de Henry Brulard, Œuvres intimes,* ed. Henri Martineau (Bibliothèque de la Pléiade, Gallimard, 1961), pp. 176–177.

15. *Vie de Henry Brulard,* p. 144, also pp. 94–95; and *Souvenirs d' égotisme, Œuvres intimes,* p. 1398? note i, p. 1611.

16. Stendhal, *Napoléon,* ed. L. Royer (Champion, 1929), Vol. I, p. 346.

17. Stendhal, Letter to Sutton Sharpe, 11 July 1827, *Correspondance,* ed. A. Paupe and P. A. Cheramy (Charles Bosse, 1908), Vol. II, p. 465.

chapter 7 revolutionary desires and fears: Heine

1. *Heinrich Heine's Memoirs from His Works, Letters and Conversations,* ed. Gustav Karpeles, trans. Gilbert Cannan (Heinemann, 1910), Vol. I, p. 248.

2. Letter to Karl Immermann, 14 January 1823, *ibid.,* p. 117; also Letter to Moses Moser, 21 January 1824, *ibid.,* p. 145.

3. *Ibid.,* p. 251; *De l'Allemagne, Œuvres Completes* (Calmann–Lévy, 1891), Vol. II, p. 32.

4. Alexander Herzen, *My Past and Thoughts,* trans. Constance Garnett (Chatto and Windus, 1968), Vol. I, p. 122.

5. Letter to J. F. von Cotta, 31 October 1831, *Memoirs,* Vol. I, p. 271.

6. *Religion and Philosophy in Germany,* trans. John Snodgrass (Beacon Press, 1959), p. 75.

7. *Ibid.,* p. 78.

8. *Ibid.,* p. 24.

9. Letter to H. Laube, 7 November 1842, *Memoirs,* Vol. II, p. 129.

10. *English Fragments, the Sword and the Flame,* ed. Alfred Werner (Yoseloff, 1960), p. 495.

11. *Ibid.,* p. 496.

12. *Ibid.;* also *De la France,* 19 April 1832, *Œuvres Completes* (Calmann–Lévy, 1884), p. 128.

13. *Lutèce,* 4 November 1840, *Œuvres Completes* (Calmann–Lévy, 1892), p. 135.

14. Letter to H. Laube, 23 December 1835, *Memoirs,* Vol. II, p. 23.

15. *Religion and Philosophy in Germany,* p. 79.

16. Letter to Varnhagen von Ense, 3 January 1846, *Memoirs,* Vol. II, p. 185.

17. *Religion and Philosophy in Germany,* p. 91.

18. Preface to *Lutetia, Memoirs,* Vol. II, p. 268.

chapter 8 revolutionary violence: George Sand and Lamartine

1. Quoted by André Maurois, *Lélia*, 1952, trans. Gerard Hopkins (Pyramid Books, 1968), p. 529.

2. Alexander Herzen, quoted in E. H. Carr, *The Romantic Exiles*, 1933 (Peregrine, 1968), p. 106.

3. *Ibid.*

4. Heinrich Heine, *Lutèce*, 30 April 1840, *Œuvres Complètes* (Calmann–Lévy, 1892), p. 37.

5. Letter to Charles Meure, 25 February 1831, *Correspondance*, ed. Georges Lubin (Garnier, 1964–   ), Vol. I, p. 810.

6. Letter to Laure Decerfz, 13 June 1832, *ibid.*, Vol. II, p. 103.

7. Letter to Charles Meure, 6 July 1832, *ibid.*, p. 112.

8. *Histoire de ma vie, Œuvres Autobiographiques,* ed. Georges Lubin (Bibliothèque de la Pléiade, Gallimard, 1970–1971), Vol. II, p. 332.

9. Letter to Gustave Papet, 12 April 1835, *Correspondance,* Vol. II, p. 848; Letter to Adolphe Guéroult, 12 April 1835, *ibid.*, p. 855.

10. *Histoire de ma vie, op. cit.*, Vol. II, p. 326.

11. *Ibid.* (as translated by Gerard Hopkins with some variations of my own).

12. *Ibid.*, p. 327.

13. *Lettres d'un voyageur*, VI Lettre à Everard, *Œuvres Autobiographiques,* Vol. II, p. 806.

14. Letter to Louise Colet, 19 November 1841, *Correspondance,* Vol. V, p. 506.

15. Letter to Louise Colet, 25 (?) February 1843, *ibid.*, Vol. VI, p. 61.

16. Letter to the Parisian Saint-Simonist family, 2 April 1836, *ibid.*, Vol. III, pp. 326–327.

17. Alexander Herzen, *My Past and Thoughts*, trans. Constance Garnett, rev. H. Higgens (Chatto and Windus, 1968), Vol. III, p. 1484.

18. Letter to Apolline and René Vallet de Villeneuve, 19 January 1848, *Correspondance,* Vol. VIII, p. 251.

19. Letter to Giuseppe Mazzini, 25 January 1848, *ibid.*, p. 257.

20. Mazzini, Letter to George Sand, 16 February 1848, *ibid.*, Vol. VIII, p. 257, note 3.

21. Quoted by Maurice Toesca in *Lamartine ou l'amour de la vie* (Albin Michel, 1969), p. 311. For Coleridge, see H. Crabb Robinson, *Blake, Coleridge, Wordsworth, Lamb, etc.*, ed. E. J. Morley (University of Manchester Press, 1922), p. 128.

22. Quoted by Henri Guillemin in *Lamartine en 1848* (Presses Universitaires de France,

1948), p. 15; see also Arsène Houssaye, *Les Confessions* (E. Dentu, 1885–91), Vol. II, p. 343.

23. Letter to René Vallet de Villeneuve, 6 January 1848 *Correspondance,* Vol. VIII, p. 241.

24. Quoted by Maurice Toesca in *Lamartine ou l'amour de la vie,* p. 433.

25. Letter to René Vallet de Villeneuve, 4 March 1848, *Correspondance,* Vol. VIII, p. 316.

26. Letter to Charles Poncy, 8 March 1848, *ibid.,* pp. 329–331.

27. Letter to Maurice Dudevant-Sand, 23 March 1848, *ibid.,* p. 359.

28. Letter to Charles Poncy, 25 November 1845, *ibid.,* Vol. VII, p. 193.

29. Bulletin No. 16, 15 April 1848; see *Correspondance,* Vol. VIII, illustrations (as translated by Gerard Hopkins with some variations of my own).

30. Letter to Maurice Dudevant-Sand, 16–17 April 1848, *ibid.,* p. 418.

31. Letter to Maurice Dudevant-Sand, 18–19 April 1848, *ibid.,* p. 421.

32. Letter to Théophile Thoré, 28 May 1848, *ibid.,* p. 477.

33. Letter to Armand Barbès, 10 June 1848, *ibid.,* p. 498.

34. Quoted by Maurice Toesca in *Lamartine ou l'amour de la vie,* p. 494.

chapter 9 the parting of the ways

1. Alexander Herzen, *My Past and Thoughts,* trans. Constance Garnett (Chatto and Windus, 1968), Vol. III, p. 1063.

2. *Ibid.,* p. 1340.

3. *Ibid.,* Vol. II, p. 822.

4. *Ibid.,* p. 814. See also *From the Other Shore, Selected Philosophical Works,* trans. L. Navrosov (Moscow, 1956), pp. 376–377; *To an Old Comrade, ibid.,* p. 586.

5. *My Past and Thoughts,* Vol. II, p. 815.

6. Quoted by Edmund Wilson in *To the Finland Station,* 1940 (Fontana, 1960), p. 277.

7. Quoted by George Woodcock in *Anarchism,* 1962 (Penguin, 1970), p. 139.

8. Mikhail Bakunin, *The Political Philosophy of Bakunin: Scientific Anarchism,* ed. G. P. Maximoff (Free Press of Glencoe, Collier-Macmillan, 1953; paperback, 1964), p. 381.

9. *Ibid.,* p. 372.

10. Quoted by E. H. Carr in *The Romantic Exiles,* 1933 (Peregrine, 1968), p. 267.

11. *To an Old Comrade,* p. 587.

12. *Ibid.,* p. 594.

13. Natalie Herzen, "The Diary of Natalie Herzen," trans. Hilary Sternberg, *Encounter,* Vol. XXXIV, no. 5, May 1970, p. 6.

14. *Ibid.,* p. 21 note 7.

chapter 10 salvation through art: Baudelaire

1. Quoted in P. Martino, *Parnasse et Symbolisme* (Armand Colin, 1938), p. 52.

2. *Mon Coeur mis à nu, Œuvres Complètes,* ed. Y.-G. Le Dantec and Claude Pichois (Bibliothèque de la Pléiade, Gallimard, 1968), p. 1280.

3. "Edgar Allan Poe, sa vie et ses œuvres," *L'Art Romantique,* ed. Henri Lemaitre (Garnier, 1962), p. 598.

4. *Mon Coeur mis à nu,* p. 1287.

5. Joseph de Maistre, *Soirées de Saint-Pétersbourg,* vii, in J. S. McLelland, *The French Right* (Cape, 1970), p. 52.

6. *"Les Misérables* par Victor Hugo," *L'Art Romantique,* p. 799.

7. Letter to Manet, 28 October 1865, *ibid.,* p. 797 note 1. See also Letter to M. Ancelle, 12 February 1865, quoted in Jules Mouquet and W. T. Bandy, *Baudelaire en 1848* (Emile-Paul, 1946), p. 325.

8. "Notes sur l'art philosophique," *Curiosités Esthétiques,* ed. Henri Lemaitre (Garnier, 1962), p. 527.

9. Alexander Herzen, *My Past and Thoughts,* trans. Constance Garnett (Chatto and Windus, 1968), Vol. II, p. 673.

10. *Baudelaire en 1848,* p. 11.

11. *Ibid.,* p. 19.

12. *Plans et notes, Le Spleen de Paris, Œuvres Complètes,* pp. 316–317.

13. *Mon Coeur mis à nu, ibid.,* p. 1273.

14. *Baudelaire en 1848,* p. 21.

15. *Le Mauvais Vitrier, Le Spleen de Paris, Œuvres Complètes,* pp. 238–239.

16. *Mon Coeur mis à nu, ibid.,* p. 1274.

17. *Sur la Belgique, ibid.,* p. 1456.

18. *Fusées, ibid.,* pp. 1263–1264.

19. "Puisque réalisme il y a," *L'Art Romantique,* p. 825.

chapter 11 literary commitment versus revolutionary tradition: Flaubert

1. *Intimate Notebook 1840–1841*, trans. and ed. Francis Steegmuller (W. H. Allen, 1967), p. 37.

2. Quoted in Frank Jellinek, *The Paris Commune of 1871* (Gollancz, 1937), p. 314.

3. Letter to Amélie Bosquet, November 1867, *Correspondance* (Conard, 1926–1933, 1954), Vol. V, p. 338.

4. Letter to George Sand, 31 March 1871, *ibid.*, Vol. VI, pp. 215–216.

5. Letter to George Sand, 29 April 1871, *ibid.*, p. 228.

6. *The Goncourt Journals 1851–1870*, trans. and ed. Lewis Galantière (Cassell, 1937), pp. 231–232. Entry of 21 December 1866, *Journal* (Flammarion/Fasquelle, 1935), Vol. III, pp. 71–72.

7. *La Première Éducation sentimentale* (Seuil, 1963), p. 246.

8. *Ibid.*, p. 256.

9. *Intimate Notebook*, p. 26. See also Mario Praz, *The Romantic Agony*, trans. Angus Davidson (Oxford University Press, 1970), p. 190 note.

10. *Intimate Notebook*, p. 18.

11. *Ibid.*, p. 36.

12. Quoted in Francis Steegmuller, *Flaubert and Madame Bovary*, rev. ed. (Macmillan, 1968), p. 121.

13. Letter to Mlle Leroyer de Chantepie, 23 January 1866, *Correspondance*, Vol. V, p. 197.

14. *L'Éducation sentimentale*, ed. Edouard Maynial (Garnier, 1964), p. 112.

15. *Ibid.*, p. 139.

16. *Ibid.*, p. 177.

17. Letter to Michelet, 2 February 1869, *Correspondance*, Vol. VI, p. 10.

18. *L'Éducation sentimentale*, p. 137.

19. *Ibid.*, pp. 233–234.

20. *Ibid.*, p. 375.

21. *Ibid.*, p. 27.

22. *Ibid.*, p. 307.

23. *Ibid.*, p. 303.

24. *Ibid.*, p. 339.

25. *Ibid.*, p. 378.

26. Quoted in *Flaubert and Madame Bovary*, p. 278.

27. Letter to George Sand, 18 October 1871, *Correspondance*, Vol. VI, p. 297.

chapter 12 the liberal dilemma: Turgenev

1. Letter to Flaubert, 6 May 1871, *Ivan Tourguéneff d'après sa correspondance avec ses amis français*, ed. E. Halpérine-Kaminsky (Charpentier, 1901), p. 57.

2. Quoted in David Magarshak, *Turgenev: A Life* (Faber, 1954), p. 16.

3. "Reminiscences of Belinsky," *Literary Reminiscences*, trans. David Magarshak (Faber, 1959), p. 128.

4. Quoted in *Turgenev: A Life*, p. 240.

5. Alexander Herzen, *My Past and Thoughts*, trans. Constance Garnett (Chatto and Windus, 1968), Vol. IV, p. 1763 note 17.

6. "Reminiscences of Belinsky," p. 128.

7. Quoted in Avrahm Yarmolinsky, *Turgenev: The Man, His Art and His Age*, rev. ed. (Orion Press, 1959), p. 76.

8. "A Propos of *Fathers and Sons*," *Literary Reminiscences*, p. 170.

9. Letter to Pauline Viardot, 8 December 1847, *Lettres à Madame Viardot*, ed. E. Halpérine-Kaminsky (Charpentier, 1907), p. 16.

10. Letter to Pauline Viardot, 19 December 1847, *ibid.*, p. 25.

11. Letter to Pauline Viardot, 30 April 1848, *ibid.*, p. 47.

12. Eyewitness account of 15 May 1848, *ibid.*, p. 59.

13. "My Mates Sent Me!" *Literary Reminiscences*, p. 209.

14. *Ibid.*, p. 203.

15. *On the Eve*, trans. Gilbert Gardiner (Penguin, 1950), p. 197.

16. *Ibid.*, p. 121.

17. *Fathers and Sons*, trans. C. J. Hogarth (Everyman's Library, 1921), p. 71.

18. "A Propos of *Fathers and Sons*," p. 169 note 1.

19. "Enough! An Extract from the Memoirs of a Deceased Artist," quoted in Richard Freeborn, *Turgenev: The Novelist's Novelist* (Oxford University Press, 1960), p. 139.

20. *Smoke*, trans. Constance Garnett (Heinemann, 1928), p. 294.

21. Quoted in *Turgenev: The Man, His Art and His Age*, p. 355.

*chapter 13 spiritual versus revolutionary
salvation: Dostoevsky*

1. *The Diary of a Writer*, 1873, trans. Boris Brasol (Cassell, 1949), Vol. I, p. 148.

2. *Ibid.*, 1873, p. 7.

3. *Ibid.*, 1876, p. 342.

4. Quoted in David Magarshak, *Dostoevsky* (Secker and Warburg, 1962), pp. 151–152.

5. *Ibid.*, pp. 153–154.

6. *Ibid.*, pp. 159–160.

7. Letter to A. E. I. Totleben, 24 March 1856, *Correspondance*, ed. Dominique Arban and Nina Gourfinkel (Calmann–Lévy, 1949–1961), Vol. I, p. 225. Quoted in J. A. T. Lloyd, *Fyodor Dostoevsky*, p. 53 (Eyre and Spottiswoode, 1946).

8. Letter to S. A. Ivanovna, 29 September–11 October 1867, *ibid.*, Vol. III, p. 135 (Magarshak, Dostoevsky, p. 381). See also Letter to A. N. Maykov, 15 September 1867, *ibid.*, Vol. III, p. 125.

9. Letter to N. D. Fonvisina, circa 20 February 1854, *ibid.*, Vol. I, p. 157 (Magarshak, Dostoevsky, pp. 191–192). See also *The Possessed*, trans. Constance Garnett (Heinemann, 1914), p. 225.

10. Edmund Burke, *Reflections on the French Revolution* (Methuen, 1923), pp. 79–80.

11. *The Diary of a Writer*, 1873, Vol. I, p. 149.

12. Letter to N. A. Lyubimov, 10 May 1879, quoted in Edward Wasiolek, *Dostoevsky: The Major Fiction* (M.I.T. Press, 1964), p. 163. See also *The Brothers Karamazov*, Part II, Book V, "Pro and Contra," chapter iv.

13. *The Possessed*, p. 366.

14. *The Diary of a Writer*, 1873, Vol. I, p.13.

15. *Ibid.*, 1877, Vol. II, p. 787.

16. Letter to M. N. Katkov, 8–20 October 1870, *Correspondance*, Vol. IV, p. 196. Quoted in *Dostoevsky: The Major Fiction*, p. 136.

17. *The Diary of a Writer*, Vol. I, p. 147. Version of Ernest J. Simmons, *Feodor Dostoevsky* (Columbia University Press, 1969), p. 14.

18. Letter to A. A. Romanov, February 1873, quoted in *Dostoevsky: The Major Fiction*, p. 112.

19. *The Diary of a Writer*, 1873, Vol. I, p. 379.

20. *The Possessed*, pp. 380, 478.

21. *The Diary of a Writer*, 1877, Vol. II, p. 939.

22. *The Diary of a Writer*, 1877, Vol. II, p. 939.

23. Quoted in *Dostoevsky*, p. 100. See also Dostoevsky, *Occasional Writings*, trans. D. Magarshak (Vision Press, 1964), p. 68.

24. Letter to A. N. Maykov, 25 March–6 April 1870, *Correspondance*, Vol. IV, p. 163. Quoted in *Dostoevsky: The Major Fiction*, p. 209.

25. *The Possessed*, p. 102.

26. Avrahm Yarmolinsky, *Turgenev: The Man, His Art and His Age*, rev. ed. (Orion Press, 1959), p. 275.

chapter 14 literary decadence and revolutionary anarchism

1. George Moore, *The Confessions of a Young Man*, 1888 (Heinemann, 1937), p. 94.

2. Swinburne, "Anactoria," ll. 182–184, *Poems and Ballads*, 1866, ed. Morse Peckham (Bobbs-Merrill, 1970), pp. 66–67.

3. Lautréamont, "Les Chants de Maldoror," Chant 2, strophes 3 and 6, *Œuvres complètes*, ed. P.-O. Walzer (Bibliothèque de la Pléiade, Gallimard, 1970), pp. 83, 92.

4. Swinburne, *Atalanta in Calydon*, l. 1151, ed. Morse Peckham (Bobbs-Merrill, 1970), p. 249.

5. Swinburne, *William Blake: A Critical Essay* (John Camden Hotten, 1868), p. 158 note.

6. *Ibid.*, p. 166 note.

7. *Ibid.*, p. 217.

8. "Before a Crucifix," *Songs Before Sunrise, The Poems of A. C. Swinburne* (Chatto and Windus, 1905), Vol. II, p. 86.

9. "Hymn of Man," *ibid.*, p. 104.

10. "To Walt Whitman in America," *ibid.*, p. 124.

11. Letter to Thomas Purnell, 15 February 1877, *The Letters of A. C. Swinburne*, ed. Edmund Gosse and T. J. Wise (Heinemann, 1918), Vol. I, p. 302.

12. "A Year's Burden," 1870, *Songs Before Sunrise*, Vol. II, p. 224.

13. Rimbaud, "Soleil et chair," *Œuvres complètes*, ed. Antoine Adam (Bibliothèque de la Pléiade, Gallimard, 1972), p. 7.

14. Rimbaud, "Mauvais sang," *Une Saison en enfer, ibid.*, pp. 96–97.

15. Rimbaud, "Délires," I, *Une Saison en enfer, ibid.*, p. 104.

16. Rimbaud, *Les Illuminations, ibid.*, p. 131.

17. Victor Hugo, *Quatre-vingt-treize*, 1874 (Garnier-Flammarion, 1967), pp. 367–368.

18. *Ibid.*, pp. 371–372.

19. Quoted in Mario Praz, *The Romantic Agony*, trans. Angus Davidson (Oxford University Press, 1970), p. 278.

20. Barrès, *Souls l'œil des barbares*, 1888 (Plon, 1922), p. 279.

21. Barrès, *Un Homme libre*, 1889 (Albert Fontemoing, 1905), pp. 164, 181. See also pp. 188–189.

22. Barrès, *Les Déracinés*, 1897 (Plon, 1922), Vol. I, p. 235.

23. Barrès, *L'Ennemi des lois*, 1892 (Emile-Paul, 1910), p. 16.

24. *Ibid.*, p. 22.

25. *Ibid.*, p. 200.

chapter 15 from Prometheus to the hooligan

1. J.-K. Huysmans, À *Rebours*, 1884 (Fasquelle, 1968), p. 268. Version of Robert Baldick.

2. Marx, *Paris Manuscripts*, quoted in David McLellan, *Marx Before Marxism* (Macmillan, 1970), p. 183.

3. Henry James, *The Princess Casamassima*, 1886 (John Lehmann, 1950), p. 104.

4. *Ibid.*, p. 260.

5. Joseph Conrad, *The Secret Agent*, 1907 (Everyman's Library, 1961), p. 311.

6. Joseph Conrad, "A Familiar Preface," *Some Reminiscences* (Everleigh Nash, 1912), pp. 20–21.

7. Joseph Conrad, *Under Western Eyes*, 1911 (Dent, 1971), p. 356.

8. *Ibid.*, pp. 134–135.

9. Pío Baroja, *Aurora Roja* (Caro Raggio, Madrid, n.d.), p. 266.

10. Alexander Blok, quoted in Introduction by translators Jon Stallworthy and Peter France, *The Twelve and Other Poems* (Eyre and Spottiswoode, 1970), p. 29.

11. Alexander Blok, "A Voice from the Chorus," *ibid.*, p. 103.

12. Quoted in C. M. Bowra, *The Heritage of Symbolism* (Macmillan, 1943), p. 169.

13. Quoted in Jürgen Rühle, *Literature and Revolution*, trans. and ed. Jean Steinberg (Praeger, 1969), p. 6.

14. *The Twelve and Other Poems*, p. 147.

15. Leon Trotsky, *Littérature et révolution*, trans. P. Frank, C. Ligny, and J.-J. Marie, (Collection 10/18, 1971), p. 138.

16. Quoted in Introduction to *The Twelve and Other Poems*, p. 35.

17. Maxim Gorky, *Untimely Thoughts*, trans. Herman Ermolaev (Garnstone Press, 1970), p. 85. See also pp. 86–89.

18. Quoted in Malcolm Cowley, *Exile's Return* (Bodley Head, 1961), p. 150.

19. Quoted in Maurice Nadeau, *The History of Surrealism*, trans. Richard Howard (Cape, 1968), p. 62.

20. André Breton, *Second manifeste du surréalisme*, 1930, *Manifestes du surréalisme* (Collection Idées, Gallimard, 1971), p. 78. Version of Richard Howard.

21. *Exile's Return*, pp. 169–170.

22. Louis Aragon, quoted in *The History of Surrealism*, p. 111.

23. Louis Aragon, "Red Front," 1931, *ibid.*, pp. 289–290.

24. *Ibid.*, p. 291. See also *ibid.*, p. 294, and *Aurora Roja*, p. 147.

25. Paul Éluard, *La Révolution surréaliste*, No. 4 (1925), quoted in Nadeau, p. 111.

26. Nadeau, pp. 143–144, 197, note 10.

27. *Déclaration du 27 janvier 1925, ibid.*, p. 103.

28. André Breton, *Prolégomènes à un troisième manifeste du surréalisme ou non*, 1942, *Manifestes du surréalisme*, p. 165.

29. Quoted in Nadeau, p. 195, note 5.

30. André Breton, *Second manifeste du surréalisme*, 1930, *Manifestes du surréalisme*, pp. 76–77. See also Michel Carrouges, *André Breton et les données fondamentales du surréalisme* 1950 (Collection Idées, Gallimard, 1967), pp. 22–34.

31. Antonin Artaud, quoted in *Le Monde*, 11 September 1970.

chapter 16 revolutionary resurrection: D. H. Lawrence

1. Frank Kermode, "D. H. Lawrence and the Apocalyptic Types," in *Continuities* (Routledge and Kegan Paul, 1968), p. 125.

2. Letter to J. O. Meredith, 2 November 1915, *Collected Letters*, ed. Harry T. Moore (Heinemann, 1962), Vol I, p. 374.

3. Letter to Edward Garnett, 22 April 1914, *ibid.*, p. 273.

4. Letter to Barbara Low, 11 (?) February 1915, *ibid.*, p. 316.

5. Letter to Ernest Collings, 17 January 1913, *ibid.*, p. 180.

6. Letter to Willard Johnson, 9 January 1924, *ibid.*, Vol. II, p. 769.

7. Harry T. Moore, *The Intelligent Heart*, 1955 (Penguin, 1960), p. 261.

8. *"The Dragon of the Apocalypse* by Frederick Carter," *Selected Literary Criticism*, ed. Anthony Beal 1956 (Heinemann, 1967), p. 158.

9. Letter to A. W. McLeod, 26 April 1913, *Collected Letters*, Vol. I, p. 204.

10. Letter to Bertrand Russell, 26 February 1915, *ibid.*, p. 324.

11. *The Rainbow*, 1915 (Penguin, 1949), p. 285.

12. Bertrand Russell, *Autobiography* (Allen and Unwin, 1968), Vol II, p. 54.

13. Letter to Ottoline Morrell, 1 February 1915, *Collected Letters*, Vol I, p. 312.

14. *Fantasia of the Unconscious*, 1923 (Penguin, 1971), p. 180.

15. *Women in Love*, 1921 (Penguin, 1971), p. 140.

16. Letter to Ottoline Morrell, 7 February 1916, *Collected Letters*, Vol. I, p. 424.

17. *Selected Essays* (Penguin, 1950), p. 112.

18. "How Beastly the Bourgeois Is," *Selected Poems* (Penguin, 1950), p. 138; Letter to Rolf Gardiner, 9 August 1924, *Collected Letters*, Vol. II, p. 801; Letter to Bertrand Russell, 2 March 1915, *ibid.*, Vol. I, p. 327.

19. "The Good Man," *Selected Literary Criticism*, pp. 258–259.

20. Letter to Bertrand Russell, 12 February 1915, *Collected Letters*, Vol. I, p. 317.

21. *Ibid.*, p. 318.

22. *Ibid.*, p. 320.

23. Letter to Mary Cannan, 24 February 1915, *ibid.*, p. 323.

24. Letter to Viola Meynell, 2 March 1915, *ibid.*, p. 328.

25. Letter to S. S. Koteliansky, 8 (?) April 1915, *ibid.*, p. 331.

26. Letter to Bertrand Russell, 29 (?) April 1915, *ibid.*, p. 336.

27. Letter to Ottoline Morrell, 5 (?) July 1915, *ibid.*, p. 351.

28. Letter to Cynthia Asquith, 16 August 1915, *ibid.*, p. 363.

29. Bertrand Russell, *Autobiography*, Vol. II, p. 53.

30. Letter to Ottoline Morrell, 26 September 1916, *Collected Letters*, Vol. I, pp. 475–476.

31. Letter to Mark Gertler, 5 December 1916, *ibid.*, p. 490.

32. Letter to Cynthia Asquith, 11 December 1916, *ibid.*, p. 491.

33. Letter to Mark Gertler, 21 February 1918, *ibid.*, p. 542.

34. Letter to Eleanor Farjeon, 20 January 1921, *ibid.*, Vol. II, pp. 639–640.

35. *Kangaroo*, 1923 (Penguin, 1950), p. 105.

36. *Ibid.*, p. 150.

37. *Fantasia of the Unconscious*, p. 88.

38. *Ibid.*, p. 115.

39. Letter to Richard Aldington, 18 (?) April 1926, *Collected Letters*, Vol. II, p. 902; Letter to Montague Weekley, 31 (?) October 1926, *ibid.*, p. 945; Letter to Rolf Gardiner, March 1928, quoted in H. M. Daleski, *The Forked Flame*, 1965 (Faber paperback, 1968), p. 229, note 1.

40. Letter to Waldo Frank, 15 September 1917, *Collected Letters*, Vol. I, p. 525.

chapter 17 literature or revolution? Victor Serge and André Gide

1. Victor Serge, *Memoirs of a Revolutionary 1901–1941*, trans. and ed. Peter Sedgwick (Oxford University Press, 1963), p. 334.

2. *Ibid.*, p. 114.

3. *Ibid.*, p. 358.

4. *Ibid.*, p. 47.

5. *Ibid.*, p. 69.

6. *Ibid.*, p. 152.

7. *Ibid.*, p. 177.

8. *Ibid.*, p. 374.

9. *Ibid.*, p. 10.

10. François Mauriac, "Qui triche," *L'Echo de Paris*, 16 July 1932, in *Correspondance: André Gide–François Mauriac 1912–1950*, ed. Jacqueline Morton, *Cahiers André Gide* 2 (Gallimard, 1971), p. 153.

11. André Gide, *Journal* (Bibliothèque de la Pléiade, Gallimard, 1951), Vol. I, p. 1193.

12. *Ibid.*, p. 1176.

13. André Gide, Appendix, *Pages de journal (1929–32)* (Gallimard, 1936), p. 190.

14. *Journal*, Vol I, p. 1262.

chapter 18 revolutionary neo-romanticism:
Malraux and Drieu

1. L.-F. Céline, *Bagatelles pour un massacre* (Denoël, 1937), p. 289.

2. Drieu la Rochelle, *Le Feu follet,* 1931 (Livre de Poche, 1967), p. 164.

3. John Lehmann, *New Writing in Europe* (Penguin, 1940), p. 126.

4. Alfred Kazin, *Starting Out in the Thirties* (Atlantic–Little Brown, 1965), pp. 20–21.

5. T. E. Lawrence, Dedicatory poem to S.A., *Seven Pillars of Wisdom;* Saint-Just, *Ecrits posthumes,* in *Œuvres choisies,* (Collection Idées, Gallimard, 1968), p. 310.

6. Marcel Arland, "Concerning a New 'Mal du siècle,' " 1924, in *N.R.F.,* ed. Justin O'Brien (Eyre and Spottiswoode, 1958), p. 34.

7. Malraux, speech of 8 June 1929, in debate on *The Conquerors,* quoted in Janine Mossuz, *André Malraux et le gaullisme* (Armand Colin, 1970), p. 253. See also Malraux, "D. H. Lawrence and Eroticism, 1932, in *N.R.F.,* p. 196, and Dennis Boak, *André Malraux* (Clarendon Press, 1968), p. 178, note 4.

8. Marcel Arland, p. 36.

9. Malraux, *La Tentation de l'Occident,* 1926 (Grasset, 1964), pp. 216–217. See also pp. 100–101.

10. Drieu la Rochelle, *Genève ou Moscou* (Gallimard, 1928), p. 217.

11. Drieu la Rochelle, *Sur les écrivains,* ed. Frédéric Grover (Gallimard, 1964), p. 175.

12. Drieu la Rochelle, "Malraux, the New Man," 1930, in *N.R.F.,* p. 188.

13. Quoted in Frédéric Grover, *Drieu la Rochelle* (Gallimard, 1962), p. 53.

14. Drieu la Rochelle, "The New Fact of the Twentieth Century," 1939, in *N.R.F.,* pp. 377–379.

15. George Orwell, review of F. Borkenau, *The Totalitarian Enemy,* in *Collected Essays, Journalism and Letters,* ed. S. Orwell and I. Angus (Penguin, 1970), Vol. II, p. 40.

16. Quoted in J. Plumyène and R. Lasierra, *Les Fascismes français 1923–1963* (Seuil, 1963), p. 96.

17. Drieu la Rochelle, *Gilles,* 1939 (Livre de Poche, 1967), p. 490.

18. Malraux, *L'Espoir,* 1937 (Gallimard, 1948), p. 124.

19. Drieu la Rochelle, *L'Homme à cheval,* 1943 (Livre de Poche, 1965), p. 52.

20. Malraux, "Saint-Just et la force des choses," 1954, in *Le Triangle noir* (Gallimard, 1970), pp. 121, 123, 126, 132.

21. Malraux, "Réponse à Trotsky," 1931, in *Les Critiques de notre temps et Malraux,* ed. Pol Gaillard (Garnier, 1970), p. 46.

22. Leon Trotsky, "De la Révolution étranglée et de ses étrangleurs," *Littérature et révolution* (Collection 10/18, 1971), p. 406.

23. Malraux, *La Condition humaine,* 1933 (Gallimard, 1946), p. 73.

24. Malraux, *Les Conquérants,* 1928 (Livre de Poche, 1966), p. 68.

25. Leon Trotsky, "Céline et Poincaré," *Litterature et révolution,* p. 439. English version from Edmund Wilson, *To the Finland Station* (Fontana, p. 436).

26. *L'Espoir,* p. 355.

27. *Ibid.,* p. 283.

28. Malraux, *Antimémoires* (Gallimard, 1967), p. 125.

29. Quoted in Janine Mossuz, *André Malraux et le gaullisme* (Armand Colin, 1970), p. 96.

30. *Ibid.,* p. 134. See also Malraux's interview with Emmanuel d'Astier in *L'Evénement,* September 1967, p.61.

31. Quoted in *André Malraux et le gaullisme,* p. 225.

32. *Antimémoires,* pp. 127, 132.

chapter 19 *dirty hands: Sartre, Camus, Orwell*

1. Sartre, "Situation de l'écrivain en 1947," *Qu'est-ce que la littérature?* 1948 (Collection Idées, Gallimard, 1966), p. 371 note 10.

2. Camus, "Nous autres meurtriers," *Franchise,* no. 3, 1946, in *Essais,* ed. R. Quilliot and L. Faucon (Bibliothèque de la Pléiade, Gallimard, 1965), p. 1569. Also *Carnets 1942–1951,* trans. Philip Thody (Hamish Hamilton, 1966), p. 88.

3. Norman Mailer, *Advertisements for Myself,* 1959 (Deutsch, 1961), p. 28. For Orwell, see Letter to Roger Senhouse, 17 March 1945, *Collected Essays, Journalism and Letters,* ed. S. Orwell and I. Angus (Penguin, 1970), Vol. III, p. 407.

4. Arthur Koestler in *The God That Failed,* ed. Richard Crossman (Hamish Hamilton, 1950), p. 58.

5. Orwell, "Looking Back on the Spanish War," written 1942, published 1943, *Collected Essays, Journalism and Letters,* Vol II, p. 305.

6. Orwell, *Homage to Catalonia,* 1938 (Penguin, 1962), p. 7.

7. Orwell, "Why I Joined the Independent Labour Party," June 1938, *Collected Essays, Journalism and Letters,* Vol. I, pp. 373, 374.

8. Orwell, "Inside the Whale," 1940, *ibid.,* p. 576.

9. Camus *Carnets 1942–1951,* p. 14.

10. Camus, *ibid.,* p. 46.

11. Sartre, *Les Mots* (Gallimard, 1964), p. 210. See also interview with M. Contat and M. Rybalka in *Le Monde,* 14 May 1971.

12. Sartre, interview with Jacqueline Piatier, *Le Monde,* 18 April 1964, quoted M. Contat and M. Rybalka, *Les Ecrits de Sartre* (Gallimard, 1970), p. 64.

13. Sartre, *Les Mots,* p. 159.

14. Sartre, *La Nausée,* 1938 (Folio 1972), p. 223. See also "Matérialisme et révolution," *Situations III* (Gallimard 1949), p. 184ff: *Les Ecrits de Sartre,* p. 65.

15. P. Wyndham Lewis, *The Writer and the Absolute* (Methuen, 1952), p. 109.

16. Sartre, *La Mort dans l'âme,* Vol. III of *Les Chemins de la liberté* (Gallimard, 1949), p. 197.

17. Sartre, *Qu'est-ce que la littérature?,* p. 193.

18. *Ibid.,* pp. 195–196. See also p. 105.

19. Simone de Beauvoir, *La Force des choses* (Gallimard, 1963), p. 333.

20. Sartre, interview with Bernard Pingaud, "Sartre aujourd'hui," *L'Arc,* no. 30, November 1966, p. 96.

21. Eugène Ionesco, *Notes et contre-notes* (Collection Idées, Gallimard, 1966), p. 127.

22. Sartre, "Merleau-Ponty," *Situations IV* (Gallimard, 1964), pp. 226–227.

23. Alfred de Musset, *Lorenzaccio,* 1834, *Comédies et proverbes,* ed. Alphonse Séché (Nelson, 1937), Vol I, p. 505. Also pp. 500, 501.

24. Sartre, *Les Mains sales,* 1948 (Folio 1971), 3d tableau, scene 4, p. 104.

25. *Ibid.,* 6th tableau, scene 2, p. 218.

26. *Ibid.,* 5th tableau, scene 3, p. 194; Saint-Just, "Discours concernant le jugement de Louis XVI," 13 November 1790, *Œuvres choisies* (Collection Idées, Gallimard, 1968), p. 80.

27. Sartre, interview with Guy Dornand, *Franc-Tireur* 25 March 1948, quoted in *Les Ecrits de Sartre,* p. 178.

28. Sartre, interview with P.-A. Baude, *L'Aube,* 1 April 1948, *ibid.,* p. 180.

29. *Ibid.,* p. 183.

30. Mailer, *Barbary Shore,* 1951 (Ace Books, 1961), chapter xxv, p. 172.

31. Sartre, *Les Mots,* p. 122; also pp. 144–145.

32. Sartre, *Les Mains sales,* 5th tableau, scene 3, p. 190.

33. Koestler, *The Gladiators,* 1939 (Hutchinson Danube edition, 1965), p. 232.

34. *Ibid.,* p. 297.

35. Orwell, *Collected Essays, Journalism and Letters,* Vol I, p. 372.

36. Koestler, *The Yogi and the Commissar*, 1945, (Cape, 1964), pp. 225–226.

37. Simone de Beauvoir, *La Force de l'âge* (Gallimard, 1960), p. 34.

38. Sartre, *Critique of Dialectical Reason*, in R. D. Laing and D. G. Cooper, *Reason and Violence: A Decade of Sartre's Philosophy 1950–1960* (Tavistock, 1964), p. 114. (This résumé was approved by Sartre himself.)

39. Sartre, *Les Séquéstrés d'Altona* (Gallimard, 1960), Act 5, scene 3, p. 222.

40. Sartre, *Le Diable et le bon Dieu*, 1951 (Folio 1972), Act 3, 11th tableau, scene ii, p. 251.

41. Sartre, "Nizan," *Situations IV*, pp. 173–174; "Merleau-Ponty," *ibid.*, p. 230. See also *Les Ecrits de Sartre*, pp. 353, 408.

42. Sartre, Preface to Franz Fanon, *Les Damnés de la terre*, 1961, *Situations V* (Gallimard, 1964), p. 183.

43. *Ibid.*, p. 185.

44. Orwell, "Inside the Whale," *Collected Essays, Journalism and Letters*, Vol. I, p. 566.

45. Orwell, "My Country Right or Left" Autumn 1940, *ibid.*, p. 591.

46. Camus, in *Combat*, 20 October 1944, *Essais*, p. 1533.

47. *Ibid.*, November 1946, pp. 332–333.

48. Camus, "Lettres sur la révolte," *ibid.*, p. 753.

49. Camus, 11 September 1944, quoted in Biographical Note, *Carnets 1942–1951*, p. 180.

50. Camus, *Les Justes* (Gallimard, 1950), p. 46.

51. Camus, *Essais*, p. 1725. See also *Les Meurtriers délicats*, *L'Homme révolté*, *ibid.*, p. 571ff; *Les Pharisiens de la justice*, *ibid.*, p. 720 ff; *Carnets 1942–1951*, p. 102.

52. Camus, *Carnets 1942–1951*, p. 111.

53. Camus, *La Chute* (Gallimard, 1956), p. 156.

54. Sartre, "Merleau-Ponty," *Situations IV*, p. 251.

epilogue: revolution as the modern shibboleth

1. Samuel Taylor Coleridge, Essay VI, *The Friend*, ed. B. E. Rooke, Vol. I of *The Collected Works of S. T. Coleridge* (Routledge and Kegan Paul, 1969), p. 226.

2. Goethe, quoted in Ernst Robert Curtius, *European Literature and the Latin Middle Ages*, 1948, trans. Willard R. Trask (Routledge and Kegan Paul, 1953), p. 266, note 49.

3. Victor Hugo, "Réponse à un acte d'accusation," January 1834, *Les Contemplations*, Book I, vii.

4. Raymond Williams, *Modern Tragedy* (Chatto and Windus, 1966), p. 77. See also *Culture and Society,* 1958 (Penguin, 1963), p. 193.

5. Marguerite Duras, interview with Nina Sutton, *The Guardian,* 13 July 1971.

6. Thucydides, *The Peloponnesian War,* trans. Rex Warner (Penguin, 1956), p. 209.

7. Pierre Trotignon, "Le dernier métaphysicien," *L'Arc,* No. 30, November 1966, p. 31.

8. Andrew Sinclair, *Guevara* (Fontana, 1970), pp. 90–91.

9. John Berger, " 'Che' Guevara," 1967, *Selected Essays and Articles* (Pelican, 1972), p. 44.

10. Emmanuel Berl, *Mort de la pensée bourgeoise* (Grasset, 1929), p. 161.

11. Jerry Rubin, *Do It! Scenarios of the Revolution* (Ballantine Books, 1970), p. 109; also Abbie Hoffman, *Revolution for the Hell of It,* 1968 (Pocket Books, 1970), p. 13.

12. Tom Wolfe, *The Electric Kool-Aid Acid Test,* 1968 (Bantam Books, 1969), p. 339.

13. Pieter Geyl, "French Historians For and Against the Revolution," *Encounters in History* (Collins, 1963), p. 184.

14. Julien Benda in Maurice Rouzaud, *Où va la critique?* (Editions Saint-Michel, 1929), pp. 196–197.

index

Joachite, xxxiv-xxxv, 5, 215, 244
and libertarianism, xxxv, 6
modern mentality of, 215, 219, 244,
248, 250, 251, 276, 280, 290
of Puritans, 6
of Swedenborg, xxxvii, 5
Wordsworth and, 23
Arago, Étienne, 143
Aragon, Louis, 241-242, 282
Arland, Marcel, 280, 281
Artaud, Antonin, 241, 246
Association of Revolutionary Writers and
Artists, 271
Atheism, 216-219, 231, 243, 312-313, 318
and communism, 125
young Dostoevsky and, 198, 202
Sartre, 300, 312-313
Shelley, 51
Auden, W. H., and "necessary murder,"
xxxii, 309
"Auguries of Innocence" (Blake), 8
Aurora Roja (Baroja), 235, 242
Authoritarianism:
accommodation of libertarians with,
xxvi, 100-103, 104-105, 108
in Soviet Russia, 265, 271, 284
See also Despotism

Babeuf, François Noel ("Gracchus"), 132,
133, 148, 152
Babouvism, 133
Baden, Grand Duchy of, 1848 revolution in,
187
Bakunin, Mikhail, 49, 130, 148-149,
150-152, 186, 190, 195, 201, 206
anarchism of, 148-149, 150-152, 216,
230, 235, 239
Balzac, Honoré de, 99, 104, 107, 108, 118,
124, 270
Barbary Shore (Mailer), 294, 305
Barbès, Armand, 143, 144, 176
Baroja, Pío, 235
Aurora Roja, 235, 242
Barrès, Maurice, 224-228, 240, 244, 268,
276, 281
The Cult of the Ego, 224
Les Déracinés, 225
L'Ennemi des lois, 226
Un Homme libre, 225

Baudelaire, 156, 158-168, 215, 245, 297,
318
aesthetic views of, 166-168, 170
biographical data, 159, 165
and 1848 Revolution, 138, 161,
162-163, 164-165
Les Fleurs du Mal, 159, 165
view of human depravity, 159-160, 165
view of nature and the natural, 159
Bauer, Bruno, 149
Beaupuy, Michel, 25-26, 28
Beauvoir, Simone de, 294, 300, 304, 306,
307, 316
Belinsky, Vissarion G., 136, 186-187, 191,
195, 198, 201, 205, 207, 263, 297
Berger, John, 324-325
Berl, Emmanuel, 279
Bible, xxxii, xxxvii. *See also* New Testament;
Old Testament; Revelation of St. John
Birth of Our Power (Serge), 264
Blake, William, xxii, xxxviii, 4-19, 23, 24,
35, 58, 74, 86, 216, 319
aims of, 4-5, 18-19
"Auguries of Innocence," 8
biographical data, 5, 6
Coleridge on, 33
defense of sexual freedom, 11-13, 323
dialectic of contraries, 15
Divine Humanity, 7, 18, 217-218
"The Divine Image," 15
Dostoevsky compared to, 202
The Everlasting Gospel, 14
The French Revolution, 6
Gide compared to, 19
"The Grey Monk," 17
Jerusalem, 5, 7, 15, 17
and Last Judgment and resurrection, 4,
8-10, 18
Lawrence compared to, 19, 251
The Marriage of Heaven and Hell, 5, 14
quoted, on Thomas Paine, 6, 17
religion of, 13-14, 18
self-image of the prophetic poet, 7
Songs of Experience, 15
Songs of Innocence, 15
"The Tiger," 15
on trial for sedition, 16
Vala, or the Four Zoas, 9-10
"William Bond," 12

Blanc, Louis, 130, 140, 141, 143
Blanqui, Louis Auguste, 142, 143, 158, 163, 181, 216
Blessington, Lady, 97, 104
Blind, Karl, 218
Blok, Alexander, 236-238, 241, 263
  The Twelve, 236, 237-238, 239
Boehme, Jakob, xxxvii, 7, 15
Bolsheviks, 153, 236, 238-239, 244, 260, 265, 268
  foreseen by Dostoevsky, 203, 209
  See also Russian Revolution
Bonaparte. See Napoleon Bonaparte
Bonnot gang (anarchists), 264
Book of Revelation. See Revelation of St. John
Borderers, The (Wordsworth), 30
Börne, Ludwig, 121
Borodin, Mikhail M., 263, 279, 287, 288
Botkin, V. P., 129
Bouilhet, Louis, 175, 177
Boulanger, General G. E., 227
Bourges, Michel de (Louis-Chrysostome Michel), 132-135, 136, 137, 141, 149
Brawne, Fanny, 69
Breton, André, 212, 230, 237, 240, 241, 243-246, 249, 252
Brothers Karamazov, The (Dostoevsky), 203, 300
Browning, Robert, 66
Büchner, Georg, 117
Bulletin de la République, 141
Buonarrotti, Filippo Michele, 132, 133
Burke, Edmund, xxiv, 5, 6, 45
  quoted, 112, 202
Burns, Robert, 39
Butor, Michel, 315
Butts, Thomas, 12
Byron, George Gordon, Lord, 69, 71, 81, 83-97, 99, 115, 151, 158, 216, 295, 305
  an activist, 66, 83-84, 87-89, 91-96, 97, 106, 168, 277
  "The Age of Bronze," 104
  biographical data, 83, 85, 88
  Cain, 86, 203, 319
  called manic-depressive, 84
  Childe Harold's Pilgrimage, 71, 87, 88, 93, 95-96, 107
  death of, 83, 97
  The Deformed Transformed, 92-93

Don Juan, 90, 92, 96, 104
  and Dostoevsky, 203, 204, 206-207
  an elitist, 89-90
  and French Revolution, 90-91
  Goethe and, 96-97, 105
  and Greek cause, 83, 96, 97
  and Italian cause, 91-92, 96
  libertarian causes of, 83
  Malraux compared to, 276-277, 279, 281
  Manfred, 89, 191
  Marino Faliero, 91, 203
  and Napoleon, 93, 103-104, 105
  outlaw heroes of, 86, 89, 93-94, 107
  politics of, 89-90
  religion of, 85-86
  Sardanapalus, 96
  and Shelley, 61, 66, 88, 89
  view of human nature, 90
Byronism, 207, 281

Cabet, Étienne, 142-143, 148, 179
Cain (Byron), 86, 203, 319
Caleb Williams (Godwin), xxx, 106
Camus, Albert, xxviii, 208, 293, 294, 297, 310-312, 316
  biographical data, 294, 297
  The Fall, 312
  The Just, 311
  The Outsider, 297
  The Plague, 300
  The Rebel, 310-311, 312
  and revolutionary violence, 304, 306-307, 310-312
Capital (Marx), 150
Capitalism, 256
  Gide's attacks on, 268, 270
  Malraux's attacks on, 278
Carbonari, 91, 92, 107, 108
Carlyle, Thomas, 29
Case of Comrade Tulayev, The (Serge), 266
Cause du peuple, La (Sand), 143
Cavaignac, General Louis Eugène, 144
Céline, Louis-Ferdinand, 275, 299
Chambers, Jessie, 251
Champfleury (pseudonym of Jules Fleury-Husson), 133, 162, 163, 167
Charles I, King of England, 5
Charterhouse of Parma, The (Stendhal), 107